# SAILING THE WATER'S EDGE

# SAILING THE WATER'S EDGE

## THE DOMESTIC POLITICS OF
## AMERICAN FOREIGN POLICY

## HELEN V. MILNER & DUSTIN TINGLEY

PRINCETON UNIVERSITY PRESS | PRINCETON AND OXFORD

PUBLISHED BY PRINCETON UNIVERSITY PRESS
41 William Street, Princeton, New Jersey 08540

IN THE UNITED KINGDOM: PRINCETON UNIVERSITY PRESS
6 Oxford Street, Woodstock, Oxfordshire OX20 1TW

press.princeton.edu

Library of Congress Cataloging-in-Publication Data

Milner, Helen V., 1958–
   Sailing the water's edge : the domestic politics of American foreign policy / Helen V.
Milner and Dustin Tingley.
      pages cm
   Includes bibliographical references and index.
   ISBN 978-0-691-16547-9 (hardback)
   1. United States—Foreign relations—Decision making.   2. United States—Military
policy—Decision making.   3. Executive power—United States.   4. United States—For-
eign relations—1945-1989.   5. Presidents—United States—Decision making.   6. United
States—Foreign relations—1989–   I. Tingley, Dustin, 1979–   II. Title.
   JZ1480.M555 2015
   327.73—dc23                                                                          2015017560

British Library Cataloging-in-Publication Data is available

This book has been composed in Sabon Next LT Pro with
Berthold Akzidenz-Grotesk for display

Printed on acid-free paper. ∞

Printed in the United States of America

10  9  8  7  6  5  4  3  2  1

# CONTENTS

# 1

## INTRODUCTION 1

# 2

## A THEORY OF PRESIDENTIAL POWER
## AND US FOREIGN POLICY 33

# 3

## FOLLOW THE SAND DOLLARS:
### Interest Groups and American Foreign Policy Instruments    77

# 4

## FROM THE FLOOR TO THE SHORE:
### Budget Politics and Roll Call Voting on US Foreign Policy    121

# 5

## CONTROLLING THE SAND CASTLE:
### The Design and Control of US Foreign Policy Agencies    157

# 6

## THE VIEW FROM THE PUBLIC BEACH:
### Presidential Power and Substitution in American Public Opinion

185

# 7

## AMERICAN FOREIGN POLICY TOWARD SUB-SAHARAN AFRICA, 1993–2009:
### A Case Study of Policy Instrument Politics and Substitution

209

# 8

## CONCLUSIONS

255

# TABLES

**1.1** Policy instruments covered in each chapter 30

**2.1** Predictions of presidential strength by distributional and ideological dimensions 67

**2.2** Predictions of presidential strength by policy instrument 70

**3.1** Interest group research questions and data sources 81

**3.2** Congressional testimony sources by policy instrument 91

**3.3** When do interest groups bypass the White House? 109

**4.1** Research questions and data sources for chapter 4 123

**4.2** Budget analysis with current action table data 128

**4.3** Types of roll call data used in chapter 133

**4.4** Vote margin analysis of foreign policy votes 136

**4.5** House of Representatives voting by policy tool 145

**4.6** House of Representatives voting by policy tool 146

**5.1** Chapter 5 research questions and data sources 159

**5.2** Bureaucratic control analysis 166

**6.1** Chapter 6 research questions and data sources 189

**6.2** *Why* respondent would punish a legislator for voting against president on foreign policy 195

**6.3** Median percentage budget change across policy tools as a function of party 205

**7.1** Millennium Challenge Account funding, 2004–2008 241

**7.2** Economic agreements concluded by the Bush administration 249

# FIGURES

# PREFACE

Writing this book has been a wonderful intellectual journey. It began when Dustin arrived at Princeton University as a graduate student in the fall of 2005. Originally, our focus was on each policy instrument in foreign policy by itself, and only later in comparison to one another as we uncovered the deep similarities and differences among them. We began working together on a series of papers on foreign aid. At that time, foreign aid was not much studied in the political science literature and especially not in the field of international political economy. Over the next decade this was to change greatly; the political science literature on foreign aid is now quite extensive. We began working on congressional voting on aid, following in the footsteps of some seminal research by Lawrence Broz, Christopher Kilby, and Benjamin Fordham on congressional voting on foreign policy. This collaboration led to a series of papers on a range of topics that we eventually published.[1]

Following our work on foreign aid we decided that a comparison with the area of international trade policy would be instructive. This arose from a suggestion by an APSA discussant, Jeff Frieden, noting that we had an interesting cross-tabulation between aid voting and trade voting in Congress in our early work but that we had said nothing about it. This led us to further expand our US congressional district–level data containing a wide variety of economic and political variables. We had expected that scholars in American politics who work on Congress would have collected all of this already, but we found that that was not the case for many of the variables we needed, or that our reviewers told us we needed. Over time we realized we had a wonderful resource in the form of a district-level dataset on Congress during the period from the 1970s to the present. And this allowed us to compare the politics of international trade and aid policy. Our efforts here led to the publication of our article in *International Organization*, bringing together the political economy of trade and aid with the foreign policy dimension as represented by the role of the president in the United States.[2]

Our next step was to ask about immigration policy.[3] We viewed immigration as another form of economic foreign policy. The admission of foreigners into the United States and the conditions for their livelihoods there were not just a function of domestic politics; they affected relations

1 Chaudoin, Milner, and Tingley, 2010; Milner and Tingley, 2010; Milner and Tingley, 2011; Milner and Tingley, 2013a; Milner and Tingley, 2013b; Milner and Tingley, 2013c; Hicks, Milner, and Tingley, 2014; Tingley, Xu, Chilton, and Milner, 2015.

2 Milner and Tingley, 2011.

3 Milner and Tingley, 2008a.

between the United States and other countries as well. And they certainly could be used to improve or degrade those relations. We again found our dataset on congressional districts useful. But the politics of immigration was very complicated. The issues and groups involved seemed much more numerous and heterogeneous than did the ones in aid and trade. But again the role of economic interest groups and ideological factors stood out as they had in aid and trade policy.

This led us to wonder whether other areas of US foreign policy looked similar or distinct. We then embarked on a journey to add military components of foreign policy to our set of comparisons. We gathered information on geopolitical aid as distinguished from the kind of development-oriented aid we had originally examined. And then we added military interventions by the United States that had been acknowledged by Congress. And finally we brought in domestic military spending. These three military-oriented areas of foreign policy turned out to be different from one another in interesting ways and fit nicely into our developing ideas about how to understand the ensemble of US foreign policy.

Our last foreign policy instrument was sanctions. This of course should not have been last, but turned out to be the most difficult. Sanctions do not follow some easy legislative or executive pattern; rather, they mix the two branches and combine different policy goals. But adding sanctions to the mix was highly useful since they bridge the economic and military instruments we had previously compared.

Our original research had covered congressional voting and the president's role in it. We then realized that there is much more to foreign policy making than this aspect, although it is key. Without congressional assent, the president cannot carry on much foreign policy for very long. Most every instrument requires funding or legal sanction if carried out over any period of time. In addition, we had long been interested in American public opinion on foreign policy. Again this is an important long-term constraint on the president, but it is not the only key to everyday decision making. Hence we decided to expand our overview into congressional and presidential budgeting, which also highlighted the variance in presidential power across foreign policy instruments. This research was made much easier by building upon the shoulders of those going before us in the "two presidencies" literature, namely, work by Brandice Canes-Wrone, David Lewis, and William Howell.[4] Bureaucratic politics has been known as a fundamental element of foreign policy making for a long time; we also considered it to be critically important. And this led us to delve into the literature on congressional and presidential control over the bureaucracy in foreign policy. An important contrast between presidential and congressional control over

4 Canes-Wrone, Howell, and Lewis, 2008.

different foreign policy instruments arises when one looks at who controls the bureaucracy.

Another critical input into foreign policy making is interest groups and their activity. This has been well documented time and again, but we hoped to add more systematic research. The development of new empirical methods using text analysis has been a boon here. Collaborative work between Dustin, Molly Roberts, and Brandon Stewart in part produced the Structural Topic Model that allowed us to understand what topics are most likely to be taken to the White House and which bypassed the White House.[5] We were also able to look at variance across foreign policy instruments and the role of interest groups using congressional testimony. Again, contrasts across the foreign policy instruments revealed how these groups exercised influence through lobbying and information provision, underlining how interest group battles over policy could undermine presidential control of policy.

Meanwhile, as we developed these empirical approaches we were also building a case studying US policy in Sub-Saharan Africa and seeing whether the twists and turns in this set of policies followed what our other conjectures and findings had uncovered. Looking over the presidency of two different leaders (Presidents Bill Clinton and G. W. Bush), we saw that in many ways it showed the contrasts among policies very clearly. Highlighting the role of material interests and interest group politics in aid and trade, it also demonstrated the underlying tendency for presidents to reach for the military option because it was less constrained by domestic politics and hence less costly to use, at least ex ante. The case gave us stronger confidence in our other findings.

We received much help in this long process. Raymond Hicks, Torben Behmer, and David Francis provided substantial research assistance over many years. Indeed, under Raymond Hicks, Dustin was trained in innumerable "on the ground" issues in data collection and management. David provided substantial insight into development issues, and Torben's rigor combined with unflappable cheeriness helped us round out substantial parts of this book. Dana Higgins, Amanda Kennard, Connor Huff, Jetson Leder-Luis, and Christopher Xu also provided tremendous research help.

We have presented various papers and chapters over the years and received invaluable feedback from these presentations. We thank the scholars in the department of political science at Columbia, Caltech, Harvard, UCSD, UC Berkeley, USC, UCSB, Stanford, CSDP, Princeton Niehaus Center, Yale, and the 2012 IPES Conference for valuable feedback. We also thank the participants at various panels at APSA and MPSA for their very useful comments that improved our research. In July 2014, we held a conference on the book

5  Roberts, Stewart, Tingley, et al., 2014.

to obtain more feedback and we were very lucky to have exceptional scholars who gave us long, detailed, and very constructive comments. We thank David Baldwin, Brandice Canes-Wrone, Stephen Chaudoin, Allison Carnegie, Benjamin Fordham, Christopher Gelpi, Joanne Gowa, Edward Mansfield, Jon Rogowski, Elizabeth Saunders, and James Vreeland for their willingness to give us such tremendous feedback. Jim Vreeland was the overall winner of the best book conference attendee; he gave us more than twenty-five single-spaced pages of comments! Many of our colleagues have also contributed much to this book. At Princeton and Harvard we thank Robert Keohane, Brandice Canes-Wrone, Amaney Jamal, Christina Davis, David Carter, Jacob Shapiro, Kosuke Imai, Ken Shepsle, Beth Simmons, and Jeff Frieden for reading various drafts and providing important comments. We also thank Adam Chilton, Jim Fearon, Judy Goldstein, Saum Jha, David Lewis, Phil Lipscy, Yon Lupu, Rose McDermott, Lisa Camner McKay, Jon Pevehouse, Ken Schultz, Virginia Tingley, Michael Tomz, James Vreeland, Meredith Wilf, and Jeremy Weinstein. It is a great pleasure having superb graduate students with whom to work; and we thank graduate students (at the time of writing this preface!) Ryan Brutger, John Chin, Julia Morse, Tyler Pratt, Alexander Slaski, Robert Schub, and Connor Huff. We thank Stephen Ansolabehere for arranging the CCES surveys. Pat Trinity has been a stalwart source of support over the years, protecting Helen from endless details and making things at Princeton run ever so well, and Tom Murphy was always there at Harvard for any number of logistical supports. We thank the Weatherhead Center for International Affairs, Niehaus Center for Globalization and Governance, Princeton University and Harvard University for financial support, and the Donofrio family for logistical support for our book conference. We also thank Eric Crahan, who has made the process of publication an enjoyable one, Elisabeth Donahue and Ticiana Jardim Marini for helpful comments, and Lisa Camner McKay for help with some editing.

Helen wishes to thank her husband, David Baldwin, who has once again provided the invaluable support, gentle guidance, and space to allow her to complete another project. She also wishes to thank Rachel, Luke, and Theo for their tireless contributions to the happiness of the author. And she thanks Dustin for being a tremendous inspiration and sparkplug; on those days when she thought that being chair of the department was going to end her research career he'd come sailing into her office with fresh ideas, revised papers, and plans for future assaults on the kingdom of knowledge, and she would know it was all going to be ok. It has been a great partnership. We depend on many sources of support and inspiration, some of which we realize and some of which we only come to understand later when they are gone. For all of them, many thanks, and may I return the favor.

Dustin thanks most of all his wife, Alice Hsiaw, who has provided the intellectual and spiritual comradery it takes for someone to write their first book. In the final year of this book's preparation Dustin met his new son Dylan. Dylan provides daily inspiration, but also the special opportunity for brainstorming at 3 a.m. on a yoga ball while bouncing. Dustin also thanks his sisters Katie and Madelyn, parents Dave and Ginny, and grandparents for support and willingness to let him chart his own path through life. Intellectual shepherding for this book stems from Joanne Gowa, Robert Keohane, Raymond Hicks, Kosuke Imai, Stephen Chaudoin, and especially his adviser Helen. He came out of graduate school thinking that being a chair also allows for ample time to spend with graduate students producing research. Dave McClure, VT, and RMD are thanked for their hands, and Adam Band for his funny emails about US foreign policy.

Dustin and Helen wish to thank all the men and women—civilian and military—who serve this country in support of a healthy US foreign policy, including those who have given their lives and livelihoods for this goal.

# SAILING THE WATER'S EDGE

# 1

# INTRODUCTION

President Obama, in one of his most significant speeches since taking office, [presented] an ambitious vision—one that eschews a muscle-bound foreign policy, dominated by the military and intelligence services, in favor of energetic diplomacy, foreign aid and a more measured response to terrorism.[1]

[f]or all the focus on the use of force, force alone cannot make us safe. We cannot use force everywhere.... Foreign aid is one of the least popular expenditures—even though it amounts to less than one percent of the federal budget. But foreign assistance cannot be viewed as charity. It is fundamental to our national security and any sensible long-term strategy to battle extremism.[2]

An Obama administration plan to change the way the United States distributes its international food aid has touched off an intense lobbying campaign by a coalition of shipping companies, agribusiness and charitable groups who say the change will harm the nation's economy and hamper efforts to fight global hunger.... The only thing getting in the way is politics and special interest.[3]

## Motivation and Focus

"Politics Stops at the Water's Edge." This popular adage stands for the idea that when it comes to foreign policy, American political leaders should speak with one voice—a distinction from the cacophony that marks domestic policy making. Yet as we demonstrate in this book, while there are times when political leaders do appear unified on foreign policy, there are just as many examples of when foreign policy debate looks much more like a contentious domestic policy discussion. Sailing the water's edge is what our political leaders do.

The above quotations highlight the main purpose of this book, which is to analyze the process of making American foreign policy. How is foreign policy made in the United States? And why is it made that way? American leaders have a wide range of policy instruments available to them, from foreign aid to sanctions to airstrikes. We study how and why they choose a particular set of foreign policy instruments to address a given international problem or opportunity. This choice of policy instruments is important because it affects the ultimate outcome of American involvement in foreign affairs.

1 Landler and Mazzetti, 2013.
2 Obama, 2013.
3 Nixon, 2013.

Our study focuses on domestic politics and the role of the president. American political institutions play a crucial role in how policy is made in the United States. The powerful position of Congress and the salience of interest groups and public opinion critically influence how presidents make foreign policy. We seek to understand this process using rigorous theory and systematic empirical evidence.

The United States can engage with other countries in a wide variety of ways. Indeed, a major change in American diplomacy in the twentieth century was the development of different types of policy instruments, such as foreign aid and international trade agreements. Today, US foreign policy employs myriad policy instruments, including immigration, economic and military aid, monetary interventions, international trade, sanctions, diplomacy, military force deployment, and domestic defense spending. Why do American leaders sometimes choose trade agreements and other times foreign aid? More generally, why do American leaders choose the specific set of foreign policy instruments considering the wide range of tools available to them? Given America's many resources, American presidents have many different policies they could use in any situation, but they choose one particular set. Why is this set chosen from among the many available options? We offer a view that rejects the claim that politics affects only domestic policy making, i.e., that "politics stops at the water's edge." Instead, domestic politics affects elements of foreign policy and does so differentially. Politics thus occurs all along the water's edge, with the use of some policy instruments more constrained by domestic politics than others.

Consider a few cases. From about 1985 onward, the United States has been trying to keep North Korea from first developing and then deploying nuclear weapons. More recently, it has been trying to make North Korea relinquish these weapons. In this long and so far unsuccessful process, US leaders have considered and eventually used many different foreign policy instruments: trade sanctions, foreign aid, military maneuvers and troop movements, negotiations, international cooperation and inspections, silence and unwillingness to negotiate, threats of force, promises of recognition and reassurance, financial inducements, supplies of oil, covert operations to destabilize the government, and other tools of statecraft. And throughout the Clinton, G. W. Bush, and Obama administrations, there has been constant debate over which instruments to use when and how much.[4]

To simplify, two camps have often formed—one advocating negotiations and positive inducements and the other counseling sanctions and the use of force. While the United States has yet to use direct force, the coercive strategy seems to have generally prevailed over the more cooperative one.

4 The basis of this discussion is from Sigal, 1998; Nincic, 2010; Cha, 2012; and Henriksen, 2012.

Part of the reason for this has been domestic politics in the United States. As Sigal notes in his study of US policy toward North Korea, "Coercive bargaining is the natural inclination of the US government. A stern negotiating record suppresses the domestic dispute that would be associated with any explicit political accommodation with North Korea."[5] Efforts at using positive inducements, such as economic aid and trade, have often found bitter opposition within the United States. And this opposition—often from Republicans—has hamstrung presidents, especially Democratic ones. For instance, Clinton's engagement policy resulted in the 1994 Agreed Framework, which expanded diplomatic relations and economic ties including energy assistance to the North in exchange for shutting down its plutonium production facilities. Facing domestic criticism and North Korean intransigence, the Bush administration once in office radically changed policy, ending the Framework Agreement, halting oil shipments, enacting sanctions, and contemplating military interdiction.[6] This case illustrates that when presidents face international problems, they have many instruments available to address them—but the ultimate choice of policy often depends heavily on domestic politics in the United States.

Another interesting case is Iraq. After the 1991 Operation Desert Shield freed Kuwait from Iraq's invasion, the US government left Saddam Hussein and his party in control following a negotiated cease-fire agreement. Over the next twelve years, the United States had to contend with this decision. Here too the United States feared that Hussein would develop and deploy weapons of mass destruction. Other concerns about Hussein's behavior included his treatment of Kurds and Shias, his threats against Saudi Arabia, Kuwait, and the oil pipelines, and his belligerence toward Israel. The G. H. W. Bush, Clinton, and G. W. Bush administrations all discussed using, and finally ended up employing, many different foreign policy instruments to contain Hussein. Many of these were of the coercive variety. The United States and other countries imposed strong economic sanctions, used the diplomacy of deterrence, imposed no-flight zones within the country, developed covert operations to topple the regime, and opened Iraq to inspections by the UN. Negotiations with Hussein to disarm and end his international provocations continued but achieved little. Clinton's later efforts to resolve the Iraq problem without the use of force were criticized by Republicans.[7] In 2003, the G. W. Bush administration decided to invade Iraq and deposed Hussein in pursuit of the regime's purported weapons of mass destruction. Apparently the sanctions and other policies had been more successful than anticipated and made Hussein's reacquiring these more difficult than anticipated.

5   Sigal, 1998, p. 170.
6   Ogden and Anderson, 2008.
7   Henriksen, 2012, pp. 49–54.

As in the case of North Korea, the US government considered many policy instruments to deal with Hussein; they ended up using coercion and military force by and large. In part this was a reaction to Hussein and the belief that his behavior was dangerous, but it was also conditioned by domestic politics, where military means tended to be politically easier for the president to employ.[8]

A more recent case showing these domestic constraints involves US policy toward Pakistan. Just prior to 2001, US policy toward Pakistan emphasized sanctions and limited engagement in response to the nuclear tests and military coup in the late 1990s. Following the 9/11 terror attacks in the United States, the Bush administration changed direction and sought to make Pakistan an ally. After a meeting with President Musharraf, Bush agreed to seek $1 billion in debt relief, greatly expanded economic and geopolitical aid, and reduced trade barriers to Pakistani goods, especially textiles.[9] Bush was able to secure debt relief from Congress, but he had a much harder time getting the economic aid funds and trade liberalization that he desired. Congress approved substantial geopolitical aid but in the end refused to grant greater trade access. The United States and Pakistan have also been unable to sign a free trade agreement or a bilateral investment treaty.[10] Hence, despite being an important strategic ally, the US government has been unable to combine this with more liberalized trade with Pakistan and has faced continuing pressures to reduce economic aid. Although immediately following 9/11 some efforts were made, trade liberalization on products that would threaten textile producers was staunchly opposed.[11] President George W. Bush and the Pakistani government wanted to open American markets to Pakistani trade, but were unable to because of congressional and interest group resistance; domestic interests in the United States worked to prevent further trade liberalization with Pakistan, undercutting US foreign policy goals.[12]

Another case that we develop at length in chapter 7 concerns US policy toward Sub-Saharan Africa. After the end of the Cold War and apartheid in South Africa, the US government had the opportunity to reshape its policy toward the region, which suffered from too much conflict, too little democratization, and too little development. The Clinton administration wanted to engage with the countries in the region to address these prob-

---

8   As Douglas Kriner notes, ex ante, presidents may pay few domestic costs for military action. But if those deployments last long and do not appear successful, the domestic costs and Congress's involvement may grow greatly. Sometimes presidents can and do anticipate this; other times they appear not to. Kriner, 2010.

9   Shah, 2006.

10   Iqbal, 2014.

11   Pomper, 2001.

12   Brulliard, 2010.

lems; thus the president decided at first to use foreign aid as a main element of his policies toward Africa. In this he was frustrated time and again by a Republican-controlled Congress that opposed development aid. Unable to pursue his goals via aid, Clinton shifted to trade policy. With Republicans in Congress favoring trade over aid, this choice became easier for him to advance. The African Growth and Opportunity Act (AGOA), signed into law on May 18, 2000, unilaterally expanded access to the US market for African exports. With aid policy restricted by Congress, Clinton pushed ahead with a trade strategy, though even this was difficult as evidenced by the many years of domestic political wrangling over AGOA. Clinton then turned to a strategy that relied more heavily on military engagement and began to build the military footprint of the United States in Sub-Saharan Africa in the late 1990s.

This process continued under President George W. Bush. During his presidency, the 2001 terrorist attacks in the United States and the global war on terror (GWOT) accelerated the movement toward military involvement in Sub-Saharan Africa, finally establishing AFRICOM, a Unified Combatant Command for the continent. AFRICOM represents the militarization of US policy in the region. Bush was also able to increase aid to the continent, although never in the full amounts he desired. The Millennium Challenge Corporation (MCC) and the President's Emergency Plan for AIDS Relief (PEPFAR) were policy innovations that were necessary to induce Congress to resume substantial aid to the region, and Congress became deeply involved in shaping these aid operations over time. Bush also pushed trade policy forward, revising and expanding AGOA several times. Again he faced domestic resistance to making AGOA an even larger element of US policy, as we describe at length in chapter 7. Thus, as with the Clinton administration, the Bush administration also ended up substituting military engagement in place of greater aid and international trade due to American domestic political pressures.

Of course, these cases are but a very small sample of the policy choices the US government has made in its approach to foreign countries and international problems. Indeed, there is a large literature describing American foreign policy.[13] The purpose of this book is to explain US foreign policy in a rigorous fashion. As Jervis notes, many studies of foreign policy, especially of the United States, tend to be descriptive or prescriptive.[14] Instead, we offer an analytical and explanatory study. We use multiple methods to

---

13   As a recent description of US policy toward Iran notes, "Over the years the US has shown considerable ingenuity in its efforts to slow Iran's production of nuclear fuel: it has used sabotage, cyberattacks, and creative economic sanctions. Now, mixing face-saving diplomacy and innovative technology, negotiators are attempting a new approach." Sanger, 2014, p. A4.

14   Jervis, 2005, p. 5.

explain fundamental aspects of American foreign policy. Case studies, quantitative methods, text analysis, and surveys all inform our research. Such an approach is rare in this area, but it is important in order to better understand policy choices and their outcomes. Throughout we try to connect our findings to important descriptive and prescriptive accounts of American foreign policy.

## Core Contributions

Governments have many policy instruments they can use to address foreign relations, but they must contend with the fact that domestic politics matters for foreign policy. American presidents have to negotiate and interact with Congress and interest groups to enact the foreign policies they prefer. Different policy instruments have different politics associated with them. Two aspects are very important in shaping the domestic politics that affect foreign policy: the nature of the distributional impact that different policies have and the degree of ideological divisions. The extent of distributive politics also affects the asymmetry of information about a particular policy between the president and Congress. These features affect how powerful the president will be, and thus whether he can pursue his internationalist agenda.

One basic but fundamental point we make is that foreign policy needs to be understood in terms of the different policy instruments it comprises. These different tools vary in their utility and their impact on a given international problem, but they also vary considerably in how they affect domestic groups. The distinct politics that shape different policy instruments is key to understanding what policies are chosen and why. The domestic politics of foreign policy accounts for why we sometimes see the militarization of US foreign policy, by which we mean defining foreign issues as military ones, and thus letting military planning and military tools dominate all aspects of foreign policy making.

Our study is progressive in a number of ways. First, we synthesize and further develop important research in a number of different areas, from the "two presidencies" theory in American politics to the open economy politics literature in comparative and international political economy. We focus on a wide variety of domestic actors, including the public, bureaucracies, interest groups, the executive branch, and Congress. Each of these actors has important implications for the president's ability to implement an internationalist grand strategy. We extend the literature on foreign policy issue areas by focusing on specific policy instruments and then theorizing about what makes these instruments different and showing how this affects the fungibility of power resources for a nation. We also unpack the common idea of "high" and "low" politics in foreign policy studies. In addition, our study highlights differences across foreign policy instruments rather than temporal changes in American foreign policy. Finally, we present a systematic study of American foreign policy. We use multiple types and sources of data to develop a more convincing argument about presidential power and foreign policy. We analyze hundreds of thousands of lobbying reports, data on presidential and congressional budgetary politics, roll call voting, data on the design of bureaucracies, public opinion data, and case studies. Thus our analysis covers a broad set of relevant institutions. Our ability to bring together such a diverse range of data about many different political institutions is unique in the study of American foreign policy, but is also rare in other areas of political science.

## What Is Foreign Policy?

Foreign policy is the means by which a sovereign nation interacts with other sovereign nations and non-state actors outside its borders. Foreign policy consists of many different policy instruments. A country can engage with other nations and non-state actors operating beyond its borders in a wide variety of ways. Today the US government employs a gamut of foreign policy instruments, including immigration, economic and geopolitical aid, international trade, sanctions, military spending, and military force. We show how these policy instruments have different politics associated with them. In turn these politics influence the ability of the president to implement the policies and grand strategies he desires.[15]

Other scholars have examined related questions using a broader conceptualization which focused on issue areas rather than policy instruments. This literature shares a number of our intuitions and emphases.[16] As scholars in

15 We generated a list of all such policy instruments from a wide-ranging review of textbook accounts of US foreign policy. These instruments emerged as key ones and they cover considerable ground. They are also instruments that are often directly linked to decision makers, agencies, in the government, which facilitates their analysis. We do not take up "diplomacy," which refers to the actions and signals sent by a country to others. While diplomacy is important in its own right, many of the instruments that diplomacy refers to relate to our core policy instruments. Hence, this book examines the implications of domestic politics for diplomacy, but is not a definitive treatment of this broad subject.

16 There are several examples of defining issue areas in abstract terms. James Rosenau defines an issue area as a cluster of values, the allocation of which through policy choices leads the actors affected to differ greatly over either the way in which the values should be allocated or the levels at which the allocations should be authorized and that the actors engage in distinctive behaviors designed to mobilize support for their particular values. Robert Keohane defines issue areas as problems about which policy makers are concerned and are determined by the "extent to which governments regard sets of issues as closely interdependent and treat them collectively. Decisions made on one issue must affect others in the issue area, either

this tradition, we think the key issue areas are development, international economic relations, diplomatic relations, and military defense.[17] Each of our policy instruments maps into one or more of these issue areas. For example, economic aid most clearly operates in the issue area of economic development. At times, these instruments can affect multiple issue areas. For example, economic aid can contribute to both development abroad and diplomatic relations. Or a trade agreement with an important ally might contribute to development, international economic relations, and diplomatic ones. Our theory helps to explain the different politics around each instrument, but also the politics of selecting a portfolio of policy instruments. Thus our analysis builds on but disaggregates further this more traditional focus on issue areas in foreign policy. Indeed, the political differences across foreign policy instruments are critically important as they shape the long-term trajectory of American policy.

Our focus on foreign policy instruments is more specific and granular compared to earlier work on issue areas. This disaggregation is important because foreign policy instruments that primarily affect one issue area may have very different politics.[18] Our focus on economic aid, international trade, immigration, geopolitical aid, sanctions, domestic military spending, and foreign military deployments reveals the politics around foreign policy more clearly compared to the traditional issue area literature. Furthermore, as we discuss later, our focus on instruments lets us connect with the literature on policy substitution in a more direct manner. Finally, our focus is less on changes in the determinants of American foreign policy over time, but more squarely on understanding differences across policy instruments.

through functional links or through regular patterns of bargaining." According to William Potter, this means that different issue areas evoke participation in the decision-making process from different actors. Rosenau, 1966, p. 81; Keohane, 1983, p. 525; Potter, 1980, p. 407. Also see Zimmerman, 1973; Evangelista, 1989; Gowa, 1998.

17  Similar lists of "issue areas" have also been generated by other scholars. For example, Brecher, et al. divide issue areas into military-security, political-diplomatic, economic-developmental, and cultural-status. Brecher, Steinberg, and Stein, 1969.

18  For example, one might aggregate military spending with other military instruments like geopolitical aid and deployments because they relate to the same issue area. We show how domestic military spending, which includes funding for bases and contracts for military weapons programs, has distinct politics surrounding it compared to geopolitical aid and foreign military deployments. Defense spending is crucial to American military strength and as such is a vital element of deterrence. For example, "the political aim of military preparations is to make the actual application of military force unnecessary by inducing the prospective enemy to desist from the use of military force." Morgenthau, 1960, p. 30. But defense spending also has substantial distributional consequences, and involves an extremely assertive Congress. Take, for example, the recent push for major new spending on overhauling the US nuclear program. While Obama wanted to downsize the arsenal, Congress pushed for much higher spending in part because of the substantial district level spending it would generate, as evidenced by press releases by legislators like Lamar Alexander. Alexander, 2014; Broad and Sanger, 2014.

Many international relations theories suggest that the constraints on presidents and foreign policy lie elsewhere, mainly in the international system and other countries. Realism, for instance, argues that countries behave according to their relative power positions and the threats that other states pose to them.[19] But realism also admits that for a better understanding of foreign policy, one has to look not only at these two components but also at *the ability of leaders to extract and direct resources from their societies to foreign policy ends*.[20] We focus on the latter element here, making our argument compatible with realism. Indeed, our theory helps realist claims to be more specific by considering when and how the domestic political system deploys resources to address foreign policy ends.[21]

Extracting and directing resources from their societies to foreign policy ends depends in the US case on the president's ability to get his policies through Congress. A government needs tax revenues, war materiel, and an extensive workforce to engage internationally using a wide gamut of foreign policy instruments.[22] To a great extent, then, the president's ability to obtain his desired foreign policy depends on negotiations with Congress as well as public opinion and interest group support. So we ask under what conditions the president can get the resources he needs to fashion foreign policy in the direction he desires. This varies a great deal by policy instrument, not so much because of factors like presidential popularity, economic conditions, or external pressures, but, we argue, as a result of the political character of the policy instruments that are involved. Other scholars have noted that power resources may not be fungible across issue areas and policy instruments, and we show why domestic politics may be one reason for this.[23] When political leaders cannot substitute one policy instrument for another, they face a problem similar to the lack of fungibility of power resources on the international level.

19   Waltz, 1979; Walt, 1998.

20   Walt, 1998; Snyder, 2002; Jervis, 2005; Taliaferro, Lobell, and Ripsman, 2009.

21   "Once raised, the notion that international power analysis must take into account the ability of governments to extract and direct the resources of their societies seems almost obvious, and in fact it simply involves incorporating into international relations theory variables that are routine in other subfields of political science." Rose, 1998, p. 161.

22   As one scholar notes more specifically about military policy, "because the state must negotiate with domestic actors for access to these societally controlled resources, our attention is directed toward state-society relations, that is, toward the process by which the state attempts to mobilize these resources. Thus, when the state participates in foreign conflict, it engages in two kinds of battles: the defense of the country's borders against foreign adversaries and the struggle with society for access to its desired resources. Consequently, the state's war preparation strategies are a function of both its objectives in the international and domestic arenas and the socioeconomic constraints on its actions." Barnett, 1990, p. 535.

23   Keohane and Nye, 1977; Baldwin, 1986; Keohane, 1986.

# Presidential Power in Foreign Policy

The main focus of this book is presidential power in US foreign policy making. Presidential power is defined as the president's ability to exert "influence over all the various doings of government: writing policy, designing the administrative state, interpreting and then implementing the law, or any combination thereof."[24] This is a broad conception of power that focuses on outcomes and the president's ability to achieve specific outcomes that would not otherwise occur in the absence of his actions. Neustadt in his classic definition of presidential power argues that it is the power to persuade. And we agree: through persuasion in part, the president comes to influence the "doings of government."[25] But we move beyond this argument about persuasion to also look at structural sources of power. For example, in chapter 6, we examine how the structure of presidential control over bureaucracies influences presidential power.

The president and presidential power are important because the executive branch is the place where the external pressures and constraints from the rest of the world are most clearly registered; it is also often the main source of American responses to those pressures. The president and the executive branch are the main conduits into the US political process for international influences on the one hand and out to the broader world for American foreign policy responses on the other. The president operates at the fulcrum of the two-level game that foreign policy exemplifies.[26] The president's primary responsibility is to guard American interests, and his competence in doing so is an important factor affecting his popularity and re-electability.

Some studies of American foreign policy make it seem as if the president is the sole force devising policy and that he can implement whatever policies he wants.[27] As Krasner wrote in a seminal book, "For US foreign policy the central state actors are the President and Secretary of State and the most important institutions are the White House and State Department. What distinguishes these roles and agencies is their high degree of insulation from specific social pressures and a set of formal and informal obligations that charge them with furthering the nation's general interests."[28] These studies view the president and executive branch as likely to dominate foreign pol-

---

24  Howell, 2013, p. 13.

25  Neustadt, 1960. Others have argued that presidents have power less through persuasion than through "going public." Kernell, 1993. Others dispute this claim. Edwards, 2003. And others see presidential power as varying more with the external conditions, or the political environment. Schlesinger, 2004. See, e.g., Skowronek, 2008.

26  Milner, 1997.

27  Krasner, 1978; Ikenberry, Lake, and Mastanduno, 1988; Legro, 2005; Brooks and Wohlforth, 2008.

28  Krasner, 1978, p. 11.

icy and able to make autonomous choices; i.e., they are able, as Krasner long ago put it, to "defend the national interest."[29]

One reason for this view is that the president and the executive branch are often assumed to be more immune to public and/or interest group pressure than the legislative branch is. Indeed, studies suggest that Congress is much more susceptible to domestic pressure from public opinion and interest groups than is the executive branch, but this makes Congress a primary vehicle for injecting these internal pressures into the foreign policy process.[30] This heavy focus on the executive overlooks Congress, the bureaucracy, interest groups, and the public, all of whom may play important roles in shaping foreign policy. Rather than neglect these actors, we place them squarely into the foreign policy-making picture.

Previous work in American politics also makes the claim that the executive branch and the president are dominant in foreign policy. The literature on the "two presidencies" is one example of this.[31] The two presidencies literature argues that because of the requirements of secrecy, timeliness, and information, presidents are more able to set the agenda in foreign than domestic policy and to move forward on it without congressional interference. It is as if there were two separate presidencies. A number of other studies have extended this argument.[32]

Recently, Canes-Wrone, Howell, and Lewis used new data to show that there exists a difference in presidential power between domestic and foreign policy issues.[33] In chapters 5 and 6 we use their data to show that presidential control varies significantly among foreign policy instruments, with some being much more like domestic policy ones. Other studies have also raised questions about the two presidencies, finding limited, if any, support for the claims and showing that presidents' abilities to gain support in Congress on foreign policy issues is often quite constrained.[34] Hence the debate

---

29   See also Krasner, 1972; Art, 1973; and Wildavsky, 1991.

30   Jacobs and Page, 2005, p. 108.

31   Wildavsky, 1966; Wildavsky, 1969; Peppers, 1975; LeLoup and Shull, 1979; Sigelman, 1979; Lee, 1980; Shull and LeLoup, 1981; Sigelman, 1981; Zeidenstein, 1981; Cohen, 1982; Carter, 1985; Carter, 1986; Edwards, 1986; Fleisher and Bond, 1988; Oldfield and Wildavsky, 1989; Renka and Jones, 1991a; Renka and Jones, 1991b; Shull, 1991; Sullivan, 1991; Canes-Wrone, Howell, and Lewis, 2008.

32   Others have asserted that the president dominates the policy process when it comes to the use of force and have noted the "imperial presidency" at least in military policy. Schlesinger, 1973; Hinckley, 1994; Meernik, 1994; Peterson, 1994; Fisher, 1995; Gowa, 1998; Gowa, 1999; Rudalevige, 2005. Howell, as well as Howell, Jackman, and Rogowski, show that during war, presidents seem to get more deference from Congress and are able to build support for their policies more easily. Howell, 2011; Howell, Jackman, and Rogowski, 2013.

33   Canes-Wrone, Howell, and Lewis, 2008.

34   Peppers, 1975; LeLoup and Shull, 1979; Sigelman, 1979; Fleisher and Bond, 1988; McCormick and Wittkopf, 1990; Howell and Pevehouse, 2005; Howell and Pevehouse, 2007; Kriner, 2010; Howell, 2011.

over the power of the president in foreign policy, and especially relative to domestic policy, continues.[35]

Other scholarship has examined the role of Congress in foreign policy.[36] Our research and these other studies show that, domestically, the president cannot always get what he wants in terms of foreign policy.[37] In fact, one piece of our data points out that close to a third of the time when the president endorses a crucial foreign policy vote, he is unsuccessful in obtaining congressional approval. This represents a small slice of foreign policy actions in the United States (the president often does not take a position on congressional votes on foreign policy, and some policies do not get voted on), but it should give pause to those who believe the president commands American foreign policy. Moreover, this is the average for all of our foreign policy votes, and for each policy instrument the rate of congressional disapproval varies greatly. Thus, presidents do face domestic constraints on their foreign policy choices. We explain when and why presidents are unable to realize their preferences for foreign policies.

Our project then moves beyond this simple divide between domestic and foreign policy-making processes by arguing that presidential power over foreign policy depends on the policy instrument and his relations with interest groups, Congress, and the public within it. Thus our focus is on the factors that allow presidents to have more influence over some policy instruments than others. In doing so, we will abstract from, or control for, many of the variables offered in the previous literature for the factors that increase or decrease presidential power.[38] We focus less on changes over time and much more on differences across foreign policy instruments.

35  Past research has also focused on other factors such as his popularity. See, e.g., Rivers and Rose, 1985; Rohde and Simon, 1985. Others conclude that its impact is marginal. Bond and Fleisher, 1984; Edwards, 1989; Bond and Fleisher, 1990. Again others consider economic conditions. Hibbs, 1982; Powell and Whitten, 1993; Lewis-Beck and Paldam, 2000; Dorussen and Taylor, 2002; Duch and Stevenson, 2008. And others look at war. Howell, 2011; Howell, Jackman, and Rogowski, 2013.

36  For example, Lindsay and Ripley, 1992; Lohmann and O'Halloran, 1994; Trubowitz, 1998; Howell and Pevehouse, 2007. An earlier literature on the competition between Congress and the president over foreign policy as suggested by Lindsay and Ripley includes Franck, 1981; Spanier and Nogee, 1981; Rourke, 1983; Johnson, 1984; Muskie, Rush and Thompson, 1986; Warburg, 1989; Mann, 1990; McCormick and Wittkopf, 1990; Caldwell, 1991; Thurber, 1991; Wirls, 1992.

37  Howell and Pevehouse, 2007; Mearsheimer and Walt, 2007.

38  Other literature focuses on presidential strategies for maximizing his influence. As Jackman points out, "An extensive literature has explored the different governing tools presidents use to pursue their policy objectives. . . . A variety of strategic tools have been found to influence policy, including: proposing a legislative program (for a recent review, see Beckmann, 2010); centralizing policy-formulation within the executive branch (Moe, 1985; Rudalevige, 2002); politicizing the bureaucracy through the appointments process (Lewis, 2008); 'going public' with an issue (Canes-Wrone, 2006); vetoing legislation passed by congress (Cameron,

Descriptively, our position is closest to the "intermestic" account of US foreign policy.[39] The president interacts strategically with legislators, interest groups, and other domestic actors in designing his policies. Congress, interest groups, and the public constrain the president in foreign policy, but, crucially, the extent of this constraint varies across policy instruments. Some foreign policy instruments have characteristics that heighten or lessen the president's ability to influence policy choices. Likewise, legislators face different incentives for each policy instrument. The need to win elections forces presidents and legislators to contemplate the domestic consequences of different types of foreign policy choices.

As discussed previously, the importance of issue areas in politics—which the policy instruments we study relate to and affect—has long been acknowledged.[40] In thinking about foreign policy, Rosenau wrote, "Systematic analyses of the functioning of all types of political systems—from local to national to international on the geographic scale and from party to legislative to executive at the functional level—are also converging on the finding that different types of issues elicit different sets of motives on the part of different actors in a political system."[41] However, as he and others noted, one cannot let the plethora of issue areas overwhelm systematic theoretical analysis, which depends on identifying their key features, an important step we take that is facilitated by focusing on policy instruments.[42]

Many scholars focus on how the cost and benefits of a policy are felt domestically. Like them, we too examine how the distribution of costs and benefits of policies affect the politics around different instruments. Others have pointed to a realm of "high politics" and one of "low politics" in foreign policy.[43] Others, like Keohane and Nye, have argued about the importance of issue areas in terms of the fungibility of power resources. They, like us, note that in certain issue areas, which use the policy instruments we focus on, leaders may have more trouble bringing some of their power resources to bear than in other areas with other resources. Our analysis explains not only why these foreign policy instruments differ, but also why there may be low fungibility across instruments and why so-called high and

2000); engaging in unilateral action by issuing executive orders (Howell, 2003); and altering legislation by issuing signing statements (Savage, 2007)." Jackman, 2012, p. 4. Cites from original passage omitted.

39   Manning, 1977.

40   Schattschneider, 1935; Lowi, 1964; Wilson, 1973; Zimmerman, 1973; Almond, 1977; Keohane and Nye, 1977; Keohane, 1983; Keohane, 1986; Evangelista, 1989; Hinckley, 1994; Lindsay, 1994; Gowa, 1998; Gowa, 1999; Henehan, 2000; Lapinski, 2013.

41   Rosenau, 1967, p. 14.

42   For different attempts, see Brecher, Steinberg, and Stein, 1969; Mansbach and Vasquez, 1981, p. 35; Meernik, 1993, p. 585.

43   Peppers, 1975; Hughes, 1978; Evangelista, 1989, p. 150; Meernik, 1993, pp. 576–577.

low politics are shaped the way they are. Presidents have more discretion over using military force not (solely) because of the nature of the external problem or threat, but because of domestic politics; high and low politics is just as much about the nature of domestic politics as it is about international relations.

We propose two criteria for understanding the politics surrounding different policy instruments. In particular, as developed in detail in chapter 2 and then illustrated throughout the rest of the book, we focus on (1) the extent to which a policy instrument engenders large costs and benefits for domestic actors—i.e., the extent of distributive politics, and (2) the extent of ideological divisions that are present. These characteristics exert an important influence on the president's ability to get what he wants. Both ideas and interests matter.

Our perspective is not entirely new. But one new feature is that we bring the scholarship in the field of international and comparative political economy to bear on this topic.[44] Much of this literature considers the distributional consequences of different policies. Relying on economic theory about the ways that policies affect incomes of different groups, the open economy politics (OEP) literature links the preferences of domestic groups for different policies given their distributional impacts.[45] This allows one to hypothesize about the policy preferences of different groups and to explore the impact of these groups on foreign policy making in a more rigorous fashion. These groups can lobby and provide information to Congress to impede or assist the president, often affecting the president's ability to use different policy instruments. Hence we link the preferences of domestic

44  See the open economy politics literature; for instance, the discussion of it by Frieden and Rogowski, and David Lake. Frieden and Rogowski, 1996; Lake, 2009.

45  Lake, 2009. A large literature on trade policy exists, which has examined on how various domestic groups define their policy preferences and how leaders respond to this. Schattschneider, 1935; Rogowski, 1987; Milner, 1988a; Magee, Brock, and Young, 1989; Lohmann and O'Halloran, 1994; Epstein and O'Halloran, 1996; Bailey, Goldstein, and Weingast, 1997; Scheve and Slaughter, 2001b; Hiscox, 2002b; McGillivray, 2004; Scheve and Slaughter, 2004; Chase, 2005; Hainmueller and Hiscox, 2006; Gawande, Krishna, and Olarreaga, 2009; Lü, Scheve, and Slaughter, 2010. A similar literature explores monetary and financial policy, examining how domestic groups and the state interact to produce policy. Gowa, 1988; Frieden, 1991; Broz, 2005. And immigration has recently come under study in a similar vein. The debate there has centered around whether economic interests are most important for defining preferences or whether other types of factors, like nationalism or culture, matter more. Citrin, Green, Muste. and Wong, 1997; O'Rourke and Sinnott, 2001; Scheve and Slaughter, 2001a; Mayda, 2006; Dustmann and Preston, 2007; Hainmueller and Hiscox, 2007; Hanson, Scheve, and Slaughter, 2007; Hainmueller and Hiscox, 2010; Tingley, 2013. Finally, a smaller literature exists that examines foreign aid. Lumsdaine, 1993; Therien and Noel, 2000; Fleck and Kilby, 2001; Noel and Therien, 2002; Fleck and Kilby, 2006; Bueno de Mesquita and Smith, 2007; Bueno de Mesquita and Smith, 2009; Milner and Tingley, 2010; Wright and Winters, 2010; Milner and Tingley, 2011; Paxton and Knack, 2012; Milner and Tingley, 2013a.

interest groups and constituents to the foreign policies that the president is considering, and we show when and how these domestic influences can affect his ability to choose and substitute foreign policies. In a sense, we are adding the president's role to comparative and international political economy models. We are thus bringing foreign policy back into international political economy.

Our second innovation is to try to explain presidential power in foreign policy making. When does the president have the most influence? Under what conditions does he have the least? We show that his influence varies by policy instrument. Our answer focuses on how distributional and ideological politics drive congressional actors. Policies that create large and concentrated gains and/or losses for domestic groups weaken presidents because they create incentives for these groups—both winners and losers—to organize and lobby the government. They thus activate the electoral concerns of legislators and presidents. These policy instruments and the issue areas they impact look much like domestic political ones where the president is constrained by Congress. In areas with less distributive politics, as in more policies that entail more public goods, the president's role in setting policy is easier; few, if any, domestic actors have incentives to collect and transmit information and/or block the president's policy choices by lobbying Congress in this case. As we discuss later, ideological politics plays a similar role. Presidents will face strong opposition to using certain policy instruments and ideological divisions will also make it harder to substitute that instrument for another.

A third important feature of our book is the attention to the distribution of information about foreign policy within the US government. In the United States a large bureaucracy has developed over time that collects, analyzes, and feeds information to the executive branch. Characteristics of policy instruments and the issue areas they impact affect how much information presidents have about policies and their ramifications relative to other groups, like Congress. Foreign policies tend to generate information asymmetries between the president and other actors because the feedback loop between domestic constituents and interest groups and Congress is unavailable. We argue, however, that the extent of this asymmetry depends on the policy instrument. Does the president have access to resources that enable him to command much more information about a specific policy proposal than Congress has? Presidents may have both the constitutional prerogatives and the bureaucratic capacity to amass much more information than Congress or other social groups when it comes to policy instruments that generate few distributional incentives. These informational advantages enhance his ability to control policy choices. For other policy instruments, he will have much less advantage as distributional concerns make other actors willing to gather and transmit information.

## Policy Substitution

A second focus of our book, and one largely absent in the "two presidencies" literature as well as much of the comparative and international political economy literatures (including the issue area literature mentioned previously), flows naturally from the previous questions just discussed: policy substitution.[46] Policy instruments can be substitutes: for example, a country can offer foreign aid instead of using military force to try to resolve an international problem. As Most and Starr pointed out, policy substitutability means that leaders can use a variety of different policy instruments to achieve a similar goal.[47] This implies that any one problem can be addressed through different policy instruments. An ideal package of policies for any particular problem would allow for tradeoffs among the instruments at optimal marginal rates of substitution. As Clark et al. point out, "there are potentially many policy paths to any foreign policy goal, and leaders make their decisions based in large part on the costs associated with those policies."[48] When and why does substitution happen, when does it fail to occur, and how do domestic politics affect this process?

More generally, what incentives do leaders have to substitute one policy for another? Why, for example, might a leader utilize economic sanctions instead of foreign aid or military intervention in order to coerce another state? Many scholars answer this question by looking mainly at the external environment and the likely reactions of other states,[49] whereas others see it as a mixture of international and domestic factors.[50] We focus more on domestic factors.

One interesting example to illuminate the role of domestic politics comes from US food aid to foreign countries. The quote at the start of this chapter gives a flavor of the issues involved with this type of instrument. Food aid from the United States is substantial, but it is delivered in an inefficient way if its goal is to reduce hunger abroad. Many scholars have concluded that such aid serves domestic economic interests and geopolitical ones rather than actually helping to reduce food shortages in poor coun-

---

46   "The foreign policy substitution argument generally posits that leaders choose foreign policies from a set of possible alternatives, depending on the circumstances they face at any given time; leaders have multiple policy tools from which to choose, and they will choose the policy tools they think are most likely to succeed." Clark and Reed, 2005, p. 609. The major works are Most and Starr, 1984; Most and Starr, 1989; Bennett and Nordstrom, 2000; Morgan and Palmer, 2000; Palmer and Bhandari, 2000; Regan, 2000; Starr, 2000; Palmer, Wohlander, and Morgan, 2002.

47   Most and Starr, 1984; Most and Starr, 1989.

48   Clark, Nordstrom, and Reed, 2008, p. 765.

49   For example, Bennett and Nordstrom, 2000; Clark and Reed, 2005; Clark, Nordstrom, and Reed, 2008.

50   Regan, 2000, p. 104.

tries.[51] Fariss, for instance, asks, "why [is] food aid used in this way if other more powerful economic aid instruments are at the disposal of policy makers?"[52] He immediately raises the issue of policy substitution. He shows that a central reason that food aid is deployed in a particular way by the United States is because of Congress. Congressional legislation that restricts what the president can do with economic aid and how he can use food aid have forced the president to turn to a peculiar method of disbursing food as a foreign policy instrument. As Fariss notes, "If the US Foreign Assistance Act or sanctions restrict the use of certain economic aid programs then policy-makers may consider food aid as a substitute."[53] Highlighting our themes, this example shows that constraints on the president's choices do exist, they are often domestic in origin, and they can even influence foreign policy in perverse ways.

What explains this? Domestic politics is our answer. The president makes choices about foreign policy with domestic considerations in mind. The economic interests of core constituents and their ideological preferences drive part of the choice of policy instruments. Problems in making the optimal substitution among policies are attributable in part to domestic politics. The president often cannot craft the ideal package of policies where he balances the costs and benefits of using different policy instruments because of domestic politics. Ideology plays an important role here, in addition to material interests and interest groups. Conflicts between liberals and conservatives, who for various reasons may prefer different types of instruments, can hinder the use of different combinations of them for addressing foreign policy problems. Both material and ideological constraints can thus influence policy substitution. In sum, presidential power and policy substitution are related. Where presidents are weak because of these constraints, policy substitution is much more difficult. Wielding different power resources in international politics is thus not only problematic because of the lack of fungibility of different policies at the international level, but also because of constraints associated with domestic politics.[54]

Given our focus on substitution, it is helpful to dispense with a common misunderstanding of what drives the use of particular foreign policy instruments over others. Some argue that the specific details of an international event determine what policy instruments should be used. If a situation

---

51 See, e.g., Wallerstein, 1980; Ball and Johnson, 1996; Zahariadis, Travis, and Ward, 2000; Neumayer, 2005.

52 Fariss, 2010, p. 108.

53 Ibid.

54 Of course policy instruments can also be thought of as being complements. In many cases this might be the case. However, we note that our same arguments apply in this case, as an optimal complement might be blocked for the same domestic political reasons, and that ultimately budget constraints will force some degree of substitution.

poses a security threat, it deserves a military answer. We believe this view is dangerously misleading, as do others.[55] We of course do not suggest that presidents should consider signing trade agreements with terrorist organizations in lieu of conducting military operations. How an international problem or threat is defined and which bureaucracies and instruments are considered for addressing it are critical issues in shaping a country's foreign policy. Non-military instruments are almost always useful—sometimes alone and other times as part of a larger foreign policy package. Indeed, throughout the book we engage with arguments about the need for US foreign policy to be broad-based in any situation. But, to be able to do so, domestic support is necessary. Even in situations that pose a national security threat to the United States, it might be wise to substitute away from some military instruments of statecraft and toward instruments like trade and economic aid. Our brief example of US-Pakistan relations following 9/11 at the start of this chapter illustrates this. Whether US domestic politics allows this substitution—or complementary use of many instruments—is the more interesting question, and one that we take up throughout the book.

## Overview of Our Theory

We examine a key requirement for the conduct of foreign policy: how American presidents extract and direct resources from the domestic political system to meet international challenges.[56] As realists acknowledge, "International imperatives are filtered through the medium of state structure and affected by how top officials assess likely threats, identified viable strategies in response to those threats, and ultimately extracted and mobilized the societal resources necessary to implement and sustain those strategies . . . Unit-level variables constrain or facilitate the ability of all types of states—great powers as well as lesser states—to respond to systemic imperatives."[57] Domestic political institutions are critical to this process. The set of political institutions in the United States that constitutes the policy-making process is unique and has been rather stable over time. The distinctive package of American institutions, including a presidency, the separation of powers, a two-party system, and executive bargaining with Congress over resources, has not changed much over the past thirty years. Ideological polarization may have increased, and the committee system in Congress may have evolved.[58] But the critical institutions and overarching institutional framework remain the

55   Campbell, 2014; DeGennaro, 2014; Holshek, 2014.
56   Taliaferro, Lobell, and Ripsman, 2009, pp. 3–4.
57   Ibid.
58   See Lindsay and Ripley for changes in the 1970s and 1980s. Lindsay and Ripley, 1992, pp. 427–429.

same. And despite changes during the era we study, American foreign policy has remained oriented to an internationalist program. There have been ups and downs in the degree of unilateralism in its policies, but there has been continuity overall. Thus we focus on differences across policy instruments and in the overall package of policies chosen.

Our theory looks at two characteristics of policy instruments to understand how presidential power across foreign policy instruments varies. First, we examine the degree of distributive politics associated with each instrument. High levels of distributive politics are found where policies generate large, concentrated economic losses and gains for domestic groups. For these policies, Congress, interest groups, and the public may all be motivated to be active, lobbying and transmitting information for and against the president's position.[59] Some groups may favor the president's preferred policy and others may oppose it, setting up the conditions for strong political contestation. This will then have an impact on the distribution of information about the policy and will likely further weaken the president's ability to use this instrument.

A second characteristic of importance is the extent of ideological divisions. The greater these divisions are, the more conflict among domestic groups, and the harder it is for the president to control policy. Actors with the opposing ideological preferences will be more highly motivated to resist the president's preferred policies. In sum, for instruments fraught with distributive politics and ideological differences, presidents will be the weakest and least able to adopt the foreign policies they desire. Our main hypothesis then is that where distributive politics is muted and ideological divisions are low, presidents will have the greatest room for influence. In chapter 2, we spell out these conditions and the hypotheses that flow from them in greater detail.

Presidential power affects the ability of presidents to substitute one type of policy for another. The dynamic of policy substitution is obscured by much previous work in IR and IPE that focuses on one issue area or policy instrument at a time (e.g., see literature on trade, finance, military force).[60] Foreign policy instruments are often interrelated. Trade and aid policy were intimately linked in discussions about engagement with regions like Africa and the Caribbean. And military or economic aid can be used in lieu of

59 Lindsay comes close to our position when he notes that foreign policy can be divided into three types of policies. One of these is similar to our category of policies that are highly distributive and asymmetric, where Congress plays the largest role. Lindsay, 1994, p. 156.

60 Hiscox, 2002; Frieden, 1991; Howell and Pevehouse, 2007. Many studies of public opinion on foreign policy focus on a particular issue area or policy instrument. For instance, a sizable literature exists on public attitudes toward international trade. Scheve and Slaughter, 2001b; Beaulieu, 2002a; Mendelsohn, Wolfe, and Parkin, 2002; Mayda and Rodrik, 2005; Hiscox, 2006; Mansfield and Mutz, 2009.

military deployment.[61] Indeed, a major reason to depart from the issue area approach is to better understand the substitution of one policy instrument for another, which may depend substantially on domestic politics. In particular, the ability to substitute one policy for another will depend on the degree of preference overlap between supporters of different policy instruments and how influential the president is.

Theories of foreign policy often argue that substitutability among policies is high; one policy instrument can be used for many purposes and many policies can substitute for each other to achieve the same goal.[62] If legislators, interest groups, the president, and members of the public all had the same preferences, then substitution would be easy; there would be no political costs to it. But if there are different coalitions around different policy areas, then shifting to different policy instruments may be more difficult. Politics plays out differently for each of them. The president's ability to substitute one policy instrument for another greatly depends on the nature of these politics. Not all power resources of a country can be used in any instance; domestic politics may render some too politically costly for political leaders to employ at times. If they operate consistently, such domestic constraints may bias foreign policy toward some instruments more than others.

Our theory suggests a further implication. Substitutability not only depends on the possibilities of forming coalitions, but also on the president's influence. In areas where the policy has large, concentrated costs and benefits and interest groups are thus very active, the president's influence will be limited: his ability to freely substitute will be constrained because different domestic groups will oppose and support his preferred policies. It will also be much more limited if the ideological divisions surrounding the policy instruments are large. That is, if the groups that support and oppose policies have strong ideological bases for their views that divide them, then the president's ability to substitute will be extremely limited. He will have to forge new coalitions across the ideological divisions in the policy areas, and forging these new coalitions will be difficult and costly. Differing material consequences and ideological predispositions toward policy instruments shape the president's influence and thus his ability to use them in place of one another.

Our theory brings together material and ideological sources of preferences. Both ideas and economic interests matter in shaping the politics of

---

61  For instance, in an analysis of US efforts to deal with the rise of terrorist groups in Africa, the *New York Times* notes one such set of choices: "Wary of committing a large number of troops, the United States has sought to use more diplomatic and development instruments than military force in Africa." Shanker and Schmitt, 2011, p. A8. As we note in chapter 7, this wariness was soon overridden and the United States began a much more military-oriented strategy, in part because of domestic constraints on the economic strategies.

62  Most and Starr, 1984; Palmer and Bhandari, 2000.

foreign policy. We show this in our various empirical chapters. Our study does not examine the origins of these ideas; instead we explore more which policy instruments have greater and fewer ideological divisions associated with them. These ideas sometimes crosscut actors' material interests and this makes them a more independent source of political action. But ideas and interests both contribute to the politics surrounding foreign policy in our view.

# Implications for US Foreign Policy

## Internationalism and American Grand Strategy

Why does the choice of foreign policy instrument matter? Our focus on the politics around specific foreign policy instruments is anything but microscopic. Instead, it informs broader debates about the direction of US foreign policy. We care about presidential power in foreign policy because it affects the overall direction of American policy. Since World War II, presidents have been the prime proponents of a grand strategy of international engagement, sometimes labeled "liberal internationalism." The debate about the persistence and success of this strategy turns on presidential power and the use of a variety of foreign policy instruments.

American policy has followed a liberal internationalist grand strategy since World War II. Defining liberal internationalism is a difficult task.[63] We adopt a definition of it based on the consensual elements of the term as used by mainstream scholars.[64] "Liberal internationalism" implies two features of a foreign policy: first, that the country engages with other nations as opposed to being isolationist; and second, that it pursues an agenda that involves promoting "open markets, international institutions, cooperative security, democratic community, progressive change, collective problem solving, shared sovereignty, and the rule of law."[65]

The instruments that can be used in pursuit of an internationalist strategy span military and economic ones. Yet without understanding the politics around these policy instruments, we have little insight into the future trajectory of this long tradition. Recent work has questioned whether the United States will retreat from its sixty-year-old policy of "deep engagement," which is necessary to protect a liberal world order.[66] One question

---

63 Busby and Monten, 2008.

64 Holsti, 2004; Kupchan and Trubowitz, 2007; Busby and Monten, 2008; Ikenberry, 2009.

65 Ikenberry, 2009, p. 71. Some have disaggregated internationalism into cooperative and militant forms. Wittkopf, 1986. Others into multilateral and unilateral forms. Claude and Nuechterlein, 1997, p. 125. Whichever version one prefers, there is a strong consensus that such internationalism has been a defining characteristic of US policy.

66 Brooks, Ikenberry, and Wohlforth, 2012; Craig, Friedman, Green, et al., 2013.

often raised is whether this policy direction can or will change.[67] Will the United States become isolationist, as it was prior to World War II? American domestic politics is crucial to the maintenance of its internationalist policy and its deep engagement with the rest of the world. Specifically, the ability of the president to extract and direct significant amounts of resources to foreign policy is critical to maintaining the US posture of liberal internationalism. But American domestic institutions shape when and whether the president can muster the resources to engage abroad. Many scholars believe that the domestic requirements for sustaining such a policy require support from a large majority of the public and a bipartisan coalition in Congress.

To pursue a liberal internationalist policy, a president needs broad domestic support because such a policy necessitates costly, long-term strategies that involve credible commitments to mutual adjustments of policies among countries (i.e., cooperation). Support in Congress is thus necessary for several reasons. First, a liberal internationalist policy depends on the use of treaties and other international agreements that require explicit legislative support, sometimes supermajorities. Trade and investment agreements, military alliances, overseas military bases and operations, foreign aid, and economic sanctions all require congressional consent. Second, sustaining commitments to multilateral partners implies that continuity over time matters. A policy of foreign engagement through multilateral cooperation requires a long-term commitment by domestic constituencies. Third, a liberal internationalist policy agenda requires that substantial resources be allocated from domestic sources to fund overseas commitments. Congressional approvals of such spending and public support for it will be more difficult for some policy instruments compared to others.

The types of policies that comprise liberal internationalism are intended to promote an open capitalist economy, democracy, and stability. Our attention to the debate about liberal internationalism is related to our attempt to understand the choices made among the set of foreign policy instruments that are necessary for international engagement: international trade, economic aid, immigration, geopolitical aid, sanctions, domestic military spending, and military deployments. An inability, for instance, to be able to use trade policy because of domestic constraints would erode a liberal internationalist grand strategy. The president's desire to use these types of policies, and Congress's willingness to go along with them, signals a commitment to a grand strategy of liberal internationalism. But a departure from liberal internationalism could happen, for example, if the president was unable to muster the resources necessary to sustain such a policy because of domestic political constraints.

---

67    See Chaudoin, Milner, and Tingley, 2010; Kupchan and Trubowitz, 2010.

Presidents, as we point out, tend to accept the need for such international engagement. But Congress, interest groups, and the public may be more skeptical. In chapter 4 we look directly at the influences on legislators' choices about policies for and against international engagement. For each policy area, we show the factors that seem to push legislators toward more engagement and those that push them away from it. Our theory highlights the main influences on this. In chapter 6 on the public and in chapter 7 on case study research we also show which types of factors are related to more pro-international engagement. In sum, we demonstrate that our theory has important implications for the continued pursuit of liberal internationalism by the United States.

## Militarization

Some observers posit that the United States's external position as a superpower and its domestic institutions have led to the militarization of its foreign policy since World War II.[68] By militarization, we mean the injection of military planning and instruments of statecraft into all aspects of foreign policy making.[69] As Bacevich notes, it is "the tendency to see all international problems as military problems and to discount the likelihood of finding a solution except through military means."[70] It implies a heavy emphasis on the military capabilities of states and their deployment. And it relies on a tendency to define all foreign policy problems in terms of security threats that depend on the military and threats of force for their resolution. The simultaneous analysis of multiple foreign policy instruments in this book is crucial in light of these claims about militarization.

Militarization has at least five important aspects. It means the military forms a regular and critical part of the institutional establishment for foreign policy making. As we discuss later, the bureaucracy and its capacity matters for foreign policy. When the military has an overwhelming bureaucratic position relative to other agencies, it can exert much influence, both in problem definition as well as policy choice and implementation. It also implies that the military occupies a central element of the budgetary allocations for foreign policy. It furthermore acts as a principal means or instrument for realizing foreign policy goals.[71] Policy instruments controlled by the military become the "go to" instruments for every problem. Militarization takes on a

---

68   Sherry, 1995; Bacevich, 2002; Bacevich, 2007; Bacevich, 2010.

69   Constructivists employ a similar concept called "securitization". Waever, 1995; Buzan, Wæver, and de Wilde, 1998; Williams, 2003.

70   Bacevich, 2005, p. 2.

71   In recent literature on conflict and war initiation, militarization means "state decisions on which fraction of their resources they allocate toward military assets," primarily weapons, troops, and infrastructure necessary for using them. Debs and Monteiro, 2014, p. 6. For

central and powerful role in all decision making about foreign policy. Military leaders come to occupy key positions in the foreign policy decision-making process. And, critically, the use or threat of force dominates problem definition in foreign policy making. Every foreign issue comes to be defined as a military one or one best subject to military resolution. Such militarization has strong institutional foundations throughout the government.

If militarization happens during periods of time or has happened in general over time, then domestic politics may matter much in explaining the militarization of American foreign policy because such politics makes some policies easier to enact than others. We show that the president has more capability to shape the use of military and national intelligence instruments than other foreign policy instruments, which *may* lead to an overreliance on military instruments of statecraft. These differences among policy instruments have critical implications. Some of these instruments, such as geopolitical aid and deployments, allow the president greater freedom from domestic constraints and thus a greater ability to use them for foreign engagement and as substitutes for other foreign policy instruments. For any foreign policy problem then, the president may be tempted to use military instruments of statecraft because doing so may make it easier to persuade Congress to authorize. Other instruments may face greater contestation among domestic groups and hence legislative constraints and less presidential discretion. Domestic politics may bias foreign policy toward a dependence on military instruments of statecraft. Thus while non-military means of statecraft may be less expensive to employ and sometimes more likely to yield positive results in international affairs, presidents may choose not to use them because of their greater domestic political costs.

Militarization in our view is not necessarily a process that has to unfold over time. It may be a process affecting decision making at each point in time. Consider an international problem at any given point in time. The president has choices among different instruments to use to address this problem. The net costs vary by instrument. If much of the time the military option is less costly domestically, it may be more likely to be chosen. Think of this calculation holding the international costs and benefits of each instrument constant. If the domestic political costs of different foreign policy instruments vary in much the same way for each country and problem, then for each choice the president is more likely to choose the military option. If this happens over and over again with each new international problem the country faces, the result is militarization.

One indicator of the militarization of US foreign policy is the relative size of the Defense Department and related intelligence agencies compared

---

other discussions, see Slantchev, 2005; Meirowitz and Ramsay, 2010; Slantchev, 2011; Bas and Coe, 2012.

**Defense and State Department**
Spending in billions of 1996 dollars, 1865–2002

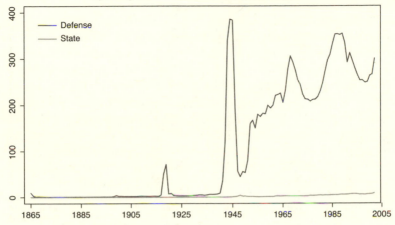

**Figure 1.1.** Department of Defense and State Department spending over time. Data show increasing trend over time in DoD spending but not State Department.

to the departments of State and Treasury. Given budget constraints, the dominant role of the military in the American foreign policy process occurs largely to the detriment of the State and Treasury departments, which are responsible for many of the non-military instruments of statecraft. Looking over time, one can see the way in which individual decisions may cumulate into a very asymmetric outcome. Figure 1.1 shows that since World War II, annual spending by the Defense Department dwarfs that of the State Department; and figure 1.2 shows employee numbers, excluding the military itself, for the main foreign policy bureaucracies, again suggesting Defense Department dominance in US foreign policy since World War II.

Why does militarization occur? Again, we argue that American political institutions are an important part of the answer. And why are the domestic costs and benefits likely to create a bias in favor of military means? We claim it is because the president has more discretion and more information relative to military instruments. Congress can't constrain the president so much as on other instruments where distributional issues arise, interest groups conflict with one another and intervene with Congress, and ideological battles break out. And the president has a bureaucracy that has been built up to provide him with information which gives him a strong advantage in the domestic political game.

Our theory then can help explain decisions leading to militarization. Militarization implies some kind of failure of policy substitution; it implies that one is using military force beyond its point of highest utility. The

25

**Defense and State Department**
Civilian Employment in thousands, 1900–2010

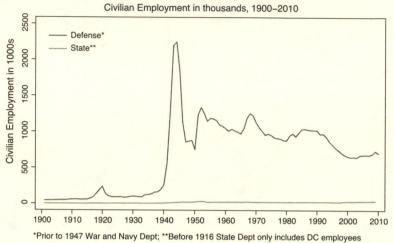

*Prior to 1947 War and Navy Dept; **Before 1916 State Dept only includes DC employees

**Figure 1.2.** Civilian employment in Department of Defense and State Department over time. Data show roughly flat employment in DoD post-1950 that is markedly greater than State Department employment.

difficulty of foreign policy substitution in the American political system has been such that military means and solutions become easier for the president to employ. Other instruments might be more effective internationally to use at this point. And as other research has shown, such investment in and use of military means may lead to greater international problems and increase the likelihood of war.[72] While our empirical focus is not on militarization as such, it is an important implication of our theory.

In our view, the militarization that has occurred since the end of World War II has as much to do with domestic politics as with international relations.[73] As one analyst of the military wrote years ago, "Given the complexities involved, it is plausible that the actual military capabilities which the US has maintained . . . owe more to the end products of the bureaucratic and Executive-Congressional politics of acquisition policy than they do to the formal guidelines . . . associated with the strategic doctrines of sufficiency, equivalence, and countervailing power."[74] The distinct political coalitions that undergird different foreign policy instruments make policy substitution in the US political system problematic and help explain the domestic pressures for militarization.

72    Debs and Monteiro, 2014.
73    Clark and Reed point to more international factors in influencing policy substitution, although they mention domestic politics. Clark and Reed, 2005.
74    Schilling, 1981, pp. 65–66.

# Organization of the Book

The book consists of eight chapters in total, five of which present empirical evidence examining our hypotheses. Our empirical chapters all draw on distinct types of data; together these give a comprehensive view of the US foreign policy process. Each chapter focuses on a different aspect of the process and on different sets of agents. We use these to explore foreign policy instruments from different angles. But in each one we seek to provide evidence for our main hypotheses, which we lay out in the next chapter.

Chapter 2 presents our theory. It engages with the debate about the role of the president and US foreign policy. We lay out arguments for why the debate about "two presidencies" is misconstrued because presidential power varies substantially across foreign policy instruments. Our theory highlights that the president's influence is moderated by the extent to which a policy instrument is characterized by two factors: (1) large distributional consequences that provide concentrated costs or benefits for domestic groups (versus public goods types of qualities), and (2) ideological divisions. We then argue that the degree of distributive politics partially accounts for the extent of informational asymmetries in favor of the executive for some policy instruments but not others. We derive several testable hypotheses from this theoretical framework. Given this theoretical structure and our hypotheses, it is important to focus on a range of core actors in our empirical chapters: interest groups, Congress, the bureaucracy, and the public. Furthermore, we also address important alternative explanations, such as those that focus on the international system as driving foreign policy and the role of the Constitution in hard-wiring in the subsequent politics we observe.

In chapter 3 we turn attention to interest groups and US foreign policy, with a focus on the extent of distributive politics present for different policy instruments.[75] We claim that for policy instruments where organized groups can obtain large, concentrated benefits or may have to pay large costs, economic interest groups will be active and lobby fiercely. Interest groups will have an incentive to collect information, testify before and lobby Congress, bypassing the White House, in order to overcome the executive's informational advantages. We aim to show how interest group activity varies across

---

75  This is important for us because interest groups are intimately linked to particular policy instruments. As Mahoney and Baumgartner point out, lobbying behavior varies not just by the interest group but that the same group may behave differently in different contexts as determined by the institutional structure and by the characteristics of a particular issue. Mahoney and Baumgartner, 2008, p. 1264. This interaction between political institutions, issue areas, and interest group characteristics is critical to recognize. Many studies of individual foreign policies show the importance of interest groups. Jacobs and Page, 2005, p. 121. Interest groups of different types matter differentially across policy arenas, and interest groups target different political actors in different issue areas. Our study shows this in a new way.

our core policy instruments (immigration, trade, economic aid, domestic military spending, sanctions, geopolitical aid, and military deployments). One way we do this is by exploring when the White House is more likely to be bypassed. Our hypothesis is that the president is less likely to be bypassed by interest groups when the issue has fewer distributive politics and ideological divisions associated with it. If interest groups are rational, then such targeting of lobbying should be evident if our theory is correct. To do this, chapter 3 draws on a rich new dataset of lobbying activity reports, which we analyze to understand who is lobbying whom in different areas of foreign policy issue. We are unable to pinpoint the preferred policy of each interest group in this process, but we generally know that for the instruments with high levels of distributive politics, groups will tend to form both in favor of and opposition to the policy.

In chapter 4 we turn to the Congress and its relationship with the president. We explore presidential power across policy instruments here in terms of whether the president can realize his preferences in legislation in Congress. In chapter 2 we state our hypotheses about when the president will be most influential and in chapter 4 we examine them empirically. Our hypothesis is that the president should be most powerful when issues have fewer distributive politics and ideological divisions. We examine two different types of data about elite behavior: agency budget data comparing presidential requests to congressional allocations, and roll call voting in the US Congress. Our focus on budgetary dynamics between Congress and the president follows earlier work in the American politics literature that uses differences in presidential budget requests for executive agencies and congressional budget allocations to assess whether the president has more influence in foreign versus domestic affairs.[76] We also examine both the universe of House votes on foreign affairs from 1953 to 2008, as well as carefully selected important votes on all of our foreign policy instruments for the House from 1979 to 2008. Our analysis of this data shows how the influence of the president, as well as local constituency-level factors and ideological divisions, varies across different types of foreign policy, providing support for our theory in chapter 2. We expect this variation in support to affect his ability to substitute policies, which the case study findings in chapter 7 make evident.

In chapter 5 we focus on the design and historical evolution of the US foreign policy bureaucracy. Relatively few studies of American foreign policy focus on the bureaucracy.[77] Here we inquire whether the patterns

---

76   Canes-Wrone, Howell, and Lewis, 2008.

77   There are notable exceptions. Allison, 1969; Destler, 1972; Krasner, 1972; Art, 1973; Bendor and Hammond, 1992; Drezner, 2000; Halperin and Clapp, 2006. And accompanying debate on their role. McCubbins, Noll, and Weingast, 1987; McCubbins, Noll, and Weingast, 1989; Lindsay, 1992.

of presidential power that we theorize about are also present in the bureaucracy. From our theory we expect that Congress should play a much stronger role over bureaus that deal with instruments having substantial distributive politics and ideological divisions, which applies to trade and economic aid in contrast to military deployments and geopolitical aid. We demonstrate the importance of control over information as well as changing patterns of relative influence in bureaucracies over time.

In chapter 6 we focus on public opinion and US foreign policy and whether it comports with the two elements of our theory. First, we ask whether empirical support exists for the way we classify policy instruments and whether in doing so presidential influence is seen to vary as suggested in chapter 2. Specifically, we inquire whether the public sees greater or less information asymmetries between the president and Congress across our policy instruments and whether the president or Congress has more control over each instrument. Second, we provide evidence for the degree of ideological divisions across different instruments. Using public opinion data, we characterize which groups support and oppose the difference policy choices for engaging with the international system and how sizable those differences are. This examination allows us to show that our coding of instruments in chapter 2 is borne out to some extent by evidence from the public's views. The public understands that foreign policy instruments differ, and they too recognize the differences that we attribute to these areas. This gives us more confidence that we have identified differences that are perceptible and that matter. The findings provide some micro-foundations for our arguments about when and why the president has a greater ability to exert influence over policy.

In chapter 7 we present an extensive case study of US foreign policy in order to explore our theory and hypotheses in greater detail. We focus on US policy toward Sub-Saharan Africa from 1993–2009, over the course of two presidencies. We detail how the presidents tried to use various policy instruments to deal with the serious problems arising in Africa after the end of the Cold War. We show how domestic cleavages around ideology and material interests in the United States shaped debates and the president's choice of policies, and how control of information by the president was important in this process. The case provides detailed illustrations of the main themes we developed earlier in the book.

Throughout the book, we focus on different policy instruments. For some types of data we can investigate all of the instruments of interest, but in others we are more limited. Table 1.1 gives an overview by chapter of the types of foreign policy instruments we engage with. We emphasize that all of our empirical chapters face different types of limitations, which we discuss both within the chapters but also in concluding. But as a whole the different types of data help to reinforce each other. For example, while Congress

**Table 1.1.** Policy Instruments Covered in Each Chapter

| POLICY TOOL | CHAPTER 3 | CHAPTER 4 | CHAPTER 5 | CHAPTER 6 | CHAPTER 7 |
|---|:---:|:---:|:---:|:---:|:---:|
| Economic aid | ★ | ★ | ★ | ★ | ★ |
| Trade | ★ | ★ | ★ | ★ | ★ |
| Immigration | ★ | ★ | | ★ | |
| Sanctions | ★ | ★ | | | |
| Domestic military spending | ★ | ★ | ★ | ★ | |
| Geopolitical aid | ★ | ★ | ★ | ★ | ★ |
| Military deployments | ★ | ★ | ★ | ★ | ★ |

Because of data availability, not all policy instruments are featured in each chapter.

may determine who testifies before Congress, it has less control over who lobbies and on what. And while presidential position taking on roll call voting might be fraught with strategic interaction on a vote-by-vote basis, our work on the institutional design of bureaucracies is less affected by such strategic position taking. We argue that as a whole our argument best fits this variety of data.

## Conclusion

For sixty-plus years, guarding America's interests abroad has taken the form of pursuing an internationalist agenda. To do so, presidents have used the types of foreign policy instruments that we focus on: international trade, economic aid, immigration, domestic military spending, geopolitical aid, sanctions, and military deployment policies. These policies have allowed him to engage with the rest of the world in order to secure and advance American interests. The designation of high and low politics does not adequately explain the choice of these different types of policies. Our theory shows why as a result of domestic politics foreign policy instruments and presidential power over them differ. This matters because American grand strategy depends on the president's ability to use all of these instruments. As Skålnes notes more generally, foreign economic policy is an important element of grand strategy, and these instruments are at times equally if not more important than military means.[78] We see the two-level game of foreign policy in the United States then being played domestically through the different preferences, ideologies, and information sets that the executive and other domestic political actors hold.

In our focus on different policy instruments, we, of course, do not dismiss the role of changes over time. There have been a number of secular trends unfolding over the course of our study. One is the growing inequality and partisan polarization within the United States.[79] Another is more external and relates to globalization, or the integration of the US national economy into a much larger global one. The US economy is still heavily domestic in its orientation, with total US trade equaling less than one-third of GDP, but it has become much more globalized in the past thirty years, as have most other economies. There have also been significant changes in the threats and structure of the international system in the roughly thirty-year period from the end of the Vietnam War era to the end of the George W. Bush administration, which is our primary focus. First, the end of the Cold War occurred in the middle of it (1989–1991), and then the start of the War of Terror in 2001 marked a turning point. Despite these changes, little about the American external position has changed over this thirty-year period. US GDP as a percentage of world GDP has stayed close to 30% during the entire time; US trade as a percentage of world trade has stayed between 12% to 15% consistently; and US military expenditures as a percentage of total world military expenditures ranged around 35% during the period, except for the five years right after the fall of the USSR.[80] Its external position thus has not dramatically shifted.

While America's external position did not shift greatly in this period, it is still worth asking whether changes in the threats and structure of the international system have affected US foreign policy, and whether they have influenced presidential power. We would argue the answer is yes. But this bears on our claims only insofar as these trends have changed the dynamics as to how the United States makes foreign policy with different policy instruments. We consider this possibility. Foreclosing a focus on issue areas and policy instrument differences, however, by stipulating that the interesting political variation is due to temporal changes ignores the rich political dynamics that we theorize about and then document.

---

78  Skålnes, 2000. Brian Pollins notes how "it will be interesting to see whether the United States formulates a new grand strategy that makes meaningful, long-term economic concessions in trade, aid, investment, and technology transfer—especially toward poor nations now on the front lines of this conflict." Pollins, 2002, p. 477.

79  McCarty, Poole, and Rosenthal, 2006.

80  Prior to this period there is some variation in US military spending and higher GDP in the 1960s.

While our approach emphasizes domestic politics, it does not neglect the international system and its influences. The president is the main conduit for such pressures to enter foreign policy considerations. This is one reason why presidents have been the main advocates for a liberal internationalist strategy in the United States since World War II, much as in the two-level games literature we see the executive as the focal point for international and domestic influences.[81] The executive branch is where international and domestic politics collide and commingle. The president generally is more sensitive to the pressures and opportunities of the international environment. His standing depends in part on being seen as a competent leader of the country in international affairs and in protecting American national security.[82] The average congressperson is less likely to be judged or held accountable for these international outcomes than is the president. Yet, as we show throughout the rest of the book, Congress can wield considerable power in many areas of foreign policy. Presidents are simultaneously at the center of foreign policy, but can also be highly constrained.

81  Putnam, 1988; Milner, 1997.
82  Murphy and Topel, 2013.

# 2

# A THEORY OF PRESIDENTIAL POWER AND US FOREIGN POLICY

In this chapter, we first discuss the different types of foreign policy instruments the president can employ. We point out how the politics of these policy instruments differ; these differences have important implications both for the presence of informational asymmetries between the president and Congress and for policy substitution. We also demonstrate the role of information and the politics of substitution in determining the president's ability to get his way in constructing foreign policy.

We develop a theory about how the politics concerning foreign policy instruments differ depending on two features: the extent of the instrument's distributional consequences and the extent of the ideological divisions. Both ideas and interests matter. We also examine the extent of the informational asymmetries connected to the policy instruments we look at; these asymmetries mean that certain actors, such as the president, may have better information about some policies. An implication of these informational asymmetries is that they provide an advantage to the actor possessing the most information. These three elements then are central to predicting presidential power in foreign policy.

Presidents are usually seen as taking into account the international environment more than legislators. "As members of Congress care foremost about their reelection prospects, they tend to invest more of their resources into *directing domestic policy benefits to their home districts and states,* for which they can claim clear credit come election time, than in monitoring distant threats to US security interests, which *amount to a public good.*"[1] Executives are more able and likely to pursue the international goals that such external pressures generate. "Since the executive *receives privileged information from state agencies,* it is frequently more aware of the national interest and the dictates of the international system than are other domestic actors."[2] As long as the United States remains powerful and deeply embedded in world affairs (which we discussed in chapter 1), guarding a favorable world order will be among its key national interests. To accomplish this, the United States needs

---

1  Howell, 2013, p. 135 (emphasis added). Some research though points to how when it comes to federal spending, presidents can also adopt "particularistic" strategies and try to reward their co-partisans rather than focusing on more universalistic considerations. Kriner and Reeves, forthcoming.

2  Taliaferro, Lobell, and Ripsman, 2009, p. 27 (emphasis added).

an active foreign policy with an internationalist orientation. Presidents are likely to adopt such an internationalist posture, but only if they can overcome their domestic constraints.[3] Congressional support for internationalism, on the other hand, is not a given; legislators always face the constant question of how to pay for international engagement, and the costs of foreign policy must be traded against domestic goals. Of course, legislators may have their own international priorities that differ from those of the president. Hence we think that the president and Congress have different incentives and preferences with respect to foreign policy, with the president favoring international engagement more strongly.

In order to realize his objectives in foreign policy, the president must convince Congress to go along with his policy program. Presidents focus on selecting policy instruments to deal with the external problems they face. But at the end of the day, Congress controls budgets and the financing of all government policies in addition to enacting laws regarding all policies. The executive can thus be checked by the legislature in his pursuit of any goal if he requires funds or laws to do it. This is even true for military-oriented policies.[4]

We argue that presidential power depends on the issue at hand. It is common to assert that presidential power is more extensive concerning the military and use of force.[5] The distinction between high and low politics echoes this notion. In high politics it is *assumed* that the president has supreme power because national survival and core national interests are at stake. Yet, as one critic of the distinction has noted, "The implicit assumption is that 'high politics,' [which means] a state's security relationship with other states in the international system, is autonomous and therefore distinct from 'low politics,' societal pressures, and the domestic political economy. These studies almost uniformly assume that the domestic political economy and national security issues are separate and distinct spheres."[6] In contrast we

3  "Limitations on executive autonomy in different national contexts, however, may undermine their ability to respond as necessary to shifts in the balance of power." Ibid.

4  "Most states must also frequently bargain with social actors in order to secure the provision of key national security goods to implement foreign policy." Ibid. We recognize that Congress and the executive branch are not unitary actors. In other chapters, we focus explicitly on the differences among legislators and show how these differences matter. For the executive branch, we do assume more hierarchy, with the president tending to dominate, although in chapter 5 we note variance in his extent of control across different agencies in the executive branch.

5  As Howell argues, "Presidents can justifiably expect to encounter less legislative or judicial interference on matters involving wars than on purely domestic issues, not because they have a special preference for these powers, but because other political actors are more willing either to grant them outright or simply to accede to the president's power claims." Howell, 2013, pp. 135–136.

6  Barnett, 1990, p. 531.

do not assume that policy instruments are independent; because of policy substitution in part, leaders will analyze the use of military and economic measures simultaneously. A contribution of our work is to bring these different areas of foreign policy together and explain why their politics differ.

Other studies have identified a variety of factors that might differentiate policy instruments, but few have tried to theorize about and test these directly, as we do here. As one analyst notes, "There are many kinds of foreign policy, however—war, diplomacy, trade, international development, foreign assistance. These policy areas vary in their stakes, in their visibility to the American public, and in their ties to domestic politics. It follows that Congress might be more assertive—and more changeable in its influence—in some of these areas than in others."[7] *But what makes the policy instruments vary in terms of presidential influence?*

## Foreign Policy Instruments

The US government has many policy instruments it can use to deal with international problems. We focus on seven main instruments: international trade, immigration policy, economic aid (including multilateral aid from the IMF and World Bank), geopolitical aid, sanctions, military spending, and military deployment. While military spending is not as frequently thought of as a foreign policy instrument, it directly relates to military strength and deterrence.[8] Below we discuss these tools and how they differ in greater detail. Each of these can relate to the main issue areas as we see them (economic development, diplomatic relations with other countries, defense and international economics), though for some pairings the relationship will be more indirect than others.

One issue area we do not examine in as much detail is diplomacy. "Diplomacy is the use of language and other signals by one state in an attempt to convey information to another. It is a kind of communication—the use of language by representatives of one state, aimed at influencing the actions of one or more others."[9] It is often associated with the other instruments that we do look at. For example, trade negotiations are diplomacy, but they tend to result in agreements that are included in our trade policy instrument. Diplomacy is mostly about persuading, or conveying information to, other governments about the willingness to use the other foreign policy

---

7  Hinckley, 1994, p. 6.

8  As Morgenthau notes, "The political objective of military preparations of any kind is to deter other nations from using military force by making it too risky for them to do so." Morgenthau, 1960, p. 30.

9  Sartori, 2005, pp. 3–4.

instruments that we examine. Finally, diplomacy is omnipresent and as such we acknowledge its importance but leave it for other scholars to address more directly.[10]

## Choosing and Changing Foreign Policy Instruments

Each of these seven sets of policy instruments can be used to a greater or lesser extent. As discussed, this book examines who has control over these tools. Before proceeding, we describe the ways these different policy instruments can be employed and changed. Presidents can try to use all of these instruments, and can try to adjust their use over time, but they often must contend with Congress and interest groups. Understanding the process by which policy is made can help bring to light when and how other political actors can affect the president's ability to obtain his preferred policies. We describe these instruments in greater detail and then discuss the political processes leading to their use.

Trade policy involves a wide variety of government actors. Congress, the president, and various bureaucratic agencies, such as the International Trade Commission, all play a role in shaping trade policy. One way this happens is through negotiating and passing trade agreements with other countries, or through unilaterally changing tariff rates, invoking escape clauses, or imposing non-tariff barriers.[11] Trade flows can also be affected through sanctions, which either the president or Congress can try to use. The Constitution gives Congress control over trade, but at times Congress has delegated this control, in varying degrees, to the president.[12]

Economic foreign aid works differently given its budgetary role. Each year the president proposes a budget and then Congress passes the main foreign aid legislation, titled the "Foreign Operations, Export Financing, and Related Programs Act." In addition, some types of economic aid are passed through the annual Department of Defense appropriations process that tends to be geostrategic in content (which we discuss below). Foreign aid can also be affected through the passing of sanctions that reduce or eliminate aid. Such sanctions can be pushed by the president or Congress.

Immigration policy is usually set by Congress and can change via amendments to visa systems, access to social benefits, physical barriers such as border fences, and directives that govern day-to-day implementation of immigration limits. All of these immigration policies can have foreign pol-

---

10  See, e.g., Saunders, 2011.

11  Since joining the GATT, the president has however put further constraints on trade policy. The United States has legally bound most of its tariff rates and cannot increase them above these levels within the agreement. Rates can be lowered and those on goods and services not subject to binding can be changed. And there are national security exceptions.

12  Goldstein, 1993; Bailey, Goldstein, and Weingast, 1997; Epstein and O'Halloran, 1999.

icy consequences.[13] Immigration policy can also be used to sanction countries or foreign groups; costly visa requirements can be imposed or visas can be denied to keep certain groups out of the country.[14] Immigration policy also includes decisions, typically made by the president, to enforce (or not) certain laws, such as those that deal with family re-unification.

The process governing domestic military spending resembles the procedure for foreign aid. Congress takes presidential budget proposals, modifies them in various ways, and votes on their annual passage of the Defense Authorization, Appropriation, and Military Construction bills. This process is subject to heavy lobbying by domestic groups, as we discuss in chapter 3. It is also an important element of congressional roll call voting, which we explore in chapter 4.

Sanctions are often related to the other foreign policy instruments we highlight, such as aid and trade. Sanctions tend to get made in one of three ways. First, the US president has broad authority to impose sanctions under four main congressional acts that have been on the books for a long time.[15] The president can also use executive orders to impose sanctions. Finally, Congress has increasingly intervened in the process over time, proposing its own sanctions on various countries.[16]

For the deployment of US troops abroad, the initial decision to deploy troops involves several steps. US intelligence agencies and the military will collect information and assess the need for deploying troops. Presidents can then make a decision to send troops or deploy military assets. Typically, though not always (e.g., air strikes in Laos during the Vietnam War), this will involve the formal notification of Congress. After deploying troops, permission to remain committed is typically passed by Congress, which must fund such efforts, often through special appropriations bills. During this time intelligence agencies and the military will continue to collect information that will be directly reported to the president, and Congress may call hearings in an attempt to obtain this information.

---

13   Teitelbaum, 1984; Tucker, Keely, and Wrigley, 1990. As Teitelbaum notes, "American foreign policy (i.e., World War II) led to domestic pressures from employers seeking Mexican labor; these pressures were resolved in foreign-policy initiatives that sought the best terms for the provision of temporary labor; and they in turn stimulated what has become one of the most sensitive foreign-policy issues between the United States and Mexico." Teitelbaum, 1984, p. 435.

14   Lyman, 2014.

15   These laws are: The International Emergency Economic Powers Act (IEEPA) of 1977; the Export Administration Act (EEA) of 1979; the U.N. Participation Act (UNPA) of 1945; and the Trading with the Enemy Act (TWEA) of 1917. Malloy, 2000.

16   Kaempfer and Lowenberg, O'Sullivan, and Hiscox argue that these reflect domestic economic, ethnic, or humanitarian interest groups and are mainly symbolic. Kaempfer and Lowenberg, 1988; Kaempfer and Lowenberg, 1989; Kaempfer and Lowenberg, 1992; O'Sullivan, 2003; Hiscox, forthcoming.

Geopolitical aid is handled by the US political process in several ways. Some of it is passed through the main Foreign Operations bill, while other geopolitical aid goes through the Department of Defense appropriations and authorization bills each year. Well-known components of geopolitical aid include the Economic Support Fund and the International Military Education and Training (IMET) program, which are both passed through the Foreign Operations bill. When passed through the Department of Defense, many of these programs involve paying for the training of foreign military personnel or paying foreign governments for participation in logistics and security operations (such as the Coalition Support Fund). Others deal more with infrastructure efforts in geopolitically important countries, like Afghanistan, or with counter-drug operations.[17] As we discuss in chapter 3, on average this type of aid, which includes training and budget support, is less subject to distributive politics and interest group pressure compared to some of the other policy instruments.

Making foreign policy involves a combination of different political processes, usually including lobbying, proposals from the president, and hearings and voting in Congress. Lobbying, whereby interest groups seek to provide information and persuade decision makers, as well as testimony in Congress from other actors, are important inputs into the policy process. We focus on these processes in chapter 3. For the president to make proposals in all these areas, he needs information from the various executive bureaucracies that deal with each issue area and policy instrument. Presidential control over these departments is very important to developing foreign policy and legislative proposals. We focus on the bureaucracies and his control over them in chapter 5.

Many foreign policy decisions involve congressional votes, which reveal preferences of both the legislative and executive branches. Members of Congress signal their preferences by casting a yea or nay ballot, and the president communicates his preference by endorsing, signing or vetoing the bill. Congressional votes may deal with complex policy packages that involve multiple instruments intended to meet multiple foreign policy problems, or with narrow policies targeted at specific countries. We examine congressional roll call voting over foreign policy in chapter 4.

Of course, not all foreign policy involves voting. Political actors can also issue threats, such as the threat of sanctions or military action, which are not subject to votes. For example, our analysis of the Threat and Imposition of Sanctions database shows that legislative actors, when they issue threats, primarily issue threats for sanctions that cover the *importation* of goods or

---

17   See http://securityassistance.org/ for more information. We also coded the long format descriptions in this database of each program, which shows the patterns we discuss.

restrictions on economic aid.[18] In contrast, threats to sanction by the executive branch concern a broad range of policies, including the restriction of US technology exports to a foreign country. Indeed, according to Leidy, a majority of sanctions imposed by the president are not about restricting imports, but rather restricting US exports to the target country.[19] Such sanctions are easier to implement because they do not violate GATT or WTO rules, and they are usually implemented under the statutory framework allowing the president to use export controls without seeking approval from Congress. When moving from threat to action, these actors can of course bring sanctions policies to a vote in Congress. Presidents can also use Executive Orders (EOs) to bypass Congress on foreign policy, such as when President Obama in 2014 issued a series of EOs that penalized specific Russian actors as a result of the hostilities in Ukraine and Crimea.[20] With this background about the political process for making foreign policies in mind, we turn to our key theoretical foci.

## Distributive Politics and US Foreign Policy

Instruments of foreign policy vary in at least two important respects which we will develop in more detail. As we show, both ideas and interests matter. We first focus in this section on the distribution of material costs and benefits across social groups from different policies. Then we discuss the implications they have for informational asymmetries and presidential influence. Next we discuss ideological sources of preferences and the extent of ideological divisions.

First, *policy instruments vary in the extent to which they have domestic distributional consequences and whether these costs and benefits are concentrated or diffuse*. Some instruments, like trade policy, often have large and identifiable distributional effects that are distributed unevenly across the country. These gains and losses tend to be concentrated on various domestic groups and not spread broadly across the population. This affects the politics surrounding the policy instrument. Presidents face more constraints when the distribution of gains and losses is large and concentrated. The extent to which costs and benefits from the different policy choices are concentrated and directly affect interest groups and local constituencies is of great importance. Some domestic groups may lose from some use of a policy instrument, while others may gain. When these losses and gains are significant, these groups will

18   Morgan, Bapat, and Kobayashi, 2013.
19   Leidy, 1989.
20   From the 79th to 112th Congress on average there are 40 Executive Orders related to foreign policy per Congress. Many are relatively minor, which is well known. Prokop, 2014.

battle for influence over policy. They are likely to lobby Congress and some may create significant resistance to policy at times. Others, of course, may support the president's desired policy. These distributional battles can hamper the president in pursuing his desired policy.

In this book we take this argument further, and connect it to how different policy instruments then have different *informational structures*. The amount of information the president has relative to other actors, such as Congress, differs depending on the extent of distributional consequences that a policy instrument generates. In some areas where distributive politics are less apparent, presidents have informational advantages that give them a stronger hand and invite congressional acquiescence.

## Distributive Politics and the Distribution of Costs and Benefits

Whether foreign policies have important and varying material consequences at the domestic level is a prime factor in differentiating among policy instruments. All foreign policies have material consequences since they require resources. But some create winners and losers within the country, and some have very large effects on certain domestic groups and little effect on others. This variable shapes the politics around a foreign policy instrument. When policies cause substantial shifts in material benefits or losses for different domestic groups, it is likely that these groups will be activated on the issue. Winners and losers from a policy may both attempt to influence Congress and the president. These distributional battles will make policy choice more costly. And they will affect how constrained the president is.

The first step in this argument is to note that the distributive effects of policies are associated with the preferences of domestic groups.[21] The role of material factors in explaining support for different types of policies has a long tradition.[22] Material or economic factors refer to the effects that policies can have on the national economy (relative to other economies) or on the income or wealth of individuals or groups, depending on their characteristics (mainly their endowments of capital and labor and their productivity). Various economic theories suggest how individuals' incomes and assets are affected by different economic policies. Preferring more income and wealth to less, individuals form preferences in support of (or opposition to) policies that increase (lower) their incomes or assets. Economic theory can thus deduce the preferences of individuals with different economic characteristics depending upon the economy in which they are embedded.

21  Milner, 1988a; Rogowski, 1989; Frieden and Rogowski, 1996.
22  Schattschneider, 1935; Scheve and Slaughter, 2001b.

A main claim in the literature has focused on how concentrated or diffuse the costs and benefits of policies are for social actors.[23] On one end of the spectrum, there are policies that provide public goods, which are non-rival and non-excludable. This means that everyone can enjoy the benefits of the policies, but no one can be excluded from them. The classic public goods problem then is to get people to pay for these policies, or even to lobby for them. Social actors are less likely to organize and lobby for a good when it has more qualities resembling a public good, for the simple reason that they have few or no incentives to do so. Moreover, actors are also less likely to search for information about the policy and its consequences and to pass that information along (often via lobbying).

On the other end of the spectrum are policies whose costs and benefits fall unevenly, with certain groups gaining or losing greatly. These types of policy outputs encourage groups to organize to obtain the benefits and/or to avoid the costs. They also provide incentives for groups to lobby, as well as to collect and provide information to policy makers. As Gowa notes,

> We can easily explain prevailing patterns of interest group activity in the US foreign economic policy process by examining the very different collective action problems presented by trade and monetary policy. . . . Because it is more excludable, however, trade policy presents fewer problems for collective action than does monetary policy. As a consequence, interest groups are far more active in it, and the trade policy process appears more fragmented than does its financial counterpart. . . . The avenues of protection provided by Congress and implemented by the executive branch suggest that trade policy can be and has become in some instances a highly excludable good.[24]

Policies that produce such excludable and rival costs and benefits have political ramifications. These policies have highly (re)distributive consequences, and political leaders will be attentive to this as it affects their office-holding prospects.[25] These distributional considerations for example mean that a

23   Wilson, 1980.

24   Gowa, 1988, pp. 22, 24. Gowa also claims that the character of policies is determined much by the institutional environment. "Institutions strongly influence the character of political goods and associated patterns of interest group activity. Whether a good is public or private is not only a function of its attributes; it is also a function of the institutional framework that produces it. Political rules of the game, in part, establish whether the government controls exclusion over what could be treated as non-excludable goods." We agree to some extent, but policies are not infinitely malleable in this sense. Ibid., p. 28.

25   A common way to frame this is that different legislators weigh local versus national outcomes differently. See, e.g., Howell, Jackman, and Rogowski, 2013. This is different from our conceptualization. We assume, instead, that distributional considerations mean that a policy produces different utility across districts.

policy may produce different effects across legislative districts. Changes in trade policy are an example where some districts (because of their economic composition) may benefit or lose more than others. In addition, interest groups can be mobilized by these distributive consequences. The winners and losers may struggle for influence over Congress and the president, creating great contestation over the policy choice. These distributional issues then have electoral consequences, and they ensure that legislators and the president have keen and sometimes opposing interests in how they are resolved. A president will have a much harder time convincing legislators, even those from his own party, to concur with his preferred foreign policy if the policy has diverging distributional consequences at the local level and for interest groups.

We rank our seven policy instruments according to their distribution of benefits and costs on social actors. In general, we claim that immigration, trade, and economic aid should have sizable, highly concentrated costs and benefits where specific domestic groups experience salient gains and losses from different policy choices.[26] They should provide incentives for interest groups to organize, collect information, and lobby. These interest groups should be particularly active at the local level, that is, through their congressional representatives, since many of the distributive effects will have local consequences. Because of this Congress is likely to be attentive to these groups and to be well informed by them about policy consequences. Some groups will lobby in favor of, and some will be opposed to, the president's preferred policy, thus polarizing debate over the policy. In this situation the president is likely to be highly constrained by domestic politics. Next we provide more detail about the concentrated nature of the costs and benefits from these types of policy instruments.

## CONCENTRATED COSTS AND BENEFITS: TRADE, ECONOMIC AID, AND IMMIGRATION

International trade is well known to have distributional consequences on the domestic level. Trade accounts for roughly 30% of the American economy, and most sectors of the economy are affected by it even if they are not directly traded. Trade and globalization are having major effects on all national economies, even the largest ones, including the United States. The large debates these days over growing inequality and (long-term) unemployment in the US economy usually refer to the possible effects of trade on these problems. Many studies suggest that these distributive consequences affect public support for trade policy. Specifically, they argue that the public votes based on their perception of how the policy will affect them, their

---

26    Below we discuss how military procurement also fits into this category.

family, or, more broadly, their country.[27] Standard arguments about the role of economic interests in determining trade policy preferences tend to draw on the Heckscher-Ohlin (HO) theorem and its related Stolper-Samuelson (SS) one.[28] The theorems suggest that owners of relatively scarce factors lose from trade liberalization, whereas owners of relatively abundant factors gain. In a developed country such as the United States, then, the expectation is that capital and skilled labor, as abundant factors, gain most from trade, while unskilled labor loses. This suggests that skilled labor and capital holders will support trade and its liberalization, while unskilled labor will oppose it and push for protection. Numerous studies find support for such predictions about trade preferences.[29]

Foreign economic aid, whether bilateral or multilateral, also has distributional consequences.[30] These consequences are less extensive than those for trade since aid is a smaller fraction of the American economy. The United States gave more than $20 billion in foreign development assistance in 2013, the most of any donor country. While a small fraction of American GDP, the amount the United States spends on foreign aid has regularly been close to, or even greater than, funding for other important budget items. In the 1990s, for instance, foreign economic aid claimed on average 0.5% of the US government budget, while much talked about spending categories, like farm income support and higher education funding, took up roughly the same magnitude of spending (each at 0.9%).[31] Aid is not an insignificant part of American foreign policy. Nor is economic aid spending small compared to several major domestic policy areas.

Some scholars have argued that the Heckscher-Ohlin model can be extended to predict that just as in trade, capital-abundant individuals in a rich

---

27   Balistreri, 1997; O'Rourke and Sinnott, 2001; Scheve and Slaughter, 2001b; Beaulieu, Yatawara, and Wang, 2005; Mayda and Rodrik, 2005.

28   Scheve and Slaughter, 2001b; Beaulieu, Yatawara and Wang, 2005.

29   O'Rourke and Sinnott, 2001; Scheve and Slaughter, 2001b; Mayda and Rodrik, 2005; Milner and Tingley, 2011. The main alternative specification of trade preferences comes from the so-called Ricardo-Viner (RV) model. This model assumes that factors of production may not be mobile and predicts cleavages along export versus import competing lines. In either model, trade has concentrated distributional consequences. And this has political implications for the president when he tries to use trade policy. Not all the evidence supports these economic models; some studies show that other variables matter as well or more for trade preferences. Hainmueller and Hiscox, 2006; Mansfield and Mutz, 2009. These studies, however, do not dispute that trade may have distributional consequences; they are more interested in whether these are the primary source of preference formation by members of the general public.

30   McKinlay and Little, 1977; McKinlay and Little, 1978; McKinlay and Little, 1979; Kemp, 1995; Morrissey, 1996; Fleck and Kilby, 2001; Mayer and Raimondos-Møller, 2003; Broz, 2005; Milner and Tingley, 2010; Milner and Tingley, 2011; McLean, forthcoming 2015.

31   Government Printing Office, 2009.

country will support foreign aid.[32] Using a standard HO trade model, scholars have shown that aid benefits certain groups within the donor country (e.g., highly skilled exporting interests or constituencies), hence making donor governments more willing to provide aid.[33] When foreign aid leads to a terms-of-trade change, individuals are affected both as consumers and recipients of factor income. If, as is likely, the distribution of factor ownership varies widely among individuals in the donor country, then the indirect effects of foreign aid can have different impacts on different groups' welfare. Some groups will gain from the country's giving of foreign aid.[34]

Furthermore, many studies of economic aid point out that domestic interests within donor countries seem to have a significant impact on how much and where aid is delivered, as domestic groups presumptively gain from these flows.[35] Aid policy may not directly engage voters, but it can have domestic distributional consequences that do affect voters' lives and politicians' fortunes. Chapters 3 and 4 provide extensive evidence to this end. Furthermore, roughly 70% of national elites sampled in the 1975, 1979, and 1982 Chicago Council on Foreign Relations (CCFR) surveys felt that US economic aid had positive effects on the US economy (in later years this question was not asked).[36] When the survey identified House members (in 1975 and 1982), more than 75% of them felt that aid had a beneficial impact on the US economy. In sum, aid seems both to have real economic effects and to be perceived to have such effects on America's political economy.

32   Milner and Tingley, 2010; Milner and Tingley, 2011.

33   See, e.g., Brakman and Van Marrewijk, 1998; Mayer and Raimondos-Møller, 2003.

34   In particular, an increase in a person's income through the terms-of-trade effect will occur if the recipient country's propensity to consume exceeds the donor's for the good that uses relatively intensively the factor that the person owns relatively more of than the average person in the donor country. For example, a transfer will increase a person's income in the rich country if the recipient country has a higher propensity to consume the capital-intensive good than the donor does *and* the person's capital ownership ratio exceeds that of the average person in the donor country. In particular, for aid transfers from rich to poor countries those groups who are relatively well endowed with the rich country's abundant factor—capital—will benefit when capital or capital-intensive goods and services are exported as foreign aid. Since aid's indirect effect is to raise the price of the capital-intensive good, relatively abundant owners of capital in the donor should benefit from and favor aid. Thus, while all factor owners in the donor country may pay more taxes to finance foreign aid, the factor owners who benefit from the terms-of-trade effect receive extra gains at the cost of factor owners who do not. For economic aid, some evidence seems to support the Stolper-Samuelson assumptions. Almost all US aid is given to low- and middle-income countries; and US exports to these countries tend to be concentrated on capital-intensive goods. Different marginal propensities to consume between the United States and its economic aid recipients exist and thus that capital versus labor endowments may drive the distributional effects in donor countries. Analysis on this point based on analysis of COMTRADE and WDI data is provided in Milner and Tingley, 2010.

35   See, for example, Dudley and Montmarquette, 1976; Alesina and Dollar, 2000; Irwin, 2000; Therien and Noel, 2000; Fleck and Kilby, 2001.

36   CCFR, 1975/1979/1982.

Our category of economic aid also includes aid given to the multilateral banks, such as the IMF, World Bank, and regional development banks. This type of aid can also have concentrated economic effects. While some see such aid as an international public good to provide systemic stability, it is also evident that such aid benefits some groups within the United States disproportionately.[37] One group that gains in a very concentrated way is financial capital, especially international lenders.[38] But, more directly, Broz and Hawes document the influence of a group of key beneficiaries of IMF bailouts: international "money-center" banks that have high exposure to international credit markets and receive de facto insurance from IMF financial rescues.[39] Demirgüç-Kunt and Huizinga have even found evidence that unanticipated increases in US financial commitments to the IMF are associated with increases in the stock market capitalization of the exposed money-center banks.[40] As concentrated winners from a policy of funding aid for the IMF and World Bank, we expect these banks to organize, collect information, and lobby Congress heavily.

These types of distributional consequences should be most apparent for economic aid—whether multilateral or bilateral—whereas this may be less the case for other forms of aid, such as geopolitical aid. That is, we expect the distributional consequences to be most evident for economic aid, in which capital or capital-intensive goods and services are shipped abroad to poor recipient countries. For military aid and related aid given for explicit geopolitical purposes, where the United States is providing budget support to allies, or providing training for foreign military personnel, we anticipate fewer direct distributional consequences.[41] We argue that distributive politics is less central to geopolitical aid; rather, foreign policy priorities as seen by the president are likely to be more powerful. Of course, we do not argue that there are no distributional consequences to this type of aid, especially when it comes to the transfer of arms, only that they will be more modest and indirect and have more public goods qualities, which we discuss below.[42]

Not all policy related to the military falls outside the distributional politics arena. Military spending on weapons, troops, and bases within the United

---

37   Broz, 2005; Broz and Hawes, 2006; Gould, 2006.

38   Frieden, 1991.

39   Broz and Hawes, 2006, p. 374. Gould and Oatley also note how important banks are to the politics of the IMF and the US position within it. Oatley, 2002; Gould, 2006.

40   Demirgüç-Kunt and Huizinga, 1993.

41   As we discuss below, there will be greater distributional consequences when it comes to the transfer of military hardware, which will benefit US defense contractors.

42   For agricultural aid where American farm goods are shipped abroad, we expect the particular interests engaged here—namely, agricultural producing groups and districts—to have strong preferences for this form of aid. Interest group and roll call analyses in chapters 3 and 4 support this connection.

States is highly distributive. And this spending is large: in recent years, the base budget for the Department of Defense has been around $500 billion per year, and this did not include sizable funds for the wars in Afghanistan and Iraq.[43] In chapter 3 and 4 we discuss this in more detail and show how this policy area also has important local domestic consequences and thus engenders much congressional and interest group activity, constraining the president. Contractors for the military are a powerful set of interest groups, and congressional attention to military bases and contracts in their district is extremely intense. Presidents, we conjecture, should have much less capacity for influence in this area than in others connected to the military. Policy instruments connected to the military are not all the same; they have different politics associated with them because of their distinct characteristics.

Like economic aid and trade, immigration is a foreign policy instrument but also has powerful domestic distributional consequences.[44] Like trade, we expect immigration policy to have very large distributive effects since it has a big impact on the economy. Estimates are that by 2012 there were 40 million immigrants in the United States, accounting for close to 15% of the total US population.[45] Because immigration adds workers to the labor pool—since 1970 the share of foreign-born workers in the US labor market has tripled, from about 5% to nearly 15%—the pattern of support and opposition to immigration might be expected to depend on its economic effects. An extensive literature has examined the effect of immigration policies on economic outcomes, such as wages and unemployment, in the receiving country. The labor market theory expects that those who gain from immigration economically will support it and those who lose will oppose it. Using results from the Stolper-Samuelson theory of trade, scholars have noted that in a capital-rich country that is importing unskilled labor, groups well-endowed with capital and skills will profit from immigration, while unskilled labor will lose.[46]

---

43    Office of Management and Budget, 2014.

44    Immigration is also an important potential substitute. For example, Peters argues, "trade and immigration policy cannot be studied as separate policies but instead scholars must take an integrated view of these two foreign economic policies. Trade and immigration policy are substitutes." Peters, 2015, p. 1.

45    Migration Policy Institute, 2014.

46    Hoskin and Mishler, 1983; Ruffin, 1984; Abowd and Freeman, 1991; Borjas and Freeman, 1992; Scheve and Slaughter, 2001a; Borjas, 2003; Borjas, 2006; Mayda, 2006; Facchini and Mayda, 2008; Facchini and Mayda, 2009; Milner and Tingley, 2011. Other work that looks at the relationship between immigrants and fiscal policy, especially in the form of the welfare state, has also been studied in Western economies. Borjas, 1999a; Borjas, 1999b; Dustmann and Preston, 2007; Hanson, Scheve, and Slaughter, 2007; Facchini and Mayda, 2008; Facchini and Mayda, 2009. These findings about economic determinants are not undisputed. Others have found that US workers in general experienced either no loss or even an increase in their wages as a result of immigration. Gaston and Nelson, 2000; Ottaviano and Peri, 2008. Several studies

Economic models also posit a strong relationship among the trade, aid, and immigration.[47] In standard trade models, flows of capital or labor can be substitutes for trade in goods and services. The theoretical consequences are also the same: in capital-rich countries such as the United States, more trade, more immigration, and more aid cause labor, especially unskilled labor, to lose while skilled labor and capital benefit. We thus expect the same types of domestic divisions on these issues and potentially the same coalitions to form around them.[48] However, we expect that trade and immigration will have more sizable distributive effects than aid.

These models then predict that domestic groups will both favor and oppose policies that lead to engagement with the international system through these policy instruments. Interest groups, the legislators that ally with them, and the local constituencies affected will be likely to organize and lobby for and against the policy under consideration. These distributional struggles may then pit parts of Congress against the president, although some groups likely will support his position. These political struggles can make the domestic costs of a foreign policy instrument higher for the president to employ.

## PUBLIC GOODS AND PRESIDENTIAL POWER: GEOPOLITICAL AID, MILITARY DEPLOYMENTS, AND SANCTIONS

Some foreign policy instruments have characteristics more like public goods: their domestic effects are characterized more by non-rival and non-excludable effects. This means they tend to not have large, concentrated costs or benefits for particular social groups. Rather, they have widespread effects that affect almost everyone in at least a small measure. Military deployments and geopolitical aid are the two most common policy instruments that fit this pattern.

The international deployment of military assets, including troops, to protect national security interests is a textbook example of a public good. There can be very sizable costs to military deployments for the country. The war in Iraq begun in 2003 is calculated to have cost $2 trillion and caused the deaths of close to 5,000 American soldiers, in addition to many more wounded (and many non-American deaths).[49] Obviously the deaths of these Americans are borne most heavily by the departed and their families, but

---

show that an array of ideological and cultural beliefs plays a more important role, or at least an interactive one. Citrin, Green, Muste, et al., 1997; Hainmueller and Hiscox, 2007; Hainmueller and Hiscox, 2010.

47  Faini and Venturini, 1993; Schiff, 1994.

48  Peters however notes that because they are substitutes, policy may thus go in different directions: open trade may lead to restricted immigration policies. Peters, 2014.

49  Crawford and Lutz, 2014.

these soldiers come from across the country, and not from any single domestic group.[50] Most of the economic costs as well are borne by the country as a whole through taxes. A central benefit of deployments likewise is said to be increased American security, and again this benefit is conferred on the country as a whole, if actually realized. Legislators and the president can all claim the benefits for themselves and their electorate. That is, the costs and benefits of deployments are closer to being non-excludable and non-rival than those resulting from trade, economic aid, or immigration policies.

The public goods nature of deployments means interest group and public pressure are much less likely to dominate the policy process. Hence legislators are less constrained by the domestic situation and less informed relative to the executive. While legislators may support or oppose these uses of force, they are less likely to see these issues as the target of lobbying efforts. Saunders, in her 2013 article on the "Electoral Disconnection in US Foreign Policy," argues that in the military area, three sets of elites can affect policy: members of Congress; key members of the bureaucracy, particularly the leaders of the key departments for foreign and defense policy (State, Treasury, Defense, and the National Security Council); and military leaders (such as the Joint Chiefs of Staff, leaders of particular missions, or combatant commanders).[51] Notable is the omission of interest groups from this characterization. Indeed, we provide more evidence for this view in chapter 3 on interest groups. We show by looking at congressional testimony that military deployments rarely attract the level of interest group activity that other policy instruments do. Instead, congressional testimony is dominated by the military and the executive branch.[52] This means that information is tightly controlled by these actors, which tends to reinforce presidential control rather than provide independent information to Congress. When interest groups do get involved, it is mostly NGOs testifying about human-

---

50   There is debate over whether the military reflects American society broadly. In terms of gender, this is clearly not the case; only 16% of the military is female. In terms of age, they are also younger. In terms of race, non-whites seem to be overrepresented: the white population of the United States is roughly 77% according to the US Census, while in the active military overall it is only 72%, according to the Department of Defense.  US Department of Defense, 2012; US Census Bureau, 2014. In terms of education, the active military is less educated: only 19% have bachelor's degrees compared to 29% of the US population, according to the same sources as above. Heritage Foundation data suggest there is no overrepresentation of racial groups within the active military. Watkins and Sherk, 2008. It seems to be that many officers come from the South. But more research on this topic is clearly warranted.

51   Saunders, 2013, p. 12.

52   Congressional testimony is obviously strategically allocated, but this still provides one interesting piece of evidence about Congress's attention. We recognize that the military might be seen as an interest group, but they are a government organization also involved in implementing and making policy, and so we believe it is quite different from private/NGO type interest groups.

itarian concerns or ethnic groups looking for support for their co-ethnics in the dispute.[53]

Geopolitical aid does not share all the non-rival and non-excludable qualities of military deployments, but neither does it cause the concentrated distributional effects that trade, aid, and immigration do. US geostrategic assistance refers to a diverse collection of programs administered by both the Department of State and the Department of Defense (DoD). These programs share a common aim of developing military capacity in recipient nations; historically, however, they have also been used to reward and win over allies. Traditionally, military assistance policy has been developed via the Department of State, with varying levels of DoD participation. More recently, DoD's role and autonomy in providing security assistance have increased dramatically, and several programs are now fully funded and implemented by DoD alone. DoD officials have actively lobbied for these programs, pushing steadily for greater authority and funding for DoD-led security assistance.[54]

Such aid often involves the transfer of US weapons, military expertise and training, or budget support (via the Economic Support Fund) to allied countries. On the one hand, the production of military hardware is done by US companies, which of course experience local economic consequences.[55] However, an important part of this aid involves training of foreign militaries. In recent years such programs have included IMET,[56] as well as new innovations under the aegis of the DoD, such as the Combatting Terrorism Fellowship Program. Funds from these programs go in part to supporting foreign military personnel during their training.[57] The local-level distributional consequences of such programs are minimal and indirect at best. And programs like the Economic Support Fund generally provide budget support to foreign governments.[58] Other military assistance programs include ones that reimburse coalition partners for their support, such as

53  Sarkesian, Williams, and Cimbala in their review of US national security policy point out that few interest groups are involved, and they note that the main ones providing information are often human rights organizations. Sarkesian, Williams, and Cimbala, 2008, p. 217.

54  Tarnoff and Lawson, 2011; International Security Advisory Board, 2013.

55  Simon, 2013. A major mechanism for this type of aid is through the Foreign Military Financing Program which contains a grant component. Such grants typically require purchasing funds through US contractors, though importantly the president can interrupt the delivery of purchased items. Philips, 2013.

56  Atkinson, 2014.

57  Some countries pay full tuition for IMET training, but many countries receive tuition support as well as financial and benefit support for their students during training. See Defense Institute of Security Assistance Management, 2007.

58  Part of this support can come from access to commodity imports or other forms of material support, which free up recipient government funds. But other ESF funds come in the form of cash transfers. For example, 53% of Jordan's ESF funds are cash transfers that service its

the Coalition Support Fund.[59] The material consequences of programs like these do not produce concentrated economic gains and losses for some American groups more than others in the way that trade, immigration, and economic aid policy can. Thus geopolitical aid has some components that will have distributional characteristics but other important parts that do not.

In our research on what legislators said about geopolitical aid and in analyses by the *Congressional Quarterly* of geopolitical aid legislation, its domestic economic consequences were rarely, if ever, discussed. Rather, it was geopolitical concerns that were highly salient. This contrasts with economic aid, where Treasury secretaries repeatedly extolled the positive consequences of aid for the US economy.[60] We also note that the policy and geopolitical consequences of such geopolitical aid are non-excludable and non-rivalrous, similar to the deployment of US troops. Interest group activity is much less in this area than in trade or economic aid. In chapter 3 we show how in geopolitical assistance policy debates, one finds mostly executive branch agencies and the military, foreign governments, and diaspora groups lobbying and testifying.[61]

Not all military-related policies, however, are more like public goods in their distributive consequences. It is important to note that domestic military spending more generally may not have the quality of a public good. Instead it is usually highly distributive in nature. This spending is large

foreign debt. Sharp, 2014. Historically other schemes have been set up with ESF funds in order to simply fund government operating budgets. Schoultz, 1987.

59 We exclude programs that cover the sale of US military systems to foreign countries. While the US government, through programs like the Foreign Military Sales program, provides procedural and logistical support for these activities, ultimately these arrangements are often between contracting suppliers and customers.

60 This is consistent with evidence that military contractors directly lobby the Pentagon and have a smaller impact on the legislature. Goss, 1972; LeLoup, 2008. Congress is involved in geostrategic assistance since it must authorize and appropriate all such funds. The executive branch presents budgets for all military aid to Congress, and Congress can amend them. The president retains veto power over all appropriations bills. During the appropriations process the executive branch negotiates closely with Congress and executive branch officials regularly testify before the various budget committees. The president can also formally signal his position on budgetary issues by providing Statements of Administration Policy (SAPs). Witnesses at congressional hearings on geopolitical aid tend to include high-level officials from the Department of State, White House or OMB officials, and the Department of Defense. This highlights how this type of aid might be appropriated by Congress but under the strong influence of the president.

61 Some studies note the influence of foreign governments on the allocation of security assistance. Related research has noted that the most influential foreign groups are those with large immigrant populations already in the United States. Newhouse, 2009; Pevehouse and Vabulas, 2012; Bermeo and Leblang, 2013. However, Foreign Government Lobby Registrations data, which are recorded when foreign government retains a new lobbyist and includes a brief description of legislative interest, show how security or military assistance is infrequently listed in these reports. For example, see CQ Weekly, 1989.

in magnitude and can affect local districts powerfully. Congresspersons fight very hard to prevent base closures and troop movements out of their districts. And military contractors lobby hard for procurement opportunities. These types of activities are much more distributive in nature than deployments or geopolitical aid. Congress tends to know much more about them, in part because people and interest groups in their districts tell them about these military programs. In chapters 3 and 4, we show in more detail that Congress does know and care about such spending programs and that the president's control over this area is much weaker than in deployments or geopolitical aid.

A final policy instrument we look at is sanctions. Usually these involve reducing or ending trade or aid relations with another country, embargoing the sale of weapons and military equipment, or disrupting financial flows to them. Sanctions clearly have economic effects; their goal is to hurt the other country, but in the process they often have costs for the country imposing them. But sanctions tend to be limited and affect either only the country or a few firms or products. This limited reach means that they often have only small economic effects on the imposing country, thus reducing their distributive consequences. Interest groups affected by them often protest and complain to Congress, but these groups tend to be much fewer in number and less affected than those targeting trade and immigration policy. As a consequence, we argue that sanctions have an intermediate position in terms of distributive politics. They may engender some concentrated economic costs in the United States, but these tend to be more narrow and limited, as compared to more general trade and immigration policies.

As a result of these public good characteristics, a president should have more influence on policy instruments involving military deployments and geopolitical aid, and to some extent sanctions, than he does on trade, immigration, and economic aid. Interest groups, legislators, and local constituencies will be much less likely to organize and lobby to battle over these policies, and they will have less information about them as well. We also expect the president to have greater control over bureaucracies that deal with the deployment of US troops, sanctions, and geopolitical aid to US allies, and on congressional voting (at least by his co-partisans). We are not the first to make this point. But in this book we show empirical implications of this argument in a more rigorous and systematic way than has been done to date. However, the president's influence over military-related policies varies. For example, when it comes to decisions to close US bases at home or to develop or dismantle weapons systems, which can have large distributive effects, the incentives of congresspersons are magnified and local constituency pressures will be more pronounced.[62]

---

62  For example, in chapters 3 and 4 we show this with respect to interest group behavior and roll call voting on defense appropriations bills.

## Distribution of Information

With distributive politics in mind, we next turn to its implications for the distribution of *information* among policy makers. By information, we mean factual information but also analysis and perspective. Policy making in a complex world is a highly uncertain endeavor. The relationship between means and outcomes is complicated and often highly contested.[63] Will more trade bring greater prosperity or economic or social volatility? Will a military strike work, and is it justified in terms of costs? Is a larger military a source of increased stability or conflict? Policy makers must make their best guesses about these causal connections. What will be the effects of a policy? They may in particular be uncertain about how it will affect their own constituency or the country as a whole. Many policies have unclear consequences and non-dispositive justifications, ex ante.

Beliefs about the relationship between policies and outcomes are shaped by many factors. But political leaders want information to try to adopt the best policies possible. Decisions might not turn out the way decision makers want, but information is valuable in order to assess costs and benefits and make an argument for a preferred position. And as we discuss, access to information about different policy instruments is not always freely available. It can be costly to collect, and perhaps risky to share.

Information is important not just for making better decisions, but also because it has the capacity to affect the influence of different actors. As the saying goes, information is power. The actor who has more information often has more capacity to influence the outcome. In our case, when the president has an informational advantage, he may well be able to induce Congress to accept policies that he prefers. As one argument about presidential power puts it, "If, '[i]n the information age, information is power,' then most of that power rests with the executive. Because of its vast resources, the executive branch has far greater access to information than do the co-branches of government. In addition, the executive branch has far greater ability and expertise to gather, examine, and cull that information than do the transitory legislative staffs in the Congress."[64] We think that presidential advantages in information vary by policy instrument; presidents may always have more information than Congress but for some policy instruments, they have much more while in others the asymmetries are much less.

Earlier work suggests that this need for information drives the development of bureaucracies. The literature on bureaucratic politics and foreign policy points out the importance of information provision by different bureaucracies to the executive.[65] In a different vein, principal-agent models

63  Goldstein and Keohane, 1993b.
64  Marshall, 2008, p. 515.
65  Halperin, Clapp, and Kanter, 1974; Drezner, 2000.

see political leaders as facing high policy uncertainty and thus needing to hire knowledgeable agents who can provide them with information. These agents then populate the bureaucracies that serve political leaders but also pose issues about agency slack.[66] We abstract from the precise principal-agent mechanics elucidated by scholars to focus on how some policy instruments pose very high information asymmetries between the executive and the legislature. That is, unlike this previous literature, we disaggregate the set of foreign policy instruments much more systematically in order to show important variation unexplored by these authors.

*Asymmetric* information arises because legislators do not always have access to information about the effects, or justification, of a policy. Sometimes this is because legislators do not have incentives to collect costly information. Other times it is because they do not gain access to institutions and the information they collect, because of various institutional firewalls or executive branch actions. As a result in some areas the president holds much more information and much greater capacity to obtain information than in other areas. Where the asymmetry favors the president, he has more influence and policy is easier for him to shape.

As Howell notes in his study of presidential power, one key way that presidents maintain or gain control over policy is by guarding or keeping control over information.[67] And this control over information gives him the ability to influence other actors and to get his way in terms of policy.[68] This book provides systematic evidence for these claims. Conversely, in areas where organized interests are actively involved because they face concentrated benefits or losses from policies, they are likely to gather information and to pass this along to sympathetic political actors like Congress.[69]

Interest groups are most likely to be involved in providing information when it involves a policy that strongly affects their interests. When distributive politics are fierce, winning and losing groups will both be more likely to collect information and lobby Congress, often counteractively. Information is costly to collect *and* provide to others, and when groups see little impact from a policy, they are unlikely to bear the costs of collecting information

---

66   Epstein and O'Halloran, 1999; Huber and Shipan, 2002; Gailmard and Patty, 2013.
67   Howell, 2013, pp. 50 and 142.
68   Ibid., p. 135.
69   See literature on fire alarms in politics; e.g., McCubbins and Schwartz, 1984. Fire alarm oversight of executive programs by legislatures occurs when interest groups complain about how programs are administered, the media expose programmatic waste or abuse, or constituents report problems with government services that reveal flaws in program design or implementation. It is highly decentralized and relies on outside actors to "sound an alarm." Bauer, de Sola Pool, and Dexter note that interest groups tend to provide information to legislators who agree with them. Bauer, Pool, and Dexter, 1972. And many interest group theories since then have argued that the central item provided by interest groups to legislators is information.

about its effects. "[Legislator] preferences depend also on policy-relevant information, and interest groups are one important source of such information. Interest groups routinely collect specialized information and conduct technical analyses; write and distribute reports of their research to members of Congress; and call upon members and their staffs to answer questions, make clarifications, and counter any opposing information or concerns that might arise."[70] When interest groups believe that policy choices will have concentrated benefits or costs, they are highly motivated to collect and disseminate information. This is more likely to be true for foreign policies that have distributional consequences and are less public goods–like in nature. In this situation presidents will not have an information asymmetry in their favor.

We thus expect interest groups to be most active at providing information to Congress on budget issues, and for them to concentrate more on policy issues when lobbying the executive branch. So we expect interest groups to lobby and provide different types of information to different branches of the US government. Interest groups then will themselves help drive these information asymmetries as they lobby the different branches in different ways.

In addition to relying on interest groups, legislators have a number of different mechanisms for gathering information, including creating specialized committees, relying on their party or the media, and mandating reports from executive bureaucracies to Congress. Some issues, however, may be much easier for legislators to collect information about than others. In part interest groups who are implicated in them and affected constituents may be willing to inform them without any effort on their part. But some issues may be much harder for them to both understand and collect adequate information about. Furthermore, for some issues legislators get access to information from interest groups, because they have a strong incentive to supply this information. For other policy instruments, these incentives are much lower and hence collective action problems may limit their supply of information. Congress, however, may have incentives to pass various reporting requirements for agencies, such as we discuss in chapter 5 about USAID, but there may be fewer incentives to do this, and it will be much more difficult to pass and enforce, for some policy instruments. In these areas the president may possess an asymmetric informational advantage.

Military deployments and geopolitical aid should be the areas where the president has the strongest informational advantages. Sanctions should also be an area where he has powerful advantages. As previously discussed, Congress faces fewer distributional concerns when it comes to these policy instruments. As a result, over time the US executive has built up a very large

---

70    Wright, 1996, p. 70.

bureaucracy to support the military and president and to develop intelligence about foreign affairs. On some foreign policy issues, the NSC, the Pentagon, and national intelligence agencies directly and regularly report to the president. Thus the president and his administration have the most direct access to the best information about military issues. The president has a strong informational advantage over Congress because of these agencies and the information they provide him.[71] This allows him to shape policy more generally because the public and legislators both agree that the executive has better information about the effects of policy choices.

Immigration, trade, and economic aid are likely the ones where he has the least advantage in part because of the salient role of distributional concerns. Distributional gains and losses will drive groups to collect information and provide it to Congress, setting up polarized debates over policy that reveal much information. For example, congressional involvement in trade is well known. In an article discussing congressional resistance to US-Pacific Rim trade deal, US Trade Representative Froman said, "Everything we do with trade policy is done hand-in-glove with Congress."[72] Congress also wields a considerable degree of control over USAID, which we discuss in detail in chapter 5. Because distributional costs and benefits are highly concentrated in these areas, interest groups are likely to be very active and to lobby Congress, as we show in chapter 3. Part of their activity is to collect and transmit information. Domestic military spending is another area where we do not expect the president to dominate in terms of information; Congress and interest groups have strong incentives to be involved and will know how much is being spent where and will have an important influence over this. Hence in these areas it is unlikely that legislators will lack information relative to the president. Since this information is power, it seems likely that these areas will see a much more balanced relationship between the president and Congress.

Other scholars have emphasized this asymmetry in discussing how delegation to the president from Congress operates.[73] We argue that this may be especially true for some foreign policy areas where the president has a large, specialized bureaucracy to inform him (e.g., the Defense Information Agency, Department of Defense, National Security Council, CIA, NSA, among others). Asymmetric information then can dominate some policy areas. Interestingly, though, the IPE literature has not focused as much on

---

71  As Kriner notes in discussing the second Iraq war, "The course of the national policy debate in the lead-up to the invasion testified to the stark informational asymmetries enjoyed by the president at the conflict initiation phase. . . . Congressional opponents of the administration's plans simply lacked the resources and information needed to rebut effectively the president's justifications for war." Kriner, 2010, p. 273.

72  Lowrey, 2013.

73  Epstein and O'Halloran, 1999; Huber and Shipan, 2002.

how factors like distributional politics can have an impact on the distribution of information between key political actors. Our research helps fill this gap.

Of course, asymmetries in information could exist for reasons other than domestic distributional politics. For example, there may be differential needs for secrecy when dealing with foreign countries; transparency may not always be preferred in some issue areas.[74] Informational asymmetries may also be associated with the need for secrecy, rapid responses, or the deeply institutionalized considerations that stem from constitutional design.[75] These exogenous considerations certainly account for some of the variation across policy instruments that we see. While our focus is more on how distributional and ideological considerations shape informational politics, we do not dispute their importance but also do not expect our alternative focus to bias our conclusions.[76]

## Political Ideology and the Extent of Ideological Divisions over US Foreign Policy

Our arguments above about distributional politics focus on winners and losers in terms of material, economic consequences. However, there are other important factors at work that arise from ideological differences among the agents. Just as the magnitude of distributive politics matters, so

---

74   Stasavage, 2004.

75   See Gailmard and Patty, 2013, pp. 206–222.

76   An additional reason, rather than exogenous feature, for delegation by Congress in some areas is that in some circumstances Congress might not have an incentive to have control because these agencies are more likely to produce better policy outcomes if Congress does not meddle. Gailmard and Patty develop such an account using a set of principal-agent models and historical case studies. A key intuition of their model is that if you want bureaucratic agents to develop expertise (and hence be able to select better policies in the future) then an incentive to do so is to give them some degree of policy autonomy. Applied to relationships with the president, they argued that "(i)n the case of foreign affairs, our theory makes a crisp prediction. Because execution, and indeed an important part of foreign policy making generally, must be under the president's influence, Congress has a strong incentive to support the president's capacity with institutions to gather, analyze, and faithfully transmit information to the president. In fact, this point is true whether we can locate presidential prerogative over foreign affairs in the Constitutions, or whether its most expansive readings are extra-constitutional . . . Regardless of the source, if presidential prerogative is generally accepted by all three branches of the government, Congress has powerful incentive to support presidential decision-making capacity. This in turn underpins the often-noted presidential informational advantage over Congress on these issues." Ibid., p. 209.

We note that the Constitution itself was designed in light of trade based distributional considerations. Furthermore, we note that logically the need for secrecy does not preclude material motivations.

do ideas. Scholars have long argued that non-economic factors such as ideas can help explain foreign policy.[77] Unlike a pure focus on ideas, however, we propose a more political view that sees divisions across ideologies as critical. The extent of these ideological divisions is the metric of importance for us.

Ideology can have a sweeping set of meanings;[78] below we lay out the role of ideology in our theory. Using Gerring's ideas, we define ideology as the set of beliefs held by an individual about politics and foreign affairs that is consistent internally, contrasts with others individuals' beliefs, is relatively stable through time, and is non-expedient—that is, it does not reflect their immediate, short-term material interests.[79] For foreign policy this means beliefs about the dispositions of foreign actors and the appropriate way to deploy government resources to deal with them. It involves beliefs about how much of a threat foreign states pose to the United States, how cooperative they are, and given these beliefs, what the priorities are for government spending. Broadly, ideology about politics and foreign affairs concerns the proper role of the government in the economy and in protecting American citizens and their way of life. We expect that ideology in this sense motivates people to support or oppose the president as he chooses foreign policy instruments to deal with foreign policy problems. And ideology thus matters since it affects citizen evaluations of their leaders and hence the electoral prospects of both legislators and the president.

The public may care more about whether a foreign policy problem is solved successfully in the end. But they may also care about what instruments are used to deal with it, especially for long-term problems. Why? Excluding consideration of immediate economic interests, they may care because they have ideas about which policy instrument will work best; they have different causal stories in their heads about how policies connect to outcomes. That is, they connect policies to outcomes, believing that certain policies are more likely to achieve resolution of the problem. Ideology thus matters for preferences among policy instruments.

The functional role of ideology in our theoretical setup is similar to the role played by distributive politics. Individuals and legislators hold ideological commitments, which may translate into concrete policy preferences. Below we discuss the content of such ideologies for foreign policy. But the key for us is the extent of ideological *divisions* on the use of a policy instrument. We present how different policies may evoke different levels of ideological divisions. We do not focus on ideas as such and where they come from, but rather on the political dimension of ideas: how they create divisions among American political leaders and shape the politics around foreign policy.

77  Goldstein and Keohane, 1993b; Lumsdaine, 1993.
78  Gerring, 1997.
79  Ibid.

As part of our definition of ideology, we note that, following Gerring, two factors critically constitute ideology: the *internal consistency* of the ideas and the *external contrast* with others' ideas.[80] Without some internal consistency, there is no set of ideas, but rather many disconnected ones. And without contrast to an opposing set of ideas, ideology does not function as a guide to choices. These two elements help determine the existence and content of ideologies.

Both of these elements of ideology are very important. They vary across policy instruments, and thus the extent of ideological differences varies with them. For instruments where the policy instruments link back consistently to the content of one's ideology and contrast sharply with the opposing ideology, there will be strong ideological differences. When the policy instruments are vaguely related to the main tenets of the ideology or are related in a contradictory way and the contrasting ideology is also ambivalent, then ideological differences will be smaller. We outline how our policy instruments vary according to their internal consistency and external contrast in terms of competing ideologies, and thus how they differ in terms of the extent of ideological divisions.

This variance in the extent of ideological differences is key. Ideological divisions often condition whether policy substitution can happen. If sharp ideological divisions exist on a policy instrument, then it will be very difficult for the president to employ that instrument and especially so if he wishes to use it instead of another instrument with fewer ideological differences. Resistance to policy choices out of ideological dislike can be as strong as resistance due to economic interests. Not only may shifting from one policy instrument to another entail shifting ideological coalitions, but it can also incur large political costs in overcoming sharp ideological divisions. Hence ideology is an important factor in considerations of policy substitution. If ideological divisions over these instruments are wide, crafting coalitions across such instruments may be very difficult for presidents.

Ideological divisions may exist in policy areas that have distributional consequences (e.g., often conservatives are more favorable to free trade than are liberals), but they *may* also exist for policy instruments where distributional implications are muted. Theoretically, there are four possible cases, with either high or low distributional consequences and high or low ideological cleavages. In terms of our model, we expect that presidential influence will be greatest when ideological divisions and distributive politics are both low in intensity. When distributive politics and ideological divisions over an issue are very strong, the president will be extremely limited in his ability to use that policy instrument. In these cases, Congress and interest groups (and public opinion) will play very constraining roles. While ideological resistance can

80   Ibid.

be fierce, policies that have strong distributive consequences can be doubly constraining for the president, since they also tend to undermine his informational advantages.

Next, we discuss the role of ideology generally. Then we set out the content of the two distinctive ideological positions in US foreign policy, suggesting how each policy instrument fits into this schema. And finally we identify the extent of ideological divisions that inhere in each instrument. This then sets forth our second main explanatory variable in this study.

## Ideology in American Domestic and Foreign Politics Research

In the domestic context, most scholars divide the ideological world into liberals and conservatives.[81] Given our focus on US domestic politics, this is the best starting point. A common conceptualization of ideology in this literature deals with ideas about the role of government in the economy. In our context this involves the left-right orientation of political ideology. Political beliefs about the efficacy of government intervention in the economy and the importance of governmental efforts to redistribute income (at home or abroad) may play an important role in guiding opinions about policy instruments that are largely economic, like international trade, foreign aid, and immigration. Individuals or interest groups holding right-wing views want to minimize the role of government, especially the government's redistribution of resources; those holding left-wing views prefer a more expansive role for government in society and often favor redistribution to the poor.[82]

In a recent book on US foreign policy and public opinion, Gries shows evidence for the important role of ideology in US foreign policy.[83] He demonstrates that foreign policy divisions among the public are just as ideologically driven as in domestic politics. Politics does not stop at the water's edge.[84] Conservatives and liberals disagree on many aspects of foreign policy. They disagree on which countries can be trusted and they feel

81 Hartz, 1955; McCarty, Poole, and Rosenthal, 2006; Desch, 2008.

82 Relatedly, partisanship is a fact of life in the American political system and has long been so. Partisanship reflects this left-right divide as the two main parties hold these contrasting views. So-called independents are an important part of the American electorate, though at the end of the day Congress is almost entirely made up of members of the two parties.

While foreign policy may be more bipartisan than domestic policy, it still has a strong element of partisanship attached to it. Even debates about its temporal trends recognize this. Kupchan and Trubowitz, 2007; Chaudoin, Milner, and Tingley, 2010.

83 Gries, 2014.

84 Ideology, which he sees having a deeper psychological structure than partisanship, shapes foreign policy debates powerfully. Party identification matters as well since the parties tend to encapsulate individuals with different ideologies, although not perfectly. It is not possible from what is reported in Gries to pull out whether ideological cleavages are larger

close to. They disagree on which foreign policy instruments and policies are best to employ. They disagree on the utility of foreign aid, the benefits of trade, and the usefulness of diplomacy. They disagree on how involved internationally the United States should be, and on whether to use international organizations and multilateral policies in general. And this division sometimes cuts along the lines of domestic ideological debates.[85] But how does this map onto our policy instruments, and should we expect the effect of ideology to be stronger in some than others?

## How Does Liberal-Conservative Ideology Map onto Foreign Policy Instruments?

In trade policy, the use of trade barriers can be seen as an inappropriate intrusion by the government, affecting the flows of goods and services among individuals, firms, and countries. Thus right-wing individuals should oppose trade barriers. Individuals with left-wing ideologies may be more worried about the implications of trade for workers and inequality and hence less likely to support free trade and more willing to use trade barriers for protection. Trade policy fits neatly into the left-right ideological divide in the United States. It has internal consistency and external contrast for both groups.

Foreign aid involves the taxation and redistribution of money by the donor government. Instead of allowing money to flow where individuals see the best investment opportunities, foreign aid redistributes money through a centralized governmental system. Thus right-wing conservatives are likely to oppose foreign aid as an inappropriate role for the government and liberals are more likely to support it.[86] Similar arguments have been made about the influence of ideology on support for multilateral aid organizations like the IMF.[87] This ideological divide over the use of trade and aid policy is explicable according to the divergent views about the appropriate role of government intervention in the economy, which here is both the domestic and world economy. These views toward trade and aid flow naturally from the basic values of each ideological position concerning the appropriate role of the government in the economy. There is thus high consistency within each ideology for views on trade and economic aid; and there is much contrast between the two ideologies about opinions of these two instruments.

---

for some issues compared to others due to the types of mediation analyses he almost exclusively utilizes. Ibid.

85  This holds controlling for obvious confounding factors like age, gender, education, region, ethnicity, etc.

86  Noel and Therien, 1995.

87  Broz and Hawes, 2006.

The connection between left and right ideological viewpoints on immigration policy is much less clear. Immigration policy is about the flows of people from abroad into the United States and their rights and responsibilities. Immigration is thus like trade policy in many ways. Using government policies to limit the flow of people does not accord with right-wing ideological principles since it means government interference with the market. On the other hand, like aid, immigration policy has implications for government redistribution. Allowing immigrants to occupy jobs in the United States and benefit from social services is a form of redistribution. And all of this should make conservatives oppose more liberal immigration policies. Immigration does not consistently fit within a conservative ideological framework. Similarly, for left-wing individuals, the story is unclear. The use of restrictive government policies regarding immigration will depend on the perceived effects of immigration on citizens. If immigration has a negative effect, e.g., by displacing workers in the rich country, then as with trade policy, left-wing individuals might find government policies to limit immigration appropriate. If immigration is seen as beneficial to the poor, or in some way fulfilling other redistributive goals, then those holding left-wing beliefs may not see immigration as a threat and hence may not support government restrictions. The ideological divide on immigration should be less than in trade or economic aid; the values of traditional left-right ideologies in terms of role of government intervention in the economy do not provide *internally consistent* views on it, and the contrast across the ideologies is also confused.

Sanctions also have less clear ideological bases. Conservatives might be opposed to them since they involve government intervention to halt or reduce economic relations. But they might support them if the country targeted is trying to disrupt the global capitalist system by promoting communism or socialism, as many countries were sanctioned during the Cold War. More left-leaning individuals may dislike sanctions since they are intended to hurt the economy of another country, and that includes innocent civilians. On the other hand, they may support sanctions that try to end inhumane or unjust practices like slavery, apartheid, repression, and other human rights violations. There is limited internal consistency on sanctions within each ideological tradition and unclear contrasts across them. Hence we expect that left-right divisions on sanctions will be smaller.

For the military policy instruments that we consider, left-right ideology also maps uneasily onto them. Deterring attacks on the American homeland and generally securing American territory are outcomes every American wants. Having adequate military capacity to do that is supported by almost every citizen. The use of military force beyond that is always contentious. Right-wing individuals may want to make sure the world is safe for capitalism and thus they may see the need for foreign military intervention. While both Democrats and Republicans have advocated for the deployment of troops, a common finding in the American public opinion literature is that on average Republicans are more hawkish. Some argue this arises from differences in threat perception between liberals and conservatives due to underlying psychological attitudes.[88] But war and military interventions tend to hurt the economy, generating public debt, higher taxes, and inflation in addition to destruction. And as various studies have shown, leaders of the business world, who tend to hold more conservative views, do not favor military conflict; indeed, they have an aversion to it.[89] On the left, support for military intervention is likely to depend much on the context. In line with their concern for taking care of the least well off in society, more liberal individuals are likely to support military interventions that stop gross human rights violations and/or assist democratic governments. But again the basic elements of liberal ideology do not speak directly to the proper use of military force. The traditional values of liberal and conservative ideologies in the United States do not seem internally consistent on supporting or opposing the use of military force. And contrasts across the ideologies seem more muted as well. At certain times practically everyone will support maintaining military might and favor military intervention. We thus expect the ideological divisions between liberals and conservatives to be mild on this policy instrument most of the time.

Geopolitical aid is also likely to have limited ideological divisions for many of the same reasons. While one might think that geopolitical aid should be as ideologically divisive as economic aid, we do not think this is correct. The values in liberal and conservative ideologies in the United States do not produce straightforward positions for individuals on this policy instrument. This type of aid is explicitly not about redistribution or government intervention; it is about American security and geopolitics. The basic elements of the American left-right ideology do not comfortably fit with a strong position on this policy instrument. For conservatives, military aid has elements of government intervention in the economy, but it also may help anti-communist groups and promote trade and investment. For liberals, this is aid that is not going to the poorest countries or individuals, but it might still support human rights and other humanitarian goals. If geopolitical aid can be seen as doing many of these tasks at once, it should be less ideologically charged than economic aid. We do not expect large ideological divisions over geopolitical aid since it does not produce internally consistent preferences within each ideology and produces much less contrast between the ideologies.

88   Jost, Glaser, Kruglanski, and Sulloway, 2003; Jost, Banaji and Nosek, 2004; Jost, 2006; Carney, Jost, Gosling, and Potter, 2008; Rentfrow, Jost, Gosling, and Potter, 2009; Gerber, Huber, Doherty, Dowling, and Ha, 2010.

89   Brooks, 2005; Kirshner, 2007; Brooks, 2013.

One military-related policy instrument that should have much more of an ideological divide is domestic military spending. While it is a truism that military spending benefits every electoral district in the country (though not necessarily to the same extent), military spending has a strong ideological foundation. Some level of military spending is obviously necessary for basic national security, and for this public good all citizens tend to support it (even if they would prefer not to pay taxes for it). But what level is appropriate? How much is enough? These are questions that immediately raise the broader issue of government spending overall. And on this liberals and conservatives differ sharply along ideological lines. Liberals are more in favor of government spending generally as they believe the government can foster growth and social goals. But they prefer spending that addresses domestic social goals and redistributes in favor of the worse off. Above a certain level, military spending is just a brake on domestic spending and creates a tradeoff with domestic goals. Conservatives on the other hand are much more averse to paying taxes for domestic social goals and redistribution. They believe the proper role of government is national security, not redistribution. It is better to have a big military that can deter all sorts of threats than a large social welfare state.

The ideological divide over government spending and taxation is especially telling with respect to domestic military spending. In 2012, the United States went through a budget crisis, as Republicans refused to raise the debt ceiling to enable greater US borrowing and spending. In the political brinkmanship that followed, a deal was reached that, if a long-term agreement wasn't achieved later, deep budget cuts would be imposed that would penalize each party on something they cared about the most. For Republicans, this was military spending. For Democrats it was mostly in the form of social spending programs, including foreign aid.[90] Domestic military spending falls neatly along the liberal-conservative divide over the role of the government in the economy; it is highly consistent with the main tenets of each ideological tradition; and it presents a vivid contrast across the two ideologies. We thus expect deep ideological divisions over domestic military spending, much like that in economic aid and trade.

In summary, ideology seems to define the other major dimension of cleavage around foreign policy instruments. This depends on how internally consistent the policy is with the basic tenets of the ideology and with its degree of contrast with other ideological systems. Beliefs about the dispositions of foreign actors and the appropriate means to deal with them are intrinsic to attitudes toward US foreign policy. But these must align consistently with the basic tenet in the ideology about the proper role of government in the economy, which tends to form the left-right spectrum in

90   Morales, 2013.

the United States. As discussed, we expect ideological divisions around economic aid, trade, and domestic military spending to be quite strong. And evidence from American public opinion suggests this is the case.[91] On the other hand, left-right ideology does not provide as much consistent framing for how to view military interventions, geopolitical aid, immigration, or sanctions.[92] It is important to remember that not all political conflict in the United States between the parties is ideological. Some is just the opposition party versus the incumbent. Opposition parties may criticize incumbents for policies they would have adopted as well just to score electoral points. We assume some of this occurs all the time, but some disagreement is driven by ideological differences, where the opposition would rarely ever adopt the incumbent's position.

### Relationship between Distributional and Ideological Factors

How do material and ideological factors fit together? Ideology can be related to an individual's economic interests, and class may partially define the way people choose parties.[93] Republicans tend to come from the strata that own capital or have high human capital, while Democrats come from the strata that represent labor. This relationship is by no means perfect, though, and may change over time.[94] For example, in our district level data there is not a very strong correlation between class and partisanship. We adopt an approach then that separates out the impact of ideology and material variables. There may be some overlap, and in a number of our analyses we take this into account.

Both ideology and distributive politics then shape the central cleavages around foreign policy instruments that we capture here. In a sense they are two different lenses through which one individual can view a policy instrument and its impact. For instruments where the distributive consequences are minimal, ideological divisions may dominate the cleavage structure. Even when distributive consequences are apparent, both factors

91   Wittkopf, 1990; Program on International Policy Attitudes, 2005; Nincic, 2012; Tingley, 2013.

92   Political competition among the parties can sometimes drive conflict over policy, even if the ideological bases are not strong: if the president is from one party and expresses one preference, the opposition may take an opposite stand just because it is in opposition. We and others think this is more likely to occur on military issues. Howell and Pevehouse, 2005; Howell and Pevehouse, 2007. Previous research anticipates such situational partisan differences on military deployments. For example, presidential scholar William Howell writes that "[a] substantial body of research shows that Democrats within Congress regularly and predictably support Democratic presidents who are contemplating military action, just as Republican members of Congress back Republican presidents." Howell, 2013, p. 101.

93   McCarty, Poole, and Rosenthal, 2006.

94   Alvarez and Nagler, 1995; Bartels, 2005; Abramowitz and Saunders, 1998.

could matter. Policy substitution and bundling will be very challenging for a president bent on international engagement because of the ideological cleavages around these policy instruments. While *some* material preferences will entail an internationalist orientation (like those associated with skill effects in trade, aid, and immigration), a pro-internationalist president could nevertheless still be constrained by ideological cleavages. Just as with the material forces present in our account of distributional politics, ideology plays a central and independent role in shaping preferences and thus affects the politics of US foreign policy.

What might this imply for how we should think about informational asymmetries? In short, they may allow the president to exercise influence, but they do not necessarily mean he will be able to influence all legislators. For example, some models of information transmission show how information uptake is more likely when there is some degree of preference similarity between the agents.[95] Signals are more informative and credible to cue-seeking audiences, like legislators, when they come from their own party, when they go against expectations, or when they are costly in some way to the signaler.[96] In our context, preference similarity between the president and legislators could arise due to similar distributional preferences; few, if any, distributional consequences; or some other closeness between presidents and legislators. An obvious candidate for this latter category is belonging to the same party as the president. Belonging to the same party as the president brings with it a host of institutional consequences as well as associations between a legislator and the president in the mind of the public. As such, beyond any potential ideological affinities, it is much more likely that members of the president's own party listen to him and trust that he speaks the truth. Hence we expect that presidential informational advantages will be most salient for co-partisans.[97] In situations where information asymmetry favoring the president is high, and ideological divisions are low, legislators may seek out other forms of guidance, along partisan lines, and presidential endorsements may be important.

### Summary about Presidential Power

We have argued that presidential power varies by policy instrument and we try to explain why. Unlike much of the previous literature on the "two presidencies," we do not expect all foreign policy instruments to be governed by

---

95   See e.g., Crawford and Sobel, 1982; Meirowitz, 2007.

96   Baum and Groeling, 2010, pp. 27–28; Trager and Vavreck, 2011, p. 532.

97   Importantly, just because a legislator is in the same party as the president does not mean they automatically share the same preferences. This is not the case, and indeed, estimated ideal points in general of the president and the legislator can differ.

the same politics. Nor do we think that the distinction between high and low politics tells the most important story. In the three areas dominated by the military, we expect different levels of presidential influence; it should be highest in military deployments and lowest in domestic military spending, with geopolitical aid somewhere in between. Our classification of policy instruments reveals more about their politics and hence about presidential power. First, in areas where the distributional impact of policies is smaller and more diffuse, especially at the district level, the president will have more leeway to push for policies he prefers since legislators will feel less concerned about the electoral consequences of these policies. When costs and benefits of policies are concentrated on social groups, distributional politics will prevail and interest groups will organize and lobby for their interests. They will thus mobilize and inform legislators, and presidents will have less leeway to realize their preferred policies. Second, an important and understudied implication of this classification concerns who has information about the policy instrument. In areas where the president has, or is seen to have, the advantage in gathering and analyzing information about the problem and its policy responses, he will have greater influence. Asymmetries of information in favor of the executive empower him over Congress.[98] Third, ideological divisions can create serious political costs for policies the president would like to enact. Resistance by legislators especially can be a critical source of constraint on presidents.

In table 2.1, we simplify our theoretical framework and set out our expectations about presidential power. When distributive politics is less at play and ideological divisions are small, presidents will have maximum influence and be able to use the policy instrument with much less domestic political cost. This is the top left-hand cell. In the bottom left, ideological divisions will be large and distributive politics will be strong; in this case presidents will be weakest. They will face strong opposition from the opposing party and elements of the public because of these ideological differences; additionally, they will face strong interest group pressures and congressional resistance combined with a lack of informational advantages. In the bottom left-hand cell, presidents will also be weak since interest groups will lobby and inform Congress and the public about policies, eroding the president's informational advantage. But ideological divisions should be less of a constraint. And finally in the top right-hand cell, presidents will retain their informational advantages because interest groups will have less incentive in low distributive politics policy instruments to collect information and dis-

98    For example, Joshua Rovner, a scholar of the intelligence community, noted how in the lead-up to the second Iraq war, "The White House had restored its credibility by bringing intelligence into the policy consensus and had exploited the persuasive power of intelligence to overcome congressional and public doubts about the need for war." Rovner, 2011, p. 160.

**Table 2.1.** Predictions of Presidential Strength by Distributional and Ideological Dimensions

|  | LOW IDEOLOGICAL DIVISIONS | HIGH IDEOLOGICAL DIVISIONS |
| --- | --- | --- |
| **LOW DISTRIBUTIVE POLITICS** | Strongest President | Second Strongest President (information advantage remains with president) |
| **HIGH DISTRIBUTIVE POLITICS** | Second Weakest President | Weakest President (interest groups transmit information to Congress) |

tribute it. But they will be weakened by the ideological divisions besetting the instrument.

## Connecting to Policy Substitution

The extent of distributive politics and degree of ideological divisions can also help explain the politics of policy substitution. Previous work in IR and IPE that focuses on one instrument at a time (e.g., see literature on trade, finance, military force[99]) obscures an understanding of policy substitution and its importance.[100] We expect the type and extent of domestic constraints on the president to vary with the nature of the policy instruments he chooses. When policy instruments, for instance, provide more public goods types of benefits (i.e., they are non-rival and non-excludable), presidents will be more influential. In contrast, shifting toward policy instruments that have distributional consequences could encounter opposition. For example, as we discussed in the previous chapter, it was difficult to get trade liberalization with Pakistan because of resistance from domestic economic interests. Furthermore, when ideological divisions are large for a policy instrument, presidents will be less able to employ it.

Political leaders cannot assume that a switch from one instrument to another will be easy. Ideological cleavages and material interests might interfere. Similarly, the ability to compliment the use of one instrument with another might face important political constraints. Where ideological divisions are large, the use of various inducements to sway the opposition will be less successful and more costly. Indeed we find that ideological divisions over trade and aid are sizable enough to block presidential efforts to use these instruments when he might want to do so.

99   Hiscox, 2002b; Frieden, 1991; Howell and Pevehouse, 2007.
100   Though some work considers the policies around policy bundles within IPE. See, e.g., Simmons, 1994.

In terms of our policy instruments, we can rank the degree of substitutability among them according to our theory. Instruments that are highly substitutable for one another have low levels of distributive politics, high informational asymmetries favoring the president, and/or low levels of ideological conflict. Given our theory, this identifies military deployments, geopolitical aid, and sanctions as more easily substitutable. Presidents should have greater flexibility using these three types of instruments and moving back and forth between them. Congress and interest groups will be less likely to object; presidents will have informational advantages in using them; and ideological divisions will be less clear and more muted. Building coalitions to adopt and implement such policies will thus be less politically costly for the president. More than the other two instruments, we expect sanctions of certain types to engender more distributive conflict and interest group activity. When sanctions affect sizable swaths of the American economy, they should generate more political resistance and reduce presidential influence. But in general presidents will be able to control the balance between sanctions, military aid, and military deployments.

In contrast, immigration, economic aid, and trade policy should be much more difficult to substitute for one another or for the other three policy instruments. Immigration, we predict, has high distributive politics but lower ideological divisions, meaning that interest groups, Congress, and the public will act as strong constraints on the president. He will not have much of an informational advantage since these groups will do their best to collect and transmit information about the policy to Congress and other important actors. For economic aid, we expect both distributional and ideological politics to matter, but for ideology to play a critical role. Ideological divisions over economic aid should render it very difficult to employ and to substitute for other policies. Building a coalition will require overcoming partisan boundaries, which is difficult and politically costly. Trade policy will also engender strong ideological and distributional politics. Substitution among trade, economic aid, and immigration will be costly for presidents as they face congressional and interest group opposition, and partisan politics divides leaders over the best choice of instruments. Presidents will also not have informational advantages that assist in building optimal packages of policies. Furthermore, substituting any one of these policies for geopolitical aid, sanctions, or deployments will be even more difficult. This is part of what may drive the militarization dynamic in foreign policy decision making.

Finally, defense spending in the United States will be a very divisive issue. With large distributive consequences and high ideological polarization over spending priorities, defense spending will be one point where the president has limited control and Congress dominates. Trying, for example, to cut military spending to increase economic aid will be a politically costly and challenging task for any president. Or, offering trade concessions in lieu of geopolitical aid will be a type of policy substitution that is rarely implementable. The domestic characteristics of the policy instruments matter; they shape the politics around the policy instrument. These in turn condition the influence presidents can wield over the policy choice. And in turn this affects policy substitution. In the end this theory is important because the success of American foreign policy depends in part upon the policy instruments chosen. Success is more likely where policy substitution can occur.

## Hypotheses: Presidential Influence and the Characteristics of Policy Instruments

When does the president have the ability to obtain his preferred policies? Although we argue that foreign policy instruments should be considered jointly, we also think that the domestic politics surrounding each of them may differ. Throughout the book, we show that the politics surrounding our main foreign policy instruments—international trade, immigration, economic aid, geopolitical aid, sanctions, domestic military spending, and military deployment—differ. As a result presidents will sometimes be more able to employ their preferred policy instruments; other times they will be frustrated. We offer a series of hypotheses to explain these differences. Our first set of hypotheses focuses on explaining the variance in presidential power. Our second set presents differences across foreign policy instruments in terms of the politics they entail, which allows us to understand variation in presidential power.

### PRESIDENTIAL INFLUENCE

Ceteris paribus, when distributive politics are very significant, presidents will be more constrained; Congress will be more likely to intervene; interest groups on both sides of the issue will be more likely to testify and lobby Congress passing along information; and Congress will be more likely to try to wrest control over the executive branch bureaucracies and agencies that deal with the area.

Ceteris paribus, when the extent of ideological divisions over a policy instrument is very significant, presidents will be more constrained.

When distributive politics is not significant and ideological divisions are small, the president will have the most control over foreign policy. In this setting, Congress will be least likely to intervene; interest groups will target the executive branch, not Congress, for their lobbying; the president will

**Table 2.2.** Predictions of Presidential Strength by Policy Instrument

|  | LOW IDEOLOGICAL DIVISIONS | HIGH IDEOLOGICAL DIVISIONS |
|---|---|---|
| LOW DISTRIBUTIVE POLITICS | Military deployment, Geopolitical aid, Sanctions |  |
| HIGH DISTRIBUTIVE POLITICS | Immigration | Economic aid, Trade, Domestic military spending |

be most able to substitute policies for one another; and in roll call voting presidential influence will be strongest on co-partisans.

## POLICY INSTRUMENT CHARACTERISTICS

Where distributive politics are very significant, ceteris paribus, we should see (1) a lot of interest group activity in terms of PAC contributions and lobbying; (2) Congress as a focal point for information transmission by economic and social groups through testimony and lobbying and hence bypassing of the White House; (3) economic interests lobbying according to the distributive consequences of the policy; and (4) active contestation by Congress over control of executive branch bureaucracies.

Where policy instruments generate internally consistent and externally contrasting views, ideological divisions will be very large, and ceteris paribus, we should see legislators voting on foreign policy largely according to their general ideology.

As detailed above, we expect distributive politics to be very significant for international trade, immigration, domestic military spending, and somewhat less so for economic aid. Military deployments, geopolitical aid, and sanctions should be less affected by distributive politics. Ideological differences should be most extreme for domestic economic aid, domestic military spending, and trade. They should be less important for military deployments, geopolitical aid, sanctions, and immigration. Table 2.2 is a summary of our expectations.[101]

As we discussed earlier, all of these hypotheses have important implications for policy substitution. The more the domestic economic interests and/or the ideological divisions for any two policy instruments matter, the

101 This classification of policies almost exclusively places policy instruments along the diagonal. Nevertheless, our theoretical formulation sketches out the complete set of logical possibilities. We think the two dimensions are fairly independent of one another. And we do not see one dimension as dominating the other, in the sense of making any deeper claims about one causing the other. See section "Relationship between distributional and ideological factors" for additional discussion.

more difficult it will be for the president to substitute one policy instrument for another. Shifting policy instruments then means greater shifts in the supporting coalitions, which may be costly to do. Because of the nature of these policy instruments, decision making faces a tendency to use military means. We provide illustrative examples of this dynamic, and how it relates to a tendency to use military instruments, especially in chapter 7, which is an extensive case study of American policy in Sub-Saharan Africa over the period from 1993 to 2009.

## Alternative Explanations

### International System

The dynamics of the international system, it is claimed, dictate the responses of states. As argued most often by Realists, policy makers have limited choice in how they respond to international problems. As Mearsheimer says, "Great powers that have no reason to fight each other . . . nevertheless have little choice but to pursue power and to seek to dominate other states in the system."[102] Other countries or non-state actors take actions, and the United States must respond in a particular way. "Survival mandates aggressive behavior."[103] Or as Waltz would seem to argue, in anarchy states must balance (or die).[104] So the United States must respond in a certain way to foreign actions.

Systemic theories clearly have a very different focus from ours, but we feel it is still important to engage with this perspective. First, the international system is not an agent and it cannot take action; and anarchy is not a condition forcing all states to behave similarly.[105] All actions are the choices of policy makers and other agents. How and whether they choose to respond to the international system and the behavior of other states is a matter of debate. The president and the executive branch are a focus of most foreign policy studies because they are the ones who feel the pressures of the international system most clearly. They are the ones who have to craft responses to this pressure. All international events and pressures get filtered through them first. And it is unlikely that they will all respond the same way. In fact, Realism has no single answer as to what means they must or will respond with, except to note that the use of force is always a possibility. We do not disagree with this, but rather ask when and why this possibility sometimes becomes a reality.

102   Mearsheimer, 2001, p. 3.
103   Ibid., p. 21.
104   Waltz, 1979.
105   Milner, 1991; Wendt, 1992. It is notable that even the two leading Neorealists—Mearsheimer and Waltz—do not agree on what states will be forced to do in the same type of international system: balance or dominate.

Second, presidents have a choice once they feel this pressure in whether and how to respond. This is reflected in the deep and long-standing debates that occur within the executive branch over policy responses to other states and external events. One has only to think of the fierce debates about major crises among Secretaries of State and Defense, the generals in the Pentagon, and the NSC over the past fifty years to realize this.[106] It is not automatic that they must select the military instrument of statecraft. This is a choice, and efforts to cast it as automatic are political in their own right.

### Some Events Require Military Instruments

A second possible view of American foreign policy, which makes concerns about substitution and militarization less interesting, is that some problems require a military solution and only a military one. We reiterate our response to this claim that we made in chapter 1. It is unclear what the logic is for the claim that a foreign policy problem or opportunity is a "military" one. The claim that the only possible action to take in a situation is one involving the use of the military is not plausible. The use of military means is a choice; it is not dictated by some external force or actions. It is one among many policy instruments that policy makers can utilize. As Clausewitz pointed out, war is politics by other means. It is one and only one means of carrying on the political negotiations over a dispute. And this is echoed by Fearon's rationalist war claim: there is always a [range of] negotiated settlement to a foreign policy problem that is cheaper than the use of military force.[107] And between a negotiated settlement and the use of military force, there are many other policy instruments, like aid, trade, and sanctions, that fall somewhere in between in terms of costs that can help end a dispute. In many if not most cases, presidents have a choice. Furthermore, most problems cannot be solved by military means alone, either.

### The Constitution

The Constitution gives certain powers to the president; and these include the military, as he is the commander in chief. Congress, it is claimed, is not

---

106    Examples include Secretary of Navy and then Defense Forrestal and first Undersecretary and then Secretary of State Acheson in the late 1940s; Secretary of Defense McNamara and Secretary of State Rusk in the 1960s during the Vietnam War; Acheson at State, President Truman and General MacArthur during the Korean War; National Security Advisor Kissinger and Secretary of State Rogers; Secretary of State Vance and National Security Advisor Brzezinski in Carter's presidency; and more recently Secretary of Defense Rumsfeld and Secretary of State Powell in the Bush administration concerning Iraq. Carter, 1982; Rearden, 1984; Condit, 1988; Isaacson, 1992; McMaster, 1997; Chace, 1998; Woodward, 2004; Kaplan, Landa, and Drea, 2006.

107    Fearon, 1995.

entitled to interfere constitutionally with this policy area.[108] And this is why the War Powers Act is so often debated. This is not accepted in all legal circles. As John Yoo maintains, "Thus, in the war powers context, the Framers did not rest the sovereign power of making war in one department, but divided it between the executive and legislature and gave each branch the means to check the other's designs. The president could not wage war without funds; Congress could not initiate hostilities without a Commander in Chief."[109] More generally, the Constitution has been described as an "invitation to struggle" between the president and Congress over the making of foreign policy.[110]

But even if true about the military, this claim can't explain what policy instruments (which include non-military instruments) the president chooses and Congress approves. First, many policy instruments are not specifically discussed in the Constitution; they were developed later (e.g., foreign aid). This leads to ambiguities in who has control. Moreover, there has been an evolution in the de facto and de jure control of policy instruments over time. Trade policy is no longer just the domain of Congress; delegation of authority to the president on and off since 1945 has created a larger role for the president, but Congress and interest groups still hold considerable sway. And aid has grown from a one-time policy in the Marshall Plan to a wide-ranging set of bureaucracies (e.g., USAID, MCC, and PEPFAR)— often under shared control of the two branches. Chapter 5 makes this clear: over time, control of new and old bureaucracies waxes and wanes between the Congress and the president. The Constitution sets broad boundaries but does not dictate who controls the policy instruments we focus on.

Furthermore, we note how even in the "high politics" domain of the military, the Constitution cannot account for the different politics we see. Our theory and empirical evidence suggest that the three military-oriented policy areas we examine should have different politics associated with them. Military deployments overseas give the president greater discretion since they are least linked to distributive politics and ideological divisions; geopolitical aid has more of a distributional element and hence somewhat less presidential discretion; and domestic military spending looks just like domestic politics with strong constraints on the president because of its powerful distributive politics and ideological divisions. The president may be commander in chief according to the Constitution, but in different foreign policy areas related to the military his influence varies greatly. Simple appeals

---

108   Louis Fisher's dismantling of the executive branch's claim to be the "sole organ" in foreign policy shows that the Constitution provides no grounds for the idea of a privileged role of the president in making foreign policy, as opposed to implementing and executing it. Fisher, 2007.

109   Yoo, 1996, p. 303.

110   Corwin, 1940; Crabb and Holt, 1989.

to the Constitution do not render a complete understanding of who controls US foreign policy.

## The Need for Secrecy

Another possible answer is that the need for secrecy demands that the president have control over certain policy areas, and everyone understands this.[111] This differentiates the military sphere from all other foreign policy areas, it is claimed. While few argue that secrecy in foreign policy is never important, most of the debate concerns how much secrecy and secrecy about what. Two points raise questions about whether this need can explain foreign policy choices. First, secrecy is not undesirable in areas outside the military. In trade or environment negotiations, for example—or really any international negotiations—secrecy about the American position is most probably in its national interest.[112] Furthermore, we know that the United States collects secret information on the economic capabilities and negotiating positions of other countries.[113] So the need for secrecy in some aspects is common across policy areas. Second, the question of how much secrecy is necessary even in the military and intelligence is hotly debated. Numerous studies suggest that presidents desire secrecy as a way to increase their domestic power and to mislead publics about the external situation.[114] Hence it seems unclear that there is some agreed upon level of secrecy that is necessary for the president in any area.

# Conclusion

Governments have many ways they can engage with the rest of the world. They can use a variety of foreign policy instruments, separately or simultaneously. Were countries run by a unitary rational executive, they would choose the set of foreign policy instruments that best fit the external problem they faced. They would choose the "cheapest" set of instruments that would address the problem most effectively; i.e., they would look for the biggest bang for the smallest buck. Most governments, however, are not governed by a unitary rational executive who can adopt the best set of in-

111   The US Constitution does not explicitly grant executive secrecy in the list of Article II powers; however, presidents have enhanced their powers through legislation and the federal courts' recognition of legal defenses to conceal information, recently often in responses to the threat of terrorism. The PATRIOT Act, the Homeland Security Act, the state secrets privilege of 1953 are all means by which the executive can hide its activities from public view.

112   For example, negotiations over TTIP are kept secret. Jasper, 2013.

113   Mazzetti and Sanger, 2013; Vidal and Goldenberg, 2014.

114   Franck and Weisband, 1974; Gibbs, 1995; Mearsheimer, 2011.

struments for a given external problem. Rather, they face domestic political constraints that may affect their ability to use any particular instrument.

There are two characteristics of foreign policy instruments and the issue areas they impact that shape presidential power. First, the extent to which a policy instrument creates large, concentrated gains and losses for different domestic groups is important. Where policy instruments are associated with such strong distributive politics, they will incentivize the affected groups who may support or oppose the policy to organize and collect information and lobby the government. These distributional struggles will create political contestation and often polarized debates over policy choices, which raise the costs of choosing that policy. Where the effects of policy are more public goods–like in nature, these groups will be less likely to organize and lobby. In areas with high interest group lobbying, presidents will tend to be more constrained and less able to implement policies they prefer. A second characteristic involves the influence of ideology. For many instruments there will be strong ideological divisions among the political actors. Presidents will face powerful resistance to their preferred policies in this case. The larger these divisions, the more difficult it will be to substitute one policy for another because such divisions will make it very costly to adopt and change policies; they will in effect greatly lower the marginal rate at which presidents can substitute one policy for another.

In addition, distributional politics then creates incentives for political actors that affect informational asymmetries. Because of external factors presidents often have built-in informational advantages that allow them to implement policies more to their liking. These asymmetries of information, relative to Congress in particular, are important in foreign policy and are maintained through the extensive bureaucracies that the executive branch runs. They make it hard for Congress to develop independent sources of information and thus to contest the president. For policy instruments where distributive politics is limited, interest groups will be less active and thus other sources of information may not be available for Congress. As we see in many intelligence gathering agencies, it is very difficult for Congress to control them and gather information from them. The distribution of material gains and losses and of information thus shapes the politics in ways that significantly affect the president's control over different foreign policy instruments.

In turn, these characteristics have two important implications for US foreign policy. On the one hand, they affect policy substitution and the president's ability to put together an optimal package of policies for any international problem, which further influences his ability to pursue a liberal internationalist agenda. Second, they may produce a tendency for the president to opt for military means since they are politically less costly, at least ex ante. When distributive politics and ideological divisions are important for a policy instrument, the president will face high domestic political costs in attempting to use it. This may dissuade him from doing so and bias his choice instead toward those instruments with lower domestic political costs. Militarization of foreign policy may be the result. Our empirical evidence has less to say about these two consequences than we would like. But we do try to draw out how these implications affect US policy in our various chapters.

Determining presidential power is difficult. Presidents and the Congress are interacting strategically and know they are being watched and judged on their behavior by the public and media. The behavior we observe is thus colored by this process of strategic interaction and common knowledge of it. And several other potential explanations for the question we ask about presidential power in foreign policy exist, including the pressures of the international system that may align congressional and presidential preferences.[115] In subsequent chapters we examine a variety of types of data to address these issues. Using many different sources and exploring different institutions, we seek to build confidence in our claims about presidential power, substitution, and American foreign policy.

115　This argument, however, cannot account for variation that we do observe, nor does it acknowledge that the international environment is a product of US foreign policy decision making itself. Furthermore, in subsequent chapters we examine this claim empirically and in many cases find surprisingly little effect. We employ a range of control variables and fixed effect strategies that allow us to see the effects of our domestic explanatory factors, holding the international environment constant.

# 3

## FOLLOW THE SAND DOLLARS
### Interest Groups and American
### Foreign Policy Instruments

The US Constitution was written with the role and influence of interest groups in mind, and interest groups have played a central role in the American political system. While Madison's concerns about factions helped generate a separation of powers system to keep them from dominating the government, it is rare for discussions of politics in the United States to exclude the role played by formally organized groups. Individuals in these groups tend to have similar preferences and thus strong incentives to seek policies that will disproportionately benefit themselves.

The role of interest groups has never been limited to domestic politics. During the interwar period, interest groups played a key role in determining US engagement with the international monetary system.[1] As Schattschneider pointed out, it was interest groups lobbying Congress that helped induce the protectionist turn in American trade policy—i.e., the infamous Smoot-Hawley Tariff—that deepened the Great Depression.[2] And with increasing trade relations between countries after World War II, powerful internationally oriented groups started to influence US policy.[3] As Goldstein and Gulotty show, protectionist interest groups have remained active throughout the post–World War II period in US trade policy.[4] This chapter helps advance our understanding of American foreign policy by looking at interest group politics for each of our core foreign policy instruments. Interest groups play a major role in the construction of American foreign policy, as our focus on distributional politics makes clear, but they also play a role in policy substitution.

In this chapter we highlight the first of our two key variables: distributive politics. Most interest groups are associated with attention to the material gains and losses from policies. They form and act because they are protecting, or hoping to gain, benefits from the policy process for their members. This attention to distributive politics is also connected to information collection and provision, as we noted before. Interest groups testify and lobby

---

1   Frieden, 1991.
2   Schattschneider, 1935. See also Kindleberger, 1973.
3   Milner, 1988b; Jacobs and Page, 2005.
4   Goldstein and Gulotty, 2014.

to both shape policy according to their preferences and provide "expertise" that often leans in the direction of their favored policy.[5] Our hypotheses and evidence in this chapter focus on the role that interest groups play in these areas according to the extent of distributive politics present. We do not touch upon the ideological aspect of our theory here. Some important interest groups in foreign policy however are not mainly motivated by material interests. These groups representing diasporas or foreign countries are better thought of as religious and ethnic identity groups whose means are similar to economic interest groups but whose goals differ. Others, such as NGOs, may have more mixed motivations as they can receive material benefits from some instruments like economic aid, but are not for-profit firms. These interest groups are important in foreign policy, but they are less central to our theory.

In the US political system today, interest groups remain extremely important, as well as controversial. In this chapter we consider a variety of groups inside and outside of government, including economic interest groups but also others such as officials from particular branches of the government as well as diaspora groups and non-governmental advocacy groups. Some of these groups may lobby for policies that leave the country better off as a whole, while others pursue particularistic interests that may be harmful. These groups come in a broad variety of forms and with a variety of motivations. Some interest groups represent particular economic interests. For example, in seminal work about the congressional politics of international financial bailouts in the 1990s, Broz shows how campaign contributions from individual banks that had a high degree of international financial exposure affected policy.[6] Other interest groups represent collections of firms, such as the National Association of Manufacturers, or even foreign countries.[7] While banks and manufacturers represent groups with material motivations, others have ideological agendas, such as the pro-Israel organizations including the American Israel Public Affairs Committee (AIPAC) or J Street.[8] In this chapter, we discuss both materially motivated groups and to some extent those motivated by religious and ethnic identity.

This book's core thesis explains the contrast in politics around different types of foreign policy instruments. Unlike previous studies of interest groups that focus on one set of policy instruments (such as in the trade and international finance literatures discussed above), we are interested in deter-

---

5 Austen-Smith, 1987; Baron, 1989; Austen-Smith, 1993; Baron, 1994; Grossman and Helpman, 1994; Grossman and Helpman, 2002.

6 Broz, 2005.

7 Pevehouse and Vabulas, 2012.

8 Smith, 2000.

mining whether and how interest group activity differs across these instruments.[9] In doing so, we provide a needed descriptive accounting of interest groups across multiple different foreign policy instruments. For some policy instruments, such as trade, the interest group landscape is well known in the literature; for others it is not. For example, much less has been written in the contemporary literature on economic interest groups behind US economic aid. More important, we show how our central explanatory variable involving distributive politics and its concomitant influence on information asymmetries shape not only interest group activity (who they lobby in the federal government), but also the decisions political actors make about how to best acquire information (e.g., who to admit for formal testimony).

Our theory suggests the following testable propositions about interest groups and US foreign policy. First, interest groups should be more active on policy instruments that have greater distributional consequences. They should testify and lobby for their preferred policies and collect and provide information to Congress to reduce any asymmetries of information between the president and Congress. Hence we should see high levels of congressional lobbying on things like budgets, as interest groups jockey to make sure appropriations bills contain funding for goods and services that they can offer. For example, we expect that when lobbying of USAID occurs, much of it will be about budgetary items. Trade policy should show similar patterns. Exporters and those wanting protection will lobby and testify before Congress in order to make sure US trade policy protects their material interests. For both cases of economic aid and trade, we expect interest groups to have less interest in targeting the president and executive branch. As we discuss in greater detail below, this is because these groups know that the president is less influential on these instruments.

These patterns change, however, when we look toward the distribution of geopolitical aid, sanctions, and the deployment of US troops. On these instruments, the president is more firmly in control. There are greater information asymmetries and fewer material distributional consequences. While diaspora-based interest groups will be active in pursuing their religious and ethnic identity–based agenda when it comes to some geopolitical aid and some firms will testify to Congress against sanctions, overall we expect less economic interest group activity for these issues. Furthermore, in order to influence, or even gain information about, the direction of US military policy, we expect that the executive branch will be targeted. In these cases interest groups know that while Congress is still relevant, they should spend some of their time and resources targeting the executive branch.

---

9   There of course are some exceptions. The literature on ethnic lobbies tends to be more multifaceted in the types of policy instruments it considers, but the traditional IPE literature is much more uniform in this regard.

The data in this chapter illuminate congressional versus executive branch politics in several ways. To better understand the politics around different foreign policy instruments, we want to know which actors testify before Congress on which issues, which branches of government lobbyists target and bypass, and which issues they choose to bring to that branch's attention in their lobbying. To answer these questions, we analyze new data on two important political processes: testimony before Congress and lobbying activity. First, we collected systematic data on which groups testify before Congress for several of our instruments. For example, for each military deployment decision that we examine in chapter 4, we collected testimony leading up to the deployment vote.[10] Then we classified the groups lobbying into different categories, such as members of the executive branch, economic interest groups, non-governmental organizations, and diaspora groups.[11] Our theory suggests that when it comes to geopolitical aid, sanctions, and troop deployments, executive branch officials will be dominant, but for economic aid and trade, economic interest groups will play a greater role than they do for the other policy instruments. While our testimony data do not cover domestic military spending and immigration, below we draw on other work and data that allows us to make connections to those policy instruments.

This classification is useful for a variety of reasons related to our overall project. It lets us identify a broader set of social actors compared to only looking at actors in government and at public opinion (as done in subsequent chapters). As such it enables comparisons across foreign policy instruments.

Second, we analyze lobbying activity to understand (1) the foreign policy topics that are the subject of lobbying, (2) lobbyists' summary of these foreign policy topics as classified by federally mandated "categories," and (3) the decisions of lobbying groups about what branches of the federal government they choose to lobby. When, for example, do interest groups bypass the White House? When lobbyists register to lobby on a given topic, they almost always list Congress. But they do not always list the White House. What explains this variation in lobbying decisions? Our theory about distributional politics and its impact on informational politics suggests that when it comes to policy instruments that entail greater distributive consequences, interest groups will be less likely to expend resources in targeting the White House. This type of "institutional targeting and bypass" is a novel way to examine the strategies of interest groups.

---

10   These deployments took place in the following countries: Bosnia, Afghanistan, El Salvador, Haiti, Kosovo, Iraq, Somalia, Lebanon, and Kuwait.

11   For completeness, we also code experts, foreign governments, and legislative officials, though these groups are less connected to our theory.

**Table 3.1.** Interest Group Research Questions and Data Sources

| QUESTIONS | DATASETS |
|---|---|
| *Who* testifies to Congress across policy tools? | Manual coding of testimonies |
| On what issues do lobbyists bypass the White House? | Web scrape of all Lobbying Disclosure Act files, 2007–2014 |

To answer these questions about lobbying, we analyze an original data-set collected by "web-scraping" the universe of lobbying reports from 2007 to spring 2014. These reports indicate not only what agencies are lobbied, but also what they are lobbied about. We show, for example, that lobbying of USAID often concerns distributional issues, such as for funding for programs that rely on contracts with interest groups. This empirical pattern is consistent with, and reinforces, a range of more qualitative evidence about development-oriented economic aid which is less connected with geopolitical concerns. In contrast, when a geopolitically relevant country is identified in the description of the lobbying content, it was extremely rare (4%) that the report dealt with budget-related issues.[12] This highlights how distributional issues are much less salient for geopolitically relevant countries. When such countries are involved, it is rare that the issue deals with budgetary matters that have distributional consequences. We summarize our data and core questions in table 3.1.

The data presented in this chapter illuminate the politics of policy substitution in several ways. First, some of our data corroborate the material as well as the religious and ethnic identity motivations of these groups. They show how some groups prefer international engagement with one instrument, while others oppose the use of the same tool. For example, we show how economic aid often benefits highly skilled US contractors and exporters.[13] But as shown in other chapters, ideological support and opposition to economic aid, with liberals supporting and conservatives opposing, will create cleavages and constraints for policy substitution. We expect different coalitions of interest groups to support and oppose different foreign policy instruments. A shift from one instrument to another, for example from economic aid to trade, creates transaction costs for the president as coalitions must be reformed.

We do not endeavor to "prove" that interest groups are influential in shaping policy. We can, however, show that they do transmit information. But we suspect they are also influencing policy, otherwise they would not

12   We parsed the data to look at reports mentioning geopolitically important nations like Saudi Arabia, Afghanistan, Iraq, Israel, Egypt, and Pakistan.

13   Aid can also build up a country's capacity to export to the United States low-skill products, which can create opposition to aid. When this occurs, groups such as US labor which are more liberal will begin to oppose it.

spend the money and effort that they do.[14] Even if at the end of the day their influence is limited, they still create costs that the president must pay in creating policy when they oppose him. Of course, showing such influence quantitatively is difficult. Instead we focus on explaining the behavior of interest groups across the different instruments, something the literature has not done.

## What Are Interest Groups and What Do They Do?

Interest groups face a very different incentive structure for trying to influence policy compared to individual members of the public. Interest groups have usually solved their collective action problems because they have a significantly salient set of common interests, but also because the policies they pursue often have excludable benefits associated with them.[15] As part of their ability to persuade policy makers, interest groups also provide policy makers with information.[16] For example, interest groups around trade policy seek restrictions or opening of markets with respect to particular goods and they provide information to policy makers to support their preferences. These groups lobby branches of the government that the groups see as central for making decisions; they target the institutions of government that they believe are the most likely to be able to shape the policy. For budgetary issues, this will be Congress. For the policy instrument of trade, this will include Congress but also the executive branch because of its role in negotiating international agreements. For some military policy instruments and sanctions, the executive branch will be crucial.

Our theory suggests several patterns of interest group activity. First, policy instruments that have large distributional consequences will see more lobbying activity focused on securing material advantages. This activity could stem, for example, from securing contracts for domestic spending on maintaining US military capacity. These contracts, as we show in this and the next chapter, are highly distributional and hence quite distinct in character from other political decisions about the use of military force. Additionally, lobbying can be about budgets for economic development aid. In less of a

---

14　In presenting our work to colleagues, some seminar participants have questioned whether interest groups actually transmit information. Recent work argues that indeed this is the case: "while primarily politicians maintain relationships with lobbyists of the same political orientation, they do appear more likely to cross the aisle when talking to experts, as would be expected if the politicians were trying to improve their information acquisition." Bertrand, Bombardini, and Trebbi, 2014, p. 3887.

15　Olson, 1965.

16　Esterling, 2004.

budgetary realm, trade policy can also have sizeable distributional impacts. Hence we expect interest groups that lobby on trade, economic development aid, and domestic spending on the military to be focused on such distributional issues. Furthermore, legislators and officials should be aware of these distributional issues such that the domestic economic consequences of these policy instruments are mentioned when they are discussed. Conversely, interest group activity on geopolitical aid, sanctions, and military deployments will take a different form. These instruments, we argue, have less of a distributional character. Lobbying activity here will primarily be by diaspora groups that want to solidify an ethnic and religious identity based agenda and some NGOs that are concerned about humanitarian implications of using these instruments. These groups will not be the direct economic beneficiaries of these instruments and hence will focus most on policy issues. Such lobby groups will continue to target Congress, but we argue that they will also target the White House at a higher rate than those lobbying in other policy areas.

A second pattern that our theory suggests is that flows of information between institutions like Congress and the executive branch and between lobbying groups will reflect underlying information asymmetries. In areas where the executive branch holds an asymmetric advantage, Congress will try to get information mostly from it. For example, when Congress holds hearings on military issues related to geopolitical aid and deployments, they will try to get the executive branch to provide information. Executive branch officials may choose to provide information or not. Conversely, in areas where interest groups are incentivized to collect and provide information, Congress will seek their testimony and they will readily provide it. For instance, economic interest groups will be called upon by Congress to provide information in hearings about US trade agreements or trade-related issues such as tariffs. Similarly, we expect interest groups to engage in some degree of institutional targeting. The White House will not be the place where lobbyists will target their efforts about ongoing tariff disputes, for example.

## Testimony and Lobbying Data about Interest Groups across Foreign Policy Instruments

We provide several main types of data about interest groups in the next sections. First, we draw qualitatively on testimony and reporting about interest groups. For example, to establish the domestic material motivations for economic aid, we highlight what is said about the direct economic consequences of aid, either through contracts or consequences for exports.

Second, we collected information on who was called to testify before Congress in relation to several of our policy instruments. Third, we study individual interest group behavior by analyzing which issues they lobby on and who they choose to target with their efforts. Next we describe in more detail the congressional hearing and lobbying data.

We collected information on who testified before Congress on several of our policy instruments. In particular, we focus on testimony about the African Growth and Opportunity Act (a piece of legislation concerning trade preferences for African countries), USAID, the Economic Support Fund (ESF, an example of geopolitical aid), and military deployments. For each of these we used keyword search in ProQuest Congressional to identify testimony that contained keywords related to each instrument. For each policy instrument, we then either took a random sample of hearings or coded all testimony sessions. We next came up with an expansive set of categories describing different types of witnesses, including economic interest groups and the executive branch.

These data help us to establish some basic differences in which actors are involved in testimony across different policy instruments. Of course, who testifies is a function of whom Congress wants to testify and who wants to testify. Observing testimony is the result of a process of strategic interaction and is therefore not simple to interpret. For example, some actors might not want to testify and so we would not observe them in the data. Hence we do not make conclusive claims based on this data. The patterns we unearth are consistent with our theory, but we highlight below the inherent limitations of this type of observational data.

To study lobbying, we examine lobbying report data about what interest groups do. When an organization, be it an economic interest group or a policy advocacy group, engages in lobbying activity with the government, it is required by law under the Lobbying Disclosure Act of 1995 to register its activity. To register activity the group must file a lobbying report.[17] As with the testimony data, lobbying report data are helpful only insofar as there are not systematic differences between lobbying registration and all lobbying activity. Any gaps will be impossible for us to observe, and may even be illegal. Hence the less voluntary nature of these data gives us more confidence in them, but we realize there are still potential problems with this type of observational data.

Several pieces of information in the lobbying report are interesting for our purposes. First, the lobbying organization must list a single label per

---

17 An example of which is given here: http://soprweb.senate.gov/index.cfm?event=get FilingDetails&filingID=8A2D2517-1082-404F-AE72-26D95FF09629&filingTypeID=51. The instructions for filling it out listed are listed here: https://lda.congress.gov/ldwebbeta/help/ default.htm?turl=Documents%2FAppLD2.htm.

lobbying report. These labels include both domestically oriented labels, such as health care, and ones that have some bearing on foreign policy. For example, "DEF" pertains to defense, "FOR" pertains to foreign relations, and "BUD" means the organization was lobbying over budgetary items. We will describe these labels in more detail. These are not labels we assigned to the data, but are identified by the lobby group itself according to pre-specified categories. We detail in great length what each captures. Almost all lobbying reports contain a short textual description of what they were lobbying about. These descriptions were typically brief but nonetheless informative and allowed us to investigate in greater detail the topics being lobbied.

Second, the organization must list the contacted agencies. Nearly every lobbying report in our sample contacted either or both the House and Senate. But beyond this there is a lot of interesting variation. For example, an organization can indicate that it lobbied the House, the Senate, and the White House. When a lobbying report lists the White House as a target for lobbying, we expect that it is less likely that the lobbying will be about issues that concern primarily distributional consequences. Distributional issues can include topics like domestic military spending that go into annual appropriations bills, and on these things we expect the White House will be bypassed. Trade policy presents a more mixed picture, in that it is highly distributional, but the president is still involved because he negotiates trade agreements with other countries. Conversely, because Congress especially controls legislation with distributive consequences, our theory predicts that interest groups will focus their attention on Congress and bypass the White House on these issues.[18] In the next section we focus on identifying and understanding different interest groups that have bearing on the policy instruments we consider.

## Interest Groups and International Engagement

In this section we discuss the role of interest groups across the core policy instruments we consider: economic aid, trade, immigration, sanctions, geopolitical aid, and military deployments. We identify groups that support

---

18   Unfortunately, there is no single database of these reports that is publicly available. Instead, we resorted to a large "scraping" operation where we connect to the weblinks of the organization, as the example given above, and extract the above data items. To do this, we took two steps. First, we extracted weblinks from the advocacy organization Open Secrets the list of all lobbying reports. They use these to be able to post all the lobbying reports so citizens can view them online. Second, we wrote a script in Python to visit each website, over 700,000 in total, and scraped the above information. Each lobbying report can list several different activities that can each be on a separate topic. In the end, we collected 872,236 instances of lobbying activity.

and oppose these policy instruments. By understanding who supports or opposes what instruments and why, we can better understand the politics of shifting from one instrument to another. In the next section, we provide evidence about how interest groups direct their lobbying efforts toward particular institutions, such as some of the bureaucracies we discuss in chapter 5, but also when, and whether, the White House, as opposed to just Congress, gets lobbied.

To structure our argument and evidence for this chapter, we initially separate the universe of policy instruments into two larger groups: one concerning economic policy instruments and one concerning military engagement. This dichotomization differs from our more nuanced perspective used in previous and subsequent chapters and allows us to present our argument here in a more concise fashion. But within each of these two groups, we return to the same set of policy instruments central to this book. The first group involves international economic engagement. The United States has grown increasingly economically interdependent with the rest of the world. Of course, this has taken various forms over time. Our discussion in this chapter focuses on the post–World War II era, which includes the embrace of trade liberalization, the emergence of the continuous use of foreign aid, as well as the development of multilateral institutions for providing foreign assistance. The second group of policy instruments involves military engagement. Here we cover geopolitical aid, sanctions, and military deployments. We have argued in this book that these instruments entail far fewer purely distributional considerations but also reflect a more substantial information asymmetry between the Congress and president. We also discuss domestic military spending and immigration, which are not included in our testimony data but are included in our lobbying data.

## Economic Engagement

In this section we discuss three of our core policy instruments that relate to economic engagement: foreign economic aid, trade, and immigration. We identify the role of interest groups in each.

### FOREIGN ECONOMIC AND DEVELOPMENT AID

The birth of large-scale foreign aid after World War II happened in a contested political environment with a range of different interest groups wanting to shape its use. Since then interest groups remain important players in US foreign aid politics. Historically these groups include US labor but also a range of companies that have contracts with USAID, the World Bank, or other organizations. Not all foreign aid is the same. Some foreign aid is for economic development, but other aid is more strategically linked, including aid in the form of weapons and military training, which we discuss in the next section. We argue in this book, and show, how different types of foreign aid have very different constituencies, which in turn influence thinking about policy substitution and presidential influence.

Starting with the Marshall Plan, a considerable amount of US foreign aid took the form of economic development aid. Early on, as discussed in the previous chapter, the role of economic development aid had undertones of broader geopolitical considerations. Since then aid designed for development and aid designed for geopolitical purposes have been largely separated.[19] We discuss geopolitical aid in the next subsection, but here we document the domestic interests supporting and opposing economic aid.

Domestic groups that receive excludable benefits from foreign economic aid come in two forms. First are groups that benefit indirectly from development aid through an expansion in exports to aid-receiving countries. This support stems from the fact that growing markets create demand for (typically capital-intensive) US exports. These considerations were extremely salient in the development and evolution of the Marshall Plan, but also played out in subsequent years.[20] These connections are not academic. Treasury secretaries who have to justify aid requests for the multilateral development banks note this, and congresspersons do as well. For example, Rep. Evans (R-DE) noted how "(i)f we can stabilize the economies and the political structures of nations in the Third World, we can expand our export markets. Already 40% of our exports are sold in the Third World. That is important to American jobs, and for every billion dollars of exports it means 40,000 American jobs together with the dignity and the self-esteem that a job brings."[21] The general view here is that foreign aid helps open up, or somehow gives US access to, markets in developing countries that are growing. These discussions were often directly related to statements about US jobs, much in the same way that discussions on trade policy would be.

A second form of excludable benefit to economic groups from foreign economic aid is much more direct: contracts from aid agencies. This can either be mandated, as is the case for "tied-aid," or through regular contract procurement practices in which firms from other countries can also compete. For example, Congressman Long of Maryland, in discussing contributions to the foreign aid wing of the World Bank, the International Development Association, noted: "About 50% of our contributions to IDA are returned directly to the US through procurement and local expenditures.

---

19   There is a long debate over the degree of fungibility of aid. See for example Baldwin, 1986. In theory, aid is very fungible as is any kind of money. But there are various ways to make it less fungible and these have been tried by most aid organizations to gain greater control over the resources.

20   Wala, 1986.

21   Evans, 1981, p. 30793.

Procurement of goods and services by the World Bank and IDA in the US total $4.7 billion by the end of June 1976. In fiscal year 1976, IDA and the WB had a net favorable impact on the US balance of payments of $555 million. I wish there were more in the House at this time to hear that . . . This not only does good for these poor people but it also creates jobs at home, right here in the US."[22] In the 1990s, while foreign aid was being attacked by conservatives, Congressman Obey appealed to a similar argument: "I want to also point out that American firms have received 39% more in procurement last year than the US contributed to all of the development banks. We contributed $1.6 billion. American corporations wound up earning $2.2 billion from that same World Bank in their programs. That has produced for the United States 42,000 US jobs. If you want to throw that away, be my guest."[23] Linkages such as these between aid and American companies showcase how foreign aid has considerable domestic distributional consequences.

Some evidence exists that the main domestic beneficiaries are firms and organizations that produce products with a high skill premium. In the previous chapter and in the next one, we argue that economic aid benefits high-skilled industries and workers, but here we provide more direct evidence for this claim. In extolling the domestic economic benefits of USAID, USAID administrator James Atwood noted that "Developing countries are particularly good customers for our high-value exports,"[24] and Treasury Secretary Robert Rubin noted how "U.S. corporations also get major contracts from the MDBs."[25]

Quantitative analyses suggest similar conclusions. In 2001 USAID published a "Yellowbook" that provides a list of each contract from USAID with the amount and vendor.[26] We took a subsample of all larger firms listed (240 contractors that had total contracts above the mean total contract amount), researched the company, and identified the headquarters. Using each firm's web statement of what its company does, we created thirteen different categories that described the various types of organizations that get USAID contracts.[27] For each category, we then summed up the contracts and divided it by the sum of all contracts in our sample (i.e., the 240 with above average contract amounts).

---

22  Long, 1977, p. 20572.
23  Obey, 1993, p. 13158.
24  Committee on Appropriations, 1996, p. 11.
25  Committee on Appropriations, 1995, p. 332.
26  US Agency for International Development, 2001.
27  The categories, derived inductively, were health non-profit, health for profit, education non-profit, education for profit, development consulting, university, non-profit other development, ethnic lobby, labor organization, corporation, political consultant, environmental group, and government agency.

One category stood out: broad-based "development contractors." For example, the firm Chemonics, which describes itself as "an international development consulting firm that promotes meaningful change to help people live healthier, more productive, and more independent lives. Around the world, we design and implement projects in financial services, private sector development, health, environmental management, gender, crisis prevention and recovery, democracy and governance, and agriculture."[28] These broad-based development contractors get a substantial amount of USAID business. These firms employ relatively well-educated individuals.[29] In our chapter on roll call voting, we will also see that legislators from high skill districts tend to be more supportive of this type of aid.

Evidence of the major budgetary implications of US economic aid to these groups is apparent in data on what interest groups lobby about. To show this, we next draw on the lobbying data described earlier. When USAID is listed as a federal agency that was lobbied, we also know what topic is listed (e.g., budget or foreign affairs) and the description of what was being lobbied on. If our claim is correct, and foreign aid is highly distributional, then we would expect simply that a large percentage of instances in which USAID gets lobbied would receive a "Budgetary" topic. Indeed, this is exactly what we see. Of the 4,041 items that were lobbied on where USAID was listed as a target (and other agencies could also be listed), 873 of them were tagged as a budgetary item, 257 related to Agriculture (see below with respect to food aid), and 267 were tagged as Trade. In total this reflects 1,397 lobbying reports that clearly suggest distributional considerations. While the total number of items tagged as foreign policy was similar (1,340), roughly 35% (1,397/4,041) of reports that mention USAID dealt with categories that have large distributional connections.[30]

Another group of interested parties to US foreign aid is banking organizations that have investments overseas. In the late 1970s and onward these banks started to support the use of foreign aid programs as part of a larger package of instruments to deal with developing country debt crises. Negotiated settlements like the Brady Plan directly made use of funding mechanisms in organizations like the World Bank and the International

---

28   Company Twitter and LinkedIn accounts, May 22, 2014.

29   We also analyzed USAID contracts at the district level, looking at whether a firm in a district got a USAID contract, the total number of contracts, and the total value of the contracts. Using data from the 103rd and 107th Congresses, we regressed these variables onto a measure of each district's high-skill concentration. In all of these models we observed a significant positive relationship.

30   Furthermore, we analyzed not just the tagged descriptions of the lobbying items, but also their open-ended descriptions using a Structural Topic Model. Roberts, Stewart, Tingley, et al., 2014. We did not find evidence that items listed with a budgetary tag were in fact efforts to change policy via budgetary means.

Monetary Fund.[31] Lawrence Broz has, for example, documented the influence of campaign contributions from these organizations on votes funding the IMF.[32] And in the next chapter we conduct a similar analysis for votes on economic assistance programs that include the World Bank and IMF. In particular, we followed Broz and calculated the campaign contributions made to legislators from large, internationally invested banks (known as "money-center banks"). We find, like Broz, that legislators receiving these campaign contributions vote more in support of aid, but these contributions are largely unrelated to support for other policy instruments.

Do we see similar patterns when we look at congressional testimony? Who testifies to Congress on foreign aid? To focus this inquiry, we code only testimony that mentions USAID from July 31, 1969 to September 19, 2013. Table 3.2 contains the results. Not surprisingly most testimony comes from USAID administrators and members of the executive branch. As we detailed in the previous chapter, Congress has frequently tried to oversee and control USAID. Overall though, 8.5% of groups testifying in our sample of 412 individuals that testified represent economic interest groups seeking USAID funding. While this is lower than the percentage for testimony related to trade (as we discuss later), it stands in stark contrast to the only 0.5% of those who could be classified as economic interest groups who testified about the Economic Support Fund. Even in formal testimony we see the importance of domestic distributional issues when it comes to economic aid.

Additional anecdotal evidence about US food aid, another important pillar of US overseas assistance, also supports our argument. We see similar patterns for both in terms of the role of interest groups. Food aid has been serviced predominantly by the Food for Peace program under Public Law 480. This program oversees regular shipments of aid but also food that can be delivered in emergency settings. Under PL 480, US food aid was to be supplied by American farmers, and shipped by American shippers.

The restrictions on food source highlight the important domestic struggles over this instrument. Many development experts argue that American policy has dramatic negative effects on development, contra the expressed purpose of the programs. Instead, this policy instrument has long been captured by domestic agricultural interests and the congresspersons that represent them. In light of international criticism about these policies, occasionally there is an effort for reform. In 2005, for example, the Bush administration proposed joining other donor countries and adopting al-

31 Indeed, several Chicago Council on Foreign Relations elite surveys asked a question about whether US aid should be used in this manner, indicating the contentiousness of doing so. An earlier literature developed similar themes about the importance of interest groups in setting broader fiscal policy. Frieden, 1991.

32 Broz and Hawes, 2006; Broz, 2011.

**Table 3.2.** Congressional Testimony Sources by Policy Instrument

|  | TRADE (AGOA) | ECONOMIC AID (USAID) | GEOPOLITICAL AID (ESF) | TROOP DEPLOYMENTS | SANCTIONS |
|---|---|---|---|---|---|
| Diaspora | 0% | 2.9% | 5.3% | 4% | 1.5% |
| Executive Branch | 19.6% | 27.7% (24.3%) | 85.7% | 50.4% | 32.5% |
| Experts | 14.3% | 12.9% | 3.2% | 13.9% | 25.2% |
| Foreign Governments | 10.7% | 0.5% | 0% | 2.2% | 0.5% |
| Economic Interest Groups | 42.9% | 8% | .5% | 3.3% | 16.5% |
| Legislature | 5.4% | 5.3% | 1.6% | 6.6 % | 10.2% |
| NGO/IGO | 7.1% | 18.5% | 3.7% | 19.6% | 11.7% |

For USAID, we break out executive branch first into non-USAID personnel and then, in parentheses, USAID personnel. Data show substantially higher percentage of testimony coming from executive branch for Economic Support Fund and Deployments, compared to this percentage for AGOA and USAID. The percentage from interest groups is also highest for AGOA and USAID. Dates of coverage for each are as follows: Trade 10/5/1994–4/20/2004, Economic aid 7/31/1969-9/19/2013, Geopolitical aid 2/1/1979–5/17/2001, Troop Deployment dates vary depending on conflict, Sanctions 1/1/1940–9/19/2014.

ternative ways to provide food assistance. This effort was blocked "because the administration's proposal has run into opposition from three interests some critics call the Iron Triangle: agribusiness, the shipping industry, and charitable organizations."[33]

This discussion about food aid points to a broader issue about how we should best think about groups that are non-profit and work toward improving US development aid and fostering development aid overseas. Interestingly, some have argued that the purported ideological dedication of non-profit aid organizations is actually deeply material, as some, such as the Catholic Relief Services, take a large portion of their budgets in the form of food aid.[34] The same might be said about the role of these groups

33   Dugger, 2005. Recent years have been no different. In 2013, the Obama administration sought a similar set of overhauls. However, a broad cross-section opposed the reforms. For example, a joint letter from over 60 organizations stated, "Growing, manufacturing, bagging, shipping and transportation of nutritious U.S. food creates jobs and economic activity here at home." Nixon, 2013.

34   Barrett and Maxwell, 2005.

beyond food aid. As we saw earlier, they certainly compete for and get contracts from USAID. This is not to undermine their moral stature, but only to point out that it is not immediately clear that they are less motivated by material considerations compared to, for example, firms that stand to benefit from increases in highly capital-intensive exports.

In part, the domestic political economy around foreign economic aid looks very similar to the politics around trade. As documented above, there are clear connections between highly skilled exporters and consultancies and economic aid. But there are also connections on the protectionism side. For example, given any policy objective, aid can be funded in a way that serves domestic protectionist purposes. As occurred in 1978 and surrounding years, a series of amendments were entertained that stipulated that "None of the funds appropriated or made available to the International Financial Institutions pursuant to this Act shall be used for the purpose of establishing or expanding the production for export of steel, grains, sugar, palm oil, citrus crops, tobacco, or tires."[35] The goal, as pursued by labor organizations, was to prevent the International Development Agency from funding projects that would compete against US industries that favored protectionism. In the 1990s, US labor vocally complained about US aid going to support the development of "Export Processing Zones," which would directly pressure US producers, especially in sensitive areas like textiles.

Beyond the distributional nature of foreign economic aid, US economic aid has become much more transparent domestically, thus reducing informational asymmetries between the president and Congress (as we discuss in more detail in chapter 5).[36] This minimization of secrecy has also come in at least two forms. First, the US government has set up a range of ways for US companies to effectively compete to get contracts. Some of this has taken the form of setting up information sharing systems so that firms are not kept in the dark and the process is not shrouded with secrecy.[37] Second, the United States participates in international institutions that coordinate aid practices and delivery, such as the OECD-DAC. Over time, it is argued, these organizations have increased international transparency and coordination.[38] Furthermore, participation by the United States in multilateral aid

35  Mathis, 1978, p. 25958.
36  These changes do not undermine the claims made in this chapter. It only suggests that were we to only focus on the recent past, our claims would have even stronger support.
37  "US government agencies—primarily the Commerce, Treasury and State Departments—have launched a concerted effort to encourage more American companies to bid on this burgeoning business, and to assist them through information programs, arranging contracts, and intervening directly when problems arise" (cited in testimony by John Cavanaugh). Cavanaugh, 1980, p. 4963.
38  Dollar and Levin, 2006.

institutions to some extent decouples the ability of the US government to keep economic aid practices and strategies secret. Of course, none of this is to say that all US economic aid policy is completely transparent. But on these dimensions it looks very different compared to geopolitical aid, discussed in the next subsection.

## INTERNATIONAL TRADE

The role of interest groups in trade is perhaps the best studied of these types of economic engagement. As we noted in the beginning of the chapter, interest groups have a storied history in trade policy in the United States and in other countries.[39] This should be expected. Government interventions in the economy through trade policy produce distortions that create winners and losers. Because of this, the benefits (and hence harms) of policy are excludable. This provides the foundations for groups to solve collective action problems (versus, for example, consumers) and take costly actions that let them try to obtain favorable outcomes. As such, individuals that control trade are likely to be lobbied. In the United States, the control over trade policy resides within Congress. While Congress has at times delegated some power to the president, legislators have been reluctant for the president to obtain long-lasting control over this highly distributive policy instrument.[40] Undoubtedly, Fast Track authority represents a form of delegation, but this has always been closely guarded and limited in its ultimate effect.[41] With limited exceptions, the politics surrounding US trade policy has long been regarded as dominated by interest groups and Congress.

There already exists a rich literature on the role of interest groups in trade policy. One vein of this research focuses on interest groups that want international engagement and open trade. The groups, driven by firms that are highly competitive internationally, lobby Congress in order to get international trade deals and other arrangements that will better enable their wares to be sold overseas.[42] On the flip side are groups that lobby for protectionism.[43]

We introduce new evidence into this extensive literature by collecting data about who testifies to Congress on trade policy. To focus this analysis, we look at the African Growth and Opportunity Act (AGOA). Initiated during the Clinton administration, AGOA was a mechanism for increasing trade with Africa as well as facilitating African economic development.

---

39  Hamilton, 1791; Schattschneider, 1935; Irwin, 2006.
40  Lohmann and O'Halloran, 1994; Hiscox, 1999.
41  Lohmann and O'Halloran, 1994; Hiscox, 1999; Goldstein and Gulotty, 2014.
42  Milner, 1988b; Kim, 2013; Osgood, 2013.
43  Grossman and Helpman, 1994; Jackson and Engel, 2003.

AGOA is politically interesting because it highlights the political tensions surrounding policy substitution. In this case, trade liberalization was seen as a way to replace failing development aid policies. Chapter 7 discusses these issues in more detail, but here we focus on congressional testimony about AGOA.

Table 3.2 presents our results from examining a random sample of testimony about AGOA between 1994 and 2006. As is clear, economic interest groups were much more active on AGOA than other actors. Their presence was twice as large compared to the next highest category, the executive branch. The presence of executive branch officials is unsurprising given their role in negotiating AGOA with the African countries. But the strikingly higher percentage of economic interest group activity is consistent with the theory laid out in this book.

## IMMIGRATION

As we noted in chapter 1, immigration is a foreign policy instrument as well as a domestic one. Immigration policy has many dimensions, we have argued elsewhere,[44] and these different policy types can have varied foreign and domestic effects. Immigration quotas can be used to reward and punish other countries, and enforcement of immigration laws can be done with similar effects. Refugee policies can have similar foreign policy consequences. Immigration has also been tied more recently to national security policy, in the wake of the global war on terror.[45] But immigration also has domestic distributional consequences, as we have argued in chapter 2, and these are likely to affect domestic groups who have the ability to lobby and inform Congress about their preferences.[46] As discussed in chapter 2, the impact of immigration on the receiving economy is debated, but there is some evidence that immigration affects wages and employment as less expensive immigrants sometimes displace natives. Many immigrants to the United States are low-skilled workers in search of higher wages and better living conditions.[47] Migrants to the United States tend to have less education on average, be younger and have larger families, all of which can have effects on the US economy.[48] Concerns over labor market competition and fiscal pressure on the welfare state may motivate interest groups to take action in this policy arena.[49]

44 Milner and Tingley, 2008b; Tingley, 2013.
45 Ting, 2006.
46 Peters, 2014.
47 Borjas, 1989; Hanson and Spilimbergo, 1999; Chiswick, 2000.
48 Cornelius, Espenshade, and Salehyan, 2001; United Nations, 2001.
49 Goldin, 1994; Borjas, 1999a; O'Rourke and Williamson, 1999; Scheve and Slaughter, 2001a; Hanson, Robertson, and Spilimbergo, 2002.

Hence we expect that economic interest groups will be quite active in this policy area, as much research shows they are.[50] In general, one might expect that groups representing capital would favor liberal immigration laws, thus giving them cheaper and more access to low-skilled labor. Groups representing labor though might oppose such liberal policies and press for restrictions on immigration. But while these two broad groups are involved in policy, their preferences are often more nuanced. Labor is often divided into high- and low-skill groups, with different unions representing different types of workers. The expectation here is that interest groups representing low-skill labor should prefer restrictions on immigration and any policies that reward immigrants while they are in the United States. Groups representing high-skill labor might go the opposite way. And groups representing business should always want greater access to cheaper labor. Preferences do not always follow this pattern, however. For example, access to welfare state benefits has costs and if immigrants use this more than natives, then those who pay the most taxes to support these services, which tend to be high-skill individuals and capital, will oppose liberal policies in immigration on this dimension.[51] Also unions often have very complex preferences.[52] In any case, we expect economic interest groups, like labor unions and business firms and associations, to be deeply involved in lobbying and providing information about immigration policy. And research suggests that political activity by economic interest groups on immigration policy is widespread and often effective.[53]

There is, however, a second set of actors that are likely to be involved in immigration policy. Besides the economic aspects of immigration, scholars have focused on how preferences are developed toward it through a sociocultural lens. Individual-level non-economic explanations of attitudes toward immigrants have a strong foundation in the literature. In these studies, factors associated with education levels and cosmopolitan versus nationalist attitudes shape preferences toward migrants.[54] On one side here then are groups that represent nativist and nationalist associations who oppose immigration and want restrictions imposed. On the other side are groups that represent ethnic or diaspora groups and prefer more liberal immigration, but especially for their particular identity group.[55] This set

---

50    Zolberg, 1990; Gimpel and Edwards, 1999; Hanson and Spilimbergo, 2001; Cornelius and Rosenblum, 2005; Facchini and Willmann, 2005; Wong, 2006; Facchini and Mayda, 2009; Facchini, Mayda, and Mishra, 2011.

51    Facchini and Mayda, 2009.

52    Briggs, 2001; Haus, 2002.

53    Wong, 2006; Facchini, Mayda, and Mishra, 2011; Facchini and Steinhardt, 2011.

54    Espenshade and Calhoun, 1993; Citrin, Green, Muste and Wong, 1997; Money, 1999; Burns and Gimpel, 2000; Fetzer, 2000; Kessler, 2001; Citrin and Sides, 2004.

55    Schuck, 1998; Wong, 2006.

of mixed cleavages over immigration sets up a complex pattern of interest group activity, as noted by many others.[56] We thus expect to see many domestic groups active in immigration policy with economic interest groups, anti-immigration nativist ones and ethnic diaspora groups all involved in lobbying and informing Congress on immigration policy.

Existing analysis of testimony data by political scientist Margaret Peters provides some support for our argument.[57] She found that various economic interests played a strong role. Given the distributional nature of this instrument, Congress hears a range of information about the topic in hearings that it calls from these groups. When government officials were involved, they were basically under-secretaries from different agencies whose policies touch on immigration. Given the substantial research effort invested by Peters, we elected not to do testimony analysis, though below we do analyze this instrument when it comes to our lobbying report data.

## Military Engagement

We now shift to policy instruments that we identified in chapter 2 as being different from the instruments of economic engagement. Geopolitical aid and the deployment of military troops serve a national-level purpose. It is not targeted at the poorest countries and not intended primarily to speed development. Geopolitical aid, such as that delivered through the Economic Support Fund, often goes to supporting key US allies in areas of the world like the Middle East and both South and Southeast Asia. In some instances, this aid is a substitute for the actual deployment of US troops.

The clear message from this subsection is that the composition of interest groups for these policy instruments looks very different from the distributionally minded economic interests in the previous subsection. By and large, the *interest groups* here are foreign governments and diaspora communities, as we discussed previously.[58] While our evidence does not let us conclusively show there is more or less interest group activity related to these policy instruments, this is certainly apparent in our data.

### GEOPOLITICAL AID

US military assistance refers to a diverse collection of programs administered by both the Department of State and the Department of Defense. These programs share a common aim of developing military capacity in

---

56  Hoskin, 1991; Gimpel and Edwards, 1999; Tichenor, 2002.
57  Peters, forthcoming 2015.
58  Of course, there are other relevant governmental actors that we consider below, such as members of the Executive Branch and military.

recipient nations. Historically, however, they have also been used to reward and win over allies. Traditionally, military assistance has been funded via the Department of State with varying levels of DoD participation in the implementation phase. Since 9/11, DoD's role and autonomy in providing military assistance have increased dramatically and several programs are now fully funded and implemented by DoD alone. DoD officials have actively lobbied for these programs, pushing steadily for greater authority and funding for DoD-led military assistance. According to the Greenbook database on aid funding, nearly half of military assistance now comes through DoD rather than the Department of State.[59]

Military assistance programs are developed within the executive branch according to national security strategies approved by the president.[60] These then go to Congress, usually the House Appropriations Committee, for authorization and appropriation. Traditional military assistance funds are implemented and overseen by the Department of State, which either directly administers the funds itself or delegates administration to the DoD. In contrast, DoD-led initiatives are appropriated directly to DoD and implemented either by regional combatant commands or defense contractors. DoD maintains oversight over all such programs, though military officials frequently consult in-country with diplomatic personnel when designing capacity-building programs. This gives the State Department some input over these programs, though it remains limited.[61]

Post–9/11 a new class of military assistance program was created to give greater flexibility to the executive branch in administering military assistance. Proposals for these programs are submitted from the field and considered jointly by DoD and State Department officials. They must then be approved by the Secretaries of both State and Defense. These programs are novel since they place State and Defense "on equal footing to determine the best application of limited resources."[62] The implementing agency is determined in an ad hoc fashion based on the nature of the project, though both DoD and State retain joint oversight. The importance of this flexibility given to the executive branch is consistent with our theoretical expectations about when presidents will have the most control over a policy instrument.

A key part of the US geopolitical aid program is the Economic Support Fund. The ESF has long been regarded as an extremely flexible aid instrument for providing assistance to US strategic allies. ESF is also very different from other forms of development aid. Indeed, in a 1983 GAO report analyzing the ESF, a section titled "ESF Differs from Other Kinds of Economic

---

59  United States Agency for International Development, 2014.
60  Heniff, Lynch and Tollestrup, 2012; International Security Advisory Board, 2013.
61  Tarnoff and Lawson, 2011; International Security Advisory Board, 2013.
62  International Security Advisory Board, 2013, p. 13.

Aid," notes that "ESF, in contrast, is appropriated on a global basis, often with specific earmarks for selected countries clearly related to geopolitical interests, such as the Middle East and South East Asia. Functional uses are not specified,"[63] "ESF is viewed as one of several tools available to meet US foreign policy interests," and "The choice of ESF as the most appropriate source of US economic aid is also influenced by the perception held by agency officials interviewed that, because ESF can be tangibly linked to short-term security interests, it is more readily authorized and appropriated by the Congress than other types of economic aid."

What groups tend to be active when it comes to the ESF? Using the same data collection methodology that we used for USAID and AGOA, we collected the universe of 122 congressional hearings (for a total of 1,999 witnesses) that mentioned the ESF between 1979 and 2002.[64] Next, we drew a 25% random sample of the hearings, verified that each witness's testimony was indeed related to the ESF, and classified each witness into one of our categories. The results are presented in table 3.2. As mentioned, in contrast to economic aid, only 0.5% of the testimony on the ESF was from an economic interest group. Instead, almost all testimony—85.7%—came from executive branch officials. This stands in stark contrast to economic aid. It underlines the different distributional consequences between geopolitical aid and economic aid. The next highest group was diaspora groups at 5.3% of ESF testimony.

When members of Congress want to get information about geopolitically motivated aid, or have their views heard, they go to the groups that have the greatest information about policy—in this case, the decision makers with the most control over this policy instrument. And, unlike for policy instruments with a greater distributional component, there is virtually no role for interest groups.[65] The next highest level of lobbying is by diaspora groups. While the presence of these groups appears small in these data, below we discuss diaspora group lobbying in further detail.

While foreign governments do not appear in our testimony data for the ESF, there is evidence that these groups are active. Foreign governments have a role in trying to influence the allocation of security assistance. A

---

63    U.S. General Accounting Office, 1983, pp. 1–2, p. 4, p. 13.

64    We had originally intended to sample from the entire period 1979-2014, but were limited to a smaller sample, as several more recent hearings have not yet been published.

65    One potential objection to this finding and its contrast with economic development aid is that economic interest groups benefiting from geopolitical aid will not want to be seen in public because of social desirability reasons. It is somehow less acceptable to lobby about instruments related to strategic and military interests than it is to be seen as profiting from facilitating economic development. In principle, we see no reason per se that this holds, and there is of course ample lobbying, as we discuss below, when it comes to military spending more generally.

2013 State Department report on security assistance acknowledges: "Foreign governments engage the Executive Branch and Congress, both directly and through the employment of lobbying firms and supporters and friends in the U.S. population."[66] Journalistic accounts have argued that the most influential foreign groups are those with large immigrant populations already in the United States.[67]

A variety of academic studies also corroborate this account of foreign policy making. Bermeo and Leblang find that nations with large immigrant populations within the United States or with "greater political voice" receive greater levels of foreign assistance.[68] Pevehouse and Vabulas reach a similar conclusion analyzing Foreign Account Registration Act (FARA) records. They find that foreign governments who lobby more receive higher levels of foreign aid.[69] A brief review of Foreign Government Lobby Registrations also supports this idea. These registrations note each time a foreign government retains a new lobbyist and includes a brief description of legislative interest. Security or military assistance is frequently listed in these reports.[70]

A different form of interest group arises out of diaspora communities. Anecdotally, the Israeli and Armenian lobbies are two of the most frequently cited examples of foreign-backed groups with disproportionate influence over US foreign assistance. The American Israel Public Affairs Committee (AIPAC) has been described as the "model for other lobbying groups."[71] Clarke and Woehrel quote a "senior Congressional source" confirming that "there is a pervasive sense in Congress that a bill AIPAC is supporting is not something we should vote against."[72] Additional interviews with congressional staffers reveal widespread agreement with this claim.[73]

It is important to be clear about what AIPAC's prominence implies for our argument, and what it does not. The AIPAC and similar organizations have had a minor economic agenda compared to its ever-present foreign

---

66   International Security Advisory Board, 2013, p. 6.

67   Newhouse, 2009.

68   Bermeo and Leblang, 2010.

69   Pevehouse and Vabulas, 2012.

70   See, e.g., CQ Weekly, 1989. In our testimony data, though, we do not observe foreign governments testifying and mentioning the Economic Support Fund. These groups instead likely focus on other programs such as Foreign Military Financing.

71   Newhouse, 2009, p. 75.

72   Clarke and Woehrel, 1991, p. 217.

73   Ibid. The Armenian and Cuban lobbies are also very well-organized diaspora groups. For example, in 2010, the Obama administration came under heavy criticism for not setting aside funds for Nagorno-Karabakh in its draft FY2011 budget. The House Appropriations Subcommittee on Foreign Operations allocated $10 million for the region in spite of Obama's omission and instructed him to increase aid to Armenia. Finally, the Subcommittee also ensured that Armenia and Azerbaijan would receive equal military assistance though the Obama administration had proposed giving nearly twice as much to Azerbaijan.

relations presence. Certainly trade relations are important between the two countries. The first Free Trade Agreement entered into by the United States was with Israel in 1985.[74] But trade relations are less consequential to the AIPAC agenda. From 2007 to 2013, the word "Israel" was used 985 times in the open-ended lobbying descriptions. Of these, 31% were tagged for foreign affairs compared to 16% for trade. And the United States-Israel Strategic Partnership Act of 2014 (H.R. 938), which passed the House 400–1, was largely focused on security issues. None of this is to say that AIPAC members and others have no economic stakes in trade or investment with Israel, but such interests are small in comparison.

Instead, the Israeli lobby is predominantly concerned with ensuring the security and continued existence of Israel. This is an excludable benefit in a global sense. But it is not a benefit that otherwise would accrue selectively for some congressional districts versus others, other than through variations in Jewish (and perhaps Evangelical) populations. Thus the nature of who becomes a winner and loser—distributional politics—looks different compared to domestic distributional consequences of our other policy instruments. AIPAC has dominated Congress on military aid to Israel, but not because Congress provides AIPAC's constituency with excludable benefits. If a voter of whatever ethnic or religious persuasion wants the existential guarantee of a Jewish state, they can have it. Instead, the winners and losers are better defined globally, as many funds that go to Israel could otherwise be spent on alternative overseas projects and commitments.

It is also important to understand exactly the type of aid that is being given and which types lobbying groups like AIPAC seek. To do this we collected data about foreign aid that is sent to Israel.[75] Unlike foreign aid sent to most countries, Israel receives substantial amounts of budgetary support from the US government. This means that the Israeli government receives money to spend on its own domestic programs. This is in stark contrast to the types of economic and food aid that we discussed before. It would, of course, be incorrect to say that geopolitical aid has no distributional consequences within the United States. But all of the evidence we have collected thus far suggests that these consequences are minor. The motivations for sending military aid to Israel have little to do with domestic distributional politics, but may perhaps relate to electoral considerations.

Finally, while discourse in the United States has tended to focus on a very small set of diaspora groups, it is important to recognize that the United States sends geopolitical aid to many other countries that it sees as crucial

74    Office of the United States Trade Representative, 2014. This passed by a vote of 422-0 and hence we do not include it in our analysis in chapter 4.

75    Tierney, Nielson, Hawkins, et al., 2011.

to US national security. It would be a stretch to think that all these countries have extremely active and effective lobbies or extensive sway over the president. Second, even if we focus on more organized groups, the types of resources that are lobbied for will have a modest domestic *distributional* consequence. Furthermore, similar arguments hold for other diaspora groups where the United States is not engaged in sending geopolitical aid to their homelands, such as the powerful Cuban diaspora. Such groups work to influence overseas policies that relate to their homeland, rather than for distributional goods available as a result within the United States. This contrasts sharply with other types of aid, such as food aid, discussed previously.

## MILITARY DEPLOYMENT

The decision to deploy US military forces overseas for potential combat is one of the most challenging decisions a US president can make. Are the politics around this policy instrument different from others? Our theory suggests that it should be. In particular, with little distributional effect and few excludable benefits, we expect interest group activity here to be minimal. Indeed, despite an earlier literature linking economic interest groups with the proclivity to wage war, Stephen G. Brooks recently argued that "there are no longer any economic actors who will be favorable toward war and who will lobby the government with this preference."[76]

While the academic literature has not shown this, it is quite revealing that in a number of studies of the decision to deploy troops, interest groups are virtually never discussed. Take, for example, a recent scholarly contribution on this topic, Howell and Pevehouse's book, *While Dangers Gather: Congressional Checks on Presidential War Powers.*[77] While the authors conclude that Congress has put a number of constraints on the president's ability to wage wars, the operative mechanisms do not include interest groups. Instead, Congress appeals to the American public. A similar omission is contained in Howell's recent *Thinking about the Presidency: The Primacy of Power* as well as Howell, Jackman, and Rogowski's *The Wartime President.*[78] Interest group politics do not figure in these accounts in any meaningful way. Hence scholars whose purpose is to exclusively focus on military deployments, rather than contrasts across policy instrument, appear to find little role for interest groups.

This summary of the literature is entirely consistent with new data we collected on who testifies before Congress when it comes to military deployments.

76  Brooks, 2013, p. 867.
77  Howell and Pevehouse, 2007.
78  Howell, 2013; Howell, Jackman, and Rogowski, 2013.

Using the same procedures as before in this chapter, we collected testimony on deployments related to Afghanistan, Bosnia, El Salvador, Haiti, Kosovo, Iraq, Somalia, Lebanon, and Kuwait, which are the countries covered by our votes in chapter 4. Then we took a random sample of testimony for each of these events and coded who was testifying.[79] After removing those providing unrelated testimony, we coded total testimonies of 518 witnesses. As we see in table 3.2, 50.4% of testimony comes from the executive branch, second only to the percentage observed for the ESF. Furthermore, when we disaggregated this figure by the country under consideration, the executive branch was always by far the largest source of information. In some cases, such as El Salvador and Haiti, NGO groups were slightly more frequent than in other cases, such as Iraq, due to the humanitarian nature of the events.[80] Economic interest groups accounted for only 3.3%, showing the low rate of interest group engagement with this policy instrument.

Our lobbying report data show a similar pattern. For each lobbying report, we extracted whether the report mentioned Syria, Iraq, Iran, Afghanistan, or Libya, all countries that have had some degree of military contestation or involvement by the United States during the time span of our lobbying data. These countries were mentioned in 0.38% of the total lobbying reports, and in only 1.1% of lobbying reports that included any agency related to foreign affairs.

## SANCTIONS

We now focus on sanctions. Sanctions can of course be used for a variety of purposes and in a variety of situations. To explore testimony related to sanctions we used the same procedure as described earlier using a key word of "sanction." Unlike more targeted searches, such as with AGOA, this one returned more false positives, as the term sanction can be used in conjunction with many other acts. In our coding of testimony, we then had to take an extra filtering step to remove these instances.

Overall, we found that the category with the most testimony events was the executive branch, at 32.5% of our sample. This was followed up by 25.2% by experts (academics and others discussing topics like the effectiveness of sanctions) and then interest groups at 16.5%. Thus in our broad sample of testimony about sanctions dealing with foreign actors, the

79   We drew 25% random samples of all hearings on the deployments in Afghanistan, Bosnia, Haiti, Kosovo, Kuwait, Lebanon, and Somalia. In order to assign a similar weight to each deployment, we drew 15% random samples of all hearings related to Iraq and El Salvador, which had resulted in more hearings than other deployments. Within each deployment we see relatively similar distributions and so these percentages are not very consequential.

80   Our review of the events surrounding the chemical weapons attacks in Syria suggests a similar story, but there are no legislative votes on this so we did not use this event in chapter 4.

executive branch was, as expected, the most involved. Nevertheless, interest groups were active.

In the process of coding testimony and in our review of the literature on sanctions it became very clear that there are (roughly) two types of sanctions: those that involved a very direct foreign policy purpose (such as sanctions on Syria or Iran) and those that dealt more directly with economic issues (such as sanctions relating to fishing rights or intellectual property). The pattern of testimony is consistent with what our theory anticipates. Interest group testimony was decidedly more frequent for sanctions serving a more economic role (40% of all testimony versus 3% for foreign policy issues), whereas the executive branch was solicited more on issues relating to foreign policy objectives. As such, our analysis shows how sanctions fits in between our categories of military and economic engagement, and the testimony patterns reflect this.

Within this testimony we saw strong tensions between Congress and the president. At times Congress sought more control, and at other times there was a greater sense of the need to delegate control to the president. This can be clearly seen in recent discussions about Iranian sanctions. Nicholas Burns, who served in the Clinton and GW Bush administrations, said,

> Therefore, that sets up this important question of sanctions, which is at the heart of the bill that you have put forward, Senator, and that so many Senators have cosponsored. What type of sanctions and what type of flexibility should the president and the executive branch have? I would just say that you are right to consider sanctions of every kind, strong financial sanctions, economic sanctions, and energy sanctions, because those have not been tried in the past, the energy sanctions, and that is Iran's Achilles heel. I would just say two things. I think it is important that the president maintain his flexibility to conduct foreign policy because this is a shifting situation. It is a situation that is highly complex and I wouldn't favor any legislation, or I wouldn't suggest any legislation that would tie his hands, that would mandate deadlines for him. But if he is given sufficient waiver authority, then I think these types of sanctions are likely to have the greatest potential impact on the Iranian government and they may be the only thing that will convince Iran to think twice about going forward with a nuclear weapons project in the face of concerted international opposition.[81]

The point here being that were Congress to try and control the president on this issue, it would be worse for the United States and hence power should be held by the president. This discussion shows that the president retains substantial control over many types of sanctions, but sanctions arising out

81  Committee on Banking, 2009, pp. 13–14.

of economic disputes will see more economic interest group activity, as would be expected.

## DOMESTIC MILITARY SPENDING

In total the United States spent $689 billion on the military in 2010.[82] Of this amount, a large percentage goes into the US economy via paying for a broad variety of goods (weapons, material, etc.) and services. This spending is closely controlled by congresspersons, whose constituencies value the inflow of funds and provision of jobs in their communities.[83] And as one commentator put it, "it doesn't matter whether weapons are used (or usable), as long as they are bought."[84] Not surprisingly, a long literature from a variety of disciplines documents the important role played by economic interest groups in establishing the "military-industrial complex."[85] Hence this foreign policy instrument looks quite different from the other military-related instruments discussed in this section. And while we do not present testimony-based evidence of interest group involvement, our lobbying data below are extremely rich in this respect.

In this section we have sought to identify *who* are the interest groups active around each of our policy instruments. We provided evidence that interest group activity is extensive for policy instruments that have distributional consequences, but much less so for ones that have fewer distributional consequences and that necessarily have some degree of information asymmetry in favor of the president. In the next section we analyze lobbying behavior in order to understand if interest groups target specific political institutions.

# Who Gets Lobbied?

The previous section documented several empirical relationships crucial to the themes of this book. For both economic and military policy instruments we identified interest groups and spelled out their preferences. Different political actors can weigh in on how and when these instruments are used. Sometimes this happens in formal testimony, as shown previously. Other times it comes in lobbying that happens inside and outside the halls of Congress. In this section we look at lobbying in more detail. This allows us to look at interest group strategies and agendas in a much broader way

82  Pollin and Garrett-Peltier, 2011.
83  Bartels, 1991.
84  Fallows, 2002, p. 47.
85  Baack and Ray, 1985; Bernstein and Wilson, 2011.

compared to examining testimony data. In particular, we examine what they report they are lobbying about and what government agencies are lobbied.

Like others studying the American political system,[86] we think it is important to understand the "input" side to American foreign policy. We do so by looking at the revealed *strategies* of interest groups: what branches of the US government get lobbied and on what issues are particular branches/agencies most likely to get lobbied. In doing so we are one of the first studies in foreign policy to leverage the extremely large repository of lobbying report data.[87]

When groups choose to lobby agencies in the US federal government, they face constraints. It is expensive to employ a staff, research and write reports, contact representatives, and spend time advocating for policies. As such, they have to target their efforts on agencies that will help them best achieve their goals. How should they do this? Our theoretical model suggests an important pattern. If the issue is distributional, it is less likely to be on the agenda when lobbyists meet with the White House. Instead, the White House is much more likely to be targeted when the issue concerns overall policy directions. Once these policy choices have been made, which the president will be actively involved in, budgetary decisions that have distributional implications will arise.[88]

Before beginning our analysis, we briefly review our previous discussion about our lobbying data which runs from 2007 to spring 2014. First, each lobbying report can have multiple separate lobbying items. For each there is a label. Some of these labels encode what is in the content fairly clearly. For example, "BUD" stands for budgetary issues which are obviously distributional, and "FOR" stands for foreign affairs policy issues. An additional category of interest is what the federal government labels "DEF" for Defense. Before proceeding, it is useful to understand a bit more about what is captured in the "DEF" category. In reading through examples of this category, the vast majority of reports with a "DEF" coding were about domestic military spending; in particular; they deal with the annual defense appropriations bills passed by Congress each year and come from interest groups

---

86   Epstein and O'Halloran, 1995; Wright, 2002; Gawande, Krishna, and Robbins, 2006; Pevehouse and Vabulas, 2012.

87   Quite recently other scholars have made use of similar data, but not in the way we do with respect to lobbying targeting or our analysis of the textual descriptions in the data. See Kim, 2013; You, 2013; Kerr, Lincoln, and Mishra, 2014.

88   Our point is that such policy matters will have less direct distributional impacts. A similar prediction is consistent with our informational account of US foreign policy. Congress gets lobbied by economic interests on budget issues because Congress requires information that it knows it is responsible for using. This in our view is coupled with prior expectations that certain actors in the US federal government will have decision-making power on an instrument, for which the potential value of information transmission, and persuasive opportunities will be higher.

that benefit from this spending directly. A more systematic analysis of the open-ended descriptions suggests a similar conclusion. Below we present results from a Structural Topic Model to show how the vast majority of entries in this category are about distributional goods. And in chapter 4 we present roll call voting evidence on the distributional importance of this domestic spending on the military. Hence, for our purposes in the rest of the chapter, we label this category as "Military Spending" (*MilSpend*) but continue to interrogate this labeling decision.

For each topic, the report will list which agencies or institutions were contacted. Not surprisingly, nearly every lobbying report listed both the Senate and House, and 97% of lobbying reports listed either the Senate or House. However, there is substantial variation in whether other institutions and agencies of interest were lobbied. For example, only 4% of all lobbying reports listed the White House. Finally, the lobbying reports provide an open-ended topic field that describes the content of what was being lobbied on.

Before proceeding, we note that these categories do not as neatly map on to our core policy instruments. While trade ("TRD") and immigration ("IMM") have clear connections, there are not categorizations for things like "economic aid," "geopolitical aid," or "sanctions." Nevertheless, these data allow us to get at some general patterns, and in the next section we analyze the open-ended descriptions of the lobbying reports to enable greater connection with our policy instruments.

## Institutional Lobbying Focus

We now turn to a systematic investigation of who gets lobbied. Our argument is that the White House is less likely to deal with distributive issues, where Congress has the most control. However, the White House has a stronger hand in setting the direction of foreign policy and should be lobbied more often in this area. Our claim is that lobbying on items that are about spending is more likely to have a distributional aspect. To reiterate, in these data, Congress always gets lobbied, and we cannot tell how much lobbying happens between the branches, nor whether the content of the lobbying is the same. We can however examine differences across lobbying topics and whether the White House is also listed. We assume that lobbying done about budgetary concerns ("BUD") has at a minimum greater distributional impacts than does lobbying with a "FOR" issue coding. As discussed earlier, we expect that lobbying about trade will look similar to lobbying on other distributional issues, like appropriations. However, there may be a greater tendency to target the White House given its role in international trade negotiations. Nevertheless, we expect the size of this effect to be small.

We begin with some very basic summary statistics. The first is to investigate whether the White House is lobbied more frequently on matters of foreign relations (issue code "FOR") versus budgetary considerations (issue code "BUD"). In the data, 8.5% of lobbying reports that list a FOR topic code lobbied the White House. In contrast, only 2% of lobbying reports with a BUD code lobbied the White House, a difference that is highly significant.[89] Lobbying on distribution tends to bypass the White House compared to the policy issues in the FOR reports. Below we study these relationships more systematically, including understanding how targeting by lobby groups on trade policy happens.

We proceed in the following manner. First, we create a dependent variable for whether the White House is bypassed (1) or lobbied (0). It turns out that on almost every lobbying report the House and/or Senate is lobbied, and so the only other category of direct relevance is if the House and/or Senate is lobbied but the White House is not.[90] Next, we create indicator variables for several key issue labels: *Foreign* (issue code FOR), *MilSpend* (issue code DEF), *Trade* (issue code TRD), *Immigration* (issue code IMM), and *Budget* (issue code BUD).

Our prediction is that the coefficient on *Foreign* will be negative, indicating a higher probability of lobbyists not bypassing the White House compared to budgetary issues. When issues are primarily about budgets and allocating resources, this will imply there are more likely to be substantial distributional considerations at play. This will mean that the White House is less likely to be involved and that the issue is more likely to be salient to interest groups who will thus provide information (via lobbying) to Congress. Given the highly distributional nature of the *MilSpend* category, for which below we provide further evidence using a Structural Topic Model, we expect it to be no different from the Budget category. Finally, consider the *Trade* category. Trade clearly has a substantial distributional component. However, institutionally the president is the one that negotiates trade agreements. Hence the distributional aspect will make it look like domestic

89   An example of the former is "Prohibiting US sale and use of obsolete cluster munitions; reforming and expanding US international child survival programs strengthening US support for efforts to prevent child marriage in developing countries promoting US ratification of international treaties." An example of the latter is "Defense Appropriations Act– Title IV– In support of increased funding for Basic and Applied Research in all services in support of funding for Force Protection Applied Research in support of funding for Surface Ship Torpedo Defense in support of funding for Penn State Cancer Institute research initiative in support of Navy Undersea Warfare Applied Research funding in support of Navy Advanced Submarine System Development funding in support of Navy Industrial Preparedness funding in support of Navy Cooperative Engagement funding."

90   Alternatively, more complicated coding that distinguishes whether the Senate versus House was lobbied reveals the same patterns, in part because the correlations between the Senate and House being lobbied on the same item were nearly perfect.

politics, with the White House playing less of a role. But for lobbying activity on ongoing trade negotiations (which in this time period included the US-South Korea FTA, for example), we would expect the White House to be targeted. In sum, we expect that lobbying in the *Trade* category will bypass White House less than reports listing *MilSpend* or the baseline of domestic issues, but the White House will be more likely to be bypassed in these three categories compared to the *Foreign* category. Finally, theoretically we expect *Immigration* to be a topic that has less to do with the White House. We see it as largely distributional, and hence our ex ante prediction is that the White House will be bypassed. In sum, we expect the type of instrument to drive who is being lobbied.

We estimate a probit model given the binary dependent variable. Our interest is in contrasting the probability an interest group targets the White House across these three categories. We investigate several different ways of defining the overall sample (and hence the composition of the sample in the excluded category). Model L1 includes all lobbying reports. L2 only includes reports that are tagged with a Foreign, Military Spending, Trade, Immigration, or Budget code (and hence the omitted category is Budget). L3 further restricts model L2 to include only reports that listed at least one government *agency* that formally deals with foreign affairs (e.g., USAID or DoD). These different specifications guard against abnormalities introduced by including a broad array of issues in the baseline category. All models include year or quarter fixed effects (i.e., a separate intercept for Q1 2012, Q2 2012, etc.) and standard errors clustered by year. We report results in table 3.3 where we show marginal effects.

Across all models (L1–L3), we find support for some of our hypotheses. The coefficient on the *FOREIGN* variable is negative, statistically significant, and of substantively important magnitude. The executive branch is less likely to be bypassed by lobbyists when an issue concerns foreign affairs and hence has fewer distributional implications. This may also reflect some degree of information asymmetry though between the White House and Congress. Models L2 and L3, as discussed in the previous paragraph, restrict the sample to issues where we can be more confident they relate to one of our policy instruments. Our expectations are also held up for the *MilSpend* and *Trade* issue codes. For military spending lobbying, bypassing the White House is common: 1.3% of *MilSpend* issues targeted the White House. As a result, in our statistical model we see that this category is even more likely than the omitted *Budget* category to bypass the White House. For *Trade*, the estimated effect is half the magnitude of the *Foreign* variable but still different from the baseline. Substantive (rather than marginal) effect calculations tell the same story.[91]

---

91   Excluding a single quarter-year or year does not substantively change our results.

**Table 3.3.** When Do Interest Groups Bypass the White House?

|  | L1 | L2 | L3 |
|---|---|---|---|
| Foreign | −0.045** | −0.069** | −0.11** |
|  | [0.0036] | [0.0042] | [0.015] |
| MilSpend | 0.026** | 0.0086** | 0.015** |
|  | [0.0010] | [0.0016] | [0.0039] |
| Trade | −0.016** | −0.037** | −0.062** |
|  | [0.0029] | [0.0055] | [0.0038] |
| Immigration | −0.051** | −0.075** | −0.19** |
|  | [0.011] | [0.012] | [0.028] |
| Observations | 872376 | 203061 | 53171 |

Standard errors in brackets, +$p < 0.10$, *$p < 0.05$, **$p < 0.01$.

Foreign equal to 1 if report tagged with code FOR, MilSpend equal to 1 if tagged with code DEF, Immigration equal to 1 if report tagged with code IMM, and Trade equal to 1 if tagged with TRD. Model L1 includes all lobbying reports. L2 only includes reports that are tagged with a Foreign, Defense, Trade, Immigration, or Budget code (and hence the omitted category is Budget). L3 further restricts model L2 to only include reports that listed at least one government *agency* that formally deals with foreign affairs (e.g., USAID or the Department of Defense). Probit model with year and quarter fixed effects (omitted) with standard errors clustered by year. Coefficients are marginal effects.

One potentially anomalous result is that *Immigration* issues have the largest effect in our regression. Our theory argues that these issues should be more like domestic ones, rather than having a higher probability of going to the White House. We find in table 3.3 that the *Immigration* variable has an effect that is slightly greater in magnitude than the *Foreign* variable. However, as we show below this result can be explained by the fact that during our time period the Obama administration became heavily involved in the "Uniting American Families Act" and related pieces of legislation that do not have the same type of distributional consequences compared to other immigration issues that related to immigrant workers and visas.[92] We provide direct evidence in the next section that not bypassing the White House on immigration was due to these less distributional issues. Were we to have

92 For example, the "Uniting American Families Act" legislation was primarily a mechanism for helping same-sex couples; see Human Rights Campaign, 2013.

the same rich lobbying data for other eras in time, we might not expect to find the same relationship and instead would find more White House bypassing overall.

## Textual Data: Open-Ended Descriptions of Lobbying Content

The final piece of data in our new lobbying dataset is the textual descriptions about what is being lobbied. We turn to these data for several reasons. The first relates to a construct validity consideration. We want to establish that, in fact, when an item is tagged officially with DEF, which we relabeled as *MilSpend*, it is predominantly the case that this reflects military spending which we see as highly distributional. Second, and relatedly, the tags used by the US government all mask substantial additional variation within each classification. For example, we have argued, and will show, that the *MilSpend* tags are highly predictive of military spending topics, rather than military policy issues. But not completely so, and this more nuanced unpacking of the data via open-ended descriptions shows this variation. The highly aggregated official labels used by the US government in the previous regression analyses mask some variation that is interesting for us. The Structural Topic Model can help us then estimate if the White House is not targeted for these distributional issues, but is targeted for policy-driven considerations.[93]

Put differently, for each of the categories in our previous regression we want to explore the topics present in the text, and then see which of these topics are associated with targeting the White House in ways that we would expect. For example, if specific lobbying reports in our *MilSpend* category that are highly associated with distributional issues are *also* ones that target the White House, and other policy issues do not target the White House, then our theoretical expectations would not find support. Of course, the *MilSpend* (i.e., DEF) tag is one example, and we conduct our analysis for each of our category tags (*MilSpend, Trade, Immigration, and Foreign*).[94] This gives us additional evidence for our interpretation of these regression results. Within each we investigate topics that are related to the White House being targeted, or not, to see if our arguments about distributional issues holds up.

93  Importantly, and as we will see shortly, the types of policies where the White House gets lobbied will not necessarily map on to direct decisions about military deployments and other military-related power projections. In part this is, as we have argued, because there is a smaller demand side for these activities so we simply see less lobbying overall. We recognize though that the relatively (compared to other analyses in our book) short time-span of these data prevents a more systematic analysis. We note, though, that lobbying reports that listed Libya or Syria were extremely rare, which we see as consistent with our theory.

94  Which, again, correspond to the official tags of DEF, TRD, IMM, and FOR.

## TEXT ANALYSIS METHOD: THE STRUCTURAL TOPIC MODEL

Depending on the analysis below, there are tens of thousands of lobbying activity descriptions, making it difficult to read through and systematize. There are a variety of approaches that can be used when analyzing textual data, computer assisted or entirely human judgment driven, and they all have their pros and cons.[95] We adopt a new "unsupervised learning" approach known as the "structural" "topic model" (STM).[96] In the previous sentence we have put into quotations several terms that may be unfamiliar to many readers. "Topic models" are a broad class of statistical procedures that seek to establish sets of words that commonly appear together within a document (here, a lobbying report). "Unsupervised learning" refers to the fact that the STM, and other topic models, are best distinguished from "supervised learning" techniques where humans first categorize texts and then statistical techniques learn from these classifications. Finally, "structural," within the context of "structural topic model," refers to the fact that unlike other topic modeling techniques largely derived in the computer science literature, the STM incorporates "structural" information about the text. This means, for example, the date on which it was written or, as developed below, whether or not the White House is lobbied, can be related to the topics in the text.

Another important distinction that we draw on below is that the structural topic model (STM) is a mixed membership model, which means that any given document can have multiple topics that it draws on. This is typical of topic modeling techniques, but less typical of supervised learning techniques. In our case this is important especially in our analysis of lobbying reports that list specific agencies like USAID, but which could also list multiple other agencies and draw on a broad range of topics within the same lobbying report.

To tie this discussion together, consider briefly the case of Trade lobbying reports. We know that some include targeting the White House, and we want to know if those lobbying reports are about different topics compared to those that do not target the White House. Above, we suggested an expectation: given our substantive knowledge, trade should be largely distributional (and hence less likely to target the White House), but that instances such as dealing with ongoing international negotiations would target the White House. The STM lets us investigate whether or not such differences exist. Technically speaking, this is done by allowing the prevalence of a topic (what percentage of the document was about a particular topic) to be a

---

95  Grimmer and Stewart, 2013.
96  Roberts, Stewart, Tingley, et al., 2014.

function of a covariate that we know about the document itself. In our case, this covariate is simply whether or not the White House was lobbied.[97]

In practice the model will estimate topics that either (1) may be semantically distinct but theoretically similar (for example, in the cases that follow there might be several topics that relate to distributional issues, but with associated words that are nonetheless quite distinct), or (2) that may not be of substantive interest. As with any topic model, it is crucial for the analyst to carefully inspect each topic to understand its semantic meaning. This is done by looking at the words most related to the topic and other diagnostic procedures such as reading texts that are highly related to a particular topic. We did this for all our analyses. Readers wishing an introduction to the STM, including various simulation tests that show the method does not induce false positive relationships, as well as additional, more technical discussions, can consult our other work on the method.[98]

We begin with an analysis of lobbying reports that can be broken out by one of the codes used in our previous regression analyses: trade (*TRD*), immigration (*IMM*), military spending (*MilSpend*), and foreign affairs (*FOR*) (which for example we suspect will contain discussion of both sanctions and aid). For each we report two separate plots. First, in the top we provide a list of words most highly associated with each topic. This facilitates our semantic interpretation because we can contrast sets of words that differentiate the topics. In the bottom we calculate for our topics of interest the average change in the proportion of a document that is composed of a particular topic as a result of moving from the White House not being bypassed to the White House being bypassed. Positive values indicate topics where the White House is more likely to be bypassed and negative values indicate topics where the White House is less likely to be bypassed.[99]

97  One might adopt a different strategy, which is to just focus on lobbying reports that targeted the White House and unpack which topics were present in those. However, we emphasize that our STM model encompasses this approach. Lobbying reports that are tagged as targeting the White House are allowed to have different topic proportions compared to those that do not. The advantage of pooling is that we can make statistical comparisons between reports that target the White House and those that do not, something that would be unavailable if only selecting on White House targeted reports.

98  Roberts, Stewart, Tingley, et al., 2014. Preparation of the text and analysis was done using the stm package in R. Roberts, Stewart, and Tingley, 2014. We followed standard text preparation procedures by removing stop words and stemming. When using the STM, or any other standard topic model, the analyst must specify ex ante the number of topics to be estimated. The results we report below were similar when we allowed for different numbers of topics.

99  This is akin to standard "first-difference" methods and uncertainty is calculated using full global uncertainty so as to populate the estimates with both sampling uncertainty and uncertainty about the latent estimated variables. Roberts, Stewart, and Tingley, 2014.

## DOMESTIC MILITARY SPENDING (OFFICIAL CODE "DEF")

When the federal government labeled a category as "DEF" for defense, we argued earlier that this includes almost entirely domestic military spending and so we labeled this in our regressions in table 3.3 *MilSpend*. To interrogate this claim we estimated a range of STM models using varying numbers of topics using the 44,957 reports that had the official DEF code. They always showed a high number of topics that were distributional in nature. Topics where the White House was more likely to be lobbied dealt with less district-level distributional consequences, like veterans' affairs policies (rather than decisions about funding particular veteran facilities across congressional districts).

This can be seen in figure 3.1, which plots information about several key topics from an STM that used seven topics. The majority of textual content for *MilSpend* reports comes from topics about defense "appropriations" or "authorization." While the topic model separates these two different topics given the differences in language used, both clearly have substantial distributional consequences. A "Research" topic focused on funding for research and technology development. To the extent that any policy aspects of the US military were lobbied on, the "Veterans' health benefits" topic was a standout. On first pass, this might seem highly distributional. However, inspection of lobbying reports related to this topic showed that this was not about funding for specific veterans' hospitals, or other things that could have more localized distributional consequences, but instead about broader issues in veterans' affairs such as veterans' qualifications and benefit standards.[100,101]

---

100   To see how this topic doesn't deal with highly localized distributional consequences, an example lobbying report highly related to this topic was, "Lobbying in opposition to including any of the TRICARE plans in the proposed health care reform bills (including HR3590 HR3962) lobbying against any proposed increases in TRICARE co-pays deductibles or enrollment fees HR816; lobbying to end the ban of concurrent receipt of military retired pay and VA disability pay (including HR333 HR303 S546 HR811) lobbying in favor of improvements in National Guard and Reserve benefits including proper implementation of HR270 available TRICARE for Grey Area retirees; and in favor of quick implementation; HR 270; S1106; lobbying in favor of increasing pay under the National Guard and Reserve Pay Equity Act of 2009 S644; lobbying in support of reducing the minimum age for receipt of military retired pay for non-regular service HR1695 S1390; lobbying in favor of allowing the survivors of a military retiree to retain the full last month of his or her retired pay "provide for forgiveness of certain overpayments of retired pay paid to deceased retired members of the Armed Forces following death" HR613; lobbying in support of the ending of the SBP/DIC Offset (HR775 S535 HR2243); lobbying to improve military health care for veterans and retirees who live in rural areas S658; lobbying in favor of changes and improvements in the Uniform services Former Spouse Protection Act (USFSPA); lobbying in support of increased benefits for caretakers of our wounded warriors; lobbying in favor of permitting a "Special Needs Trust" for appropriate disabled SBP beneficiaries."

101   Indeed, and after we had done these analyses, a related "media event" hit the White House, dealing with VA hospitals having de facto policies that fabricated wait times (05/20/14).

## DEF tagged lobbying reports

### Topics and High Probability Words

**Research:**
fund, research, develop, dod, technolog, amp, advanc, budget, project, medic, energi, program, materi, product, appropri, initi, defens, support, center, manufactur

- - - - - - - - - - - - - - - - - - - - - - - - - - - - - - - - - - - - - - - - - - - - - - - - -

**Appropriations:**
defens, appropri, bill, author, hous, senat, report, request, fund, depart, rdtamp, armor, scienc, materi, detect, amp, matter, technolog, fuel, offic

- - - - - - - - - - - - - - - - - - - - - - - - - - - - - - - - - - - - - - - - - - - - - - - - -

**Authorization:**
defens, act, nation, author, appropri, depart, procur, issu, rampd, continu, rdtamp, secur, consolid, assist, hrs, disast, supplement, law, compani, general

- - - - - - - - - - - - - - - - - - - - - - - - - - - - - - - - - - - - - - - - - - - - - - - - -

**Veterans Health Benefits**
militari, secur, legisl, support, health, regard, servic, contract, feder, state, member, monitor, construct, amend, arm, veteran, govern, lobbi, educ, base

### White House Bypass

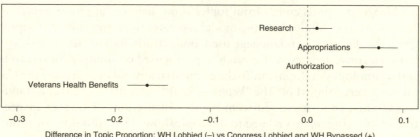

Difference in Topic Proportion: WH Lobbied (−) vs Congress Lobbied and WH Bypassed (+)

**Figure 3.1.** Structural Topic Model results from analyzing lobbying reports that list "DEF" as the substantive category (labeled "Military Spending"). 7-topic model. Top plot gives words highly associated with each topic and bottom plot gives the difference in topic prevalence for documents by whether or not the White House was lobbied. Items to the left indicate topics more likely to have lobbied the White House, and topics to the right are associated with lobbying reports that bypassed the White House.

Nevertheless, this topic was estimated as a very small proportion of the overall corpus (<10%). No topics dealt with active military campaigns.

Finally, we can estimate how the prevalence of these topics differs by whether or not the White House was lobbied. As shown in the bottom right of figure 3.1, the White House was modestly more likely to be lobbied on the Veterans topic, but dramatically less likely to be lobbied on distributional issues. We see this as further evidence of the importance of Congress in controlling military spending, which has substantial distributional consequences.

### FOREIGN RELATIONS (OFFICIAL CODE "FOR")

As we saw in the previous regressions, the White House was less likely to be bypassed when a lobbying report is tagged with the foreign relations code. What do these lobbying reports tend to be about, and what issues are associated with the White House being targeted or not? We estimated a ten-topic STM using the 8,959 "FOR" lobbying reports and report the results in figure 3.2. We focus on four topics which are illustrative. They also help focus our attention given that for each of our analyses below we will have multiple topics to potentially report on and inspect.[102] Two topics deal most directly with distributive issues. The "Foreign Operations Appropriations" topic deals primarily with lobbying on the annual appropriations bill that addresses US foreign aid, and the "Bilateral Trade Issues" topic deals primarily with various bilateral trade issues that are not connected to ongoing trade negotiations or trade-related international institutions (we will show instances of lobbying on these topics in the next section on lobbying reports tagged as "trade"). Two other topics deal less with distributive issues.

The first is a topic about "Iranian Sanctions." This gives us our first connection with this policy instrument in this chapter. While we recognize that sanctions can have distributional consequences, and in many cases Congress can hijack a sanction once initiated,[103] in this instance this is unlikely because these were efforts to impose additional sanctions related to Iran's nuclear program, to penalize foreign firms for doing business with Iran, and to bring about increased cooperation with Israel to prevent Iran from developing a nuclear weapon. We see, though, that in this case the White House is less likely to be bypassed when it comes to sanctions, pointing to the important role played by the president on this issue. Given the time period we examine, we do not get to observe behavior for earlier sanctions events.[104]

Another less distributional topic was one on "International Law" which deals with issues such as the UN's Convention on the Law of the Sea Treaty and the UN Convention on Rights of Persons with Disabilities Act. The bottom right of figure 3.2 shows how the highly distributional topics bypass the White House, whereas the sanctions and international law topics include lobbying the White House.

## TRADE (OFFICIAL CODE "TRD")

In the comparative and international political economy literature, the role of interest groups is most developed for the case of trade. Next we look at the 23,583 lobbying reports that were tagged with a trade (TRD) designation and report the results in figure 3.3. We estimated a ten-topic STM

---

102  The other six topics we do not report on largely conform to our expectations.

103  Hiscox, forthcoming.

104  We also do not examine whether increasing congressional assertiveness on the Iranian nuclear negotiations and sanctions in the early part of 2015 were precipitated by greater pressure on Congress by interest groups.

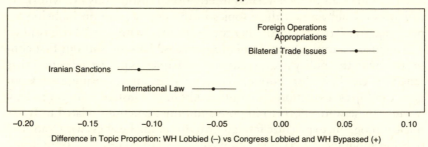

**Figure 3.2.** Structural Topic Model results from analyzing lobbying reports that list "FOR" (Foreign) as the substantive category. 10-topic model. Top plot gives words highly associated with each topic and bottom plot gives the difference in topic prevalence for documents by whether or not the White House was lobbied. Items to the left indicate topics more likely to have lobbied the White House, and topics to the right are associated with lobbying reports that bypassed the White House.

model and analyze four of those topics. The "market access and intellectual property" topic and "Tariffs/Duties" topic are both highly distributional. Both may benefit specific firms and hence excludable benefits and have a substantial distributional effect. Two other topics dealt with broader, international-level engagement through specific free trade agreements being negotiated and the World Trade Organization (WTO). Decisions about trade agreements and cases in the WTO both connect with distributional issues, but are part of a set of policy levers that the president has on trade. The president is a player in trade, as we have discussed, insofar as he can negotiate these international agreements. We indeed find this relationship in lobbying which targets the White House. Topics that deal with PTAs and the WTO are significantly more likely to be part of lobbying reports where the White House gets lobbied. In contrast, the more day-to-day distributional issues related to tariffs, duties, market access are less likely to target the White House. Instead, lobbyists bypass the White House and focus their energies

### TRD tagged lobbying reports

#### Topics and High Probability Words

**WTO**
trade, polici, wto, china, negoti, world, organ, agreement, bilater, develop, econom, govern, barrier, invest, doha

**Tariffs/Duties**
duti, bill, tariff, import, provis, product, suspens, relat, reduct, certain, miscellan, footwear, extend, propos, rule

**Market Access/Intellectual Property**
issu, relat, trade, market, access, intern, properti, general, intellectu, protect, foreign, includ, matter, pertain, regulatori

**FTAs**
trade, agreement, free, korea, fta, panama, colombia, columbia, support, sout, mexico, truck, uskoria, peru, mexican

#### White House Bypass

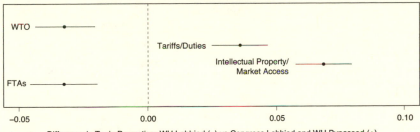

Difference in Topic Proportion: WH Lobbied (−) vs Congress Lobbied and WH Bypassed (+)

**Figure 3.3.** Structural Topic Model results from analyzing lobbying reports that list "TRD" (Trade) as the substantive category. 10-topic model. Top plot gives words highly associated with each topic and bottom plot gives the difference in topic prevalence for documents by whether or not the White House was lobbied. Items to the left indicate topics more likely to have lobbied the White House, and topics to the right are associated with lobbying reports that bypassed the White House.

on Congress. Consistent with our theoretical expectations, the most directly distributional topics are those that target Congress.

## IMMIGRATION (OFFICIAL CODE "IMM")

What topics are prevalent when a lobbying report is tagged with the immigration code? Immigration is an extremely complicated policy instrument. As discussed in this chapter, there are several different distributional issues associated with immigration. Perhaps the most salient distributional issue deals with worker access programs, such as visas and guest worker programs. These decisions are driven by Congress, rather than the White House, and so we expect that the lobbying reports that do list the White House as a target will not be about this topic. Conversely, as discussed earlier, there are several issues related to immigration that have less of a material distributional quality to them, such as those related to family unification. We

**IMM tagged lobbying reports**

**Topics and High Probability Words**

| **Visas/Jobs** |
| visa, relat, provis, issu, bill, card, stem, green, immigr, employmentbas, student, entir, foreign, employ, nation |
| **Overall Reform** |
| immigr, reform, comprehens, issu, legisl, regard, support, bill, refuge, general, detent, polici, hous, lobbi, senat |
| **Guest Workers** |
| worker, program, agricultur, support, propos, busi, everifi, regul, guest, season, labor, temporari, rule, small, legisl |
| **Family/Refugees** |
| act, state, unit, alien, immigr, provis, amend, famili, educ, nation, law, purpos, develop, relief, secur |

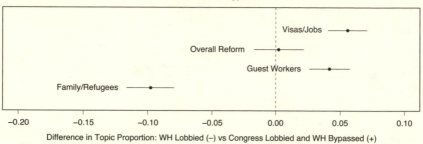

**White House Bypass**

Difference in Topic Proportion: WH Lobbied (−) vs Congress Lobbied and WH Bypassed (+)

**Figure 3.4.** Structural Topic Model results from analyzing lobbying reports that list "IMM" (Immigration) as the substantive category. 7-topic model. Top plot gives words highly associated with each topic and bottom plot gives the difference in topic prevalence for documents by whether or not the White House was lobbied. Items to the left indicate topics more likely to have lobbied the White House, and topics to the right are associated with lobbying reports that bypassed the White House.

expect, both theoretically and based on media reporting on immigration during this time period, that the White House will be targeted in these instances, which may account for the somewhat anomalous results in the regression analyses presented earlier in the chapter. We estimated an STM where the prevalence of topics is related to whether the White House gets lobbied or not for the 10,238 reports with an IMM code. This lets us see if there are some topics that get lobbied on which were directed toward the White House. It also lets us understand the distribution of topics prevalent in this sub-corpus. In figure 3.4 we present results from a seven-topic STM where we focus on several topics of interest.

We analyzed four topics. One expansive topic dealt with "comprehensive immigration reform," which constituted nearly 30% of the entire corpus. This dealt with a variety of issues, some distributional and some more policy relevant. Two other topics were more directly distributional, dealing with visas/jobs and guest worker programs. The fourth topic dealt with issues related to families and refugees.

The bottom pane of figure 3.4 lets us see which of these topics was more likely to be associated with bypassing the White House or including them in the lobbying strategy. While in our regression analysis in table 3.3 we saw that the White House was somewhat less likely to be targeted compared to the other policy codes, this may be because of the content of lobbying activity. Indeed, we see that the topic likely driving that result is not distributional in nature: the White House was substantially more likely to be lobbied when the topic was about families and refugees. In contrast, the White House was significantly more likely to be bypassed when it comes to visas, jobs, and guest worker programs. Finally, there was no significant difference for the "comprehensive reform" topic. Given its comprehensive nature, lobbyists listing this were equally likely to target the White House as not. In summary, we saw greater White House bypass on direct distributional issues. Nevertheless, some aspects of *contemporary* immigration policy have generated some focus on the presidency. This is consistent with the fact that President Obama began contemplating the use of executive action on the issue in order to sidestep a Congress gridlocked on the issue.[105]

## Conclusion

Interest groups have always been active in US domestic and foreign policy. We bring them into our theory in focusing on one key characteristic of a policy instrument: the extent of its distributive politics. Where distributive politics is very significant, economic interest groups should play a large and active role. They should also affect the degree of informational asymmetries between presidents and Congress on policy issues. Our theory makes predictions about the role of these groups, and here we present evidence about these hypotheses.

While there has been much empirical investigation of these groups in domestic policy, this has been rarer when it comes to interest groups surrounding US foreign policy. Furthermore, it is rare to integrate and analyze the role of interest groups across multiple different policy instruments related to foreign policy. This chapter introduced new data about congressional testimony to see what actors are active across our policy instruments when it comes to formal, public displays of preferences and conveyance of information. We also draw on a new dataset of the *universe* of lobbying reports to identify which issues are getting lobbied on and, most important, when the White House is the target of these lobbying efforts.

We expected and found substantial differences across our policy instruments. We found an active role of economic interest groups in areas where

---

105 We also conducted additional analyses of reports that listed either USAID or the DoD. We found similar results as those reported on for the DEF and FOR tagged reports.

there are powerful distributional consequences and low information asymmetries, whereas they played a much smaller role for areas not characterized by these variables: i.e., military deployments, sanctions, and geopolitical aid. Furthermore, to the extent that we observe economic interest group activity related to the US military, it relates to domestic military spending which is highly distributional and largely bypasses the White House. Instead, the White House gets targeted when it comes to policy issues.

There are, of course, limitations to the analyses. For example, we do not control the data-generating process behind who testifies before Congress. Strategic interaction among the various groups and political actors involved may affect who testifies and lobbies about what and when. We only observe and analyze what occurs. It might be, for example, that Congress does not want to call on groups such as arms manufacturers to testify about geopolitical aid. Similarly, we have made inferences about what motivates interest groups to bypass the White House or not. We have argued that these "revealed" preferences reflect an understanding of interest groups about what actors control either budgets or policies. As discussed at length above, while policy issues can have distributional consequences, they are less direct and immediate compared to the explicitly distributional issues like military contracts or setting tariffs on particular products. In the next chapter we continue to examine these issues, including the analysis of annual spending bills for the US military. Finally, this chapter does not engage with how ideological influences animate interest groups. It is possible, for example, that ideological scaling techniques developed for interest groups could be deployed.[106] This would enable us to match specific political organizations and companies onto a liberal-conservative scale. We could then see if ideological divisions matter; that is, we could see if ideological groups lobby against each other more on specific types of policy instruments and hence examine how prevalent counteractive lobbying is across the different policy instruments.[107] This is certainly a task for future research.

106    Bonica, 2014.
107    Austen-Smith and Wright, 1992; Austen-Smith and Wright, 1996.

# 4

# FROM THE FLOOR TO THE SHORE

## Budget Politics and Roll Call Voting on US Foreign Policy

To further examine our arguments about domestic politics and US foreign policy, we turn to interactions between Congress and the president. Our analysis in this chapter focuses on observed behavior by elected officials in a highly institutionalized setting. An advantage of this elite-level data is that they are more proximate to the actual policy outputs and politics that we analyze.

This chapter examines three sets of hypotheses developed in the book. They concern presidential influence, economic interests, and ideological factors in foreign policy. First, we examine hypotheses about presidential influence in Congress. We expect that presidents will have more influence over a foreign policy instrument when it has fewer concentrated domestic distributional consequences—and thus also features information asymmetries favoring the president—and fewer ideological divisions.

We test this first by examining the influence of the president in setting budgets. The president first proposes a budget for different foreign policy agencies, which control different policy instruments. Congress then accepts, modifies, or rejects these requests. This inquiry follows previous work that examines presidential influence in the "two presidencies" tradition.[1] Their main contrast is between all foreign policy and all domestic policy agencies. Our focus is on disaggregating foreign policy instruments. Hence we break apart the foreign policy agencies into ones that somewhat better match our policy instruments and ask whether presidential influence varies across them.

We next test this hypothesis using roll call voting in Congress, which enables a much more granular focus on our policy instruments than the budgetary data. Our theory implies that the president should be better able to compel legislators in his party to vote his preferred way when the vote deals with issues that have weaker domestic distributional concerns and fewer ideological divisions. Presidential influence over US foreign policy instruments thus should be greatest in congressional voting on military deployments, sanctions, and geopolitical aid. It should be least for votes on economic aid, international trade, immigration, and domestic military spending. Domestic military spending will also see less presidential influence vis-à-vis

---

1   Canes-Wrone, Howell, and Lewis, 2008; Howell, Jackman, and Rogowski, 2013.

Congress. The president should have more influence over his own party members in Congress since they are most likely to listen to his endorsement. The patterns of presidential influence in roll call votes are similar to what we see in budget negotiations over different government agencies. The greater the distributional consequences, and/or ideological divisions, the less influence the president has.

We also examine two other hypotheses about legislator preferences regarding foreign policy and international engagement. Our second hypothesis concerns economic interests and distributive politics across the different instruments. Legislative voting on some types of foreign policy should be strongly correlated with constituency interests. Constituent economic interests should matter; that is, legislators should vote for foreign policy instruments in part with regard to their constituents' material interests. Consistent with economic models showing the distributive consequences of policies, legislative support in the House for foreign economic aid, immigration, and trade liberalization should be higher when a legislator comes from a district that is well endowed with a relatively high-skilled constituency. Evidence of this would be consistent with the Stolper-Samuelson theorem's predictions about the economic implications of these types of policies; more high-skilled individuals should gain more from these types of policies of international economic engagement.[2] In a similar vein, we also examine how voting on domestic military spending correlates with the value of defense contracts obtained by companies in a district. We expect distributional considerations to be more muted for sanctions, geopolitical aid, and especially troop deployments.

Our third hypothesis is about the extent of ideological divisions across policy instruments. Unlike in the previous chapter, here we are able to examine the influence of political ideology more directly. Constituents' and the legislators' own ideology should affect their choices about foreign policy instruments. The more conservative the constituents of a district are (or the legislator himself), the greater the probability that their legislator votes in favor of trade liberalization, geopolitical aid, and military deployment, but the less likely the legislator votes in favor of general economic aid and perhaps immigration. In contrast, more liberal legislators should be more likely to support economic aid, and their support should wane as this aid becomes increasingly military-oriented. Liberals should also remain more opposed to trade liberalization and military deployment, but should perhaps be more supportive of immigration liberalization compared to conservatives.

The extent of these ideological divisions matters most for us. The bigger the influence of ideology, the larger the ideological divisions we find. We

2   Scheve and Slaughter, 2001b; Ladewig, 2006; Milner and Tingley, 2010; Milner and Tingley, 2011.

**Table 4.1.** Research Questions and Data Sources for Chapter 4

| QUESTIONS | DATASETS |
| --- | --- |
| When does the president get his budget targets? | Canes-Wrone et al. 2008 |
| Does presidential influence on roll call voting vary across policy instruments? | Universe of House foreign policy votes 1953–2008 and hand-selected House votes 1979–2008 |
| Does the effect of material and ideological variables vary across policy instruments? | Hand-selected House votes 1979–2008 and district level data |

expect these ideological divisions to be greater for trade, economic aid, and domestic military spending, and weaker for geopolitical aid, sanctions, immigration, and military deployment. Presidents wishing to use these instruments of statecraft will face different patterns of support and opposition domestically for these foreign policy instruments, and when the divisions between these groups are large, he will have the least influence.

The structure of the chapter is as follows. First we examine presidential influence via an analysis of the budgetary proposal and appropriation process. The next section lays out our datasets on roll call voting and tests our argument using roll call voting data from the US House and Senate on a large set of foreign policy votes. We conduct two sets of analyses. First, we examine the universe of House votes on foreign affairs from 1953 to 2008, classifying foreign affairs votes into whether they dealt with the military or not. Second, we examine a subset of these votes which sources suggested were salient and consequential. We break these votes apart by their characteristics and classify them into more substantive categories that match the policy instruments we study (i.e., trade, immigration, military deployment, economic aid, geopolitical aid, defense spending, and sanctions).

We address several core questions in this chapter and draw on a broad range of data which is summarized in table 4.1. Evidence presented in this chapter highlights how the "two presidencies" literature is misconstrued. Instead, the president's influence is moderated by the extent to which a policy instrument has large distributional consequences and ideological divisions. We provide a rich political economy account of legislative voting in American foreign policy.

## When Do Presidents Get the Budgets They Request?

We focus on congressional decision making in the shadow of the president by looking at politics of budget requests and allocations. We expect that the president will have more influence over policy instruments that have fewer distributional politics and ideological divisions. Hence we expect them to receive budget allocations from Congress closer to what they desire on these types of issues. Each year since the 1921 Budget and Accounting Act the president submits a budget proposal to Congress around February or March for all executive agencies for the next fiscal year. Congress then deliberates and appropriates funds given its constitutional role for a whole range of agencies and categories. Some of the money that is appropriated is mandatory, given previous legislative enactments. Other funding is discretionary, which means Congress has the ability to change funding amounts. We and others see this process as a form of bargaining between the president and Congress.

Does Congress fulfill the president's requests? Or does Congress appropriate amounts that are different from what the president says he wants? Here we examine how successful presidents are at getting budgets for agencies that control aid programs and international diplomatic efforts, and contrast them with presidential success over agencies that control military budgets. In all of our tests Congress is more deferential to presidential requests for agencies overseeing military efforts relative to those controlling non-military instruments. Presidential influence over budgets for the DoD is significantly more than for the State Department and other domestic agencies. Like others, we are aware of various inferential challenges arising due to strategic interaction between the president and Congress.[3] Data presented in this section are largely consistent with the claims we advance in this book, but as with much observational data of this type we recognize there are limitations in relying on solely these results for our broader claims.

## DESCRIPTION OF AGENCY BUDGETARY DATA AND FOREIGN POLICY INSTRUMENTS

The US appropriations process is complicated, and the historical record of the appropriations process is even more complicated. There are different types of appropriations and different ways they are reported.[4] Canes-Wrone, Howell, and Lewis take on the general question of the "two presidencies" by

---

3 Strategic interaction between the president and Congress can compromise the inferences we can make from analysis of budgetary data. One advantage of the appropriations data is that it is more immune to strategic maneuvering within the institutions that govern Congress. But unfortunately our data do not tell us how much the president really wants for a particular agency, or whether he intentionally asks for more or less, knowing that Congress is likely to adjust the budget. Whether this request process is strategic, or if the presence of strategic interaction biases our empirical results, depends on a variety of assumptions. Our observational data cannot address these concerns.

4 A key distinction in earlier work is between discretionary and mandatory appropriations for government programs and executive agencies. We follow this approach; hence the politics of mandatory appropriations schemes are beyond the scope of the book.

analyzing appropriations data from 1969 to 2000.[5] They find that presidents are more likely to get what they want for foreign policy agencies than for domestic policy agencies.[6] We use their data to test some of our hypotheses.

Our hypotheses suggest that the president will not be equally influential across all types of foreign policy instruments. Different foreign policy instruments will have different domestic politics associated with them. Since different agencies control different instruments, presidential budget requests for these agencies should be treated differently by Congress. Our departure from previous research is to disaggregate foreign policy agencies: foreign policy funding decisions should not all be treated the same. For example, Canes-Wrone et al. construct foreign policy agencies from the Current Action tables by grouping together the Defense Department, the Atomic Energy Commission, and the State Department into one dummy variable for these agencies in order to compare them to domestic policy agencies.[7] We instead group together the Defense Department and the Atomic Energy Commission, but have a separate variable for the State Department's funding, which is more connected to economic foreign aid and trade.[8] Our hypothesis is that the president's success will be greater in agencies that control funds for military-related instruments like the Defense Department than in domestic agencies. In contrast, for agencies like the State Department which control economic and diplomatic types of instruments, the president will be less influential and will face political constraints more like he does with the domestic agencies.[9]

---

5   Canes-Wrone, Howell, and Lewis, 2008.

6   They use a reporting document known as the Current Action (CA) table in the official budget report of the US president. The CA table listed budget requests and actual appropriations for a set of executive agencies. In 1990, the Current Action table ceased to be published, and instead a similar table dealing with discretionary budget authority by agency was published in the official presidential budget. Canes-Wrone et al. extended the Current Action table during this period. We attempted to update their data from 2000 and up, but were unable to exactly replicate their methodology. Our results, however, do not change if we simply use the published "Discretionary Budget Authority by Agency" tables (e.g., table S-13 in 1996) from 1996 and up.

7   These domestic agencies include: Agriculture, Defense (civil), Commerce, Education, Energy, Environmental Protection Agency, Executive Office of the President, General Services Administration, Health and Human Services, Housing and Urban Development, Interior, Judiciary, Justice, Labor, Legislative Branch, NASA, Office of Personnel Management, Postal Service, Small Business Administration, Transportation, Treasury, and Veterans Administration.

8   Our assumption is that the State Department account picks up more economic and diplomatic items than does the Defense Department. To the extent that we find differences between the organizations, this measurement error likely means we underestimate any differences.

9   Ideally our data would use categories that directly match our core policy instruments. Unfortunately, the available data do not allow us to disaggregate this way. For example, we are aware of no long-term historical time-series data that would allow us to measure presidential requests across agencies like the IDA, USAID, ESF, or the International Trade Commission.

The Defense Department and the nuclear weapons part of the Energy Department, which we group together in the budget data, involve funding for military policy instruments, such as military aid and deployments. The State Department and related agencies are more tied to economic and diplomatic instruments, given their focus on economic aid, sanctions, trade, and diplomacy. Presidential influence over Congress should be greater in foreign policy domains with fewer distributional politics and fewer ideological divisions. That is, the president should do better with budget requests for the Defense Department than with the State Department.[10]

While our roll call vote analyses below disaggregate policy instruments more finely, these budgetary data are helpful since they look at another aspect of presidential bargaining with Congress. Our coding scheme for the budgetary data is close to some of that which we use in the roll call data, given the available categorizations. The association between executive agencies and policy instruments allows us to draw parallels across the book's empirical sections as best we can.

## EMPIRICAL MODELS OF BUDGETARY SUCCESS

Our dependent variable is a measure of presidential success in budgeting. We adopt the operationalization used by Canes-Wrone et al.:

$$-|\% \text{ Change in President Request}_{(it)} - \% \text{ Change Enacted Appropriations}_{(it)}|.$$

Smaller values of this measure indicate that the president has less budgetary success with Congress because the absolute value expression is multiplied by $-1$. A positive coefficient on an independent variable in a regression using this measure indicates greater presidential influence. This measure takes into account the size of the requests since it is a percentage, and the previous year's requests since it includes the difference between year $t$ and $t-1$.

A range of other variables could explain the president's success in obtaining the budgets he wants. Canes-Wrone et al. include independent variables for whether there was currently a war, the presence of unified government, and the current deficit level. Other scholars use additional measures, such as the level of unemployment, the economic growth rate, and the percent-

---

Hence we employ more aggregated data, which makes this particular analysis more akin to the analysis of issue areas. Fortunately our roll call analysis and other evidence in the book do not have this problem.

10    We recognize one important tension, though. We know from chapter 3 that these defense budgets for domestic military procurement face heavy lobbying. There are domestic distributional consequences to the Department of Defense budget. But unfortunately we cannot split apart the data in a more granular way, unlike what we were partially able to do in chapter 3, and directly in some of our roll call analyses. Were we able to split the data more finely we would expect our results to be stronger.

age of Congress that is in the president's party.[11] We explore several different specifications, utilize additional covariates, and subject our results to additional robustness checks.[12] In particular, we focused on variables that might affect presidential power. The American politics literature suggests a number of such factors: presidential popularity and unexpected, exogenous shocks—including terrorist attacks, foreign crises, or natural disasters—being the most mentioned.[13] The addition of these variables does not change our main findings, and several of them had little to no impact.

We report our results in table 4.2. The key comparison is between models B1 and B2 and the rest where we disaggregate the foreign policy agencies. The budgetary data is in a time-series format containing different panel units, i.e., different agencies.[14] Models B1 and B2 replicate Canes-Wrone et al.'s original results, the first one without presidential fixed effects and the second with presidential fixed effects. Presidential fixed effects mean that we are identifying the effect of the different policy instruments off of variance within a presidential term of office. Model B3 drops the interaction term between their foreign policy dummy variable and the presence of unified government. Inclusion of this control variable is not relevant for our results, so we subsequently drop this interaction term.

Beginning with model B4, we disaggregate the original "DefenseOrig" variable. The coefficients on the dummy variable for Defense agencies are positive and highly significant. The coefficient for the State Department is negative and insignificant. Congress is more likely to accept the president's funding requests for Defense and related agencies than for domestic ones, but this is not the case for the State Department. The power of the president to get what he wants in foreign policy areas outside of the

11   Howell et al., 2013.

12   These are not reported here. For example, we estimated models with a measure of world terrorist threats and presidential popularity (averaged over a year or during the April–October period that is standard for budget negotiations). Miller, LaFree, and Dugan, 2011; Woolley and Peters, 2014. Both were insignificant. Alternative external threat measures from the CAMEO data on material conflict throughout the world do not change our results with these data. Schrodt and Yilmaz, 2007. We also explored interacting some of these variables with our agency dummies. There were some patterns that suggest greater delegation to more security-oriented agencies during times of conflict, but these results were weak. This is consistent with Howell et al.'s findings that some US wars tend to shift greater power to the president and that they affect domestic politics just as much as foreign policy. To keep our discussion focused, we do not concentrate on these control variables whose importance is minimized with our fixed effects strategies.

13   Cohen, 1999; Beckmann, 2010.

14   We follow the original authors and use panel-corrected standard errors with panel-level heteroskedasticity and analytic weights determined by an agency's previous year's appropriations to account for variation in agency size. Canes-Wrone, Howell, and Lewis, 2008, p. 8. They also use fixed effects for presidents (in some models), and we do the same but do not report these estimates in the tables. This means, for example, that the effect of an agency is identified off of deviations from a president's average level of budgetary success with Congress.

**Table 4.2.** Budget Analysis with Current Action Table Data

|  | B1 | B2 | B3 | B4 | B5 | B6 | B7 |
|---|---|---|---|---|---|---|---|
| DefenseOrig | 0.08** | 0.08** | 0.07** |  |  |  |  |
|  | [0.02] | [0.02] | [0.02] |  |  |  |  |
| StateDept |  |  |  | −0.02 | −0.03 | −0.02 | −0.02 |
|  |  |  |  | [0.03] | [0.03] | [0.03] | [0.03] |
| Defense |  |  |  | 0.07** | 0.07** | 0.07** | 0.07** |
|  |  |  |  | [0.02] | [0.02] | [0.02] | [0.02] |
| Defense OrigX Unified | −0.03 | −0.04 |  |  |  |  |  |
|  | [0.05] | [0.05] |  |  |  |  |  |
| UnifiedGovt | 0.07 | 0.10+ | 0.08+ | 0.06+ | 0.08+ | 0.33** | 0.45** |
|  | [0.05] | [0.06] | [0.05] | [0.03] | [0.05] | [0.12] | [0.15] |
| War | 0.01 | 0.06 | 0.06 | 0.01 | 0.06 | 0.09+ | −0.03 |
|  | [0.03] | [0.05] | [0.05] | [0.03] | [0.05] | [0.05] | [0.10] |
| Deficit | −0.02* | −0.02 | −0.02 | −0.02* | −0.02 | −0.00 | 0.01 |
|  | [0.01] | [0.01] | [0.01] | [0.01] | [0.01] | [0.02] | [0.02] |
| ln(Unemploy) |  |  |  |  |  | 0.03 | 0.10 |
|  |  |  |  |  |  | [0.12] | [0.13] |
| Avg. Pres. Seat Share |  |  |  |  |  | −2.64* | −3.72** |
|  |  |  |  |  |  | [1.13] | [1.41] |
| Growth |  |  |  |  |  | 1.72* | 1.99* |
|  |  |  |  |  |  | [0.84] | [0.89] |
| PresApproval |  |  |  |  |  |  | 0.00 |
|  |  |  |  |  |  |  | [0.00] |
| Constant | −0.11** | −0.14 | −0.14 | −0.10** | −0.14 | 0.65+ | 0.66+ |
|  | [0.02] | [0.09] | [0.09] | [0.02] | [0.09] | [0.39] | [0.39] |
| Observations | 607 | 607 | 607 | 607 | 607 | 607 | 607 |

Standard errors in brackets, $+p < 0.10$, $*p < 0.05$, $**p < 0.01$.

Models 1 and 2 replicate the original CWHL data, model 3 drops the insignificant interaction. Models 4–7 break out their original Defense variable into Defense/AEC vs. State Department. Models 2, 3, 5–7 include presidential fixed effects (omitted).

Defense Department—i.e., in areas like economic aid, sanctions, trade, and diplomacy—is no different than what he can do for domestic policy agencies. The use of presidential fixed effects, which control for any variables that are constant within a presidency, do not change this result. These results hold controlling for a variety of different domestic- and international-level variables.[15] Interestingly, many of the variables often claimed to influence presidential power seem to have no discernible effect. Presidential popularity, the state of the economy, war, and exogenous shocks like terror attacks do not have consistently positive effects on the president's ability to get what he wants from Congress. Rather, the factors that we focus on as shaping politics around different policy instruments seem to matter most.[16]

## The Voting-Legislating Connection

The analysis of congressional roll call voting has a long tradition in political science and economics.[17] Congressional voting is consequential for the direction and scope of US policy and provides an opportunity to observe the revealed preferences of elites.

15 Of course, we do not control for unmeasured variables that change over time, and which could interact with our fixed effect units. Econometric techniques that handle this are at the current frontiers of research in econometrics. Bai, 2009; Stewart, 2014. Our results are robust to using the statistical specification in Howell, Jackman, and Rogowski, 2013. Compared to other domestic agencies, funding for Defense and other security-related agencies was closer to what the president requested, whereas presidential influence in funding for the State Department and related foreign policy agencies did not differ significantly from other domestic agencies and was lower compared to Defense agencies. An additional potential concern is the use of weights on previous year appropriations. Not using these weights has the effect of increasing the magnitude of the StateDept coefficient and its significance. The magnitude of Defense also becomes smaller and remains highly significant. However, a test of a difference between the State and Defense department coefficients shows some significant differences, but the results are more sensitive. We note how Canes-Wrone et al.'s results did not change when they used various instrumenting strategies for presidential budget proposals. Given this, and our low confidence in the validity of such a strategy, we do not empirically engage with this issue. Finally, we also analyzed the Howell, Jackman, and Rogowski data which was an extension of data from Kiewiet and McCubbins to cover from 1933 to 2006. Kiewiet and McCubbins, 1991. These data cover a broader range of agencies than in the Current Action tables, and are collected from the Senate document "Appropriations, Budget Estimates, Etc." (ABE). For the HJR data we disaggregate their "Defense" category by breaking out items that we then label as *IntlAffairs*. "International commissions, International Organizations and conferences, Administration of Foreign Affairs." Consistent with our theory, these items were less likely to be funded in accordance with the president's wishes.

16 These control variables were also susceptible to changes when dropping the various congressional sessions, but our core explanatory variables retained their significance and substantive effects.

17 Bailey and Brady, 1998; Baldwin and Magee, 2000; Beaulieu, 2002a; Hiscox, 2002a; Beaulieu and Magee, 2004; Broz, 2005; Magee, 2010.

The logic of our argument about the power of the president flows from a series of claims that have been established about congressional behavior. First, while there have been doubts that roll call voting means much in American politics,[18] recent work has tended to show more decisively that roll call votes are important for legislators.[19] Legislators regard roll call votes as an important element in their reelection record, and they pay careful attention to such votes. "Members [of Congress] view legislative voting as an important component of the electoral connection and consider constituency cues in roll-call decisions. . . . Even safe legislators' roll-call voting affects their risk of electoral defeat. Thus members are correct in assuming that legislative votes have an impact on the probability of reelection."[20] Moreover, roll call votes reflect legislators' beliefs about their constituents' preferences. "There is now strong evidence that the electorate is responsive in the aggregate—incumbents whose voting patterns are 'out-of-step' with their districts are more likely to fail in their re-election efforts."[21]

As classic studies of the connection between Congress and the public have shown, legislators anticipate the reactions of their constituents. It is not because they think the public monitors their votes but rather that in the run-up to the next election, interest groups, challengers in the primary or general election, or the media may make a public issue out of one or more of their roll call votes.[22] It is the potential reaction of voters to this information at election time that makes legislators aware of their preferences when taking roll call votes. Many of the studies cited here demonstrate that the public lowers their evaluation of representatives who cast roll calls that they disapprove of. Since legislators cannot perfectly predict in advance which votes might generate trouble later, they have to worry about all the votes they take (and don't take). Moreover, some research shows how this concern over roll call votes affects the agenda for these votes. For instance, Cox and McCubbins, and Kelly and Van Houweling point out that if this logic holds, the majority party in Congress will seek to avoid scheduling votes that divide the majority party, and they provide evidence for this conjecture.[23] Such negative agenda control only makes sense if legislators are worried about the electoral ramifications of their roll call votes.[24]

18    Miller and Stokes, 1963; Stokes, 1963.
19    Ansolabehere, Snyder, and Stewart, 2001a; Canes-Wrone, Brady, and Cogan, 2002; Jessee, 2009; Ansolabehere and Jones, 2010; Kelly and Van Houweling, 2011.
20    Canes-Wrone, Brady, and Cogan, 2002, p. 136.
21    Kelly and Van Houweling, 2011.
22    Fenno, 1978; Kingdon, 1989.
23    Cox and McCubbins, 2005; Kelly and Van Houweling, 2011.
24    This point, of course, raises the selection issue for which roll call votes we see, as noted in our introduction. This negative agenda control by the majority may have implications for our study. However, for this to be the case and have a bearing on our claims, any bias from

Roll calls are important for legislators. They worry that the public may punish them for any deviation from their preferences, which is often the party line. Hence when foreign policy issues arise and the president wants Congress to authorize the policy instruments he needs to deal with the issue, he must sometimes convince legislators—often from his own party— that they must vote for international engagement in ways that their constituents might not support. Republican presidents, for instance, might have to appeal to Congress to provide economic aid, which is often not favored by conservatives; or Democrats may have to appeal to Congress for trade agreements that they oppose. Our claim is that for policy instruments with weaker domestic distributional concerns and/or weaker ideological divisions, the president will be more likely to get congressional assent to policies he endorses, especially from members of his own party.[25] In addition, where distributive politics is less, this may result in informational asymmetries favoring the president; and these may also promote his influence in Congress.

For any vote the president can signal his policy preference. While many have noted the importance of bipartisanship in foreign policy since World War II,[26] it is still the case that the president almost always needs the majority of his party to support him if legislation he endorses is going to pass.[27] When the president asks a legislator from his own party to vote against his local interests, the legislator risks electoral punishment. Legislators who do not share a common institutional connection, via the US party system, might not be willing to follow the president's lead. But even legislators who are in his party might be reluctant to go along with the president on issues with local distributional consequences and little reason to suspect the president has an informational advantage. Where distributional concerns are less and ideological divisions fewer, presidents should be better able to convince their own party members to vote as they want.[28]

---

this type of agenda control must operate differentially across our different policy instruments, rather than simply being a general concern.

25 Lee, 2009.

26 McCormick and Wittkopf, 1990.

27 Edwards points out that presidents have typically obtained support from congresspersons from their own party about two-thirds of the time since 1953 and that this is twice the rate of support they get from the opposition. Edwards, 2003, p. 10.

28 Previous research anticipates such a partisan gap on military deployments, but less for ideological reasons than for party politics. For example, presidential scholar William Howell writes that "A substantial body of research shows that Democrats within Congress regularly and predictably support Democratic presidents who are contemplating military action, just as Republican members of Congress back Republican presidents; and that it is nearly always across party lines that the deepest political cleavages cut . . . When members of Congress are willing to resist the president on matters involving war, as with all sorts of other issues, they do so because they have powerful political incentives to criticize the opposition president who

Our theory suggests that instruments such as military deployments and geopolitical aid will involve these informational asymmetries. An implication of this is that when it comes to legislative voting we should see divisions based on whether a legislator is in the same party as the president. And legislators not in the president's party will not have incentives to follow him. As discussed in chapter 2, legislators will be more likely to be swayed by the president when he is in the same party because information transmission is more likely when there are shared interests, which the political party label helps create. However, for other policy instruments, we have argued that distributional and ideological politics will be much more important for shaping legislators' preferences. Hence, for example, for economic aid and trade we expect legislators to be driven more by the economic composition of their districts as well as by the ideological orientation of their district. Presidential influence will be much lower in this case. Thus our focus on multiple policy instruments lets us examine the range of presidential influence in roll call voting in previously unstudied ways.

## Roll Call Samples and Results

Roll call voting patterns have been examined in a broad variety of areas.[29] Most previous studies of congressional voting go in one of two directions. One set of studies analyzes a set of voting in a single instrument, such as trade policy.[30] Scholars collect a set of votes on trade policy, code the votes in a consistent direction (pro- or anti-trade), and regress the votes on a set of explanatory variables. Other studies pool and analyze all congressional votes,[31] or a vast swath of votes across many different policy areas.[32] The analysis in this chapter combines these approaches. We both use the universe of foreign policy votes and in a second set of analyses we collected important sets of votes on each different instrument of foreign policy: economic aid, trade, immigration, geopolitical aid, sanctions, domestic military spending, and military deployment. Table 4.3 summarizes our different strategies.

### Dataset 1: The Universe of House Foreign Affairs Votes

Our first dataset uses all foreign policy related votes in the US House from 1953 to 2008, or roughly 3,900 votes (the sample size varies in ways we describe

---

takes our nation to war. Because they recognize these political incentives, presidents tend to resist the demands for information sharing that follow." Howell, 2013, p. 101.

29    Ansolabehere, Snyder, and Stewart, 2001b; Hiscox, 2002a; Hiscox, 2002b; Magee, 2010; Milner and Tingley, 2011.

30    Hiscox, 2002b; Ladewig, 2006.

31    Poole and Rosenthal, 2006.

32    Middlemass and Grose, 2007.

**Table 4.3.** Types of Roll Call Data Used in Chapter

| | SAMPLE COVERAGE | VOTE GROUPING | DV | KEY IV |
|---|---|---|---|---|
| Table 4.4 | Universe of Foreign Policy Votes 1953–2008 | Security vs. Non-Security | Own Party and Total Vote Margin (Y-N) | Pres. Position Yea vs. Nay or Y/Abstain/N **X** Security Dummy |
| Table 4.5, 4.6 | Sub-sample 262 House votes | Separate Policy Domains | Individual Leg. Vote (1 if pro-policy) | Pres. Position/ Pres. Party, District variables |

below). For these votes we analyze each vote's margin, that is, the difference in the number of yes and no votes, for legislators in the president's party and for legislators not in the president's party. We use Rohde's categorization to dichotomize votes into issues that have weaker domestic distributional concerns and that put priority on information asymmetries favoring the president versus those that do not.[33] But categorization of all these votes into issues that have weaker domestic distributional concerns and that have fewer ideological divisions versus those that do not is relatively straightforward, given their coding scheme. Votes related to the military deployments, sanctions, and geopolitical aid are coded as the former.[34] Policy instruments like economic development aid, trade policy, immigration, the IMF, and State Department funding are coded as non-military foreign policy instruments.

*As a short-hand reference, intended to efficiently encode the dichotomy*, we use the terms "military" and "economic and diplomatic" votes. Of course, any binary distinction is not perfect, which is why in subsequent analyses we focus more narrowly on specific categories of foreign policy votes. Overall, we believe this categorization is reasonable; our subsequent analyses break these categories out more finely into our policy instruments.

33   Rohde, 2010.
34   Using Rohde's numeric codes the military categories are: 110 111 112 113 114 115 116 117 118 119 121 122 123 124 125 126 145 156 190 199 250 259 300 301 302 308 309 310 311 312 313 314 315 316 319 320 321 322 323 324 325 326 327 329 330 331 332 333 339 340 341 342 344 345 347 348 349 350 353 354 355 356 357 358 359 360 361 362 363 368 369 370 371 379 380 381 382 383 385 387 388 389 397 407 408 415 418 460 464 466 468 469 470 471 472 479 480 481 482 483 489 490 491 498 530. These categories include votes on deployments, and military aid, among other things. Non-security include 101 106 140 141 142 143 149 401 402 410 411 412 413 414 416 417 419 420 421 422 423 428 429 430 431 432 433 439 441 443 449 450 451 452 532 540 543 544 545 546 547 548 549. These include votes on economic aid, funding for State Department programs, and trade policy, among other things. One difference between the security votes in this sample and the security votes in our sub-sample analysis later in the chapter is that in the latter we do not include military spending votes that are not directly connected to specific military deployments. For similar distinctions see Souva and Rohde, 2007. We analyze military spending votes later in the chapter.

In the next section, using a smaller handpicked set of votes, we code each vote by whether it is in favor of using the instrument, "pro-engagement," or not. But in this section, because the sample of votes is so large, we are unable to categorize each vote according to how it affected foreign policy; i.e., whether it was pro- or anti-engagement with the international system. So for this set of votes we do not know the content of the vote relative to the president's preferences, but we know the vote margin favoring the president. For our second dataset we are able to identify the direction of the vote and then match that relative to the president's preferences, which is almost always pro-engagement.

The Rohde data also collected whether or not the president took a position on a vote, the outcome of the vote (the margin of victory), and the vote breakdown by party. Our analysis below uses both the dichotomous categorization of votes and the president's position.[35] We ask whether the president's endorsement made it more likely that legislators voted for the bill. We examine this universe of votes to see if the president could influence members of Congress, especially in his own party, to vote for bills he wanted. Hence we focus first on the yea-nay difference (i.e., the vote margin) within his own party, and outside his party, that the bill received as a function of the president's position and other covariates. The unit of analysis is the roll call vote, which contrasts with subsequent analyses that use a legislator-level analysis.

## VOTE MARGINS ANALYSIS

We begin by looking at the margin of victory for the president's preferred policy (i.e., the vote margin) for members of the president's party and all legislators. We code the president's position on each vote (support versus oppose) by a simple indicator variable (*PresSupportVsOppose*). Using the categorization scheme described above, we create a variable equal to 1 if it has a military connection and 0 if related to a non-military foreign policy instrument, essentially economic or diplomatic, for each vote (*MilitaryVsEconDipl*). We then interact the president's position with the *MilitaryVsEconDipl* variable to create the variable *PresXMilitary*.[36] Our prediction is that the interaction will be positive for members of the president's party. Presidents will have more success influencing individual voting decisions when they concern foreign policy with low distributional consequences, higher informational asymmetries, and lower ideological divisions.

35  Our understanding is that a similar compilation for the Senate by Rohde's team is not yet complete.

36  In auxiliary models, we use a trichotomous version of the presidential variable, −1 if opposed, 0 if no position, and 1 if in favor, and find substantively similar results.

Table 4.4 presents the results of several different types of models. In the first set of models our dependent variable is the margin of votes by which the president's party supports the bill (column "Same"), which is our key focus. It subtracts the number of no votes in the president's party from the number of yes votes. This tells us how well the president did in getting his own party to vote in his preferred direction (which is almost always pro-international engagement). We also analyze an identical set of models, but use the vote margin of the other party (column "Other"). As described in the table notes, we also use several different types of models, varying the specification by using all votes or removing procedural ones (which tend to be very party line and hence could bias our results),[37] or whether or not congressional session fixed effects are included.

As noted above, we are using observational data here and it has numerous problems. The potential for omitted variables is one. Congressional session (2-year) fixed effects deal with several types of issues. First, the relationship between congressional and presidential preferences may vary across sessions as individuals and majorities change, producing results that are driven solely by preference similarity or other unobserved factors common to the era. With session fixed effects, the influence of the president is identified from deviations occurring within a session. Since preferences within a two-year session are often thought to be relatively constant, this mitigates the potential problem of changing preferences over time. The inclusion of these fixed effects also helps us deal with features of the external environment that might differ across congressional sessions, such as the degree of divided government or the polarity of the international environment. Importantly, *with regard to any potential omitted variable or endogeneity problem, it must explain not just presidential impact itself, but why it differs for military versus economic/diplomatic votes*. Hence, if it is claimed that the president's support is endogenous to the preferences of the majority, one must explain why this affects bills more tightly related to military one way and those less related another way. Finally, we also control for the average presidential popularity within a year and an interaction of this measure with the president's position.[38]

The results support our hypotheses. For the president's own party vote share the interaction between presidential position and the military policy instrument indicator is positive and significant. This indicates a larger

37  Chaudoin, Milner, and Tingley, 2010.

38  A more sophisticated analysis would link the presidential popularity time-series directly with each vote. Unfortunately this is not yet possible because the Rohde data did not include the exact vote date though with substantial work this could be done. We also estimated models with a range of other control variables relating to the economy and international events. The inclusion of our fixed effects guards against the influence of these and other variables. We also obtain similar results when including domestic votes.

**Table 4.4.** Vote Margin Analysis of Foreign Policy Votes

| | SAME1 | OTHER1 | SAME2 | OTHER2 | SAME3 | OTHER3 | SAME4 | OTHER4 |
|---|---|---|---|---|---|---|---|---|
| PresSupportVsOppose | 161.3** [56.26] | −120.6+ [62.19] | 159.5* [59.19] | −112.0 [69.11] | 181.6* [66.59] | −92.10 [77.35] | | |
| PresXMilitary | 54.84** [17.98] | −4.610 [24.22] | 64.14** [19.45] | −0.424 [24.71] | 61.06** [20.81] | 4.999 [24.63] | | |
| MilitaryVsEconDipl | −15.44 [11.63] | −1.630 [13.16] | −22.74+ [12.63] | −0.946 [14.34] | −16.61 [13.27] | −0.953 [13.70] | 26.12** [5.706] | 25.92** [7.170] |
| PresSupportAbstainOppose | | | | | | | 129.5** [36.65] | −38.52 [31.08] |
| PresSAO X Military | | | | | | | 46.56** [11.76] | 13.25 [11.35] |
| PresPopularity | 0.475 [0.470] | 0.0114 [0.650] | 0.730 [0.536] | 0.179 [0.754] | 1.249* [0.547] | 0.467 [0.740] | 0.442 [0.382] | 0.208 [0.422] |
| PresPosPopularity | −0.129 [0.880] | 1.078 [1.081] | −0.235 [0.878] | 1.056 [1.185] | −0.808 [0.988] | 0.411 [1.436] | | |
| PresSAOPopularity | | | | | | | −1.101+ [0.565] | 0.0844 [0.555] |
| Constant | −86.51** [29.26] | 77.71+ [39.12] | −91.57** [32.87] | 66.91 [44.18] | −122.5** [36.41] | 139.0** [42.00] | 68.36* [28.29] | 113.3** [33.63] |
| Observations | 1194 | 1194 | 1040 | 1040 | 1040 | 1040 | 3895 | 3895 |

Standard errors in brackets, +$p < 0.10$, *$p < 0.05$, **$p < 0.01$.

OLS with SEs clustered at Congressional Session.

Model 1 uses procedural votes, 2–4 exclude them. *Same* models use the president's party Yea-Nay as dependent variable, *Other* uses those outside the president's party. Models 1–3 use only votes where the president took a position and 4 uses a linear interaction placing abstentions between nay and yea. Models 3–4 use session fixed effects. Note: sample sizes vary because we estimated models that (1) also excluded procedural votes, (2) used a presidential position IV using only votes he took a position on or all votes including abstentions, and (3) included or excluded domestic policy votes.

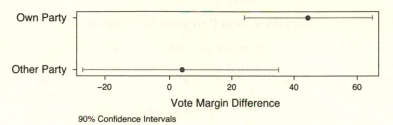

**Figure 4.1.** Difference in own and other party vote margin moving from non-military to military vote, conditional on president taking a position. Uses model 3 in table 4.4. Positive values indicate a larger difference between yeas and nays. Point estimates with 90% confidence intervals reported.

Yes-No difference when the president supports passage and the vote most directly concerns an issue connected to the military, which we argue has distinct distributional and informational characteristics. That is, the president's position is supported by more members of his party when the bill has more to do with policy directly linked to these instruments. This result holds under all of the different model specifications.[39]

Using model Own3,[40] we calculate the change in vote margin. We fix the president's position to "yes" (1), and ask, what is the difference in the vote margin for his own party between votes that are most military-oriented and those that are not. On average, military votes receive approximately forty-five more votes than non-military votes. Figure 4.1 plots this effect, as well as the corresponding effect for legislators outside the president's party. Alternative specifications that look at the *percentage* of all votes in the House that were "yes" reveal similar results.

However, the hypothesized relationship does not occur when we look at the vote margins for members of Congress outside the president's party. The impact of presidential position taking is no different across our two broad collections of policy instruments. This difference between the effects on the president's own party versus the opposition holds across the model specifications. This suggests that when we start to look at legislator-level results in the next section, we should see a partisan gap when presidents take a position on deployments and geopolitical aid and sanction related votes. This is because of the difference in results within the president's party versus the results based on those outside his party. In subsequent results we find a similar relationship corresponding to influence on co-partisans.

39  We also controlled for other variables such as dimensions of the global security environment and economic variables, and our results do not change.

40  The Clarify program does not handle the xi: prefix, and including large numbers of dummies introduces invertibility issues in Clarify, though not with the standard model in Stata. Calculation directly from slope coefficients in the fixed effects model gives similar results.

## Dataset 2: Roll Call Vote Sub-Sample

Our next dataset uses a more fine-grained analysis of individual votes that correspond most closely to our policy instruments. We created a smaller dataset of votes by selecting those that met certain a priori criteria in order to identify legislators' preferences toward each of these policy areas (via the Voteworld program, *Congressional Quarterly*, and the Congressional Record). In general, these criteria were designed to choose consequential votes that would have an important impact on the resulting policy and/or deemed salient since previous scholars had analyzed them or our investigation of the Congressional Record noted their prominence. In general, we avoided using procedural votes unless congressional debate indicated that the vote would have direct and large consequences on the policy outcome. Some votes that met these criteria had to be removed because there was insufficient variation in voting (i.e., they featured unanimous or near unanimous voting). We have 262 House votes in this sample spanning the 96th to the 110th Congresses (1979–2008), all of which are in the large universe of foreign policy votes we used above.[41] This smaller sample allows us to more finely categorize the votes. Our collection of votes also represents, to our knowledge, the most systematic collection and classification of roll call votes on foreign policy issues.

With this smaller set of votes we researched each vote to determine whether a yea or nay vote indicated support for the policy instrument. Then we code the dependent variable to be a vote in the pro direction of the policy instrument. For example, a bill that sought to increase tariffs would have those voting nay coded as a 1 and 0 for those voting to support the bill. This enables us to align our dependent variable across all policy instruments and votes in the same direction which facilitates the comparisons we want to make. It also lets us see which variables are correlated with support for engagement, which helps us understand the domestic bases of support and opposition to "grand strategies" like liberal internationalism. Since we have to do this manually, researching each vote, we were not able to do this in the preceding section. Coding their direction is important because it allows us to examine the preferences of legislators across different policy instruments.

Most important, for these votes we examine legislator-level voting decisions, linking presidential positions on votes as well as detailed congressional district–level data to individual vote choices. We ask what factors influence individual legislators when voting on foreign policy and when does the president have the most influence. Furthermore, we can investigate the extent of the partisan gap when the president adopts a position, and

---

41   One exception is domestic military spending votes which we now analyze. We also collected a comparable dataset for the Senate and found nearly identical results.

whether this gap is larger for some policy instruments than others, as our hypotheses suggest.

We classify each vote as belonging to a separate foreign policy domain: trade, economic aid, immigration, geopolitical aid, sanctions, military spending, and military deployment. Each of these represents a unique foreign policy instrument and each varies according to the extent of its distributional and ideological politics. We describe each foreign policy instrument below.

In trade, since the Constitution gives Congress explicit control over trade policy, presidents must bargain with Congress for trade negotiating authority. The president must then bring any international agreement back to Congress. In addition, legislators can introduce trade legislation since they have constitutional authority over national trade policy. We examine all three types of bills below: presidential authorization to negotiate in trade, final passage of trade agreements, and individual bills to regulate trade policy. We include trade votes that (1) had clear consequences for US trade policy (e.g., were not procedural votes or "sense of Congress" votes), (2) had been used by previous scholars in roll call vote analysis of trade policy (though we update our sample in time beyond the existing literature), and (3) did not deal with individual products unless those products involved major US industries (e.g., steel, automobiles, textiles, sugar).

In foreign economic aid, the president also needs congressional approval since this involves taxing and spending. Congress must agree to his proposals to appropriate and then allocate funds for foreign aid each year. Unlike in trade, aid appropriations are usually part of a much larger foreign operations bill, which contains spending for all forms of international activity in the US government. Committees amend the president's proposals and then these bills may face amendments on the floor. We focus on these amendments since they give a clearer picture of preferences for economic aid alone.

Our economic aid votes were ones that had clear financial consequences for economic aid distributed through key foreign aid programs, such as the main US bilateral aid agency, USAID, or key multilateral organizations such as the World Bank or the IMF. Along with the State Department and the US Trade Representative, these agencies conduct much of US foreign policy that does not deal directly with military issues.[42] Their sole intent was to affect such aid flows; they did not deal with other key issues such as AIDS, labor rights, or abortion that have on occasion come up in the legislative

---

42 Examples of these votes include a 96th Congress amendment vote that sought to cut funding for the World Bank's Inter-American Development Bank from $308,000,000 to $163,079,165, or a 104th Congress vote that sought to decrease the USAID budget by $69 million. There were insufficient votes on the Export-Import Bank to include that agency in the analysis as a separate instrument.

agenda.[43] In this category we also included votes on the International Monetary Fund. Votes on the IMF involve funding for the IMF in general but also votes on funding for particular IMF activities, such as their involvement in the East Asian currency crises in the 1990s. The IMF represents broader financial engagement. We thus expect voting patterns will be similar to aid. We expect presidential influence in this area to be less salient than in the military domains. To identify our sample, we drew on the previous set of votes Broz uses and supplemented them with additional votes identified by our search procedure.[44]

Next we consider geopolitical foreign aid. We include two types of votes. The first is country-specific economic aid votes that dealt with economic aid packages to particular countries. These votes were on aid packages to geopolitically important countries (e.g., economic aid to the Philippines or Nicaragua). The votes have a direct consequence on the president's ability to conduct foreign policy with the country and hence bear more directly on US geostrategic interests. Second, we include in this category military aid votes that were explicitly about giving US hardware and military expertise to particular countries. For example, votes on packages to Central American countries in the 1980s and Saudi Arabia in the 1990s are included in this category. The differentiation of geopolitical and economic aid is an important feature of the voting data in this chapter.[45]

Military deployment votes (and votes on spending for specific military deployments) in our sample relate to funding and authorization of troop deployments overseas in conflict arenas. During the era we study (1979–2008), this included votes on military operations in El Salvador, Bosnia, Somalia, Iraq, Afghanistan, Haiti, and Lebanon.[46] To identify votes in this category, we made sure that we were collecting the universe of key votes.[47]

43    The qualitative information we have suggests these areas were heavily influenced by domestic political factors, especially ideological ones.

44    Broz, 2005; Broz and Hawes, 2006; Broz, 2008; Broz, 2011.

45    We also collected the final passage votes on the overarching yearly appropriations bill for aid and general foreign affairs conduct (such as funding for the State Department). The bill comes out of the "Foreign Operations and Export Financing" Appropriation subcommittee and includes funding for other organizations such as the Export-Import Bank. The legislation spans a broader area of interests and issues, and hence unlike amendment activity we cannot cleanly classify voting on the bills into particular policy domains. Our analysis of these votes largely conforms to our theoretical expectations. There was no evidence of presidential influence, and moderate influence of our ideological and distributional variables.

46    We exclude votes on things that we consider more symbolic and with little legislative force, such as votes that "express a sense of Congress" in one way or the other on US military deployment, which previous scholars have also avoided.

47    This included using various Congressional Research Service (CRS) reports on votes about military deployment, the Howell and Pevehouse database on force deployment to identify potential theaters of deployment, and use of the Policy Agendas database which coded the issue area of congressional votes. Howell and Pevehouse, 2005; Mages, 2007; Policy Agendas Project, 2014.

Immigration votes in our sample deal with issues about immigrant access to the United States and policies that govern how immigrants are treated while in the United States. As with other policy domains, we reviewed a range of resources and previous scholarly work to identify the votes in our sample.[48] This group of votes covers many different types of immigration policy: high- and low-skill visas, access to welfare benefits, employer restrictions, border control, and final passage.

Our sanctions votes contained a variety of votes on different sanctions episodes during our sample. These included votes on sanctions on Rhodesia, South Africa, Cuba, and China. These of course are not the only sanctions applied during this period. But as we noted in chapter 2, the president can apply sanctions without congressional consent, and Congress can write legislation such that de facto sanctions are put in place via appropriating legislation, for example.[49] For the military spending votes we collected two sets of votes from the US House of Representatives. We collected every annual vote on the military appropriations and authorization bills, the annual military construction bill, and votes on particular weapons systems. We pool these together, though estimating them separately gives similar results. We cannot control for the president's position in domestic defense spending votes since the president never took a position on any of our votes in this area.[50]

As discussed previously, for this analysis of individual legislator voting, we code individual votes that support the use of a policy instrument for international engagement as a 1, and 0 if the vote was in opposition. This facilitates our understanding what factors push toward greater engagement. For example, the president almost always favors more engagement and this lets us see if his influence pushes legislators in this direction. If an amendment to an aid bill sought to cut aid funding, then legislators voting against the cut have their vote coded as a 1, and 0 otherwise. A vote to supply funds for military deployment would be coded as a 1 and a vote to oppose funds a 0. For our sanctions vote, we code as 1 a vote against imposing sanctions and a 0 otherwise. Making these substantive decisions requires collecting information about each vote and making a determination in each case. Many times this was straightforward, other times this was more difficult and required more intensive inspection, and finally some votes were extremely complex and a clear determination of direction could not be assigned. In

48    Gimpel and Edwards, 1999.

49    Sanctions put in place via executive action include sanctions on Iran, Libya, Iraq, Haiti, Balkan countries, Burma, and several others.

50    This is despite the fact that our sample covers many votes. The implications of this pattern for our theory are perhaps interesting, and surprising, given arguments about presidential intervention on federal spending in order to favor co-partisans. Kriner and Reeves, forthcoming.

such cases we simply do not include the votes. Hence our analysis attempts to get at general preferences toward the use of each of these policy instruments as they lead to US engagement with the rest of the world. This then in part also lets us speak to the factors that drive support for liberal internationalism.

## EXPLANATORY VARIABLES AND ESTIMATION STRATEGY

To capture the relationship between the president's positions and legislative voting, we include a variable that notes his endorsement for a bill. Following Meernik and Oldmixon, we created a variable to indicate the president's position, coded as 1 if the president was of the legislator's same party *and* the president supported a policy in favor of international engagement.[51] These *positions* (not the individual legislator positions) come from Rohde's research, which collected executive communications to Congress that related to particular votes.[52] For example, this variable would be equal to 1 if a Republican president opposed a cut to foreign aid and the legislator was a Republican. If our presidential foreign policy hypothesis is right, this variable *PresSupport* should be positive in foreign policy domains with the fewest distributive and ideological politics. In our sample of votes, presidents almost never took an "anti-internationalist" position.[53] So voting with the president means taking a pro-engagement position.

We also include other independent variables that capture district distributional and ideological variables. To capture the economic characteristics of the districts that legislators represent, we draw on the predictions made by the Stolper-Samuelson theorem by measuring capital endowments at the district level. The key prediction here is that for trade, and some types of aid and immigration policy, the greater the amount of capital (human or physical capital) used in the district (relative to unskilled labor), the more likely is a vote in favor of the pro-international engagement position. Following earlier work, we measure this by the percentage of people working in high-skill jobs in the district (*%HighSkill*).[54]

In chapter 3, we saw that interest groups were extremely active with respect to domestic spending on the military. For our votes on military spending, we created a district-level measure of contract spending using data on over 17 million DoD contracts from the General Service Administration's Federal Procurement Data System. After obtaining the data, we used the contractor's address to figure out how to map contracts onto a congressio-

51    Meernik and Oldmixon, 2008.
52    Rohde, 2004.
53    While in some issue areas presidents took positions more often than others, this did not systematically vary across our broader categories of security versus non-security forms of foreign policy.
54    Beaulieu, 2002a; Beaulieu, 2002b; Broz, 2005; Broz and Hawes, 2006.

nal district. These addresses were then passed through ArcGIS to produce a longitude and latitude coordinate. Merging these coordinates with information about the congressional district boundaries was done by using shapefiles from the National Historical Geographic Information System. In a small number of instances these files were incomplete, and so we manually created the necessary shapefiles using a congressional district atlas. Finally, for each congressional session we calculate the log of the sum of district contracts. This serves as our key distributional explanatory variable for votes on domestic military spending.[55]

Ideologically based theories suggest that legislators from more conservative districts will have different preferences for foreign policy instruments than more liberal ones. Ideology will affect the perception of cause and effect that legislators have about the different foreign policy instruments.[56] For instance, given their views on the efficacy of markets versus governments, more conservative legislators should support free trade but oppose foreign aid, while legislators from more liberal ones will have opposite preferences. But beyond this more basic identification of the direction of effect, we also discuss below whether some policy instruments are more ideologically divisive than others. Following scholars in American politics, we measure district ideology using the percentage of the previous two-party presidential vote that went to the Republican candidate.[57] We expect these variables to be negatively related to economic aid, somewhat ambiguous for immigration, military deployments, geopolitical aid, and sanctions, and positively related to trade. However, we expect some of these, such as geopolitical aid, sanctions, immigration, and military deployments, to be less ideologically divisive, even if ideology nevertheless plays some role.

In some models we include a number of control variables that others in the literature have identified. The role of organized interest groups is likely to be important.[58] PAC contributions from corporate sources (*CorpPAC%*), labor groups (*LabPAC % PAC*), and money-center banks (banks with high overseas exposure) (*BankPAC %*) are operationalized as a percentage of total PAC contributions and taken from the electoral cycle *preceding* the Congress where we observe an actual vote.[59] We include regional control variables

55  We note that these data do not let us look at subcontracting, which can be spread out across other districts. Subcontracting data were not available throughout our time-series.

56  As Goldstein and Keohane point out, "Causal ideas help determine which of many means will be used to reach desired goals and therefore help to provide actors with strategies with which to further their objectives." Goldstein and Keohane, 1993a, pp. 13–14.

57  We also examine an alternative model where we use legislator ideological scores calculated using the DW-Nominate scaling technique. McCarty, Poole, and Rosenthal, 2006. Legislators with more negative values are more liberal and those with more positive values are more conservative.

58  Grossman and Helpman, 2002; Broz, 2005.

59  Broz, 2005; Roscoe and Jenkins, 2005, p. 60.

because other foreign policy studies have concluded that regional politics in the United States are important.[60] Finally, we also included a number of demographic variables at the district level, such as district foreign born and African American percentages, and unemployment.

Before moving on we take a moment to describe our estimation strategy, as we move away from vote-level regressions used earlier. Our data are in a panel format with the legislator-vote as the unit of analysis. We estimate a series of panel probit models but note that linear probability models give similar results.[61] In our analysis across separate domains, in tables 4.5 and 4.6, we estimate panel probit models as before but also include vote fixed effects. This means that the effects are identified off the variation within each vote; hence, factors that do not vary within a vote (such as the overall partisan balance or current state of the economy) are controlled for. Put differently, in this analysis of separate policy instruments we do not use explanatory variables that are constant within votes, because this prevents the inclusion of vote fixed effects (e.g., the president's average popularity within a congressional session). In these models, inclusion of vote fixed effects is important because there is variation in the vote margins of the bills we observe. This also in principle helps us deal with the fact that we do not control for what types of votes come to the floor. If bills vary according to how divisive votes are, for example, this could create biases in our estimates, then vote fixed effects alleviate this problem.[62]

60    Trubowitz, 1998, p. 232.

61    We also estimated a series of models more akin to those presented in the previous section, but split up our vote categories into military (troop deployment, geopolitical aid) and non-military (economic aid, trade, and immigration) categories (for purposes of this analysis we excluded sanctions and domestic military spending). We estimated a panel probit model and linear probability model but instead of vote fixed effects included legislator fixed effects. Hence the effect of other variables is identified from within legislator deviations. Put differently, any contributions to the estimated parameters come from cases where legislators have different values of the explanatory variable across multiple votes. If there are omitted variables that are constant for a legislator or his district over time, then these fixed effects will control for them. For example, if a legislator has a military background and is naturally more responsive to presidential appeals related to national security, this will be controlled for by the fixed effects. Additional (unreported) models also included congressional session fixed effects for reasons described above. Our results are robust to their inclusion. We interact whether the vote is on a military or non-military tool with a variable giving whether or not the president takes a pro-international position. We expect, and find, that the interaction term, *PresXMilitary*, is positive and significant in each model and full computation of the effect given the constituent terms show this to be a substantively meaningful interaction. Note that legislator FEs is a more demanding specification compared to using state or regional FEs.

62    For example, perhaps on some issues legislator preferences are already closer to the president's and the president carefully chooses to take positions on these more popular votes. Vote fixed effects guards against such a bias.

**Table 4.5.** House of Representatives Voting by Policy Tool

| | ECONAID | IMM | TRADE | DOMMILSPEND | SANCTIONS | GEOPOL | MILDEPL |
|---|---|---|---|---|---|---|---|
| PresSupport | 0.0270 | 0.235** | 0.266** | | 0.711** | 0.331** | 0.438** |
| | [0.0172] | [0.0154] | [0.0120] | | [0.0314] | [0.0136] | [0.00913] |
| HighSkill | 0.827** | 0.182+ | 0.848** | −0.676** | −0.0476 | 0.281* | −0.146 |
| | [0.178] | [0.0972] | [0.189] | [0.188] | [0.202] | [0.114] | [0.0979] |
| PresVotePercRepub | −1.357** | −1.398** | 0.738** | 0.966** | −0.0454 | 0.0209 | −0.0500 |
| | [0.0977] | [0.0476] | [0.0827] | [0.0775] | [0.0898] | [0.0508] | [0.0550] |
| log Mil Spend sum | | | | 0.0196* | | | |
| | | | | [0.00841] | | | |
| Observations | 9588 | 25602 | 12382 | 15590 | 3907 | 14845 | 12017 |

Standard errors in brackets, $+p < 0.10$, $^*p < 0.05$, $^{**}p < 0.01$.

Panel probit with population average effects and vote fixed effects (omitted).

**Table 4.6.** House of Representatives Voting by Policy Tool

| | ECONAID | IMM | TRADE | DOMMILSPEND | SANCTIONS | GEOPOL | MILDEPL |
|---|---|---|---|---|---|---|---|
| PresSupport | 0.0193 [0.0203] | 0.252** [0.0153] | 0.288** [0.0135] | | 0.730** [0.0323] | 0.330** [0.0137] | 0.449** [0.00882] |
| HighSkill | 0.616** [0.215] | 0.209+ [0.111] | 0.894** [0.205] | -0.547** [0.199] | 0.0130 [0.243] | 0.123 [0.131] | -0.189 [0.127] |
| PresVotePercRepub | -0.960** [0.132] | -0.844** [0.0721] | 0.256* [0.123] | 0.659** [0.121] | 0.256+ [0.146] | 0.0309 [0.0830] | 0.191* [0.0901] |
| BankPAC | 2.512** [0.565] | 0.108 [0.242] | 0.372 [0.732] | -1.174** [0.389] | -0.0816 [0.691] | 0.578+ [0.306] | 0.540+ [0.324] |
| CorpPAC | 0.103 [0.0779] | -0.0709 [0.0457] | -0.147+ [0.0765] | 0.189* [0.0779] | 0.318* [0.124] | 0.215** [0.0684] | 0.0854 [0.0642] |
| LabPAC | 0.763** [0.0682] | 0.351** [0.0368] | -0.865** [0.0686] | -0.499** [0.0606] | 0.404** [0.0899] | 0.312** [0.0476] | 0.357** [0.0519] |
| Unemploy | -0.0182 [0.650] | 0.892** [0.320] | -0.706 [0.498] | 0.915+ [0.506] | -0.132 [0.758] | -0.511 [0.372] | -0.649 [0.420] |

| | ECONAID | IMM | TRADE | DOMMILSPEND | SANCTIONS | GEOPOL | MILDEPL |
|---|---|---|---|---|---|---|---|
| ForBorn | 0.567** [0.172] | 0.596** [0.0920] | 0.179 [0.142] | -0.0179 [0.110] | 0.0139 [0.172] | -0.00115 [0.114] | 0.0690 [0.0835] |
| West | -0.0566 [0.0351] | 0.0254 [0.0179] | 0.199** [0.0292] | -0.0133 [0.0277] | 0.172** [0.0358] | -0.0415* [0.0204] | -0.0406* [0.0198] |
| Midwest | -0.0561 [0.0349] | 0.0170 [0.0160] | 0.101** [0.0292] | -0.0665* [0.0270] | 0.156** [0.0345] | -0.00762 [0.0201] | -0.0358+ [0.0194] |
| South | -0.139** [0.0339] | -0.0135 [0.0170] | 0.0581+ [0.0315] | 0.0805** [0.0270] | 0.0625+ [0.0378] | 0.0236 [0.0211] | 0.0649** [0.0203] |
| Black | 0.232* [0.114] | 0.0631 [0.0610] | -0.0120 [0.0924] | -0.0354 [0.0765] | 0.220* [0.110] | -0.122* [0.0624] | 0.0873 [0.0659] |
| log Mil Spend sum | | | | 0.0187* [0.00751] | | | |
| Observations | 9455 | 25325 | 12264 | 15502 | 3879 | 14697 | 11936 |

Standard errors in brackets, +$p < 0.10$, *$p < 0.05$, **$p < 0.01$.

Panel probit with population average effects and vote fixed effects (omitted).

Including vote fixed effects prevents us from examining the president's influence in general, as this is constant for each vote. Instead, a positive co-efficient on the *PresSupport* variable then means that we see a larger partisan gap among the set of votes where the president takes a position in support of international engagement.[63] This can happen because the president is influencing his own party (which previously we showed tends to be the case) or opposition members are voting more against the president.

## RESULTS FOR LEGISLATOR LEVEL VOTING: VOTES ACROSS FOREIGN POLICY INSTRUMENTS

Here we report our results analyzing each policy instrument and use this to motivate our analysis of the alignment of legislators with the president. We use a panel probit model with vote fixed effects, and estimate relationships across different domains of foreign policy votes. We present results for the House but found similar results for the Senate. Table 4.5 includes a specification with only the three core variables: district skill composition, presidential co-partisanship, and ideology.[64] Table 4.6 adds additional control variables. These variables help guard us against potential sources of omitted variable bias.[65]

Our key variable is a measure of whether the president endorsed the pro-international position and if the legislator was a member of his party, *PresSupport*. Our theory suggests that this variable should have the greatest impact on legislators for votes in issue-areas with the fewest distributive politics and least ideological divisions. The marginal effects coefficients on this variable are, as we expected, large and highly significant in the three categories of votes that have the most to do with these types of policies: geopolitical aid, sanctions, and military deployment. It is largest for the sanctions votes. While we expected this relationship to be present for sanctions, it is larger than for the other two categories, a result we did not expect.[66]

This variable about presidential influence is also significant for trade and immigration, but the magnitudes are much smaller. We cannot estimate this for domestic military spending because the president never took a posi-

63 While the president's position is constant within a vote, not all members of Congress are from his party. We thus exploit this variation, and the variation across votes, to estimate the partisan gap when the president tries to be influential.

64 We also estimated models where we only include the president's position due to concerns that we theoretically construct presidential influence as operating where distributional and ideological cleavages are less, and so our results including these additional variables might be misleading. We find similar results with this specification.

65 We also estimated models with a legislator's own DW-Nominate score. We find largely similar results.

66 This is particularly surprising given that some of the sanctions involved had a potential economic connection with them, though this was likely small for the sanctions cases that were voted on.

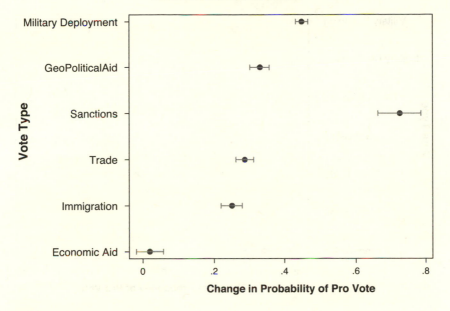

**Figure 4.2.** Change in probability of House member voting in favor of policy tool, changing presidential position variable from abstain/oppose to support. Uses models in table 4.6 *and holds all other variables at their mean*. Point estimates with 90% confidence intervals reported.

tion. Votes on economic aid and final passage of the Foreign Operations bill (which includes many items, including funding for things like the Export-Import Bank) had insignificant coefficients for this variable about the president. This pattern holds for both our sparser specification and when we include many more control variables. Figure 4.2 presents substantive effect graphs for our policy instruments. Here we change *PresSupport* from 0 to 1, holding other variables at their sample median and taking the average of the vote fixed effects. Consistent with the marginal effects coefficients, military deployment, sanctions, and geopolitical aid had the largest effects. Trade and immigration had similar magnitudes, but both were lower than for deployments, sanctions, and geopolitical aid. General economic aid saw little effect of the president.[67] We found a similar pattern in the Senate, but to keep our empirical presentation more concise we do not report those results here.

67  One criticism of this type of analysis is that presidents in fact would always prefer Congress to vote in the pro-international position regardless of whether he takes a public position. This might be especially the case for votes related to military deployments. However, it is unclear how this concern would cause a particular bias across our inferences about the different issue areas.

The effect of the *PresSupport* variable was negative for economic aid votes when the 96th Congress is excluded, and positive and significant if the 102nd or 104th Congresses are excluded. In this latter case the marginal effect remains tiny, which is consistent with our theory.

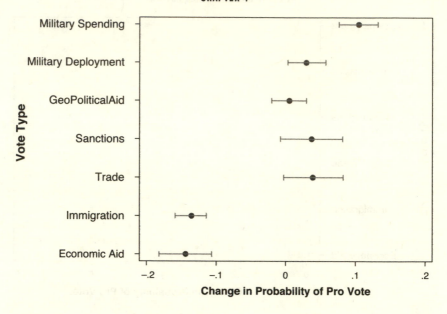

**Figure 4.3.** Change in probability of House member voting in favor of policy tool, changing ideology variable from 25th to 75th percentile. Uses models in table 4.6 *and holds all other variables at their mean*. Point estimates with 90% confidence intervals reported.

Next we discuss our ideological and economic variables. First we look at the influence of district ideology and present substantive effects in figure 4.3. We find that legislators from conservative districts are less likely to support general economic aid and immigration, and more likely to support trade. For trade and aid, the positive and significant effect of *PresVotePercRepub* is strongly consistent with conservative support for free-market ideals. As discussed in chapter 2, conservative opposition to immigration is more anomalous. These results are consistent with the public opinion data we present in chapter 6. The effect of ideology was insignificant for geopolitical aid, and sometimes significant but with a much smaller impact for military deployments and sanctions.[68]

How do these results speak to our hypotheses about ideological divisions? We see that economic aid and military spending are the most ideologically divisive. That is, they have the largest estimated substantive effects. We also expected that military deployments, sanctions, and geopolitical aid would be less ideologically divisive, and we see this. We do not observe trade policy being more ideologically divisive than these categories, which was

68 Some work on particular instances of military aid uncovers a more robust effect of ideology on this type of aid, especially with respect to military aid during the Contras. Leogrande and Brenner, 1993.

contrary to our expectations. We also see that immigration is highly divisive, which is consistent with data presented in chapter 6 but not with our initial expectations. We note, though, that when we separated our immigration votes into separate categories, such as border control versus visas for high-skill immigrants, there was great heterogeneity in the extent of ideological divisiveness, with border control and low-skill visa votes being much more divisive than votes on high- skill visas and regulations on employers. Overall, our expectations about ideological divisiveness receive some, but not complete, support.

Next we look at our economic variables. Our theory argues that these variables will be important for our economic aid, trade, and immigration votes. In the House, the percentage of district in high-skill occupations is positive and significant for our general economic aid votes and trade, as seen in table 4.5 and 4.6. Districts with greater skill endowment support deeper economic engagement with the rest of the world. This result suggests that factor endowments play a crucial role in solidifying an "internationalist" coalition. While the relationship between factor endowments and trade preferences has been explored in previous work, this evidence with respect to economic aid is consistent with our analyses in chapter 3, which disaggregate what types of economic groups are active in the economic aid arena. The *%HighSkill* coefficient was also positive for immigration, but this was not robust to the inclusion of additional control variables.[69] The skill measure (*%HighSkill*) was insignificant for votes on geopolitical aid and military deployment votes, as we expected.[70] Economic interests are much less involved in these areas.

We find support for our argument with the military contract spending votes. The more money spent in a district on military contracts, the more supportive the district's congressperson will be on military spending bills. To calculate the substantive effect of the domestic military spending variable, we calculate the change in probability of a pro-vote moving this variable from its 25th to 75th percentile, which produces a change in probability of 2.5% (95% CI: .001%, 5%). These results are consistent with our earlier evidence about interest group activity on these components of the American foreign policy machine. They highlight how defense spending

69    When we restrict the sample to votes on visas for low-skill immigrants, we find a more robust relationship.

70    These results are not quite as strong for the Senate. While we continue to observe a positive and significant coefficient for general economic aid, for other policy domains the relationship is not significant at conventional levels. For example, for trade, the effect is significant without the controls but the $t$-statistic in the model with controls is $t=1.5$. We also estimated a model that included district-level military spending for the geopolitical aid votes. We found no significant relationship. We note that, perhaps unexpectedly, the *%HighSkill* variable was negative and significant for the domestic military spending votes.

issues do not have the same distributional and informational profile as is the case with the foreign policy instruments of geopolitical aid and military deployments.[71]

In the preceding discussion we focused on comparing the effect of our key variables across policy instruments. But a similar analysis can be done within each of our policy instruments using this same information. We find that ideology and distributional factors are crucial for explaining voting on economic aid, immigration, trade, and domestic military spending, but presidential position taking was less important. A converse pattern holds for sanctions, geopolitical aid, and military deployments. These results are largely consistent with our theory.[72]

In sum, holding constant a number of factors identified as affecting legislators' preferences over foreign policy, including local constituency interests and ideology, we find support for our main hypothesis about presidential influence. Presidents have the greatest influence over instruments that are linked to issues that have weaker domestic distributional concerns and fewer ideological divisions. These types of issues also convey informational asymmetries favoring the president. These results hold using two different analyses of the roll call record and using a variety of identification strategies. For all foreign policy votes, we find that the margin of victory for the president's most preferred policy rises as the vote is more directly concerned with military instruments, which tend to have fewer ideological and distributive politics.

For our smaller subset of votes, the president is more likely to influence legislators to vote for international engagement if that vote is about an instrument linked to issues that have weaker domestic distributional concerns and less ideological divisiveness, and hence information asymmetries favoring the president. Some instruments, such as geopolitical aid, sanc-

---

71   We also collected votes on food aid which we expect to be highly distributional, as discussed in chapter 3. For our food aid votes we identified a set of four votes that sought to reduce US food aid that is delivered through the PL 480 program. For our votes on food aid, we add a measure of district-level agricultural production using data from the Census of Agriculture. This is designed to pick up on the importance of agricultural production and hence is a proxy for why a legislator might support food aid because of its local economic consequences. Across each of the food aid models, larger district agricultural production correlates with support for food aid, a change in probability of 3.6% (95% CI: 1.4% , 6.2%).

72   The main exception again being that our theoretical model did not expect the strong role of ideological cleavages for immigration. We also estimated linear probability models and calculated changes in Bayesian Information Criteria scores when we estimated a baseline model with only the presidential variable but then added our skill and ideology variables. The addition of these variables only improved model fit for economic aid, immigration, and trade. For domestic military spending, presidents never took a position so we could not perform this analysis. The addition of these variables does not improve model fit, as measured by the BIC, for sanctions, geopolitical aid, and military deployments.

tions, and deployments, allow the president greater freedom from domestic constraints and thus a greater ability to use them for foreign engagement and as substitutes for other foreign policy instruments.[73] Perhaps surprisingly, this effect was highest for our sanctions votes. In chapter 4 we were able to paint a more nuanced story about presidential influence and economic interests with sanctions.

The role of ideology was strongest for our economic aid, immigration, and domestic military spending votes; trade and sanctions saw smaller effects and geopolitical aid, and military deployments had the weakest ideological divisions. Surprisingly, immigration votes evinced very strong ideological divisions. Importantly, the direction of the effect differs between trade on the one hand and economic aid and immigration on the other. As we have argued throughout the book, this has important implications for policy substitution. Two different coalitions support these instruments then.

Finally, we also found some support for our predictions that economic aid, trade, and immigration would have economic cleavages, thus highlighting the role of distributional factors in legislative voting. The presence of distributional considerations was also salient for domestic military spending. Conversely, we did not see these material interests in the votes on geopolitical aid, sanctions, and military deployments. This is consistent with evidence presented in previous chapters. Again, it shows that not all military-oriented instruments are the same and some look very much like domestic political issues.

# Conclusion

In this chapter, we ask what conditions allow the president to have greater discretion in foreign policy relative to Congress. To do this, we look at two pieces of evidence. First, we ask when the president will be able to get budget outcomes closer to those he desired for the various domestic and foreign policy agencies in his government. Second, we look at the president's influence on roll call votes in different foreign policy issues. We ask when legislators will be more likely to vote on foreign policy issues in a manner consistent with the preferences of the president. Both of these pieces of data confirm that the president's ability to get his preferred outcomes in votes and budgets varies across foreign policy instruments. Is this result an artifact of the preferences of the president and legislators? Could it be that the president and legislators, especially from his own party, are always closer to one another on issues linked to the military than on other foreign policy

---

73   This result may also help explain the United States's revealed preference for bilateral versus multilateral aid. Milner and Tingley, 2013a.

issues? We do not think this is the case since among all foreign policy roll calls, the president issues more endorsements for bills related to economic and diplomatic policies than he does for votes on the military, suggesting his preferences are closer to legislators' on the former type of issue.[74]

Some foreign policy instruments are just as constrained by the legislature as are domestic policy ones. There aren't "two presidencies," and politics does not always stop at the water's edge. The influence of presidential endorsements is largest on policy instruments with fewer ideological divisions and distributive politics. And this distinction cuts across military-oriented policy instruments. Coupled with evidence from the previous chapters, these results paint a picture of an influential president, but only on some foreign policy instruments.

Determining presidential power is difficult. Presidents and the Congress are interacting strategically and know their behavior is being watched and judged by the public and media. The behavior we observe is thus colored by this process of strategic interaction and common knowledge of it. Much of the data we present are observational, and hence proving causality is difficult. Selection bias, simultaneity, and endogeneity all exist as potential problems.[75] The president will be selective about which votes he endorses and opposes. His anticipation about the vote may influence his endorsement. Using many types of data may help with these problems. For instance, the congressional roll call voting data may overestimate the president's influence since he may endorse bills he suspects will pass and only bills the majority thinks will pass may be put on the agenda; in contrast, the budget data may underestimate the president's role since he may in anticipation alter his requests to reduce the difference with Congress. In addition, in our models with vote fixed effects, these differences in preferences across votes are held constant; and our results still hold. Our identification strategy also controls for many factors that are viewed as important in shaping presidential influence, such as presidential popularity, war, and economic conditions.

74    Using the data used in our first analysis, the president supports twice as many roll calls in terms of percentage of those votes for economic and diplomatic foreign policy (17%) than he does for military foreign policy (9%), and he supports more roll calls for domestic votes (+10%) even than he does for military ones. In addition, if we assume that an abstention by the president implies his support (though see Lee, 2009, p. 80.), then he "supports" all three types of roll calls almost equivalently: 90% of domestic roll calls, 86% of economic and diplomatic foreign policy ones, and only 83% of military votes. These data suggest that his preferences on roll call votes relative to the median in Congress are not that different with respect to security versus non-security votes.

75    For example, presidents and legislators are interacting strategically and know they are being watched and judged on their behavior. This means that the majority party in Congress has strong reasons to control the agenda for roll call votes. Majority leaders will do their best to prevent certain votes from arising. Cox and McCubbins, 2005.

Our roll call vote analyses are only suggestive about policy substitution. In chapter 6 on public opinion we also see very different coalitions of supporters and opponents across policy instruments. However, the votes we examine do not capture actual policy substitution. We tackle this problem in chapter 7 with an extensive case study of US policy in Sub-Saharan Africa, chosen because it draws on nearly all of our policy instruments. Finally, we have not focused on how Congress tries to interfere with presidential decisions through alternative mechanisms such as hearings and bringing issues to the public, which may give Congress more influence.[76]

Presidential influence vis-à-vis Congress matters. In the post–World War II period presidents have all favored global engagement with the international system. Legislators, as we and others have argued, are often more concerned with local pressures from constituents and ideological forces. The more they act as constraints on the president, the less able the president is to engage with the instruments most appropriate to the foreign policy problem. Substitution of policy instruments in foreign policy becomes very difficult in such a political environment. This is not to argue that all domestic constraints on presidents are undesirable. Presidents may feel compelled into too much engagement for a country's own good (i.e., overextension). And presidents may choose poorly among the instruments they have at hand to deal with a situation abroad. Legislative and public scrutiny can force them to think harder about these potential pitfalls.[77] But domestic politics may also constrain them in unhelpful ways.

76  Kriner, 2010.
77  For a forceful argument about this, see Posner and Vermeule, 2010.

# 5

## CONTROLLING THE SAND CASTLE
### The Design and Control of US Foreign Policy Agencies

The president relies upon various governmental agencies and bureaucracies for making and implementing policy. Many of these provide him with critical information that allows him to make policy decisions in a more effective and timely fashion. Bureaucracies and the information they gather also help the president design policies that he proposes to Congress. And they are key in implementing these policies later. All of these functions that bureaus provide enable the president to better control the policy process. Therefore, if Congress wants to exert control over policy, Congress must deal with these bureaucracies.

Control over these bureaucracies is therefore critical to understand. The role of bureaucracies and how they relate to the president has been an important element in studies of American foreign policy.[1] Our focus in this chapter is on how much control the president or Congress can exert over these organizations. Presidential power in foreign policy depends in part on this. While the president may prefer to have maximal control over these agencies, Congress can try to prevent this in a variety of ways. Below we discuss how this can happen through the design of these bureaucracies, but also trace out a more dynamic story where Congress has the ability to prevent the president from establishing and maintaining these agencies since it can deny them funding. It can also insert clauses that make the bureaucracies more responsive to Congress. Hence the terms under which these bureaucracies are formed and persist are important in affecting congressional-presidential relations.

We seek to show that the president has more influence over some bureaucracies than others in the foreign policy area. His control differs by the policy instruments covered by an agency, as we theorize in chapter 2. In those areas where the benefits and costs of policies have large, concentrated effects on social groups, Congress will be much more reluctant to give the president strong control over the bureaucracy. This will also be true when ideological divisions over them are very high. Congress will try to grab hold of the agencies and make them more responsive to its preferences.

---

1 Allison, 1969; Destler, 1972; Krasner, 1972; Art, 1973; Bendor and Hammond, 1992; Drezner, 2000; Halperin and Clapp, 2006.

For policy instruments where ideological divisions are small and distributive effects are less central, Congress will be less likely to assert control over the agencies, and hence these bureaus will be dominated by the president. Of course, this does not mean that Congress will never try to exert control over these types of agencies; but given the president's asymmetries in information over Congress in these areas, Congress will have a harder time exerting its influence. Congress can make attempts to gain greater control over these agencies even after their creation, but its success will vary.[2]

We examine our key hypothesis about the role of the president by looking at the design of bureaucratic agencies that provide inputs into and implement US foreign policy. These hypotheses follow from earlier work in the American politics literature. Not all bureaucracies exhibit the same amount of presidential control. Previous research identified agencies associated with foreign affairs as having greater presidential control, while bureaucracies focused on domestic policies had greater congressional control compared to the president.[3] Our expectation is that the president's influence in the bureaucratic process will not be the same for all foreign affairs policy instruments. Instead it should be a function of how linked a policy instrument is to distributional concerns as well as the extent of ideological divisions.

Our goal in this chapter is to investigate whether US bureaucratic institutions are designed in a way that reflects these differences, giving the president more control over some policy instruments versus others. We expect military-related agencies that connect directly to overseas operations (e.g., deployment, intelligence gathering) to be the most under presidential control. Some military agencies are entirely connected to the economies of defense, and our theory suggests that these should be different, and less under presidential control, because they entail large domestic distributional benefits. Finally, those dealing with trade and economic aid, due to their distributive nature, should be the least under presidential control.[4] Unfortunately, this chapter does not include sanctions as a policy instrument, in part because many agencies contribute to US sanctions policies. We also present new data about average liberal versus conservative ideology of bureaucrats across sets of bureaucracies, which we argue has implications for substitution. Table 5.1 summarizes the key questions and range of data that we use in the chapter.

The structure of the chapter is as follows. First we articulate why we think it is important to study the institutional design of US agencies and

2   In such instances individual congresspersons may see no special incentive to go up against the president, or because Congress is content with delegating leadership and control over such agencies to the president.

3   Canes-Wrone, Howell, and Lewis, 2008.

4   We of course do not examine whether the public opinion patterns we see are a cause or effect of these institutional design features. This would require a very ambitious research design.

**Table 5.1.** Chapter 5 Research Questions and Data Sources

| QUESTIONS | DATASETS |
|---|---|
| Design of bureaucracy (presidential versus congressional control) | Canes-Wrone, Howell, and Lewis 2008 (with extension by Milner/Tingley) |
| Evolution of control over time (foreign aid versus intelligence) | Original case studies |
| Liberal-conservative ideology across agencies (Is there a development/trade versus security divide?) | Clinton et al. 2012 |

how these design considerations connect to our theoretical arguments. We then introduce data and analysis on how bureaucracies have been designed and the ways the president and Congress end up exerting control over these important agents in US foreign policy as a function of these design choices. The next section introduces case studies of USAID and US intelligence agencies, and we then engage with our theme about policy substitution. The final section links our results to overall themes in the book.

## Institutional Design

The construction and implementation of US policy is largely accomplished through a range of bureaucratic agencies, mainly within the executive branch of the US government. In the data we analyze there are nearly 430 separate agencies that qualified for our sample. These agencies perform a wide range of functions, from collecting information, implementing laws passed by Congress and the president, helping promote US trade interests, to planning and waging wars. The means by which these agencies were established varies considerably. Indeed some, like the National Security Agency, which was created following the Brownell Committee Report and a subsequent memorandum from the CIA with its board consisting entirely of top officials from the military and existing intelligence agencies, were deemed top secret at the time. The role of Congress in its creation appears to have been absent. Other agencies saw a more vigorous role for Congress. Explaining this variation in presidential control is important.

One theme in this literature is thinking about how the design of agencies puts them more under the control of the president or Congress.[5] If presidents

5 Epstein and O'Halloran, 1994; Huber and Shipan, 2002; Lewis, 2003; Canes-Wrone, Howell, and Lewis, 2008.

are able to exert control over a policy instrument, then this should be reflected in the way that bureaucratic agencies are created and controlled.[6] These institutional design considerations are important for a variety of reasons. To begin with, US foreign policy is implemented by these agencies. Failing to analyze the politics of foreign policy agencies would neglect a substantial portion of the political forces operative on foreign policy.[7] Looking at their institutional design features is important because, while these features may change over time, they reflect the sense at the time of implementation of what is politically feasible. Furthermore, future events can lead to change, but initial design decisions can have an impact later through a variety of processes, such as control over the ability to replace agency leadership in light of unfolding events.

Looking at the institutional design of bureaucratic agencies is also important because we can link different agencies to different policy instruments. Agencies like the African Development Foundation are clearly related to foreign aid, while the Overseas Private Investment Corporation is linked to trade and investment. As argued in chapter 2, our theory chapter, we expect Congress to be, on average, less willing to allow agencies overseeing trade and economic aid to be controlled by the president because these issues have concentrated benefits and costs for US interest groups, such as contractors and investors. They can have important distributional implications for these groups, even if on average they are small compared to other domestic issues. Defense and intelligence agencies, like the National Security Agency, are different. As discussed in chapter 2, the output of the NSA is non-excludable and hence like a public good. In our analysis below, we take advantage of the rich variation across bureaucracies in what issues they handle and how much control the president has over them.

What are the design features that we should focus on, and why are they important? It is useful in thinking about this to take a step back and look at it from the perspective of the institutional designer. Politicians care about both reelection and the implementation of their preferred policies. Consequently they will consider issues about who will lead the agency, who it will report to about what issues, who can change leadership and organization, and exactly what issues it handles. Design features have important implications for these aspects of control. For example, given the rules when these agencies were created, some agencies require partisan balancing in terms

6  The funding of agencies is something we take up in a subsequent chapter, where we contrast presidential requests and congressional authorizations by different issues areas. We arrive at very similar conclusions to the present chapter.

7  For example, a long literature in international relations documents the importance of bureaucratic actors more generally. Allison, 1969. More concretely, presidential control over intelligence agencies and the drones these agencies use in strikes typifies an important tactical turn in recent years.

of appointees. This has the effect of decreasing the impact of changes in leadership. Another example is fixed terms for commissioners. This has the effect of decreasing the influence of the executive branch as they cannot easily replace commissioners that they disagree with.[8] Below we discuss these design decisions in further detail.

Our focus on the president is somewhat different than in earlier literatures that conceptualized the design process as being driven by the nature of principal-agent relationships between Congress and the bureaucracy.[9] Given our focus on American foreign policy, it is crucial to emphasize the president. Our theoretical focus on distributional considerations connects directly with similar distinctions made by experts of agency design in the American politics literature. David Lewis, for example, writes that "Congress has delegated increasing amounts of authority to the president, both in general and specifically related to the provision of public goods ... decision making on the public goods components of foreign policy and defense has been shifting from the halls of Congress to the executive branch, as evidenced by the free hand presidents have had in committing troops, entering international agreements and setting foreign policy."[10] Our argument differs from this claim in two respects. First, we see many areas of foreign policy as having substantial distributional consequences. Not everyone benefits from a particular tariff, growing wheat for overseas food aid, or contracting for delivering technical assistance to a developing country; some gain and some lose. Some foreign policy instruments have large distributive consequences, which engender conflict and operate much like more domestic ones.

Second, some foreign policy instruments may be such that the executive branch is intimately connected to decision making on a day-to-day basis and has a substantial informational advantage over Congress.[11] As scholars note, "These [presidential] advantages are perhaps greatest in foreign policy, where the president exercises the independent constitutional authority over foreign affairs and maintains the largest informational advantage over Congress."[12] This places key agencies for executive decision making within the president's cabinet. Compared to other agencies, such as independent

---

8   Lewis, 2003, p. 3. The focus on agency design differs from a parallel, important, literature on political appointments and the policy-making process. Moe, 1982. For a model that blends insights from the design and appointment literatures, see McCarty as well as others. McCarty, 2004, McCubbins, Noll, and Weingast, 1987.

9   McCubbins, Noll, and Weingast, 1987; McCubbins, Noll, and Weingast, 1989.

10   Lewis, 2003, p. 25.

11   Similarly, presidential expert David Lewis notes, "Indeed, the president's control over information, his ability to act first, sometimes in secret, and his natural advantages over public opinion in foreign policy make it very difficult for Congress to constrain presidents." Ibid., pp. 74–75.

12   Ibid., p. 74. See also: Canes-Wrone, Howell, Lewis, and Moe, 1999.

commissions, government corporations, and legislative or judicial agencies, the president has more influence over agencies represented in his own cabinet.[13] And in particular, we argue that this influence is greater in part because these cabinet agencies keep relevant decision-making information confined to the executive branch. This informational asymmetry is very important for presidential power.[14]

Of course, by focusing on the initial design of agencies in terms of how much control the president has relative to Congress, we nevertheless acknowledge that Congress can change this relationship. For example, Epstein and O'Halloran note how "The Agency for International Development, which administers foreign aid programs, has 33 objectives and 75 priorities and must send Congress 288 reports each year";[15] and these requirements were built up over time.[16] We argue that Congress is more likely to exert control when its members see strong distributional reasons, and few reasons to allow the president to have asymmetric information. We develop this point in several case studies of particular agencies.

## Analyzing Bureaucratic Control

In this section we look at bureaucracies and ask whether their design reflects greater presidential control over some policy instruments than others. Several scholars use this approach to study questions related to our own, such as Canes-Wrone, Howell, and Lewis (hereafter CWHL).[17] Their original finding was that presidents exert a greater degree of control over foreign policy agencies than for agencies that govern domestic policies. We adopt the same strategy they used, but we disaggregate foreign policy into separate instruments. We then ask if agencies with responsibility for policy instruments having more distributive consequences are less likely to be designed in ways that give the president greater control. In turn this has consequences for information asymmetries.

We use data from CWHL that covers every executive branch agency created between 1946 and 2000, which we then updated through 2012.[18] Each

13    Emmerich, 1971; Seidman, 1998; Lewis, 2003, p. 45.

14    "When members of Congress have less information about the day-to-day workings of agencies and their policies, budgets, and programs, it is more difficult for them to publically criticize and justify opposition to the president's preferences over structure and policy, giving presidents a significant advantage (Brody 1991)." Brody, 1991. As cited in Lewis, 2003, p. 74.

15    Epstein and O'Halloran, 1994, p. 701.

16    For example, in 1993 House Resolution 2404 put in place a variety of new requirements designed to enhance congressional oversight and mandate reforms. We discuss this evolution in more detail later in the chapter.

17    Canes-Wrone, Howell, and Lewis, 2008.

18    Exactly defining what government organizations constitute an executive branch agency is somewhat complicated. We follow an expert on the issue, Lewis, and use his coding scheme.

agency was coded on four dimensions that are aggregated into a single dependent variable.

1. Is the agency headed by an administrator (implying presidential control) or a commission (suggesting more congressional control)?
2. Does the president make appointments without rules on partisan balance in the agency (presidential control) or with rules (congressional control)?
3. Can the president remove an agency head at any time (presidential control) or does the head serve for a fixed term (congressional control)?
4. Is the agency located in the cabinet or executive office of the president (presidential control) or not (congressional control)?

If the agency is structured so that the first condition for each of these four dimensions holds, then the original design of the institution is such that the president has strong control. In this case, our ordered dependent variable is equal to 4. If the second set of conditions holds for each of the four dimensions, then the president is very constrained, and our dependent variable is equal to 0. Thus larger values indicate greater presidential control, whereas lower values indicate less presidential control and instead a greater role for Congress. We also consider an alternative dependent variable below, which is just a dummy variable for whether or not the agency is represented in the president's cabinet (or executive office of the president), which should reflect the highest degree of informational asymmetry due to presence of regular cabinet-level meetings.

Next we describe our key explanatory variables. *Foreign Affairs* is simply a dummy variable for whether the agency deals with foreign affairs issues. It is taken from CWHL, where it was their key explanatory variable, allowing them to contrast foreign affairs agencies to domestic ones. Our argument is that this category should be disaggregated and recoded into different foreign policy instruments. We expect that agencies dealing with economic aid (*AidFP*), trade (*TradeFP*), and diplomacy (*DiplFP*) will look quite different from agencies directly responsible for US military policy (*MilFP*). Examples of *MilFP* agencies include the Defense Security Assistance Agency, National Security Agency, and Joint Chiefs of Staff. Examples of *AidFP* include the African Development Foundation and Agency for International Development (USAID); examples of *TradeFP* include the International Trade Administration and Overseas Private Investment Corporation; and examples of *DiplFP* include the International Communications Agency and Bureau for International Programs. The agencies in the *DiplFP* category do not fit into any of the other categories, underlining the fact that they do not match up with the policy instruments we discuss in chapter 2. Our final category, *DomMilSpendFP*, relates much more closely to what we have labeled as domestic military spending in previous chapters. This category includes the Emergency Procurement Service, Office of Minerals Mobilization, and Defense Materials Administration. Crucially, while these agencies deal with things related to the US military, they have a much more direct distributional impact compared to agencies in the *DefFP* category. Our theory suggests that they should be more controlled by Congress, but we can empirically test this.

We expect the military-related agencies to be the most under presidential control, and the trade and economic aid categories should be the least under presidential control. Our predictions about the agencies related to diplomacy were not developed in chapter 2. We suspect they lie somewhere between military and the more distributive aid and trade instruments. As such, we assign them their own category.[19] In the models then, as in chapter 4, the policy instruments serve as proxies for our two key independent variables: the extent of distributive conflict and the degree of ideological divisions.

We largely follow the statistical specifications used by CWHL. We, however, also add two additional control variables: *Pres Pop*, which is the average presidential popularity in the year the agency was created and *GDP change*, which is the change in GDP in constant dollars from the previous year. These controls seem very important; we contrast our argument about presidential power with ones that attribute his influence to his domestic popularity, which may depend on the state of the economy as well as other factors. We thus need to control for these other influences to bring us closer to the claim that it is the characteristics of the policy instrument that is shaping his relationship with Congress. We include the other control variables CWHL used,[20] and estimate models with and without presidential fixed effects.[21] We also exclude the interaction between their foreign affairs indicator and unified government, which was never significant in their analysis or in ours. We use an ordered probit model given the ordered nature of the first dependent variable and a probit model for when our dependent variable is the dichotomous indicator for whether or not the agency is in

19    In chapter 4 on the roll call votes in Congress and elsewhere we are able to observe political action on our full set of narrower policy instruments. In this chapter this is not possible for immigration, sanctions, and geopolitical aid because there are not agencies in the data that solely focus on those instruments. And categories like "diplomacy" are more akin to the issue area literature rather than our focus on particular policy instruments.

20    These include indicator variables for the presence of unified government, a time of war, whether the agency is funded by a line in the budget, deals with adjudicative issues, and whether the agency was created by statute. In separate models we also estimated models that controlled for the size (in terms of budget) of the agency. This did not change our results, but this variable is missing in the original data for nearly half of all observations.

21    The use of presidential fixed effects has relatively little impact on our core results, but helps guard against omitted variables that are constant within a presidency.

the president's cabinet. All models cluster standard errors by year. While we present results based only on their original data, we also updated the data to include agencies created after their data ends in 2000. To do this we followed their coding procedure, and drew on a variety of sources to collect the list of agencies created after 2000, up to 2012.

We present the results in table 5.2. Models B1 and B2 use the original data from CWHL, and the remaining models use new data collected to extend the coverage to the present day. Model B1 includes the original specification whereas the other models disaggregate and recode the foreign policy variable as discussed above. Models B1–B3 use the original ordered dependent variable from CWHL, and model B4 uses a binary variable indicating if the agency is represented in the president's cabinet. In all of these models the excluded category is domestic policy agencies. The dependent variable then indicates the extent to which the design of the agency gives power to the president, with higher values indicating more influence. A positive coefficient on the main independent variables relating to the type of foreign policy the agency deals with indicates greater control by the president, relative to agencies concerned with domestic policy.

The results largely conform to our predictions, showing the important need to disaggregate foreign affairs agencies. Different agencies deal with different types of foreign policy issues, and this matters and is reflected in their different designs. The coefficient on *Foreign Affairs* in model B1 is positive and significant, indicating support for the standard "two presidencies" perspective. Presidents have more control over foreign policy agencies than domestic ones. But models B2–B7 showcase our contribution. Here we see that the effect of the *Foreign Affairs* variable is largely driven by particular sets of agencies. The largest impact on presidential control comes from agencies in the *MilFP* category. These agencies, like the National Security Agency, tend to be highly controlled by the president. Agencies involved with trade, economic aid, or public diplomacy look on average like other domestic policy agencies. They were not significantly different from the excluded domestic agency category. The more anomalous result from the perspective of our theory is that agencies in charge of domestic military spending, according to our categorization, were under more control by the president than these other categories like economic aid. This is inconsistent with our results in previous chapters, and may reflect how some of these agencies were first designed in the immediate post–World War II era under heavy presidential influence.

Next we present these results graphically given that regression coefficients on ordered probit and probit models are not directly interpretable. We present a first difference analysis in figures 5.1 and 5.2. To do this, we changed each of our policy instrument variables one at a time from 0 to 1, and calculated the change in probability for *each level* of our dependent variable in the or-

## Table 5.2. Bureaucratic Control Analysis

| | B1 | B2 | B3 | B4 | B5 | B6 | B7 |
|---|---|---|---|---|---|---|---|
| Foreign Affairs | 0.38+ | | | | | | |
| | [0.22] | | | | | | |
| MilFP | | 0.67+ | 0.80* | 0.74* | 0.79* | 0.61* | 1.07** |
| | | [0.38] | [0.40] | [0.31] | [0.35] | [0.29] | [0.31] |
| DomMilSpendFP | | 0.43** | 0.65** | 0.36* | 0.63** | 0.60** | 0.90** |
| | | [0.15] | [0.18] | [0.15] | [0.18] | [0.20] | [0.20] |
| DiplFP | | −0.10 | −0.06 | −0.14 | −0.12 | −0.43 | −0.25 |
| | | [0.40] | [0.42] | [0.40] | [0.41] | [0.61] | [0.62] |
| TradeFP | | −0.21 | −0.30 | −0.19 | −0.29 | −0.25 | −0.36 |
| | | [0.38] | [0.39] | [0.38] | [0.38] | [0.38] | [0.42] |
| AidFP | | −0.16 | −0.14 | −0.31 | −0.34 | −0.23 | 0.09 |
| | | [0.43] | [0.47] | [0.39] | [0.44] | [0.48] | [0.55] |
| Unified Govt | −0.66** | 0.05 | −0.55** | −0.02 | −0.54** | −0.05 | −0.81** |
| | [0.19] | [0.15] | [0.19] | [0.15] | [0.19] | [0.19] | [0.23] |
| War | 0.07 | −0.07 | 0.00 | 0.03 | 0.02 | −0.15 | 0.10 |
| | [0.21] | [0.15] | [0.21] | [0.16] | [0.22] | [0.18] | [0.24] |
| Budget Line | 0.14 | 0.24* | 0.18+ | 0.24* | 0.22* | 0.15 | 0.04 |
| | [0.10] | [0.10] | [0.10] | [0.09] | [0.10] | [0.13] | [0.13] |
| By Statute | −1.10** | −1.03** | −1.13** | −0.95** | −1.13** | −0.66** | −0.69** |
| | [0.15] | [0.14] | [0.14] | [0.13] | [0.14] | [0.17] | [0.18] |
| Adjudicative | −1.22** | −1.21** | −1.18** | −1.01** | −1.02** | −1.03** | −0.85** |
| | [0.18] | [0.16] | [0.17] | [0.23] | [0.21] | [0.25] | [0.22] |
| Avg. Pop. | −0.00 | 0.01+ | −0.00 | 0.01+ | 0.00 | 0.01 | −0.00 |
| | [0.00] | [0.00] | [0.00] | [0.00] | [0.00] | [0.01] | [0.01] |
| GDP Change | −0.00 | 0.00 | −0.00 | 0.00+ | −0.00 | −0.00 | −0.00 |
| | [0.00] | [0.00] | [0.00] | [0.00] | [0.00] | [0.00] | [0.00] |
| Observations | 407 | 407 | 407 | 429 | 429 | 432 | 432 |

Standard errors in brackets, $+p < 0.10$, $*p < 0.05$, $**p < 0.01$.

Models B1 and B2 use the original data from Canes-Wrone et al. B2 breaks apart the foreign policy variable into different foreign policy instruments. B3–B7 use new data collected to extend the coverage to the modern day. B1–B5 use the original ordered dependent variable from Canes-Wrone et al., and B6–B7 use a binary variable indicating if the agency is represented in the president's cabinet. B1, B3, B5, and B7 include president fixed effects (omitted). Standard errors clustered at the year level.

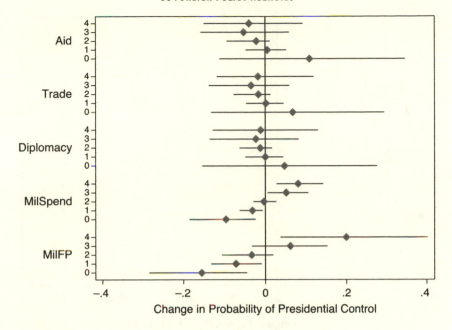

**Figure 5.1.** Simulated first differences for bureaucratic control analysis. 90% confidence intervals for each of the groups of bureaucracies that correspond to our foreign policy instruments using model B4 (ordered probit model) from table 5.2. Results obtained using estsimp in Stata.

dered probit model (using model B4), and the probability of being in the president's cabinet for the dichotomous probit model (using model B7).[22]

Interpretation of these plots is straightforward. The x-axis represents the probability scale (0 to 1). Changes in the probability of the outcome shifting each policy instrument indicator from 0 to 1 are graphed. Values further to the right illustrate greater presidential control. For example, in figure 5.1, there were 5 possible levels of the dependent variable, with a 0 the least control and a 4 the most control. A change in probability is given for each of these levels. The effect of the *MilFP* is to decrease the probability of no control by nearly .2 (on a 0 to 1 scale) and increase the probability of the highest level of control by .2. In contrast, for *Aid*, the effect is positive on the lowest level of control, though consistent with the regression table these effects were insignificant. We again see marked differences between the military and non-military agencies, as expected in the model of placement in the president's cabinet.

22   We kept the presidential fixed effects as the excluded category, set our policy instrument indicators to 0, set the continuous variables to their sample medians, and fixed the other binary indicators to 1. Calculations were performed using the quasi-Bayesian bootstrap procedure commonly known as Clarify with 1,000 simulations.

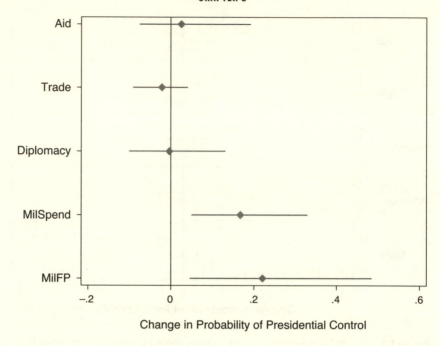

**Figure 5.2.** Simulated first differences for bureaucratic control analysis. 90% confidence intervals for each of the groups of bureaucracies that correspond to our foreign policy instruments using model B7 (probit model) from table 5.2. Results obtained using estsimp in Stata.

The preceding analysis suggests strong support for our argument that the politics of control over foreign policy agencies differs substantially by the policy instruments that an agency oversees. Neither presidential popularity nor presence of international conflict has much effect. Rather, across agencies we see differences, as we expect. Agencies that govern aid and trade policies on average—and controlling for potential confounding factors with standard variables as well as presidential fixed effects—look similar to agencies that govern domestic politics. On the other hand, again on average, agencies tightly connected to the US military establishment, which, as we have argued in chapter 2, have fewer distributional implications and ideological divisions, are designed such that the president has more control over them.

## Case Studies

In this section we focus on several important agencies for the creation and implementation of American foreign policy. This section complements our quantitative analysis. We show that if you look at the historical cases, they reveal how the design and evolution of the agency reflected concerns about distributive politics and in parts its relationship to information provision. We note debates about the degree of presidential power and design of the agency. And we give a better sense of how change over time happens, and how it is often driven by concerns over presidential power. So for several agencies we discuss their creation and evolution. First, we document the arguments, rationales, and political environments surrounding the creation of these agencies. Second, we explore the evolution of these agencies, if any, to better understand how the politics of control unfolds over time and across multiple administrations.

We focus on two cases. The first is USAID, which is the main US bilateral aid agency. The second is the Defense Intelligence Agency along with several other military and intelligence related agencies. We have chosen these agencies for several reasons. First, they provide variation across our policy instruments, giving us a broad view of the nuances of politics around these agencies. Second, as we discuss below, USAID and DIA were created around the same time and in the above data are actually coded as under the president's control. This means that if in the previous regression results USAID was coded as more under congressional control, our results would be even stronger. While our actual results already paint a supportive picture of our theory, here we show that Congress has been able to claw back control over USAID to a large extent. This is in contrast to congressional efforts to do so for agencies like the DIA, which have been much less successful.

## USAID

USAID is the main bilateral aid agency for the United States. In 2012 its staff numbered 3,658 and had an operations budget of $11 billion.[23] It is the largest bilateral aid agency in the world, and only the multilateral World Bank has a larger budget. Its current mission statement is to "(s)hape and sustain a peaceful, prosperous, just, and democratic world and foster conditions for stability and progress for the benefit of the American people and people everywhere." This USAID case shows that the agency started out under strong presidential control. But once Congress realized the importance of the agency and the distributive consequences of aid-giving, it quickly moved to take much greater control over USAID.

At its creation, USAID was relatively more under the control of the president than Congress, according to Lewis's coding scheme. It received a score of 4 out 4, with the president appointing an administrator, not having to balance party membership, able to name the head, and having the agency

23   In contrast, total World Bank lending in 2012 was approximately $35 billion.

located within the executive branch.[24] This set of initial facts is inconsistent with our theoretical predictions about economic aid, so it is essential to understand this important case historically.

During the 1950s, with the Korean War a recent memory and the spread of Communism a continual threat, the US foreign policy establishment increasingly relied on foreign aid as an instrument. This culminated in President Kennedy's reorganization and consolidation of US foreign aid programs. In part to initiate what became known as the "development decade," there were important security motivations for foreign economic aid during this era. "The expansion of the aid program leading up to and including the 1961 initiatives paralleled an increase in the perceived security threat of spreading communism. Aid was intended as a weapon to address that threat."[25] The precursor agencies used for aid delivery, Mutual Security Agency, Foreign Operations Administration, and International Cooperation Agency, were fused to become USAID, but the new Agency for International Development inherited some of the motivations of the previous agencies crafted in the early days of the Cold War. Indeed, a confidential committee draft in 1961 was called the Mutual Security Act, but was later changed to the Act for International Development, with the intent to authorize the creation of USAID. In September 1961, Kennedy signed the subsequent legislative vehicle to authorize creation of the new agency. With Executive Order 10973, Section 102, USAID was formally created.

While the commercial and economic consequences of foreign aid were well known and discussed in the run-up to the 1961 reforms, the centrality of aid to US national security was critical to the establishment and structuring of USAID. However, congressional assertiveness in controlling USAID quickly became the norm. Legislatively this was done via the Foreign Assistance Act of 1961 (P.L. 87-195), but also through the frequent refusal to pass yearly authorization legislation or enact a new law.[26] Legal scholar Jeffrey Meyer breaks down congressional control of US foreign assistance programs, including USAID, into a delegation phase (1961–1972), an investigation phase (1972–1983), and a review phase (1983–1988).[27] With each new phase, congressional assertiveness grew.

24   Specifically, USAID was installed as part of the State Department, which was a cabinet-level position.

25   Hagen and Ruttan, 1988, p. 3.

26   "In 1973, Congress amended the Foreign Assistance Act to steer funds into specific, functional categories including education, agriculture and family planning. The aid structure developed by the amendments remains largely intact today." Bristol, 2011, p. 538.

27   "During the 'delegation phase,' from 1961 until 1972, Congress extended to the president wide latitude to bypass statutory restrictions imposed on foreign assistance, reserving for itself few tools to control executive discretion. During the 'investigation phase,' from 1972 until 1983, Congress tightened its controls by instituting systematic and detailed reporting require-

The sources of the desire for control have varied over time. One major source of congressional assertiveness reflects economic interests. Congress is regularly briefed about the economic benefits of aid to the US economy, and at times tallies aid spending per congressional district. Congressional interest in economic aid then reflects the distributional nature of aid and the electoral benefits to legislators of directing aid flows. In describing the ways that Congress shapes US foreign aid, Bruce Jentleson notes "the proliferation of 'earmarking', the foreign aid equivalent of domestic entitlements . . . Given the multiple priorities injected into the process by individual members of Congress, the various executive branch actors with interests in foreign aid, and powerful interest groups, very little nondiscretionary foreign aid is left."[28]

It is no surprise, then, that the United States has resisted international efforts to "de-tie" aid; that is, Congress has refused to abide by international standards that advocate for aid contracts not to be serviced necessarily by US companies.[29] Similarly, US food aid, under PL-480, has long required US food to be sourced from American farmers and shipped by American ships. The role of economic interest groups operating through Congress is not a new phenomenon, as evidenced by various restrictions put in place on aid during the 1960s.[30] The entrenched nature of these interests was on display more recently when the Obama administration proposed relaxing these rules about food aid due to increasing evidence that these policies are deleterious to aid recipients (see additional discussion in chapter 3).

Ideological sources of assertiveness by Congress are also evident. Efforts to cut foreign aid began in earnest with the Republicans elected in 1994 and led by Newt Gingrich. At that time Jesse Helms and others squarely put their sites on USAID, attempting to slash its budgets and dictate its

---

ments and initiating expedited voting procedures to review executive action. Finally, during the 'review phase', from 1983 until the present, Congress put itself into a position to review and participate more effectively in foreign assistance policy through devices such as objective definitional limits, expanded consultation requirements, independent fact-finding, shortened authorization periods, and expansion of expedited review procedures." Meyer, 1988, pp. 72–73.

28    Jentleson, 1990, p. 172.

29    "Furthermore, Congress maintained its practice of tying specific aid programmes to the purchase of US goods and services, a practice inconsistent with the new aid regime. The 'earmarking' of aid projects to unrelated federal spending bills further limited the president's ability to pursue a coordinated aid programme." Hook, 1998, p. 169.

30    "A 1960 appropriations suggestion to deny funds for programs that compete with United States agriculture, a suggested 1964 authorization limitation requiring AID and recipient countries to purchase oil at competitive market prices, and a 1967 authorization provision requiring that all auto purchases be made from United States firms are all directly traceable to interest group pressures. . . . Although interest group pressures are probably not as strenuously and consistently applied to the foreign aid program as they are to most domestic programs, there is still evidence to indicate that 'who gets what' in foreign aid is somewhat dependent upon 'who demanded what." Morrow, 1968, p. 1006.

policies.[31] In chapter 4 we examined congressional roll call votes that were taken about some of these attempts. USAID, and the rest of the foreign aid establishment, was constantly cast by conservative leaders as inefficient and ineffective.

One politically charged set of controls included proposals to prevent USAID funds going to support anything related to abortion. Essentially, the national debate about abortion domestically was mapped directly onto the besieged USAID.[32] The first restrictions were led by Jesse Helms in 1973 in an amendment to the Foreign Assistance Act. This was reinforced by the "Mexico City Rule," which was made by the Reagan administration but pushed for by conservative congresspersons; funds from the US government for overseas family planning programs, largely administered through USAID, were restricted unless there were extreme mitigating circumstances such as rape. Under the Clinton administration the rule was rescinded but was put back in place by a Republican dominated Congress in 1999 following years of struggles.[33]

How has Congress sought to control USAID, in light of the fact that institutionally it is positioned to be under greater control by the president? One mechanism, mentioned earlier, is through reporting requirements. These reporting requirements cover a broad range of behaviors, from communicating the goals of certain aid programs to notifications of any shifts in funds from one program to another. How onerous are these reporting requirements? Reviewing the data as of 1989, Bruce Jentleson noted with respect to USAID that "(o)nly the Department of Defense has more, yet it has a budget fifty times greater."[34] This congressional involvement is in stark contrast to earlier detachment. Writing in the late 1960s William Morrow noted that "AID and its predecessor agencies have always been allowed broad authority in the use of appropriated funds. Money has often made available on an 'area' or 'fund' basis, and only infrequently are stipulations attached to earmark funds for specified activities within these categories."[35]

31    Doherty, 1996.

32    At other times, congressional pushing has gone the other way. Republican presidents have resisted efforts by congressional Democrats to provide, and increase, funds to population programs like the UNFPA. Baker, 2009.

33    "Year after year, an intensely committed anti-abortion minority in the House of Representatives sought to re-impose the policy. Their goal was not only to establish more abortion-related restrictions in foreign aid legislation, but also to limit the resources and influence of USAID's international family planning programme, the IPFF and UNFPA." Crane and Dusenberry, 2004, p. 130.

34    Jentleson, 1990, p. 174. We would argue that this contrast with the Department of Defense having more reporting requirements does not undermine our broader argument about congressional control precisely because the implication of Jentleson's statement is that relative to its size, USAID is extremely hamstrung by these requirements.

35    Morrow, 1968, p. 990.

Historically, some congressional assertiveness has been directly tied to trying to constrain the president's ability to use aid programs to advance narrower geostrategic concerns and to put more control on the conditions under which US allies receive aid. Many of these efforts were directed toward aid outside the economic development purview. But given that USAID in the 1960s had more of an explicit linkage to geo-security than it does today, it was caught up in some of these efforts, especially during the Vietnam War.[36] The beginning of these efforts can be traced back to the 1971/72 amendment to the Foreign Assistance Act (S 2819–PL 92-226). However, in subsequent debates it became clear that the president would have much greater authority when it came to security assistance funds, even though many of the reforms were an attempt to rein the president back in.[37] For example, the 1981 Foreign Aid Authorization bill "significantly strengthened the president's hand in deciding when and how to use aid as a foreign policy tool.... Carter had asked Congress to loosen its grip on the foreign aid program, saying he needed greater flexibility to provide military aid 'to meet unforeseen foreign policy and security emergencies.'"[38] Similar patterns of acquiescence to the president followed in subsequent appropriations bills.[39] This acquiescence surrounding geopolitical aid is in contrast to sustained congressional assertiveness in the same period on economic aid.[40]

The 1990s saw one of the most sustained attacks by Congress on USAID to date. Our roll call votes from this era show how Congress repeatedly sought to de-fund USAID and other aid agencies. Much of this effort was led by congressional Republicans seeking to end government spending on programs they opposed. Oftentimes the debates focused on the tradeoffs faced, with economic aid programs cast as competing with money that could be spent more directly on US schools or infrastructure. Another issue

36  Ibid.; Congressional Quarterly, 1981.
37  Congressional Record, 1973.
38  Congressional Quarterly, 1981, p. 81.
39  For example, in discussing the 1984 fiscal year appropriations bill, the *Congressional Quarterly* noted, "The bill gave Reagan much more freedom to allocate military aid among countries than any president had had in recent years." Congressional Quarterly, 1985, p. 161.
40  For example, in discussing the 1984 Authorization and 1985 appropriation, the *Congressional Quarterly* noted attempts to maintain economic aid to Africa in light of the Reagan administration considering various cuts. "Congress specified that Africa should get at least as much in no-interest loans from the International Development Association (IDA) during the next three years as it did during the previous three years. The move was made to protect Africa from the administration's decision to cut the U.S. contribution to IDA, which contributed to a projected drop in IDA's lending pool from $12 billion to $9 billion in fiscal 1985–88." Ibid., p. 173.

Recent examples of this are clear in congressional opposition to giving aid to Egypt following the turbulence in the summer of 2013, though ultimately here the Obama administration made the decision to suspend some military aid to Egypt. Given that USAID does not deliver military aid that was primarily threatened they were kept out of the fray.

taken up in the early 1990s dealt with the rewriting of the foreign aid au-thorization bill, which had not been renewed since the mid-1980s because of political struggles in Congress. While there seemed to be consensus that reform was needed, it was blocked in part because of congressional con-cern that they could be giving up control. The *Congressional Quarterly* put this bluntly: "members could not agree on a new approach to foreign aid, and they strongly resisted proposals that would reduce their own power to channel foreign aid to favored programs. Where the administration saw reform, many lawmakers saw a potential raid on their authority in foreign policy and on their power of the purse."[41] In many cases, the cuts in US foreign aid during this period focused on development aid to poorer coun-tries, leaving intact geopolitical aid (an example being HR 1561 in 1996). Throughout the 1990s and early 2000s, abortion-related issues continued to stall legislation about US foreign assistance programs.

These high levels of activity can be seen in figure 5.3. We used every *New York Times* article from January 1, 1987 to June 19, 2007 that contained the words "Agency for International Development" or "USAID." [42] We then estimated a Structural Topic Model (STM) to analyze all 1,479 of these arti-cles.[43] The STM is a type of unsupervised text analysis method derived from methods in machine learning. We introduced this model in more detail in chapter 3, where we use it to analyze descriptions of lobbying. We focus on a single topic, which can be thought of as a set of words that often oc-curred together within news articles that focused on Congress and USAID. The collection of words related to this topic includes words like "Congress," "budgets," "Helms," among others. Words that most exclusively relate to this topic are presented in the left-hand side of figure 5.3. Other topics dealt with USAID activities overseas and other things unrelated to what interests us here, which is the role of Congress. On the right-hand side of figure 5.3 we plot the estimated proportion of news articles that are dedicated to this congressional topic over time. We see a sharp spike during the 1990s. The key finding is the large increase in congressional activity during the 1990s around USAID, which is also consistent with our reading of the legisla-tive record. The news articles during this time period covered Congress's Republican-led attempts to control USAID, often through control over budgets and other mechanisms.

41   Congressional Quarterly, 1997, p. 204. Furthermore, the administration's attention was focused on military type issues and so made less of an effort to battle Congress on this issue. "The reform effort was also hurt by weak lobbying on the part of the administration. Clinton did not weigh in on the issue, and his top foreign policy advisers were preoccupied with high-stakes international crises, such as the nuclear weapons program in North Korea." Ibid.

42   Available as the "New York Times Annotated Corpus." For other researchers using this corpus, see https://groups.google.com/forum/#!forum/nytnlp.

43   Roberts, Stewart, and Tingley, 2014.

**Exclusive Words**

**Congress Topic Prevalence Over Time**

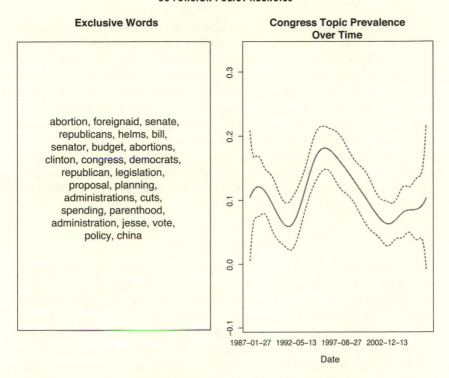

abortion, foreignaid, senate, republicans, helms, bill, senator, budget, abortions, clinton, congress, democrats, republican, legislation, proposal, planning, administrations, cuts, spending, parenthood, administration, jesse, vote, policy, china

1987–01–27  1992–05–13  1997–08–27  2002–12–13

Date

**Figure 5.3.** *New York Times* coverage of congressional intervention on USAID. All *New York Times* articles that mention USAID were analyzed with a structural topic model. We display here what we call the congressional intervention topic. The left figure displays the words most exclusive to this topic compared to other topics that highlights the salient role played by congressional actors. On the right is the expected proportion of each article that deals with this topic over time. Model estimated with stm package in R using date (in a spline to allow for nonlinearities) as a topic prevalence covariate. Results show the strong uptick of congressional interference during the mid-1990s.

In recent years the role of Congress in controlling USAID is also quite clear. USAID administrator Rajiv Shah remarked: "(l)ike an enterprise, we're focused on delivering the highest possible value for our shareholders. In this case, the American people and the congressional leaders who represent them."[44] Given Congress's history of interventions and manipulation of the agency, this vision of USAID is perhaps unsurprising. Beyond operational mandates, Congress also continues to have a central role in the reform and reorganization of the agency and US foreign aid policy more generally, a fact recognized by congressional observers.[45]

44  Shah, 2011.
45  "Congress is driving the reassessment of development policy already under way with a series of legislative initiatives from Berman and the two leaders of the Senate Foreign Relations

As this discussion shows, USAID, and the control over USAID, has changed over time. Since USAID's establishment, and certainly by the 1970s, Congress held considerable sway over the agency. Hence while the data used in the previous section accurately codes USAID to have been designed to be highly controlled by the president, Congress nevertheless has found ways to wrest control away from the president. While the observations cast some skepticism about the long-run implications of initial institutional rules, their evolution with respect to USAID is consistent with our theoretical arguments. When a foreign policy instrument involves deep ideological divisions and important distributional consequences, Congress will want to and try to exert an influential role. This is precisely what we observe in the case of USAID.

## Intelligence Agencies

The origin and functioning of US intelligence agencies have long been highly secretive. With the Cold War ramping up in the 1940s, the United States began to create agencies for military intelligence. The CIA was established in the National Security Act of 1947, the National Security Agency was established via a top secret memo in October 1952, Defense Intelligence Agency (DIA) was established on August 1, 1961, the same year as USAID. Following the creation of these agencies, congressional oversight was minimal for many years. Indeed, the first hearing on the NSA took place twenty-five years after its formation, and congresspersons charged with overseeing the CIA felt it was in the national security interest of the United States to simply trust the CIA.

The DIA, perhaps less well known, was the result of an Eisenhower-era Joint Study group seeking ways to organize military intelligence activities. The DIA was to be responsible for providing the Secretary of Defense, the staff assistants to the Secretary, the military departments, the Joint Chiefs of Staff, specialized Department of Defense agencies, unified and specialized

---

Committee: Chairman John Kerry, a Massachusetts Democrat, and top Republican Richard G. Lugar of Indiana," Cadei, 2010, p. 1728.

Other economic aid programs like PEPFAR and the Millennium Challenge Corporation (MCC) were initially presidential initiatives indicating an effort to create new aid institutions unburdened by constraints and protocol in place in organizations like USAID. However, it is well understood that organizations like the MCC were quickly subjected to congressional oversight and control. Nowels, 2003; Rose, 2014. For example, the Congressional Research Service noted that "Since its inception, Congress has closely followed MCC implementation." Tarnoff, 2014, p. 2. The contrast with geopolitical aid is seen in a 2004 *Congress and the Nation* article discussing how Congress had underfunded the MCC by nearly a billion dollars, but then went on to say that "(t)he bill met the White House requests to boost economic and military aid for U.S. allies such as Israel, Poland, Pakistan, and Afghanistan." Congressional Quarterly, 2005, p. 293.

commands, and other national intelligence community organizations with military intelligence. Formally the DIA would report to the Secretary of Defense through the Joint Chiefs of Staff. In the data coding by CWHL, the DIA was coded to be most strongly under the control of the president; it was rated a 4 in their scheme.

Beginning in the early 1970s and in response to allegations of domestic eavesdropping and other scandals, the DIA, and other national intelligence agencies, began to be attacked by Congress, largely because of their intense secretiveness.[46] In 1971 Stuart Symington (D-MO) began a campaign to remove some of this secrecy in the only real way a congressperson could: through control over their budgets. Congressman Symington offered an amendment to place a $4 billion ceiling on fiscal 1972 expenditures by the Central Intelligence Agency, National Security Agency, Defense Intelligence Agency, and for intelligence work performed for the army, navy, and air force. In explaining his amendment to the Senate, he argued that its purpose was to get an idea of the ways the intelligence community was spending the money and how much they were receiving. The only people who knew this information besides the president were a small group of senior committee persons on the Intelligence and Appropriations committees. He said he had called the Appropriations Committee and requested budget information. "I was told that, except for the five senior members of the Senate Appropriations Committee, they (the staff) had been instructed not to talk about these multi-billion dollar intelligence appropriations."[47] The DIA and other intelligence agencies had effectively shielded themselves from Congress as an institution. Senator Fulbright interjected, stating, "I have never heard of this before, except from the Executive Branch."

Symington's arguments focused on bureaucratic waste but most pointedly about how an executive branch–led reorganization of the intelligence community was putting intelligence strictly under the direction of the military and White House. "This gives Executive privilege to the final policymakers, and therefore, except for the power of the purse, enables said policymakers to, in effect, take the entire question of intelligence out of the hands of Congress."[48] "I am certain in my own mind that we would not have engaged in at least one war—killing people and having our own killed—if pressures, combined with unwarranted secrecy, had not been characteristics of our intelligence knowledge and activities in that country; because our

46  Congress held its first "true" hearing of NSA in 1975. The hearing ... "was scheduled to examine allegations that certain federal agencies [...] have regularly intercepted and copied personal telegrams and cables for at least 30 years without court order." Committee on Government Operations, 1975, p. 2.
47  Symington, 1971, p. 42924. Also see Congressional Quarterly, 1972.
48  Symington, 1971, p. 42924.

political and military actions were approved by the Congress on the basis of misinformation and a lack of information."[49]

The opposition, led by Senator Ellender, led his argument by saying, "I hesitate to have these programs submitted to the committee of the whole because of the highly sensitive nature of the material that come before us. . . . my fear is that if this material were made widely available, we would do harm to our own intelligence operations."[50] This theme is precisely in line with our discussion in chapter 2, where we argued that some policy instruments generate information asymmetries, especially if they entail few distributional consequences for interest groups. Indeed, much of the subsequent discussion focused on how little concrete information was available to the Senate on a number of matters, including US involvement in Laos. Symington's amendment failed a 31–56 roll call vote (Senate Vote 363, D: 28-20, Republican 3-34).[51]

Momentum in Congress to rein in the intelligence agencies serving under the president developed throughout the early 1970s, largely due to an array of scandals such as Watergate, US involvement in the Chilean elections of 1970, and US military activity in Laos.[52] Investigative committees were set up in both chambers with a call to bring to the public information about funding for these agencies. In 1975 the House Appropriations committee revealed that it had cut funding to some intelligence agencies, but, contra previous commitments to transparency, refused to reveal funding levels for the DIA, CIA, and other related agencies. Two committee votes in the Defense subcommittee of the appropriations committee to either reveal funding amounts to these agencies to the rest of the Appropriations committee or publish the CIA's budget were defeated. Reporting on the votes, the *Congressional Quarterly* explained the committee's decision as "Stating that intelligence operations must remain secret if they were to be successful, the committee contended that disclosure of the intelligence budget and the committee's recommendations might well lead to demands for the publication of ever-increasing data and could prove harmful to our intelligence efforts."[53]

Congressional demands for greater oversight began to increase. Following reports highlighting the lack of statutory authority of the DIA and related agencies, and minimal oversight abilities by Congress that had allowed it and other intelligence agencies to engage in unacceptable behav-

49    Ibid., p. 42925.
50    Ibid., p. 42928.
51    Debate begins on page 42923 on November 23, 1971. "I became concerned that, because of their lack of knowledge of certain intelligence matters bearing on foreign policy, members of the Foreign Relations Committee were not in a position to make intelligent judgment of certain US policies overseas." Ibid.
52    Congressional Quarterly, 1976b.
53    Congressional Quarterly, 1976a.

iors, the Ford administration preemptively began to make changes in 1975. Implementing two-thirds of the recommendation of the Rockefeller Commission,[54] President Ford began to make changes. However, many of them were focused on changes to domestic activities (mail openings, wire taps, etc.), though some focused on foreign activities such as assassinations. Ford refused to disclose budget information or "readily agree" to congressional oversight. Rather, the first Executive Order on intelligence on February 18, 1976 (E.O. 11905) established the Committee on Foreign Intelligence as part of the National Security Council and which reported to the president.[55]

Oversight committees eventually were set up in Congress, known as select intelligence committees. For the NSA, these committees arose out of concerns about unsupervised domestic eavesdropping activity. In 2013, with the leaks by former NSA contractor Edward Snowden, it is apparent that congressional constraints on the NSA did little to circumscribe NSA activities. For the CIA, committee members regularly complained. Britt Snider, the CIA Inspector General from 1998 to 2001 and counsel to the Church Committee in the 1970s, describes the relationship in a way that suggests Congress was continuously circumvented by the executive branch, despite special oversight committees.[56] Some of this is administration-specific, other problems are due to the institutional design arrangements: the president was required to inform members of key committees shortly after a CIA "finding," but he could limit this "in special cases" to only committee leaders, or the rule that the president needed to approve every CIA covert action, so as to take away his plausible deniability. Furthermore, Snider describes how overseeing members of Congress complained they weren't informed adequately (too little, too late), and that they were expected not to share overwhelming amounts of information with their colleagues (including those on the subcommittee on oversight).

More recent efforts by Congress have fallen short as well. For example, in 1994 some in Congress felt the need to establish a permanent Inspector General position at the DIA and National Security Agency as part of the 1995 intelligence authorization bill. However, the amendment was dropped from the final version of the bill.[57] In 2008, President Bush successfully vetoed the Intelligence Authorization Act in part because it called for the creation of these Inspector General positions.[58] More recently, even with

54 The Rockefeller Commission, named after its chair—then Vice President Rockefeller— was the executive branch's investigative panel charged with looking into the illegal domestic activities of the CIA. It is the executive branch's counterpart to the Church and Nedzi/Pike Committees. For more, see Federation of American Scientists, 1996.

55 For the EO, see here: https://www.fas.org/irp/offdocs/eo11905.htm.

56 Snider, 2008, pp. 60–70.

57 Congressional Quarterly, 1995.

58 Congressional Quarterly, 2009.

all of the revelations made by the leaks from Snowden, Congress remained stymied when it came to oversight of intelligence programs. Furthermore, in 2014, key members of Congress accused the CIA of spying on them. And even members of the Senate Intelligence committee admit they are overwhelmed and under-informed.[59]

Overall, we find less evidence of congressional success in constraining the president and his intelligence agencies when compared to USAID.[60] While USAID and the DIA were created at the same time, and with the same institutional design favoring the executive branch, their trajectory was very different. In the end, USAID's administrator, as quoted above, recognized the paramount role of Congress in USAID; the same cannot be said about the relationship between the intelligence community and Congress. Instead, the president remains firmly in control when it comes to policy instruments that have few distributional implications and large asymmetries in information. Agencies that have important distributional implications and small information asymmetries, like USAID, are ones where Congress has been able to legislate control over the agency away from the executive branch.

With these case studies, we acknowledge that the structure of the American bureaucratic system was not established at one point and then allowed to determine all subsequent political relationships. While our quantitative analysis suggested support for our arguments, our case studies recognize that actors like the president and Congress can and do work overtime to change institutional arrangements. While the original institutional design for USAID put it well within the control of the president, this quickly began to erode. Indeed, some have argued that the evolution of the Millennium Challenge Corporation looks no different: it was a presidential initiative that got coopted by Congress. By taking on an "outlier" in our quantitative results and contrasting it with the historical trajectory of agencies that were not outliers, we bolster confidence in our results.

## Implications for Substitution

What implications does our analysis have for policy substitution? In this section we briefly consider several implications. To revisit, foreign policy substitution involves using multiple policy instruments, each of which could be used to reach the objective. If substitution is easy, then shifting across

---

59  Senator King: "We are 15 people overseeing a $50 billion enterprise, I can't tell you I know with certainty every intelligence program this enterprise is engaged in." Quoted in Mazzetti, 2014.

60  Similarly, many have claimed that presidents have actively gained increasing amounts of power in agencies like the Department of Defense and other agencies with a high connection to national security. Howell, 2013.

policy instruments—which can also mean shifting across agencies—is less costly, and the optimal mix of policy instruments for the situation can be deployed.

Our findings about bureaucratic control suggest that presidential efforts to substitute between trade and aid, for example, will be difficult. Moving away from aid and toward trade, for example, means that congressional coalitions in support of engagement will need to be modified. Furthermore, agencies that control aid, like USAID, will have to appeal to Congress because Congress controls their funding and has, as discussed above, increasingly come to oversee the agency. Similarly, presidents may also have a difficult time controlling agencies that use the policy instrument they wish to substitute towards and subsequently use more of. If instead these agencies are required to see Congress as their main boss, then the design of aid policy will be more difficult to control. As we discuss in chapters 7 (our case study chapter) and 8 (our conclusion), this suggests one reason why presidents might be tempted to militarize American foreign policy. Indeed, we have shown in this chapter that presidents have much greater control over such agencies.

A final consideration with respect to policy substitution is whether there exist ideological differences across agencies. If on average different bureaucracies contain a similar mix of individuals, then substitution from one policy instrument to another would not favor one ideological disposition over another. But if differences do exist, this could be a source of friction and hence a constraint.[61]

To our knowledge no one has asked this question directly with respect to foreign affairs agencies, but fortunately Joshua Clinton and colleagues conducted the Future of Government Service survey in 2007–2008 of over 7,448 federal administrators.[62] In this survey they estimated ideological ideal points for civil servants based on fourteen congressional bills where they asked the civil servants to indicate how they would vote on the bill. Next they used a scaling procedure to place each individual on a scale running from -1 (liberal) to 1 (conservative) (see original paper for estimation details). For the vote-based procedure they report ideological preference averages for those in the army (.44), navy (.41), air force (.38), Department of Defense (.34), and State Department (-.24). Simply put, civil servants in the State Department were quite a bit more liberal than those in the military agencies.[63]

---

61    This data does not let us test our hypotheses about ideological divisiveness, which we turn to in the next chapter.

62    Clinton, Bertelli, Grose, Lewis, and Nixon, 2012.

63    In a more recent survey Clinton and colleagues used a self-reported question about ideological position conducted on a total of 2,400 federal executives. Clinton, Lewis, and Selin, 2013. This survey asked them to rank themselves on a liberal (=1) to conservative (=7) scale. From this survey we group together respondents in the military agencies into the category

These results are consistent with the type of bargaining process empha-sized in the "bureaucratic politics" view of foreign policy decision making.[64] Staff within bureaucratic agencies will lobby for their own self-preservation, budgets, and policy preferences, which—other things being equal—means diverting foreign policy toward using instruments that the agency controls. If ideological divisions also exist across the agencies, this will magnify the problems related to policy substitution, as decision makers will be both organizationally and ideologically entrenched.

In the next chapter we present similar results with respect to the general public. Hence, not only do members of the public have different prefer-ences for different types of policy instruments depending on their ideo-logical commitments, but personnel in bureaucratic agencies that oversee these different policy instruments also have significantly different ideolog-ical orientations. This is important for substitution, as shifting toward or away from a policy instrument may entail shifting toward or against the use of different bureaucratic agencies, which may be staffed by ideologically different agents.

## Conclusion

In this chapter we studied an area of American foreign policy that to date has been largely neglected: the structure of bureaucratic institutions that oversee the genesis and implementation of foreign policy. We began the chapter by building off of earlier chapters that gave us some theoretical ex-pectations. In particular, we expected that the politics of bureaucratic agen-cies should differ depending on the characteristics of the policy instrument that an agency deals with.

The data and analysis in this chapter are not without problems. We face the same problems as the original analysis by CWHL and follow their lead in using fixed effects to try to deal with problems of inference caused by omitted variables. We control for many potentially confounding variables that do not vary within presidential administrations. Our quantitative anal-ysis also treats the institutional design coding of each agency as fixed, but as shown in our case studies this can change in practice over time, even if there are no formal legal changes. However, as discussed in our case studies, we expect any such changes to mainly strengthen our results. Congressional

---

"Military." We also grouped together respondents that worked in either USAID, USITC, State Department, or the Export-Import Bank into a "Economic/Diplomatic" category (there were very few observations among the non-State Department agencies). Persons in the military cat-egory were substantially more conservative.

64   Allison, 1969.

control over aid has increased, but we do not see the same changes in congressional power in agencies concerned with issues like intelligence gathering. Of course, this remains an open empirical question that would require substantial additional data collection and categorization.

Finally, we recognize that these agencies may to some extent be influenced by societal pressures, such as interest groups, which this chapter does not address, but chapter 3 on interest groups does address some of these concerns. Likewise, this chapter does not examine more systematically ongoing struggles between the president and Congress on funding these agencies. We do not have data on the size and importance of each agency. Our conjecture about militarization, however, would suggest that agencies dealing with the military elements of statecraft would grow relatively larger over time and would be more likely under presidential control. We expect these two conditions to be associated with one another since Congress should be more likely to give the president what he wants in terms of budget and manpower for these types of agencies. And we find some support for this in chapter 4 on budgetary politics between the president and Congress.

The ways we expect these politics to differ are consistent with the theoretical expectations we set out in chapter 2. For policy instruments with a high degree of distributional consequences, we see that Congress plays a crucial role and agencies are relatively less controlled by the president. Conversely, when distributional consequences are low, the president has much greater control. These institutional arrangements have an impact, we argue, on informational asymmetries as well, showing the connection between distributional politics and information.

The result of our analyses is consistent with our theoretical expectations. And while these theoretical expectations in their primitive form have been the subject of various conjectures like the "intermestic" politics literature, heretofore there has been little systematic demonstration of how the agencies and their politics differ, especially one informed by explicit theoretical expectations as articulated in chapter 2. [65]

65    Manning, 1977; Lindsay, 1992; Lindsay and Steger, 1993; Fisher, 1998; Milner and Tingley, 2011.

# 6

# THE VIEW FROM THE PUBLIC BEACH

## Presidential Power and Substitution in American Public Opinion

We have shown how the politics of American foreign policy vary significantly by foreign policy instruments. This variance is important because it affects how the president forms foreign policy and ultimately whether those policies are more or less successful. The president faces a number of challenges from the external environment. Some problems involve other countries, like the Soviet Union during the Cold War; others involve large external processes that affect the United States, like climate change or global financial crises. The president often needs to address these and to resolve the problem posed by another country or some external threat. To do this, he possesses a number of foreign policy instruments that he can potentially use to exert influence abroad. In deciding which of these instruments to employ, he must, however, take into account domestic politics.

There are a number of ways in which the domestic environment affects his decision making on foreign policy. Previous chapters have shown how this happens through interest groups, the legislature, and even bureaucracies. A different set of influences concerns the public. We focus on public opinion in this chapter.

Looking at public opinion in the light of our theory is an important step. If the majority of our predictions were inconsistent with public attitudes, then it would be important to develop a more complete accounting of this incongruence given our focus on the United States, the leading democratic country on the international scene. We do not want to overstate the impact of public opinion on foreign policy, but endeavor to establish, like other scholars, a broad consistency between our theory and mass attitudes.

This chapter has two goals. First, we use it to provide additional evidence about the informational advantage hypotheses that we laid out in chapter 2. We ask whether the public recognizes the asymmetries we hypothesize across foreign policy instruments. Our evidence here compares public views on when the executive branch has more information about an issue than Congress. This evidence suggests the public also thinks that presidential control over the different policy areas varies in a way that is consistent with our theory. In some policy instruments, but not others, the president has more information than Congress and is in greater control.

Second, we investigate survey evidence that lets us see the extent of ideological divisions among the public across foreign policy instruments. This is also important in terms of how we classify the policy instruments in chapter 2. These ideological divisions are important in shaping presidential power and policy substitution. The survey data also reveal how members of the public trade off different policy instruments with each other. We focus on how decisions and support across instruments of foreign policy vary by liberal and conservative ideology. Our goal is to examine if the public makes decisions in ways that are consistent with our theory.[1]

## Public Opinion and Foreign Policy

Before moving to the empirical content of the chapter, we note that the role of public opinion in foreign policy is debated. A number of scholars have taken on the important question about the role of public opinion in foreign policy,[2] with some arguing that the public has little constraining role,[3] and others arguing it has an important influence.[4] Some scholars see the public as a constraint. Democratic governments need to act in ways consistent with the general views of the public; otherwise competing electoral actors can replace them in government as they better represent the public's views.[5] This holds just as much in foreign policy as domestic policy. "Both Congress and the President have become reluctant to actively pursue foreign policy agendas that are at odds with public opinion."[6] Political leaders pay attention to the public on foreign policy.[7] In a 2004 Chicago Council on Foreign Relations survey, a sample of House and

1  We use chapters 3 and 4 on interest groups and Congress to demonstrate more about how policy instruments feature differential levels of distributive politics.

2  Page and Shapiro, 1983; Bartels, 1991; James and Oneal, 1991; Risse-Kappen, 1991; Hinckley, 1992; Page and Shapiro, 1992; Baum, 2002; Baum, 2004b; Milner, 2006.

3  Guisinger, 2009. See also Jacobs and Page who argue that once interest groups like business and labor are accounted for, there is little influence of the public. Jacobs and Page, 2005. Lindsay and Ripley also in their survey of the role of Congress in foreign policy suggest little influence for the public: "Legislators . . . have an incentive to follow constituent opinion. But the relationship between public opinion and congressional behavior is not simple, at least not on foreign policy issues. Although two recent studies found evidence that constituent opinion influenced congressional voting on specific issues (Bartels, 1991; Overby, 1991), anecdotal evidence suggests that legislative behavior on foreign policy does not reliably mirror public opinion. The Senate approved the Panama Canal treaties by the required two-thirds majority even though polls showed over 60% of the public opposed the treaties (McCormick and Black, 1983)." McCormick and Black, 1983; Bartels, 1991; Overby, 1991; Lindsay and Ripley, 1992, p. 422.

4  Aldrich, Sullivan, and Borgida, 1989; Baum, 2004a; Aldrich, Gelpi, Feaver, Reifler, and Sharp, 2006.

5  Page and Shapiro, 1992; Erikson, MacKuen, and Stimson, 2002; Canes-Wrone, 2006.

6  Campbell, Rae, and Stack, 2003, p. 144.

7  Program on International Policy Attitudes, 2005.

Senate members were asked about the importance of public opinion in shaping their foreign policy positions. On a 0-10 scale, with 0 not at all influential and 10 extremely influential, average responses were 7 and 7.5 for the House and Senate, respectively.[8] The influence of other groups, like interest groups and foreign publics, was decidedly lower.[9]

This importance extends to sub-components of foreign policy as well, like foreign aid. The multilateral Organisation for Economic Co-operation and Development (OECD) released a report on US aid policy noting the importance of public attitudes: "Given the influence of public opinion in matters of development assistance and the public misunderstanding of the size and role of American aid, public awareness should be a priority task for the government and its development partners."[10] Hence many expect that policy will be broadly consistent with public opinion.[11] We do not expect or assume that the public has detailed knowledge of policy or global problems, only that elites care what they broadly think and try not to act in complete disregard of the prevailing majority opinion.

An alternative view of public opinion is that it reflects elite attitudes. Individuals develop beliefs based on the cues sent by elites,[12] a position most directly connected to an analysis of security-related foreign policy issues by Berinsky.[13] Elites can frame their views or use other strategies to get the public to support their positions. This rich literature suggests for our purposes, then, that data about public opinion are still helpful because much actual foreign policy decision making is elite-driven. Hence if public opinion merely reflects elite opinion, and it is hard (though not impossible) to get elite opinion, then our inferences from the public opinion data are still relevant and informative. We bracket this important debate about whether public opinion shapes elite opinion or elite opinion shapes public opinion. In reality, like most things, it is some of both. But neither perspective suggests that opinion data on either the public or elites are irrelevant for understanding the formation of foreign policy. Below we predominantly focus on the mass public, but we include several analyses of elite opinion as well, including the Chicago Council on Foreign Relations survey and the TRIPS survey of international relations scholars.

We believe that public opinion data at a minimum help us explore important elements of our arguments. Our prior expectation is that public

---

8    Chicago Council, 2005.

9    We of course recognize the potential for social desirability bias, though responses were anonymous and it is unclear ex ante if social desirability bias could cause the size of the gap we observe.

10    Organisation for Economic Co-operation and Development, 2006, p. 11.

11    Aldrich, Sullivan, and Borgida, 1989.

12    Sniderman, Brody, and Tetlock, 1991; Lupia, 1994.

13    Berinsky, 2007.

opinion has some role in shaping policy, but we do not provide definitive evidence.[14] Instead, the goal of this chapter is to show whether and when public opinion data are consistent with our theory.

## Chapter Outline

This chapter has two main parts. First we establish an empirical basis for arguments developed in chapter 2 about the president and informational asymmetries. We ask (1) if the public can identify an information asymmetry between the president and congresspersons across different foreign policy instruments, and (2) if the public sees differences in the amount of information the president has about the impact of different policies on their localities relative to Congress. Finally, we investigate two implications of these arguments about information. First, that the president will have more control over some policy instruments versus others. Second, if individuals see some types of policy as having fewer ramifications for their local area, they may be more willing to have the president determine policy rather than their congressperson.

In the second part of the chapter we show that the public has preferences about foreign policies and that their positions often differ systematically according to ideological commitments. We use this to provide evidence for our classification of foreign policy instruments in chapter 2. We expect that ideological divisions will be much greater in certain instruments than in others. If ideological divisions are large, then the president will have difficulty constructing different coalitions for different instruments. The need for different political coalitions for different types of foreign policy highlights the potential difficulties of policy substitution. If the president wants to shift instruments, or simply use more of one than another (perhaps due to changing external events), this can entail a domestic cost. Presidents will have to compensate opponents if they want to make a shift and risk alienating legislators from whose preferred policy instrument they are shifting. Identifying different preferences across foreign policy instruments is a necessary condition for claiming that constraints on policy substitution are a crucial feature of foreign policy. Coupled with our analysis of the president's informational advantage, this analysis sets up our broad view of how the de-

14 We conducted a variety of analyses like regressing congressional voting on district-level estimates of public opinion. The results were mixed, with some results showing a positive connection, and in others the null was not rejected, which was unsurprising given the nature of the statistical specifications and data availability. The more recent case of the proposed military intervention in Syria certainly portrays the saliency of public opinion.

**Table 6.1.** Chapter 6 Research Questions and Data Sources

| QUESTIONS | DATASETS |
| --- | --- |
| President/congressional information/control | CCES 2012, 2013, SSI 2014, TRIPS 2014 |
| Why support/oppose a legislator that opposes president? | CCES 2012 |
| Ideological determinants of tool preferences | CCES 2010, 2012, Chicago Council |
| Aid recipient tradeoffs | CCES 2010 |
| Choosing between aid, trade, and immigration to deal with international problems | CCES 2008 |
| Budget re-design (development/security substitution) | Program on Public Consultation 2010 |

sign of American foreign policy faces constraints in policy substitutability. Through the chapter we draw on a range of data. To facilitate an overview of these different data sources and the research questions they speak to, we provide a summary overview in table 6.1.

## The Role of the President: Information and Impact

We ask here whether the public sees differences across foreign policy instruments in the president's informational advantage, and whether these differences affect the public's willingness to let the president lead. We show that on some foreign policy issues the public does not think the president has an informational advantage and actually believes that his congressperson is more likely to know what the best course of action is. On issues like trade, economic aid, and immigration, there is a natural tendency by voters to see their congressperson as more informed about their interests than the president. But the less the issue involves distributive politics, the more the public feels the president has an advantage.

Our main hypothesis discussed in chapter 2 is that presidents will possess greater control over foreign policy instruments where the president has the greatest informational advantage over other decision makers in Congress. We argued that policy instruments with the fewest distributive politics would be the ones where the president is seen as having the most information and as being the one with the most control over the policy instruments.

Interestingly, there is very little work on these questions in the public opinion literature. Instead most scholars examine public preferences and relate them to various presidential and congressional behaviors. This does not help with our hypotheses about information asymmetries. Irrespective of their preferences about particular policy instruments, does the public think that the president has more or less information on the appropriateness and consequences of these policy instruments? Existing data cannot answer these questions.

To examine these claims, we fielded a series of questions using the 2013 Cooperative Congressional Election Study (CCES) survey.[15] This nationally representative sample was fielded in October 2013. First, we asked respondents to indicate their opinions about differences between the president and congressperson across a set of distinct foreign policy instruments. Questions probed respondents' beliefs about differences in political elites' information and to what extent each set of actors should have control over the policy instrument. We also asked questions about the perceived extent of local distributional consequences of each of the policies. Second, we shifted our questioning to perceptions of foreign policy more generally and asked individuals whether their support for their congressperson increased or decreased if they voted against the president on foreign policy, as well their reasons for taking that position.

Our first question directly engages with the information asymmetry hypothesis. Do members of the public think that the president has greater information on some policy instruments versus others? In particular, we asked:

The US government uses different tools when it makes foreign and domestic policy. These tools include the use of the US military troops, health care, trade policy, education, acquiring materials for the US military, immigration, economic aid, and military aid.

The following questions will ask you to indicate whether in general the US president/executive branch or Congress has more information on *when and how* these policy tools should be used.

Please check the box next to who you feel is more informed about when and how these policy tools should be used.

For each policy instrument respondents selected either the US president/executive branch or Congress. This lets us determine if members of the public as a whole see systematic differences in access to information across policy instruments. In particular, this question asked about the *use* of policy instru-

15    We also fielded the same questions in a parallel survey using Amazon's Mechanical Turk and obtained nearly identical results. Berinsky, Huber, and Lenz, 2012. We also fielded a similar set of questions in the 2012 CCES and obtained nearly identical results. The 2012 survey contained slight differences in question wording. We view our results as robust to these changes, as well as to any changes between 2012 and 2013.

ments. So, for example, this would include how, and what type, of foreign aid to send, what types of education policies to implement, and whether or not to send troops abroad. We included both domestic and foreign policy instruments, as our theoretical arguments suggest that several foreign policy tools should look more similar to how the public views domestic policy tools.[16]

A second way to consider informational asymmetries between the president/executive branch and Congress is to consider information about district-level effects of a policy. In chapter 2, we argued that some types of policies will have much greater domestic distributional impacts. This will lead legislators and interest groups affected to seek out and gather information about the issue. If so, then in these areas congressional representatives will likely have more information about how a particular policy will affect their district compared to an outsider. Alternatively, other policies will have fewer distinctly local consequences. In this case national-level leadership will know more about the impacts of a policy, due in part to better knowledge about the policy instrument itself and its use. To measure perceptions about district-level impacts, we asked the following question where respondents once again chose from the same set of policy instruments as in the previous question.

Please consider the impact of these policies on your congressional district.

For each type of policy, please indicate whether in general you think the US president/executive branch knows more about how the policy will affect your congressional district or your congressperson knows more.

Please check the box next to who you feel is more informed about how the policy will influence your district.

Figure 6.1 displays the percentages of the public who said the president/executive branch is more informed about each issue, and includes 95% confidence intervals based on the binomial distribution. These results show strong support for the asymmetric information hypothesis. Respondents view the two policy instruments that we see as having least distributive politics associated with them—i.e., military deployment and geopolitical aid—as the ones the president has the most information about. The president is seen to have less information about trade, economic aid, and immigration compared to the use of troops and geopolitical aid. Most of

16  In the 2012 CCES we only included the foreign policy issue areas, and contrasted the president to the respondent's own congressperson. One potential problem with this question is that individual congresspersons may rely on their congressional leadership for either information or direction, given that the leadership may have better information. Hence the overall level of informational advantage for the president in each policy area may be biased upward. Responding to these criticisms, we ran an additional nationally representative survey in 2013, but we obtain substantively similar results in 2012.

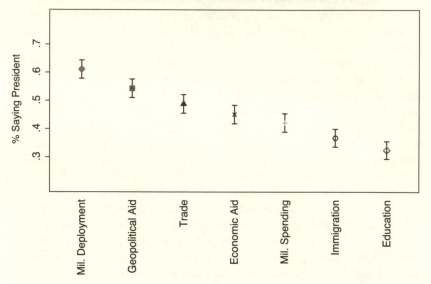

**Figure 6.1.** Whether president/executive branch or Congress knows more about when and how the policy tool should be used. Nationally representative data from 2013 Cooperative Congressional Election Study. Means with 95% confidence intervals reported.

the domestic policy areas are on average seen as having even fewer presidential informational advantages than these foreign policy instruments.[17]

An extension of the informational hypothesis is that the president will also have more information about the impact of certain instruments on the respondent's own locality as identified by their congressional district. This additional test of the hypothesis makes sure that using the reference point of a local area does not change the results.[18] Figure 6.2 plots the results which are very similar to the results presented in figure 6.1. Policy instruments that have fewer distributive politics are associated with the president having more knowledge about district-level impacts, though the difference between geopolitical aid and economic aid is more muted for this question.

17   One exception is health care, which we exclude from the plot. This is not a surprise, perhaps, given the highly politicized debate about "Obamacare" that continued during the time period of the survey. But in general we find broad support for our arguments.

We also split up the results into self-identified Democrats, Republicans, and Independents. The pattern across issue areas is identical within each partisan orientation, but the levels were lower with Republicans, not surprisingly, saying the president has less information across the issue areas. We strongly expect this pattern would shift if the president was a Republican.

18   Individual perception of impact could come both from different views of the level of impact or the saliency/importance. We do not take up this matter, as our efforts here are more to establish basic patterns in public opinion across the tools.

**Who Has Most Information About District Impact?**

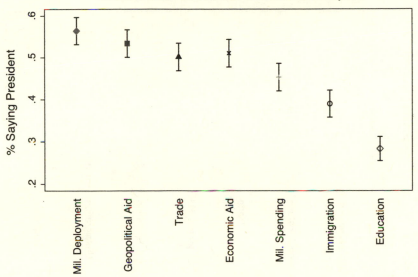

**Figure 6.2.** Whether president/executive branch or Congress knows more about the impact of tool on respondent's congressional district. Nationally representative data from 2013 Cooperative Congressional Election Study. Means with 95% confidence intervals reported.

Policy instruments like trade are seen as giving the president less of an informational advantage about district-level impacts.[19]

The preceding results suggest that the public recognizes the types of information asymmetries that our theory posits. Next, we examine attitudes about what actors control our different policy instruments. This is an important test because, while individuals might perceive the information asymmetries we document above, this might not translate into views about who controls each policy instrument the most. Hence, having documented public views about information, we turn to the crucial outcome variable dealing with presidential control.

In the spring of 2014 we fielded a nationally representative survey using Survey Sampling International where we asked the following question:

> The US government uses different tools when it makes foreign and domestic policy. These tools include the use of the US military troops, health care, trade policy, education, acquiring materials for the US military, immigration, economic aid, and military aid.

[19] For this question the district-level effects of health-care policy are seen to be more in line with other domestic tools, though education still ranks at the bottom for all respondents.

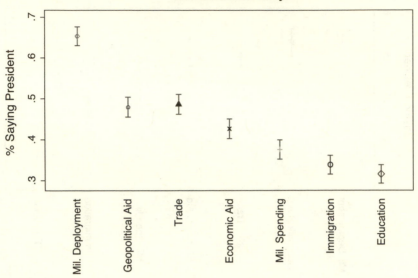

**Figure 6.3.** Whether president/executive branch or Congress controls a policy tool. Nationally representative data from 2014 Survey Sampling International survey. Means with 95% confidence intervals reported.

The following questions will ask you to indicate whether in general the US president/executive branch or Congress has more control over when and how these policy tools are used.

Please check the box next to who you feel has more control over when and how these policy tools are used.

Respondents selected between Congress or the president/executive branch. As before, we then plot the results for each of our policy instruments in figure 6.3.[20] The US president clearly is seen as having the most control over the deployment of troops. The next highest categories are geopolitical aid and trade. While the relatively high degree of control over geopolitical aid is consistent with our theory, the high level of perceived control over trade is not particularly surprising given the role of presidents in negotiating trade agreements. Nevertheless, nearly 60% of respondents felt that Congress has the most influence over economic aid. And an even higher percentage indicated Congress's control over domestic military procurements. Finally, immigration and education are seen to have the lowest levels of presidential control. These findings are largely consistent with our theory.

20   As before we drop the result for health, which, due to Obamacare had a very high percentage, indicating presidential control.

**Table 6.2.** Why Respondent Would Punish a
Legislator for Voting Against President on Foreign Policy

| DON'T VOTE AGAINST PRESIDENT | FREQ | % |
|---|---|---|
| President has more info. | 167 | 44.8 |
| Constitution | 62 | 16.6 |
| National Interest | 79 | 21.2 |
| Other | 65 | 17.4 |

Data from 2012 Cooperative Congressional Election
Study.

We also probed the opinions of international relations scholars who might be considered more "expert" or "elite" than our mass surveys. We make use of two questions in a survey fielded by the Teaching Research & International Policy (TRIP) initiative. In May 2014, the TRIP SNAP survey asked respondents two questions related to ongoing events in Egypt: "When it comes to decisions about MILITARY aid sent to Egypt, who has the most control, the president/executive branch or Congress?" and "When it comes to decisions about ECONOMIC aid sent to Egypt, who has the most control, the president/executive branch or Congress?"[21] Our prediction was that a larger proportion of people would say the "president/executive branch" for geopolitical aid compared to economic aid. We found exactly this in our sample of "elites": for geopolitical aid the split was 74% president and 26% Congress, and for economic aid the split was 51% president and 49% Congress.[22]

We also investigated whether the informational dimension is important in deciding how to reconcile any conflicts between someone's legislator and the president. In the 2012 Cooperative Congressional Election Study we asked: "When your member of the House of Representatives votes against President Obama on foreign policy, does your support for him/her rise or fall?" Following their response, we asked respondents to choose from a set of options about why they gave the answer they did. Among respondents stating their support for their legislator declines when they go against the president, the top response was "the president has access to the best information about the effectiveness of the policy." As shown in table 6.2, the most

21   http://www.wm.edu/offices/itpir/trip/snap-polls/.
22   We would further suspect that if the country was less geopolitically central, Congress would have even more control over economic aid, but not necessarily geopolitical aid. The TRIP Snap poll can only support a limited number of questions and we are very thankful to their team for access.

frequent response by those saying they do not vote against the president was that he has more information.

Overall, we find broad support for our hypotheses. When we ask the US public in a nationally representative sample to indicate their views on information asymmetries and local effects across different policy instruments, we find stark differences. And these correspond to their views on which actor has more control over the issues areas as well. We arrive at these conclusions using multiple different measures, and all point in the same general direction.[23]

# Ideological Divisions and Substitution across Foreign Policy Instruments

## Survey Questions about a Single Policy Instrument

Policy substitution becomes problematic when individuals hold very different views of policy instruments that are shaped by their ideology. When ideological divisions over an issue are very large, this ideological structuring makes substitution across the policy instruments very difficult. In this section we identify the relationship between ideology and our policy instruments. We focus on two themes. First, we try to establish the direction of the relationship. Second, we explore whether some issues are more divisive ideologically than others.

We begin with results from the 2012 Cooperative Congressional Election Study (CCES). The CCES has two components—a common section and an individual team section. In 2012, the common section had a question on support for the US-South Korea trade agreement as well as questions on a variety of different types of immigration policy proposals. In the team content section, we asked additional questions about support for economic and geopolitical aid, as well as about the use of military force.

For our dependent variables, we use the following questions. We code each response category as a dichotomous choice where a 1 indicates a preference for fewer restrictions on immigration or more support for trade. To simplify the interpretation of results, we standardize the coding of the dependent variable. The simplest way to do this, and the one we also adopt in chapter 4 when looking at roll call voting, is to code each of the eight responses such that a 1 demarcates the most pro-internationalist position; that is, it is the preference for an open world economy and one that is most likely to be supported by the president, as we discuss in chapter 2. Below we

---

23   Given our innovative questions, we are not able to analyze responses to them further back in time because they were not asked in previous years.

list the original questions, but those with an asterisk (*) are reverse coded so that a 1 is either pro-immigrant or pro-trade.

## IMMIGRATION QUESTIONS

What do you think the US government should do about immigration? Select all that apply.

- ★ Grant legal status to all illegal immigrants who have held jobs and paid taxes for at least 3 years, and not been convicted of any felony crimes.
- ★ Increase the number of border patrols on the US-Mexican border.*
- ★ Allow police to question anyone they think may be in the country illegally.*
- ★ Fine US businesses that hire illegal immigrants.*
- ★ Prohibit illegal immigrants from using emergency hospital care and public schools.*
- ★ Deny automatic citizenship to American-born children of illegal immigrants.*

## TRADE QUESTION

Congress considered many important bills over the past two years.

For each of the following tell us whether you support or oppose the legislation in principle.

US-Korea Free Trade Agreement: Would remove tariffs on imports and exports between South Korea and the United States.

For our study, the responses coded as pro-internationalist are those that allow immigrants better and easier access to the United States and that remove barriers to immigration and trade. Hence agreeing that the United States should grant legal status to all illegal immigrants who have held jobs and paid taxes for at least 3 years and has not been convicted of any felony crimes is pro-internationalist. Opposing an increase in the number of border patrols on the US-Mexican border is pro-internationalist. Opposition to allowing police to question anyone they think may be in the country illegally is pro-internationalist. And opposing fines for US businesses that hire illegal immigrants is pro-internationalist. Allowing illegal immigrants to use emergency hospital care and public schools and giving automatic citizenship to American-born children of illegal immigrants are both pro-internationalist. And finally, support for the US-South Korea FTA is pro-internationalist.

The common content section also asked a series of questions about the respondent's ideological orientation, their occupation (which we define below in greater detail), education, gender, age, and state of residence. The ideological orientation question scaled respondents along a 7-point liberal to conservative scale. With each of these binary-dependent variables, we estimate a probit regression model with these explanatory variables and state fixed effects. Sample sizes for these regression models were over 40,000, making them some of the largest foreign policy public opinion polls to date. We expect conservatives to support trade and oppose economic aid. For immigration, our theoretical development posed reasons why conservatives or liberals might oppose immigration, and hence ideology should be less divisive here. Geopolitical aid and the support for troops we expect to be less divisive but based on some earlier work may receive some positive support from conservatives. The CCES survey did not ask about military spending and sanctions.

To succinctly present our results, we plot substantive effects in figure 6.4 for our ideological variables. We calculate the change in probability of holding a pro-internationalist position on the issue when moving from the most liberal to most conservative ideological position, holding all other variables at their mean value. For instance, if an individual were to change her ideology from the most liberal to the most conservative, this would mean that her likelihood of supporting the US-S Korea FTA would rise by 5%.[24] For the common survey questions, the impact of the large sample size is immediately seen in the small confidence intervals.

Our expectations are not born out with respect to immigration. Conservative opposition to immigration (and hence to internationalism) is quite strong, though this varies across the types of immigration policy questions. The strongest effect is for the questions on police questioning, border control, and legal status. The smallest impact for ideology among the immigration questions concerned the question on fining businesses, which perhaps highlights the inherent tension in conservative economic attitudes on immigration, as this particular policy instrument directly interferes with free enterprise.

Consistent with previous results, this means that conservatives are more supportive of free trade during this time period than liberals. Hence conservatives are pro-internationalist when it comes to trade but not so for

24 We also investigated a quadratic relationship, whereby more extreme conservatives were more opposed to trade. In our data we did not see this much evidence of this relationship, but as with any covariate, there can be some degree of non-linearity in effect. For example, in our data, there was a dip in support among middle-of-the-road ideologues, and likewise for independents. But the general pattern is one of increasing support with ideology, and clear Republican/Democrat differences.

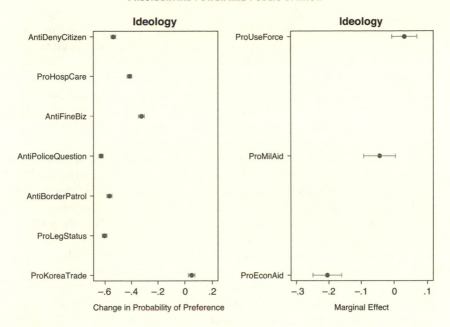

**Figure 6.4.** Change in probability of pro-international response due to changing respondent ideological self-placement from very liberal to very conservative, holding other variables at their mean. Immigration and South Korea trade question on left and foreign aid questions on right. Nationally representative data from 2012 Cooperative Congressional Election Study.

immigration, and vice versa for liberals. This splintering of support for internationalism is a problem for presidents in conducting foreign policy.

In our team survey we asked questions about support for economic and geopolitical aid, as well as support for the use of force more generally.[25] Each of these questions had ordinal response scales, and we use linear regression models to estimate the effect of ideology (ordered probit models give nearly identical conclusions). We use the same model specification as in the previous analysis with state fixed effects (regional dummies produce similar results).

We find that conservatives were significantly less supportive of economic aid, which is consistent with earlier research. In the 2012 CCES survey the

25 We asked several questions on the team section of the survey, which has a smaller sample size of 1,300, about aid and military force. The use of force question was, "Some people think that US military force should never be used under any circumstances. They are at 1 on the scale below. Other people think there are many situations in which US military force should be used to deal with problems. They are at 7 on the scale below. And, of course, other people have opinions in between. Where would you put yourself on this scale?"

effect of ideology on geopolitical aid was negative but not significantly different from zero. The negative relationship may or may not be due to the fact that a Democratic president is in power.[26,27] In other surveys, Conservatives are typically more supportive, something we have found in the analysis of previous Chicago Council surveys. Regardless, this suggests some evidence that the magnitude of the cleavage on this instrument is lower for geopolitical aid, which is consistent with our argument. We turn next to more systematically investigating whether this is true.

We collected the Chicago Council on Foreign Relations surveys starting in 1975 and ending in 2010 for both their elite and public samples. We extracted two questions that were consistently asked about economic aid and geopolitical aid. We also constructed an index based on responses to a series of questions about the use of military force.[28] For each of these three instruments we create a 0 to 1 index ranging from opposition to support. Next, we estimated a linear regression pooling over years for each of these independent variables and including survey year fixed effects and an ideology scale, gender, and college education.[29] Results are plotted in figure 6.5. We find that the estimated effect on economic aid is greater than the other two policy instruments. This is consistent with our results from the 2012

26  These results are consistent with elite attitudes. Those who occupy military positions in the US government tend to be more conservative than those in the State Department. In a pioneering paper, Clinton et al. estimate liberal-conservative ideal points of members of different government agencies. Clinton, Bertelli, Grose, Lewis, and Nixon, 2012. In chapter 6 we present results using their estimates that are average ideology scores for the State Department versus other military-oriented agencies like the Department of Defense, and military branches. The State Department elites were significantly more liberal compared to these other agencies.

27  In other survey analyses we have also studied the relationship between preferences about multilateralism in foreign policy. Consistent with other work we generally find more opposition to these institutions by conservatives, though this effect is more muted for organizations like NATO compared to the UN or the World Bank. Holsti, 2004; Broz, 2005; Broz and Hawes, 2006; Milner and Tingley, 2013a. These cleavages highlight difficulties presidents face with substitution, here across institutional mechanisms.

28  For military and economic aid, the question read, "I am going to read a list of present federal government programs. For each I'd like you to tell me whether you feel it should be expanded, cut back, or kept about the same." For each tool the responses were cut back (0) kept same (.5) and expand (1). The military force questions were preceded by the following framing. "There has been some discussion about the circumstances that might justify using US troops in other parts of the World. I'd like to ask your opinion about several situations. First, would you favor or oppose the use of US troops." Respondents were then given a range of contemporaneous issues and asked whether they opposed or supported deployment of troops. We then calculated for every respondent a 0 to 1 scale, where 1 was saying use force in every situation and 0 supporting troops in no situation, and .5 for supporting use in half of the cases, etc.

29  Different years include scales with varying numbers of options. For every year we created a 0 to 1 scale with 1 most conservative and 0 most liberal. Year-by-year analysis produced similar results.

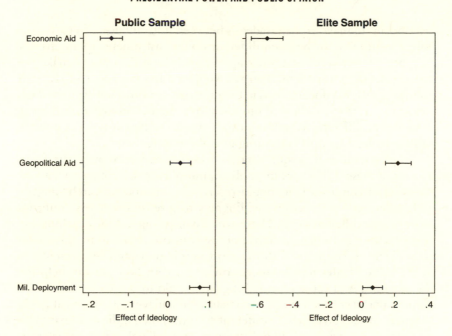

**Figure 6.5.** Marginal effect of ideology on economic aid, military aid, and use of troops in CCFR surveys, 1975–2010. Results show that the magnitude of the effect of ideology variable on economic aid is substantially greater than for the use of troops and military aid.

CCES survey, and supports our argument that instruments like economic aid have greater ideological divisions.

## Survey Questions about Multiple Policy Instruments

The previous section established that the coalitions behind important types of foreign policy instruments differ in important, and politically relevant, ways. If so, then if presidents seek to replace one foreign policy instrument with another, they may confront different political coalitions. Hence, they may be constrained in their ability to substitute. Advocates of one policy instrument that the president is shifting away from may protest, and opponents of the policy instrument the president is shifting toward may also protest. In some cases there might be similar coalitions though, and in those cases substitution, or policy bundling, could be easier.

In this section, we study this substitution dynamic more directly, rather than just relying on differences in the influence of covariates, like ideology and material interest, on support for individual types of policy instruments. The common theme in the design of these questions is to enable respondents to make explicit tradeoffs between different uses of a particular policy instrument, or between different policy instruments themselves. If everyone has the same rank ordering of policies and thus would make the same tradeoffs across them, then we would be less confident of the rich political landscape documented in the previous sections. However, the analyses in this section continue to support those results. Ideology in particular continues to differentiate public attitudes toward different types of policies and the tradeoffs people are willing to make among them.

We present several unique datasets with which we examine the foundations of these differences in public opinion. First, we contrast views on the types of countries that should receive aid. Previous research suggests such differences exist because willingness to give differs across countries according to different goals. Those who favor giving aid for development purposes want most to give to the poorest countries. In contrast, those who favor giving to countries with the most ample trade and investment ties to the United States may be more concerned with how aid can help the US economy. And those most willing to give aid to our closest allies and military partners may see aid as a means for achieving geopolitical goals. Attitudes toward giving aid to different countries then indicate in part people's views on the goals of aid policy. For example, Tingley finds using cross-national data on foreign aid budgets that when conservatives come into office in donor countries, aid shifts away from poorer countries.[30] However, this relationship does not hold for aid recipients that are middle income. Fleck and Kilby find that increases in US aid toward countries with whom Americans trade heavily occur when aid is controlled by conservative administrations.[31] Determining which countries receive aid and which don't is a political decision, one whose outcome features in a range of debates.[32] These domestic political decisions are driven by distinct political coalitions.

We ask whether our public opinion data support similar findings. We ask whether liberals and conservatives favor giving aid to similar types of countries. Second, we contrast how a nationally representative sample of the public would allocate the US federal budget across military and nonmilitary budgetary line items. This unique survey, fielded in 2010, lets us also examine how different partisan groups would change foreign policy budgets and by implication the relative use of different foreign policy instruments. Third, to delineate foreign policy preferences even further, we investigate the prioritization that individuals place on using trade, immigration, or aid policy to deal with overseas development problems.

30  Tingley, 2010.
31  Fleck and Kilby, 2006.
32  Burnside and Dollar, 2000; Fleck and Kilby, 2006.

## WHICH COUNTRIES SHOULD GET ECONOMIC AID?

We begin with the question: to what types of countries do individuals want to give aid? Foreign aid can be used for different purposes, and other studies have found that different types of individuals prefer aid for different reasons.[33] Conservatives tend to favor aid if it promotes US economic or geopolitical interests; liberals are more supportive of it when it is directed at development needs in the recipient country. To more finely gauge preferences toward aid, we asked respondents about which types of countries they preferred giving aid to. In the 2010 CCES survey we asked the following question:

The United States has decided to give foreign economic aid to two countries, country A and country B. They are both small, are democracies, and about the same distance away from the United States.

- ★ Country A has a low income level and imports very little from the United States.
- ★ Country B has a medium income level and imports a large amount from the United States.

Using the sliding scale, indicate how you would like economic aid between these countries to be divided.

Respondents then chose their preferred share, ranging from giving everything to country A (a 0 on the scale) and everything to country B (a 100 on the scale). We assume that respondents giving a larger share to country B weigh the strategic trade consequences of foreign aid more than the development ones and/or have opinions about which countries will better use the aid. Importantly, we do not have individuals set overall spending levels, just the proportions.

We examine responses by political party, which gives a simple way to consider differences in preferences by liberal-conservative ideology. The average value for Democrats was 48, showing a slight preference for country A. For Republicans the average value was 54, showing a slight preference for country B. The difference between the two groups was statistically significant in a difference-in-means test ($p<.01$).[34] The key implication of these data for our purposes is that when increasing or decreasing the relative shares of aid to different types of countries, the president will face political constraints. Different domestic groups will favor different types of countries. Characteristics of these countries, and how they relate to the different foreign policy goals of partisans, will have an impact on his ability to direct aid policy.

---

33   Milner and Tingley, 2013b.

34   The gap widens considerably when we consider the proportion of individuals from each party who said that more than 75% should be given to country B.

Indeed, as we discuss in chapter 7, a similar type of politics extends to even more direct questions about the use of development aid versus trade as a way to engage with poor countries, like Haiti and many in Sub-Saharan Africa.[35]

## HOW MUCH SHOULD BE SPENT ON FOREIGN POLICY INSTRUMENTS?

Our next evidence comes from December 2010 when the Program on Public Consultation conducted a study in which respondents indicate how much they want spent on different federal programs in fiscal year 2015. Respondents were given a projected budget for thirty-one different line items, and then could either increase or decrease the budget for each one. Among this set of line items were questions about spending on foreign policy instruments, including those with a direct military connection as well as those more connected to economic and diplomatic instruments.

For our analysis, we group these two types of policy instruments together. In the military category are spending on the general military budget, operations in Iraq/Afghanistan, intelligence services, nuclear weapons, Economic Support Fund, and military aid. In the economic and diplomatic category are spending on humanitarian assistance, development assistance, the Global Health Fund, the State Department, and the United Nations.

Next, for each of the line items we calculated the percentage change from the projected budget and then took, for each individual, the median percentage change within the military and non-military category. These two new dependent variables reflect typical changes that individuals made across the budget categories. We then regress these variables, using the survey's weights, on indicator variables for partisan affiliation as well as a set of demographic control variables.

Consistent with other evidence presented in the book, Republicans and Democrats differ significantly in how they would adjust the federal budget to reflect their preferences. We present the results in table 6.3. Simply put, Democrats want to cut military spending more and Republicans want to cut non-military foreign policy spending (such as foreign aid) more. These results hold if we include a set of control variables including age, income, education, and gender. Crucially, the magnitude of the Republican coefficient on the economic and diplomatic items was significantly larger compared to the Republican coefficient for the military items. This again provides evidence of differential ideological divisions.[36]

---

35    Of course, this survey question is just one way to investigate preferences over who gets US foreign aid. For example, one can easily examine the role of geostrategic factors as well by manipulating the geopolitical importance of countries to the United States, which parallels the research done with observational data.

36    We of course note though that these spending items also include what we term domestic military spending, which we expect to have similarly high ideological divisiveness. We

**Table 6.3.** Median Percentage Budget Change across Policy Tools as a Function of Party

| | MILITARY1 | MILITARY2 | NONMILITARY1 | NONMILITARY2 |
|---|---|---|---|---|
| Republican | 0.0572* | 0.0533* | −0.227** | −0.223** |
| | [0.0255] | [0.0259] | [0.0704] | [0.0727] |
| Independent | −0.0386 | −0.0406 | −0.167** | −0.176** |
| | [0.0301] | [0.0298] | [0.0628] | [0.0648] |
| Male | | −0.0110 | −0.0839 | −0.0732 |
| | | [0.0224] | [0.0570] | [0.0536] |
| Education | | −0.0124* | | −0.0255 |
| | | [0.00624] | | [0.0194] |
| Income | | 0.00354 | | −0.00939 |
| | | [0.00329] | | [0.00811] |
| Age | | −0.000125 | | −0.00196 |
| | | [0.000686] | | [0.00128] |
| Constant | −0.202** | −0.102 | 0.0503 | 0.486+ |
| | [0.0168] | [0.0789] | [0.0634] | [0.250] |
| Observations | 791 | 791 | 791 | 791 |

Data from 2010 Program on Public Consultation survey.

Standard errors in brackets, $+p < 0.10$, $*p < 0.05$, $**p < 0.01$. Positive values indicate increase in budget. Separate models estimated by military and non–military foreign policy categories. Omitted partisan category is Democrat.

## TRADEOFFS ACROSS DIFFERENT FOREIGN POLICY INSTRUMENTS

Finally, we ask directly about making tradeoffs across policy instruments. In the 2008 CCES we asked a question with a more direct contrast among different types of foreign policy instruments. In particular, we asked:

If the U.S. is considering helping a developing country, please rank which policy would you prefer they use.

---

note though that while we found in the defense spending categories that Republicans had significantly higher levels of spending, this was not the case for funding the wars in Iraq and Afghanistan where there was no significant difference between the parties. An alternative way to analyze the data is to examine relative budget amounts between two clearly distinct budget categories within the foreign aid line items. We ask whether Republicans, compared to Democrats, give higher budget priority for geopolitical aid versus development aid. While only 15% of Democrats dedicated more money to geopolitical aid than development aid, 32% of Republicans dedicated more to geopolitical aid than development aid, a highly significant difference ($p<.05$).

1. U.S. allow more immigrants from that country,
2. U.S. increase foreign economic aid to that country, or
3. U.S. allow more imports from that country.

Overall, we found that the most popular option was to allow more imports; that is, to engage internationally using trade policy. Overall, immigration was the least popular on average. To analyze these data further, we took each combination of policies and asked whether one instrument was ranked over the other, and regressed this on a set of common covariates including a liberal-conservative scale. We found that conservatives were significantly more likely to favor trade over aid, and trade over immigration, and aid over immigration, compared to liberals. For example, while most liberals preferred trade over aid, there were more liberals than conservatives that preferred the opposite. This again shows that different domestic political coalitions form around different foreign policy instruments, and by implication this means policy substitution is difficult. Furthermore, this ideological cleavage on foreign policy instruments may help explain why presidents are more able to convince their own party members to support them, rather than being able to win over the other party on their foreign policy. We show this more directly in chapter 4, which discusses Congress and roll call voting on foreign policy.

## Conclusion

We make three points in this chapter. First, we show that our characterization of the policy instruments in chapter 2 has empirical support in the eyes of the American public. We examined public perceptions about our informational asymmetry hypotheses. We wondered whether the public perceives the president and executive branch to have superior information over Congress in some areas, but not others. We found that such variation exists, and that it was consistent with our hypotheses in many ways. The implications of this are important. Insofar as the public puts constraints on both Congress and the president, the public ex ante will give more credence to one institution versus another. This then has direct bearing on the relative power of the president across different policy instruments.

Second, and consistent with much existing literature, there are systematic variation foreign policy preferences at the individual level. The public holds views about foreign policy (they are not disinterested) and those views are connected to ideology. Political ideology shapes these views and the extent of ideological divisions on them varies. Conservatives tend to be more sympathetic to military instruments and trade and much more opposed to economic aid and immigration. Ideological divisiveness on foreign policy instruments like geopolitical aid and the use of troops was lower since they tend to be less directly related to the sources of ideological differences. This comports with the analysis in chapter 4 on roll call voting.

Third, the way the US public trades off and prioritizes different policy instruments differs according to their ideology. We found similar results in chapter 5 showing that there are ideological differences between individuals working in the State Department versus those in defense-related departments. These results matter because it means that different foreign policies have different groups of supporters and opponents, and there may be very large ideological gaps between them on some issues that make substitution even more difficult. Shifting from aid to trade, or cutting military spending and increasing aid spending may be especially difficult because of the extent of ideological divisions over the instruments. Policy substitution can thus be problematic for presidents. When they want to construct policy packages or use one policy instead of another to deal with an external problem, they will have trouble building supporting coalitions using diverse policy instruments. Domestic politics thus constrains foreign policy, and it limits the ability of the president to respond in the most optimal fashion to external problems.

Following the theoretical propositions from chapter 2, we provide evidence here from public opinion surveys about the mechanisms by which the president can gain more influence over certain policy areas. The president has more leeway when he is seen as having more information about a policy and its implications than Congress, and when that policy is not seen as having a large distributional impact on the public's welfare in their local districts. While others have mentioned this informational advantage, our data are some of the first to demonstrate this advantage at the micro level. How the public views the informational advantage of the president can affect how Congress interacts with the president on foreign policy. The president also has more discretion over policy when ideological divisions over it are not that large, and he is more able to substitute policies for one another when this is the case.

While we presented a range of data using multiple different types of survey designs, we recognize some important limitations of this chapter. As we discussed in the beginning of the chapter, showing that public opinion translates into government policy is difficult if not impossible. Our claims are more modest: public attitudes are largely consistent with our theoretical predictions and with many of our elite level analyses in subsequent chapters. Future work might consider how our theory could help explain variation in public influence across different policy instruments.[37]

37 We also recognize that our analyses do not randomize key variables of interest, such as ideological orientation, and hence we cannot pinpoint causal relationships among these variables as well as in experimental designs.

# 7

# AMERICAN FOREIGN POLICY TOWARD SUB-SAHARAN AFRICA, 1993–2009

## A Case Study of Policy Instrument Politics and Substitution

Having shown the greater ability of presidents to employ militarized foreign policy instruments over economic ones, can we find evidence of presidents substituting a military approach to foreign policy for an economic one when the latter is thwarted by Congress and/or interest groups? We focus on American foreign policy toward Sub-Saharan Africa (SSA) during two American presidencies, Clinton (1993–2001) and G. W. Bush (2001–2009). By looking at a series of US foreign policy episodes, we seek to show how constraints on presidents vary across policy instruments depending on the extent of distributional and ideological politics which in part determine informational asymmetries between the president and Congress.

Presidential power varies across our policy instruments, as we show in these cases. Where a president is weak, it is very hard for him to substitute one policy for another and this may lock him into less appropriate policy choices. Militarization of foreign policy may be a result of this domestic political process. With other avenues to deal with foreign problems blocked, the president may resort to the use of military means more often than would be optimal. He will substitute policies that are "cheaper" in terms of domestic politics for those that may be more effective in terms of foreign policy goals.

So we expect to see that the politics surrounding trade and economic aid policy toward Sub-Saharan Africa are quite different than those around geopolitical aid and troop deployments. There should be more interest group activity in the former, and Congress should not lack information relative to the president. Under these conditions, it will be harder for the president to obtain his preferred economic aid and trade policies. He may be forced to substitute the use of the military for these other instruments, resulting in the militarization of US foreign policy toward Sub-Saharan Africa. We divide the cases to focus on our theoretically important elements: distributive politics and the role of interest groups, ideological divisions and the role of Congress, and finally presidential power in each period and for each instrument.

The time period we explore is roughly sixteen years from 1993 to 2008 inclusive. This covers the two presidencies of Bill Clinton and George W.

Bush. And it covers two very different sets of external situations: the immediate end of the Cold War in the early 1990s before the war on terror begins, and the period from 2001 onward after the 9/11 terror attacks and the global war on terror (GWOT) begins. We selected this time period because we want to see if the key features of our theory are evident for both presidents. Even though Clinton and Bush were from different political parties with different preferences over foreign policy instruments and even though they presided during different external circumstances, we expect to see strong similarities in the two periods.

Bush may have had greater overall influence because he presided mostly after 9/11 and during the global war on terror (GWOT), but we still think that differences across our policy instruments should be apparent. One reason we look at these two presidencies is to let the party of the president as well as the external situation vary. Clinton was a Democratic president during a period of low external threat, and Bush was a Republican president during a period of high external threat and pressure. Of course, a much more ambitious case-based study would be necessary for a fully factorial research design in this respect. Nonetheless, the case lets us evaluate whether the politics of foreign policies toward Sub-Saharan Africa look similar in the two presidencies, as our theory would suggest.

American policy toward Sub-Saharan Africa is a good case to examine for several reasons. First, US neglect of Africa for much of the Cold War left a void in policy that enables us to see how presidents tried to deal with the continent after a major change in the international system. Hence, given our focus on international engagement, American policy toward Africa is a good candidate. US-Sub-Saharan Africa policy was not already well defined and deeply path-dependent in 1992, as it was in other regions like Western Europe.[1] Second, policy toward Africa involves more than one country and its idiosyncrasies. By looking at the policies adopted toward a continent including forty-eight countries, we are moving away from the specifics of a single country or small region to a much broader focus. This also allows us to see how American policy makers considered a panoply of policy instruments to address a range of critical foreign policy issues. Third, like other regions, Africa also has particular connections to the American population because of its history and the legacy of slavery. Africa policy then is not sui generis; it contains, we argue, much of the same complex texture that is involved in American policy toward other countries and regions.

For instance, American policy toward Asia in the Obama administration fits many of the arguments we make. The administration's "pivot to Asia" was intended to be a strategic repositioning, involving all types of foreign policy instruments. As one study notes, "Democratic and Republican ad-

---

1  van de Walle, 2010, p. 1.

ministrations alike, with congressional support, have built and maintained strong ties that bind the United States with countries across the Pacific by dint of alliances, trade, values, immigration and family links."[2] This involved at first strong coordination across all parts of the executive branch, representing all types of foreign policy instruments and bureaucracies. "This effort . . . required a whole-of-government approach using all elements of US national power. To develop and implement it, the government's national security leaders showed strong cooperation and team work. Secretary of State Clinton, Secretary of Defense Robert Gates and his successor Leon Panetta, and National Security Advisor Tom Donilon worked closely and effectively together . . . to realize the president's vision."[3] But as the report notes, the military has come to dominate this grand strategy over time. With foreign aid growth unlikely and the Trans Pacific Partnership (TPP) stalled because of congressional opposition, the pivot has become a rebalancing of US military forces away from Europe and the Middle East toward the Pacific.[4] "The military component of the pivot has frequently been overemphasized and characterized as the driver of US policy," referring to the new Marine deployments in northern Australia, the return of the US military to the Philippines, and the rising US naval presence in Singapore.[5] We focus on Africa, but believe one could tell similar stories in other regions.

An important point regarding the nature of our analysis in this chapter is how it differs from previous chapters. Following King, Keohane, and Verba, we believe that the use of quantitative versus qualitative evidence is an uninteresting distinction.[6] But in this chapter we examine more than in the others the role of time and the changing external constraints of the international system. This attention to temporality and deep context differs from other parts of the book. In chapters 3–6, our empirical analysis typically tried to control for such temporal differences; using various fixed effects strategies that help control for differences across time periods, we pinned down the differences across foreign policy instruments. Indeed, to lend credibility to our core empirical findings about the key differences across issues areas, this approach was necessary.

But the move to a case study challenges our ability to make strong causal interpretations of a slowly evolving set of events and political dynamics. Furthermore, the ability of a case study to present more nuance lets us introduce the role of time in a way that pushes us on the implications of our theory but also sets up conditions where we can interrogate some of

---

2  Campbell and Andrews, 2013, p. 2.
3  Ibid., p. 3.
4  Matishak, 2014.
5  Campbell and Andrews, 2013, p. 8.
6  King, Keohane, and Verba, 1994.

our hypotheses in ways unavailable given the econometric strategies in the previous chapters. For example, our use of various statistical strategies (e.g., year, congressional session, and/or vote fixed effects) in previous chapters "absorbs" time so as to control for differences between time periods. And, given that these strategies were essential to examining the claims made in those chapters, our ability to investigate temporal variation was more limited.[7] Here we can show how the political dynamics of policy substitution can play out over time. Presidents get blocked in their efforts to solve external problems one way and try alternatives; both domestic and international forces affect their choices and outcomes.

## Sub-Saharan Africa Policy (1993–2001): The Clinton Years

### Transition: Understanding the Context of Policy Inherited from George H. W. Bush

The beginning of the Clinton presidency was the first period after the end of the Cold War that the United States had a chance to redefine its policy toward Sub-Saharan Africa.[8] During the Cold War, the United States had either neglected the continent or sporadically gotten involved in proxy wars there in its Cold War struggle against the USSR.[9] Following the collapse of the Soviet Union, the United States began to shift resources away from Africa's proxy political contests, toward Eastern Europe and the Commonwealth of Independent States. From 1990 to 1993, USAID's Africa desk lost 30–40 staff positions out of a total of 130 and eliminated its programs in eight African countries. The State Department also closed consulates in Kenya, Cameroon, and Nigeria, and eliminated 70 posts from the Bureau of African Affairs. According to one journalist writing in 1993, "over the past two years the word handed down in Washington has been simple: don't ask anything for Africa that costs money."[10]

The Clinton administration, however, had ambitious goals for Sub-Saharan Africa. Assistant Secretary of State Susan Rice summarized US policy on Africa as having two overarching goals: "accelerate Africa's full integration into the global economy," with the aim of accelerating growth and prosperity, and reducing social unrest and the need for costly intervention; and "protecting the US and its citizens from threats that emanate from Africa as they do from the rest of the world. In addition to weapons proliferation, we must guard against state-sponsored terrorism, narcotics flows, the

7   Wawro and Katznelson, 2014.
8   "The Clinton administration has developed the first truly post-Cold War policy for Africa." Clark, 1998, p. 12.
9   Perlez, 1992, p. 1.
10   Michaels, 1992, p. 94.

growing influence of rogue states [...], international crime, environmental degradation, and disease." Rice continued by outlining the imperatives to African integration in the world economy: Economic growth and development, the promotion of democracy and human rights, and the prevention, management, and resolution of conflict.[11] These interrelated goals required that the United States bring many different foreign policy instruments to bear in Africa.

In terms of our argument, the Clinton presidency is notable for several trends in its Sub-Saharan Africa policy. The US government began trying to expand economic relations, especially after the end of apartheid in South Africa in the early 1990s. President Clinton undertook policies that tried to enhance trade and investment relations with Sub-Saharan Africa and to provide debt relief.[12] First, as Democrats are likely to prefer, the president wanted to use foreign economic aid as a main element of his policies toward Africa. In this he was frustrated time and again by a Republican-controlled Congress which opposed development aid (as captured by several of our roll call votes in chapter 4 and as demonstrated in chapter 5 in our discussion of USAID).

Second, failing to be able to engage with aid because of deep ideological divisions over it, he shifted to trade policy. With Republicans in Congress favoring trade over aid, this choice became easier for Clinton to advance. The African Growth and Opportunity Act (AGOA), signed into law on May 18, 2000, after four years of debate, which unilaterally expanded access to the US market for African exports, was the result of this effort. As we argue, policy substitution is an important strategy for presidents, and when it is easier in terms of domestic political costs to shift to another policy instrument, presidents will choose to do so. With aid policy restricted by Congress, Clinton pushed ahead with a trade strategy in the late 1990s. But even this was difficult, as evidenced by the years of political wrangling over AGOA in the late 1990s. Ideological divisions and distributive politics also afflicted trade policy.

Third, to deal with the continuing critical problems of conflict, democratization, and development in Africa, Clinton finally turned to a strategy that also relied on military engagement. He established the basis for a US military presence in Sub-Saharan Africa beginning in the late 1990s, as aid and trade policy were stymied at home. For example, the creation of the African Crisis Response Force (ACRF), later renamed the African Crisis Response Initiative (ACRI), was the result of both internal and external forces in the late 1990s.[13] And from this small military footprint grew a much larger one over time, again revealing the tendency for US foreign policy to become militarized. Our view is that the use of trade and military

---

11   Rice, 1997. Also see U.S. Department of Defense, 1995.
12   Jones and Williams, 2012, p. 2.
13   Omach, 2000.

deployments partially substituted for Clinton's inability to pursue his first choice of policy instruments because of distributive politics and ideological divisions at home. His administration had more (but of course not complete) discretion in terms of domestic politics with military deployments compared with aid or trade.

With this background in mind, we next turn to specific discussions across aid, trade, and military instruments. In each, we lay out the main lines of the policies discussed and adopted. We examine the president's interactions with Congress and interest groups. We detail how policy evolved over time, especially in reaction to domestic pressures and ideological divisions. We pay attention to informational asymmetries in each instrument, and where the president was able to maintain them and where interest groups helped Congress equalize them. And we show how policy substitution occurred, with increasing militarization of American policy toward Sub-Saharan Africa. Each of these steps touches upon one of the hypotheses that we advance in the book.

## Aid Policy

### AID POLICY PRIOR TO CLINTON

As Cold War tensions waned, US foreign assistance to Africa began a steep decline. From a peak of $1.7 billion in 1985, aid reached a low of $1.1 billion in 1990.[14] At the same time, criticism of the US foreign assistance program was growing as was pressure for reform. In 1992, James C. Clad and Roger D. Stone opened a *Foreign Affairs* article with the sentence, "America's foreign bilateral assistance program lies dead in the water."[15]

### AID POLICY CHANGES DURING THE CLINTON ADMINISTRATION

While US foreign assistance to Africa remained relatively unchanged during the early years of the Clinton administration, the Republican takeover of Congress following the 1994 mid-term elections led to a dramatic drop.[16] Congressional critics took aim in particular at development assistance, arguing that decades of US assistance had achieved little in promoting economic growth on the continent. In FY1996, development assistance was cut to $665 million from $802 million the year before, a reduction of about

---

14   Constant 1995 dollars.
15   Clad and Stone, 1992, p. 196.
16   "Finally, foreign aid to the Africa region stagnated in current terms and declined in real terms, falling to a historic low in 1996. The US had provided as much as a fifth of all foreign aid to sub-Saharan Africa, but by 2000 it accounted for under 10 percent. By then, USAID no longer had resident missions in 22 of sub-Saharan Africa's 48 countries." van de Walle, 2010, p. 5.

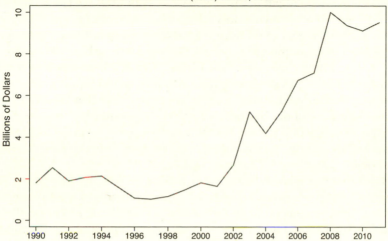

**U.S. Bilateral ODA Commitments to Sub–Saharan Africa**
In billions of constant (2009) dollars, 1990–2011

**Figure 7.1.** US Official Development Assistance to Sub-Saharan Africa. Source: Geographical Distribution of Financial Flows (OECD, 2012).

18%. Assistance gradually recovered during Clinton's second term, though by 2000, bilateral aid still remained below the level it had been in 1990.[17] Figure 7.1 shows the constant dollar amounts of US bilateral aid that went to Sub-Saharan Africa from 1990 to 2011. The decline in real aid funds in Clinton's term is notable since such aid had rarely, if ever, declined in the past. As we note below, this led the Clinton administration to deploy other policy instruments for attaining its goals in Africa. The president was pushed to substitute trade policy for aid, in part because trade policy was easier for him to develop given Republican preferences in Congress. Ideological differences between the parties prevented the president from using the policy instrument he most preferred. More than any other policy instrument or time period, foreign assistance during the Clinton administration seems to demonstrate the weakness of presidential power. Clinton faced a congressional majority ideologically opposed to foreign assistance and determined to obstruct his policy choices, which we discuss next.

## ROLE OF CONGRESS

From 1992 to 1994, foreign assistance to Africa remained relatively constant with strong support emanating from the House Subcommittee on Africa.[18]

17   Copson, 2000a.
18   Committee on Foreign Affairs, 1993.

However, Congress adopted a more antagonistic stance following the 1994 elections in which Republicans won a majority in both the House and Senate. The new Republican majority advanced its own reform agenda, heavily informed by the goal of producing a balanced budget.[19] Deep ideological divisions over economic aid appeared. During a November 1993 news conference, incoming chairman of the Foreign Affairs committee Jesse Helms noted that review of foreign assistance activities would be a priority for the new year and accused the US foreign aid program of "[spending] an estimated $2 trillion of the American taxpayers' money, much of it going down foreign rat holes, to countries that constantly oppose us in the United Nations, and many which reject concepts of freedom."[20] To begin with, Helms proposed a 20% cut in US foreign assistance.[21]

Even before the new Congress had been seated, Senator Mitch McConnell (R-KY) introduced legislation containing a variety of foreign assistance reforms, including an initiative to de-fund and eliminate the African Development Fund (ADF), a smaller aid allocation which funded non-governmental initiatives.[22] By mid-1995, Republicans in Congress talked of cutting US Africa assistance by up to one-third. The Senate passed Foreign Operations appropriation legislation (H.R. 1868), cut ADF funds from $802 million to $676 million, and eliminated the ADF earmark. The House version preserved the ADF earmark, but appropriated slightly less than the Senate. Ultimately, funding was cut to $665 million for both FY96 and FY97.[23]

Congressional Republicans similarly took aim at US multilateral assistance to Africa. In April 1995, the Government Accounting Office responded to a congressional request to audit the African Development Bank by stating that the bank was "solvent but vulnerable."[24] The GAO's report also critiqued the institution for not taking "due regard for [members'] creditworthiness" in making loan decisions.[25] Congress reacted by rescinding half of the FY1995 appropriation and refusing to appropriate any funds for FY1996 and FY1997, instead calling for sweeping reforms to lending practices.[26] That same year, Congress also cut funding for the International Development Association, the second largest channel of US development assistance to Africa.[27] While assistance levels began to rise again

19   Grant and Nijman, 1998.
20   Goshko and Williams, 1994.
21   Ibid.
22   Peabody, 1995b.
23   Copson, 1995; Copson, 2000b.
24   U.S. General Accounting Office, 1995, p. 2.
25   Ibid.
26   Copson, 2000b.
27   Copson, 1995.

slowly from 1998, the Republican majority in Congress remained skeptical of foreign assistance and antagonistic toward the objectives of the Clinton administration.

## ROLE OF INTEREST GROUPS AND DISTRIBUTIVE POLITICS

Interest groups played a significant role during debates over foreign aid, just as they did in debates over trade. During the early years of the Clinton administration, both business groups and NGOs actively supported foreign assistance reform, though for different reasons. Business lobbies, arguing that the United States received less than other countries did in exchange for foreign assistance, lobbied in favor of "assistance programs that funded capital projects, fewer cash transfers to alleviate balance of payment problems, more 'mixed credits' . . . and strengthening of 'buy America' provisions that guaranteed procurement of U.S. goods and services."[28] Business groups' opposition to cash transfers and debt rescheduling again suggests their economic interests in loans and grants that were tied to US goods and services. Advocates of development also lobbied for change, though opposite from what business groups wanted.[29] The influence of business groups led some in Congress to propose increasing bilateral foreign assistance to infrastructure projects in order to increase US exports, particularly from the construction industry. This proposal was opposed by the Clinton administration, who maintained that development objectives and export promotion should remain separate.[30]

Later in the administration, interest groups again played an important role during debates about Congress's foreign aid cuts described above. In hearings before the Subcommittee on Africa in March 1995, one private sector spokesman, Malcolm Pryor, urged the Committee to maintain funding for USAID as well as the African Development Bank, saying that "USAID has been very receptive to giving us . . . [export] opportunities."[31] Cuts in Africa assistance were also opposed by members of the Congressional Black Caucus, particularly Representative Donald Payne (D-NJ), Chairman of the House Subcommittee on Africa. In its opposition, the CBC was joined by a broad coalition of national black organizations and high-profile figures such as Rev. Jesse L. Jackson.[32]

Again, special interests, both economic and ideological, were actively engaged in the policy-making process. While most economic interests favored aid,

---

28 Grant and Nijman, 1998, pp. 33–34.
29 Ibid.
30 Lancaster, 2000.
31 Committee on International Relations, 1995, p. 34.
32 Peabody, 1995b; Peabody, 1995a.

there were ideological divisions with substantial conservative opposition. This contrasts somewhat with trade, as we discuss below, where there was greater conservative support and economic interest groups lined up on both sides.

## PRESIDENTIAL POWER

Throughout the Clinton administration, Congress consistently rebuffed the president's efforts to first reform and then increase foreign assistance to Africa. Clinton's first major initiative upon taking office was a comprehensive review of foreign assistance practices accompanied by a major reform proposal. In this he was both responding to widespread criticism of existing foreign assistance practices and attempting to win greater flexibility for the executive branch in the allocation of foreign assistance. In late 1993, after a comprehensive executive review, the Peace, Prosperity, and Democracy Act was circulated to Congress in "discussion form."[33] The bill proposed the repeal of the 1961 Foreign Assistance Act along with all amendments and country-specific provisions, and the establishment of a new, more flexible aid framework.

Initial congressional reactions were mixed. Members largely agreed on the need for comprehensive reform, but many raised concerns about the removal of country-specific legislation and the dramatic increase in presidential policy-making space.[34] The administration's FY1995 budget request reflected the proposed new aid legislation, eliminating country-specific earmarks and requesting overall funding levels instead. Ultimately the measure received little support in Congress and was abandoned entirely following the 1994 elections and the Republican takeover of Congress.

For the rest of his time in office, President Clinton lobbied against Republican initiatives to cut foreign assistance to Africa, though with little success. Shortly after congressional cuts of the foreign assistance budget, the president began to embrace trade policy more actively. He decided to substitute away from foreign assistance toward a policy where there was initially greater ideological agreement among lawmakers, though this too eventually unwound.

While foreign assistance began to rise again in 1998, Congress continued to withhold funds requested by the administration. Beginning in 1999, the president also engaged in a new battle over foreign assistance, this time in the form of multilateral debt relief. By 1998, the debt burden of African countries grew to $226 billion. As the debt burden grew, the demands of repayment increasingly choked off the provision of public services which helped retard economic growth on the continent. By the late 1990s, a broad

33  Nowels, 2007.
34  Goshko and Lippman, 1993.

international consensus began to emerge among donor countries, NGOs, and lending institutions that an aggressive debt relief program was needed. The focal point for this program became the IMF/World Bank Highly Indebted Poor Country (HIPC) initiative, through which debt relief for the world's poorest countries was coordinated by both financial institutions and paid for out of a joint "HIPC Trust Fund." Though both the World Bank and IMF contributed where possible to the trust fund, they were unable to cover the overall costs of debt reduction and thus called upon donor nations to fund the HIPC program. In February 1999, the US Treasury Department estimated that the HIPC Trust Fund faced a shortfall of around $2 billion.[35]

That same year, President Clinton requested $120 million for debt relief programs in his initial FY2000 Foreign Operations budget request. He later increased this request to $970 million over four years. The Republican majority in Congress, however, resisted any such proposals. In its initial Foreign Operations appropriations, H.R. 2606, Congress appropriated only $33 million for bilateral debt relief measures, but refused to appropriate any funds at all for the HIPC initiative.[36] President Clinton vetoed H.R. 2606, citing Congress's intransigence over debt relief as well as cuts to multilateral development banks, which would "seriously undermine [US] capacity to promote economic reform and growth . . . especially [in] Africa."[37] In H.R. 3422, Congress subsequently increased funding for bilateral debt relief to $123 million, though it continued to block the use of these funds for multilateral/HIPC debt relief and again refused to increase funding for multilateral development banks. This time Clinton relented, signing the bill into law on November 29, 1999.[38]

Clinton faced strong congressional opposition to using foreign aid as a central instrument in its Sub-Saharan Africa policy. Ideological divisions and distributive politics weakened Clinton and made him unable to use the policy instrument he most desired. As we discuss next, this led the administration to look for other policies to advance American interests in Africa. However, as we discuss below, some of these avenues proved to be much more difficult than others.

## Trade Policy

### TRADE POLICY PRIOR TO CLINTON

The lens of the Cold War meant that policy toward Sub-Saharan Africa had typically been dominated by security concerns. As these concerns gave

35  Nowels, 2000.
36  Ibid.
37  Quoted in Copson, 2000a, p. 11; see also Copson, 2000b.
38  Nowels, 2000. In particular see note 15.

way during the presidency of George H. W. Bush, a new emphasis on economic development emerged. Though the first Bush administration placed emphasis on free trade, engaging actively in the Uruguay Round and negotiating the North American Free Trade Agreement, no Africa-specific trade initiatives emerged during this period. With the foreign aid channel blocked by Congress, the Clinton administration had to consider other policy instruments for Africa.

## TRADE POLICY CHANGES DURING THE CLINTON ADMINISTRATION

Policy making during Clinton's two terms in office fundamentally changed US Africa policy, in particular by elevating the role of trade as an important policy instrument. While the Clinton administration followed in George H. W. Bush's footsteps, concluding the Uruguay Round negotiations, but paying little attention to African trade, Congress took an increasingly active approach. By the mid-nineties, a bipartisan coalition of lawmakers began to advocate a new, trade-based approach to Africa policy. This advocacy led over many years to the African Growth and Opportunity Act, signed into law on May 18, 2000, which unilaterally expanded access to the US market for African exports. As noted in a recent Brookings study:

> [The signing of AGOA] introduced a fundamental change to U.S. policy toward Sub-Saharan Africa ... AGOA moved the U.S. away from a singular reliance on development assistance as a strategy for engaging African countries and introduced [trade and investment] as stimuli for economic development and poverty reduction.[39]

While Congress took an early interest in trade policy, the Clinton administration initially paid little attention to trade, emphasizing traditional development assistance instead. However, by 1997 the administration had reversed course and firmly embraced AGOA. As will be suggested below, this reflects strategic substitution on the part of the president after being blocked from the use of foreign assistance by House Republicans. But Clinton's turn to trade policy was not easy either; it took years for AGOA to pass and it was watered down considerably in the process due to domestic opposition in the United States.

A key feature of debates over AGOA was the prominent role of economic interest groups who vocally participated in the policy-making process. Private sector interests on both sides of the debate lobbied extensively to support, oppose, or shape the legislation according to their market position. Their active role was evident in our quantitative analysis of AGOA in chapter 3.

39  Schneidman and Lewis, 2012, p. 1.

## ROLE OF CONGRESS

Clinton's first major trade initiative, conclusion of the GATT Uruguay Round negotiations, received broad bipartisan support in Congress.[40] Support was particularly strong among congressional Republicans.[41] Distributional concerns did play a role, causing some opposition to the agreements, particularly from the textile and apparel sectors.[42] In spite of this opposition, implementing legislation was successfully passed in the House on November 29 and in the Senate on December 1, 1994, both with bipartisan support.[43]

With respect to Africa, however, some members of Congress questioned the impact of the Uruguay Round agreements on poor developing countries. In line with these concerns, Representative Jim McDermott (D-WA) successfully added an amendment to the authorizing legislation requiring the Clinton administration to formulate a comprehensive US trade and development policy for Africa. Two years later, in 1996, members of both parties came together to form the congressional African Trade and Investment Caucus to "initiate a broader discussion" of trade and development issues on the continent.[44] In September 1996, Representatives Jim McDermott (D-WA), Phil Crane (R-IL), and Charles Rangel (D-NY) introduced an early version of what would become the African Growth and Opportunity Act: a package of legislative measures designed to stimulate US-Africa trade and investment. These measures included negotiation of a US-Africa free trade area by 2020, establishment of a US-Africa economic forum, and increased market access for African exports, including textiles.[45]

Turning to trade policy as an instrument for helping Africa, Clinton faced domestic opposition. Passage of the AGOA initiative, which was the main element of American trade policy toward the continent, took nearly four years and was controversial at each stage. The measure enjoyed support from a bipartisan coalition of free trade–oriented Republicans and Democrats, who were ready to embrace a new approach to African development. However, it was opposed both for distributional and ideological reasons. Representatives from textile-rich states in both houses lobbied against the measure, as did many more liberal Democrats who criticized the emphasis on trade over foreign assistance.

40    Ingwerson, 1994; Moynihan, 1994; Rostenkowski, 1994.
41    Devroy, 1994. We note though that the extent of ideological cleavage was reduced by opposition to the agreements that came from opposite ends of the political spectrum: a coalition led by Republican Pat Buchanan and Green Party leader Ralph Nader. Walker, 1994. But generally speaking here too there was clear conservative support and liberal opposition.
42    Ingwerson, 1994.
43    Dreier, 1994.
44    Committee on International Relations, 1996; quoted in Dagne, 1998, p. 1.
45    Committee on Ways and Means, 1996.

No vote was taken on the bill in 1996, but a new version was introduced the following year. In spite of President Clinton's endorsement in April 1997, again no vote was taken on the measure.[46] AGOA ran into trouble again in August 1998 when the Senate Finance Committee approved its own version of the legislation. Rather than approving a similar measure to what the House had passed, the Republican leadership once more attached several trade-related measures to the bill, including MFN for Mongolia and fast-track authority. The Committee also stipulated that only garments manufactured using US cloth could be imported under the new regime.[47] This last provision reflects lobbying by US textile manufacturers, wary of surging African imports under the new regime.[48] Finally, the Senate version also stripped the bill of provisions related to debt relief and foreign assistance, prompting at least one House Democrat, Maxine Waters (D-CA), to reverse her prior support for the bill in an open letter calling for other Democrats to do the same.[49] Ultimately, the Senate failed to vote on the bill before the end of the year, leaving it once again to be taken up the following year.

In July 1999, the House of Representatives passed its version of AGOA for the second time by a vote of 234-163. Again, the bill was the subject of heated floor debate as representatives of American textile manufacturers argued that the bill would set the stage for fraudulent transshipment of Asian textiles into the US market.[50] Textile opposition also nearly derailed the Senate version of the bill for a second time in October 1999 when Senator Ernest F. Hollings (D-SC) led a filibuster, which temporarily delayed any possibility of a vote.[51] However, on November 3, 1999, the Senate version finally passed by a vote of 76-19. The following year, after approval in both Houses of the conference report, President Clinton signed the measure into law on May 18, 2000.[52] Because of distributive and partisan politics, it took close to four years to get this trade policy initiative off the ground. Attempts to substitute away from one policy to another—in this case from aid to trade—must contend with the politics of the new policy instrument that is being proposed.

---

46    Press accounts suggest that this attempt at passage was undermined by the Republican leadership's attempts to fold in fast-track authorization, as mentioned above. Dinkins, 1997a. In mid-March 1998, the House of Representatives once again took up the measure, this time passing the proposed legislation with a vote of 233-186. The passage took place in spite of opposition from members of the House who criticized the bill for not incorporating adequate foreign assistance funds. Peabody, 1998. The House bill was also opposed by Representative Jesse Jackson, Jr. (D-IL), who argued that the bill would exploit African workers, though the Congressional Black Caucus supported the bill overall with a vote of 24-12. Schmitt, 1998.
47    New York Voice, 1998.
48    Waithaka, 1998.
49    Waters, 1998.
50    Kabugi, 1999; Schmitt, 1999b.
51    Schmitt, 1999a.
52    Ross, 2000.

## ROLE OF INTEREST GROUPS AND DISTRIBUTIVE POLITICS

The role of interest groups can be discerned during each of the major policy debates over African trade policy during this period. Interest groups played a dual role during these debates, both lobbying for and against greater engagement in Africa as well as providing policy-relevant information in the process. Information provision by interest groups is an important element in our theory. When groups are incentivized to do this, it weighs against the president having any kind of informational advantage. One reason that Clinton had such troubles getting his trade policy for Sub-Saharan Africa implemented was that Congress had a great deal of information about it, provided by these competing interest groups.

The major role of interest groups was apparent even *before* AGOA's introduction as Congress considered its options for a new approach to the region. Beginning in 1995, subcommittees in both the House and Senate held a series of hearings on US trade and investment in Africa. Private sector spokespersons featured prominently in these hearings, lobbying for greater US engagement but also providing insight into on-the-ground challenges and opportunities of doing business in Africa. Witnesses represented companies actively engaged in African markets, including Coca-Cola, AT&T, and General Motors among others, though also groups opposed to trade which we discuss below.

On the pro-trade side, many American firms described the important opportunities for trade in Africa. Many witnesses from the private sector highlighted growing opportunities for US businesses in the African market.[53] Executive director of the US-South African Business Council, Daniel O'Flaherty, offered an example of a $240 million infrastructure project upgrading rail and road links between the South African business hub of Gauteng and Mozambique's capital of Maputo. O'Flaherty warned though that US suppliers were frequently disadvantaged in the African market compared with European counterparts who received considerable policy support from their governments.[54]

Economic interest groups were also active in lobbying and advising the executive branch and Congress. From September 8 to November 10, 1994, the Corporate Council on Africa and the Department of State jointly held three roundtable discussions to "identify specific issues and recommendations to improve the commercial environment in Africa."[55] These roundtable discussions included over sixty high-level, private sector executives as well as representatives from the executive branch. The final product of these meetings was a report containing specific policy advice on how

53   Committee on Ways and Means, 1996, p. 57.
54   Ibid., p. 95.
55   Committee on Foreign Relations, 1995, p. 61.

the US executive branch could enhance support for US businesses operating in Africa. While providing guidance to the executive branch, the CCA also submitted the final report directly to Congress.[56] The reliance of both branches of government on this private sector expertise suggests that the executive branch enjoyed little or no informational advantage in debates over trade policy. Our evidence on testimony on AGOA in chapter 3 clearly shows this pattern as well.

As formal debates over the African Growth and Opportunity Act began, special interests, particularly economic interests, continued to weigh in. A March 1997 hearing on the proposed legislation drew energetic engagement from the private sector. AIG's president for Africa and the Middle East, Ralph W. Mucerino, welcomed the bill, calling it "the most important piece of legislation to Africa in many years."[57] As the legislative process continued, pro-trade groups began to organize more formally in support of AGOA. In one example, a group of sixty US corporations joined forces to form the African Growth and Opportunity Act Coalition, Inc., co-chaired by Ford Motor Company's vice president, Elliot S. Hall.[58]

However, economic actors concerned about the new policy's negative distributional consequences also became vocal participants in these debates. These interests had an important impact on the policy-making process, obstructing passage of the legislation on a number of occasions as noted above. In a letter to the House Subcommittee on Trade, the American Apparel Alliance, a national trade association of apparel manufacturers, registered its "vehement opposition" to the proposed legislation.[59] Similarly, Footwear Industries of America, Inc. lobbied against the legislation, arguing that "Africa needs to grow and prosper. But this must not come at the expense of closed shoe factories and unemployed shoe workers [in the US]."[60]

The distributional concerns just mentioned shaped the legislative process in important ways, nearly derailing AGOA on a number of occasions. As noted above, textile groups lobbied successfully in 1998 for an amendment to restrict new African textile imports to those made only from American fabric and thread. The then-ambassador from Mauritius, Chitmansing Jesseramsing, described this provision as "the death knell for the textile industry in sub-Saharan Africa," while Roble Olhaye, ambassador from Djibouti and dean of the African diplomatic corps, called the measure "a slap in our face."

---

56   Ibid. Perhaps not surprisingly, the first of these recommendations reads: "Take into account the U.S. private sector and consider commercial ramifications to U.S. exporters/importers when formulating policies." Ibid., p. 63.
57   Committee on Ways and Means, 1997, p. 124.
58   Waithaka, 1998.
59   Committee on Ways and Means, 1996, p. 197.
60   Committee on Ways and Means, 1997, p. 239.

The provision was one of several that blocked passage of the measure in 1998.[61]

Textile interests again played a pivotal role in the final showdown over passage in November 1999 when Senator Ernest Hollings (D-SC) led a filibuster, blocking the Senate's move to vote on the bill. As was widely recognized at the time, Hollings acted under pressure from South Carolina's influential textile industry. In his campaign to halt AGOA he was joined by at least six Republicans who also hailed from southern or New England textile-producing states.[62]

Interest groups were very active in the trade area, as other studies of trade policy have well documented.[63] And most of these groups had important economic interests at stake, which they lobbied strongly for. In addition, these groups provided Congress with information about what AGOA might look like and its distributional impact. This information then left Congress less dependent on the executive branch for knowledge about what the executive was proposing.

## PRESIDENTIAL POWER

The Clinton administration had a difficult time engaging Africa through a trade strategy because of domestic politics. Interest group resistance combined with ideological battles over trade limited his power substantially. In addition, the preferred strategy of the administration was at least initially one involving foreign aid. It took several years for the administration to give up on the aid strategy and turn to trade. During the early years of Clinton's presidency, there was little support from the administration for a comprehensive Africa trade policy.[64] Though the administration did complete the Uruguay Round negotiations begun during President George H.W. Bush's administration, it undertook no Africa-specific initiatives until early 1997.[65]

---

61  Quoted in Kelley, 1998.

62  Dewar, 1999. NGOs also weighed in on the debate. Throughout 1997, the Constituency for Africa held town hall meetings across the United States to advocate for AGOA's passage. Dinkins, 1997b. In contrast, another high-profile NGO, TransAfrica, vocally opposed the bill, arguing that it placed unreasonable eligibility requirements on African nations and included no provisions for environmental or labor rights. Chapman, 1998. Another voice calling for greater engagement was the National Conference of Black Mayors (NCBM).

63  For example, Milner, 1988a; Chase, 2005; Manger, 2009; Kim, 2013; Goldstein and Gulotty, 2014.

64  A 1996 report of the International Trade Commission seemed to confirm these assertions, noting that during the period 1992–1994 export promotion to Africa received little support from traditional executive branch agencies, such as OPIC and the Exim Bank, when compared with other regions. Jabara, Harman, Corey, et al., 1996.

65  One exception to the early disinterest in Africa trade policy, however, was the effort by Secretary of Commerce Ron Brown to strengthen US trade ties with the continent.

Favoring developmental aid at first, the Clinton administration was slow to change to a focus on trade for engagement with Sub-Saharan Africa. When the Clinton administration submitted its first "Comprehensive Trade and Development Strategy for Africa" in February 1996, it was roundly criticized for placing too much emphasis on traditional development instruments, rather than on new approaches.[66] As one private sector spokesperson testified during congressional hearings later that year, the comprehensive strategy resembled "more a justification of traditional development programs than a policy advocating the expansion of African trade."[67] The executive branch was initially unsympathetic to private sector actors who pushed for expanded trade relations, and it defended the status quo with its focus on aid. However, in early 1997 the administration reversed its earlier policy, embracing the AGOA legislation. The administration formally endorsed the legislation during a White House ceremony in mid-June 1997 in which it also launched a new Partnership for Economic Growth and Opportunity.[68] The timing of this reversal strongly suggests a connection with the president's frustrated attempts to achieve his policy goals through the use of foreign assistance as had been his initial preference.

Following this decision to substitute trade for aid policy, the administration launched itself into the legislative battle over passage of AGOA. The administration was active throughout the four years it took to pass the measure in spite of various setbacks along the way. Following Congress's failure to move forward on the proposal during the 1997 legislative session, the president kicked off a new lobbying effort by endorsing the measure during his state of the union address in January 1998.[69]

These efforts achieved little, and revealed a president with limited influence over the legislative process. As already described, the Senate failed to vote on AGOA at all in 1998. In early 1999, the Clinton administration mounted yet another campaign to pass the measure. In a January 22 speech, Assistant USTR for Africa, Rosa Whitaker, stated: "The Administration's top priority in 1999 is to work with the 106th Congress to ensure passage of the African Growth and Opportunity Act."[70] This new effort culminated in the weeks be-

---

Clark, 1998. From 1992 to 1996, he visited the continent six times and played an active role in strengthening US investment ties with South Africa following the 1994 election of Nelson Mandela. These efforts led to a $600 million trade and investment package for the newly democratic nation, announced in 1994.

66  Dagne, 1996; Umoren, 1996.

67  Committee on Ways and Means, 1996, p. 82.

68  Dagne, 1998.

69  "So this year we will forge new partnerships with Latin America, Asia, and Europe. And we should pass the new 'African Trade Act'; it has bipartisan support. I will also renew my request for the fast-track negotiating authority necessary to open more new markets, create more jobs, which every President has had for two decades." Clinton, 1998, p. 115.

70  Whitaker, 1999.

fore the Senate's final vote when President Clinton undertook a personal lobbying campaign, reaching out to key senators via phone to support the bill.[71]

While the final passage of AGOA is viewed as a victory for President Clinton, his influence over the legislative process was limited. Though he expended considerable political capital in lobbying for passage, his efforts were continually undermined by distributional concerns as well as political maneuvering by both parties. In particular, his personal lobbying campaign late in 1999 nearly came to nothing as some Senate Democrats unanimously opposed AGOA out of electoral concerns.

Thus presidential power in the realm of trade policy during this period seems to have been moderate. In the case of AGOA, economic interests concerned about the distributional effects of the legislation held up passage for some time in spite of the president's lobbying efforts. Economic interest groups lobbied Congress forcefully for and against passage of AGOA, providing it with much information and undermining any informational advantage the president might have had. Again, distributive and partisan ideological pressures seem to have limited the president's options and forced him to choose a policy instrument he might not have otherwise.

## Military Policy

### MILITARY POLICY PRIOR TO CLINTON

As noted earlier, America's geostrategic interests in Africa declined as Cold War tensions eased in the late 1980s. During a 1992 hearing before the House Subcommittee on Africa, Department of Defense (DoD) deputy assistant secretary for International Affairs, Jim Woods, noted: "Our strategic interests in Africa are very modest. We have no interest in establishing a major or permanent presence ... Altogether, there are fewer than 300 U.S. military personnel presently assigned in sub-Saharan Africa."[72] The United States was not very militarily engaged in Africa prior to the 1990s. But this was to change greatly over the next two decades. First, the United States began engaging via a series of multilateral peacekeeping efforts, often led by the UN. Later the United States began unilateral military missions in Sub-Saharan Africa. American foreign policy toward Sub-Saharan Africa became steadily more militarized as time passed.

### CHANGES IN MILITARY POLICY DURING THE CLINTON ADMINISTRATION

When it comes to the use of troops, the president had more control over policy internally than in aid or trade. From 1992 to 2001, the Clinton administration

---

71   Schmitt, 1999c.
72   Committee on Foreign Relations, 1992, p. 7.

engineered two important transformations of US military policy toward Africa. US military intervention in Sub-Saharan Africa had been very limited up to the end of the Cold War. From 1971 to 1983, for example, Africa was not included at all in the US military command structure.[73] And during the Reagan and Bush administrations in the 1980s, very little attention was paid militarily to Sub-Saharan Africa; Libya, however, was the nearest center of military action for both presidents in Northern Africa. The first transformation in policy was the increasing use of UN peacekeeping missions that developed in the Clinton years and the turn away from them to a more unilateral policy later.

Prior to the 1990s, the American military footprint in Sub-Saharan Africa had been very small, if not non-existent. As the Cold War ended, problems in Sub-Saharan Africa became increasingly dire and public. Following the Bush administration's example in Somalia, the Clinton administration engaged these problems through a series of UN-led peacekeeping operations in the 1990s. The Clinton administration was at first very enthusiastic about these multilateral efforts, and the US Congress was generally supportive. But over time both the president and Congress became considerably more skeptical of US direct involvement in peacekeeping missions. Though both supported US participation in Somalia at the outset of the Clinton presidency, Congress became a staunch opponent of peacekeeping as the US death toll began to rise but had little ability to determine the direction of policy. The Clinton administration also backed away from its initial enthusiasm, instead choosing to provide military training for indigenous peacekeepers as an alternative to direct participation.

A second important shift began toward the end of Clinton's presidency, instigated by the terrorist bombings of two US embassies in East Africa. The Clinton administration added a counterterrorism element to US policy, beginning with swift retaliation after the bombings via a cruise missile strike against an alleged chemical weapons facility in southern Sudan. These unilateral military measures received broad support in every branch of government and among the general population.[74] The unilateral strikes represented a new emphasis on counterterrorism in US Africa policy, a trend that became much more pronounced during the presidency of George W. Bush. They also presaged the beginning of greater militarization of US policy in Sub-Saharan Africa.

## ROLE OF CONGRESS

Initially, the majority in Congress supported US military intervention even in UN-led peacekeeping operations in Sub-Saharan Africa. But over time,

---

73 Ploch, 2011.
74 Bennet, 1998; Fidler and Suzman, 1998; Robbins and Ricks, 1998; Suzman, 1998.

Congress grew increasingly opposed to such efforts and tried to restrict the president's ability to pursue them. The president, however, was able to deflect such restrictions and continue peacekeeping operations, although executive branch enthusiasm for them also waned. Ideological divisions were fairly muted in this area compared to aid and trade; bipartisanship often prevailed.

Congressional majorities supported the president in peacekeeping operations. For instance, majorities in Congress not only supported, but even lobbied in favor of, the humanitarian mission in Somalia. Throughout 1992, Senators Nancy Kassebaum (R-KS) and Paul Simon (D-IL) called publicly for US action to address the spreading famine, leading a fact-finding mission to the country in early 1992. By midyear, both houses of Congress had adopted resolutions supporting a UN mission. Congressional support remained strong throughout the early phase of the mission. When the Clinton administration supported an expansion of the UN mandate in May 1993, both houses again passed resolutions in support.

Congressional support began to erode gradually during the summer of 1993 and evaporated following the deaths of eighteen US servicemen in Mogadishu on October 8, 1993.[75] As is described in more detail below, Congress was active in calling for an end to US involvement in light of these casualties. Informed by this experience, Congress adopted a much more negative stance on peacekeeping and made several attempts over the following years to increase its oversight of US involvement in multilateral peacekeeping.[76]

Congress's efforts to play a greater role in peacekeeping deliberations were unsuccessful, as we show below, in part because of the nature of its funding authority. Traditionally, Congress provides funding for peacekeeping operations only through its overall UN appropriations. Thus Congress could not pick and choose which operations to fund. Presidents typically agreed to a mission first and then requested supplementary funding from Congress much later.[77] To get around this, from 1994 to 1995, Congress tried to create new reporting and consultation requirements for the executive branch. Both the FY1994 and FY1995 DoD appropriations bills "stated the sense of Congress that no funds should be spent for costs incurred in UN military operations unless the President consulted with the bipartisan leadership of Congress."[78] Similarly, the FY1994 and FY1995 Foreign Relations Authorization Acts stipulated that the president must update Congress monthly on both current and anticipated UN peacekeeping missions.

As an additional measure, on January 5, 1995, legislation was introduced in both the House and Senate to prohibit funding of any US forces placed

75  MacKinnon, 2000.
76  Grimmett, 1995, p. 1.
77  Ibid.
78  Ibid., p. 4.

under the control of the UN. The Clinton administration strongly opposed these initiatives. During testimony on January 26, 1995, before the House Committee on International Relations, Secretary of State Warren Christopher noted that if the bill were passed he would recommend that the president exercise veto authority. Secretary of Defense William Perry made similar statements.[79] Though the House passed its version of the bill (H.R.7), 241 in favor to 181 opposed, the Senate version died before any vote was taken. These congressional measures to constrain the president's ability to use peacekeeping as a policy instrument were not adopted, as the president pushed hard against them.

In practice, these congressional maneuvers did little to deter the Clinton administration from supporting multilateral peacekeeping operations where it chose to. Though the administration initially opposed and then delayed action during the 1994 Rwandan genocide, it later supported UN missions in Zaire, Angola, and Western Sahara.[80] For most of its two terms in office, the administration also continued its support of the Nigerian-led Economic Community of West African States Monitoring Group (ECOMOG) peacekeeping mission in Liberia, allocating around $80 million in assistance from 1991 to 1997.[81] Congress at times tried to curtail the president's prerogative and discretion in peacekeeping activity. The president retained his informational advantages in this area, faced limited distributional and ideological pressures, and was therefore able to resist congressional attempts to constrain his authority for military action.

## ROLE OF INTEREST GROUPS AND DISTRIBUTIVE POLITICS

In the area of military policy, interest group activity was considerably less than in either aid or trade policy. For example, a review of every congressional hearing on African peacekeeping from 1993 to 2000 revealed not a single witness drawn from the private economic sector.[82] Rather, witnesses were drawn from the executive branch, the academic or think tank communities, and from various non-governmental organizations. Thus, while interest groups such as NGOs may have played a role in the policy-making process, the distributional concerns so apparent in trade and aid policy were largely absent.[83]

---

79   Ibid.
80   United Nations Security Council, 1995; Serafino, 2006.
81   Berman and Sams, 2000.
82   We searched all hearings on ProQuest Congressional for the keywords "Africa" and "peacekeeping" from 1993 to 2000. We collected all the hearings and reviewed all the speakers who testified at each.
83   This is not to imply that distributional concerns were completely absent. For example, US peacekeeping policy had important economic consequences for the defense contracting

## PRESIDENTIAL POWER

The president seemed to be more able to define policy toward Africa using military instruments of foreign policy. While the president faced some congressional opposition to peacekeeping and other military operations in the region, Clinton was able to overcome most such opposition and implement the policies he desired, unlike in aid and trade. During the 1992 presidential campaign, candidate Clinton advocated "aggressive" multi-lateral engagement and criticized the Bush administration for not doing more to promote peace in Somalia. Upon taking office Clinton ordered the National Security Council to undertake a broad, inter-agency review of US peacekeeping policy. He also extended the US mission in Somalia and supported the UN Security Council Resolution 814 which expanded the UN's original mission to include the achievement of a political settlement.[84]

Because of uneasiness over a mounting death toll, the Clinton administration began to publicly back away from its initial proposal as early as August 1993. While the deaths of US soldiers in Mogadishu accelerated the move away from peacekeeping, the decision to withdraw troops reflected a shift in the administration's preferences, apparent even before the events of October 8, as much as it reflected congressional pressure.

After the US withdrawal from Somalia, there was no trace of the administration's earlier enthusiasm for multilateral intervention. This became particularly clear in the case of US policy toward Rwanda in the spring of 1994. Though the presidential directive overhauling US peacekeeping operations, PDD-25, was not released until May 1994, the Clinton administration began invoking it as reason not to intervene in Rwanda as early as April of that year. Throughout the Rwandan crisis, the administration played down the extent of the killings and avoided labeling the crisis as a genocide.[85] At the same time, the US delegation to the UN Security Council argued against maintaining UN peacekeepers in the country and firmly backed an April 21 vote by the UNSC to withdraw most of the existing

---

industry. A large part of the administration's assistance to ECOMOG funded the provision of services and equipment to African peacekeepers through US civilian subcontractors. For example, in Liberia, International Charter Incorporated received US funding to provide helicopter transportation. Pacific Architects and Engineers also received US funding for vehicle repairs. Similar funds were provided in support of UN missions in Rwanda and Somalia, benefiting contractors including Raytheon, Dyncorp, Brown and Root, Lockheed Martin, Bechtel, and MPRI. Berman and Sams, 2000. However, there is no evidence that these groups engaged in observable high-profile lobbying around peacekeeping policy in the manner that economic interest groups did, for example, in the realm of trade policy, as we show more systematically in chapter 3.

84    MacKinnon, 2000.
85    Lippman, 1994.

peacekeeping force from Rwanda.[86] This policy reflected the Clinton administration's own inclination not to be drawn into a second, politically unpopular African crisis.

In the years that followed, the Clinton administration continued to adopt an ambivalent posture toward peacekeeping in Africa. One crucial episode came in late 1996 as tensions between Rwanda's ethnic Hutus and Tutsis began to spill over into violent conflicts in the neighboring states of Zaire and Burundi. In early November 1996, President Clinton announced his willingness to send as many as 5,000 servicemen to Zaire and surrounding nations to help deal with the refugee crisis caused by this ongoing violence and ethnic rivalry.[87] Republican opposition to this was strong in Congress. However, in early December 1996, the Clinton administration noted that around 400 US troops had indeed been deployed to the region and that US aircraft were also involved in supporting humanitarian assistance missions there.[88] Thus once again the president was able to use his military instruments without congressional obstruction.

In the mid-1990s, the Clinton administration, frustrated by congressional budget maneuvering attempting to limit its ability to use aid and multilateral peacekeeping, advanced a new proposal for an African Crisis Response Force (ACRF). Through the ACRF, the Clinton administration planned to provide military training to African peacekeepers, enabling them to provide security in Africa's own conflicts and alleviating international demands for direct US engagement. The proposal met skepticism both in Africa and among US allies. Moreover, some members of Congress opposed the initiative both on the grounds that it could lead to new US interventionism on the continent and that it would require additional funds.[89] The US Congress particularly opposed any move that could have been interpreted as American involvement in setting up a standing army.[90]

In the face of congressional opposition, the administration forged ahead. Lacking the ability to use other foreign policy instruments to deal with the serious African problems, it chose the military option. The program, later renamed the African Crisis Response Initiative, was launched that same year with training taking place in Senegal, Uganda, and Malawi.[91] In 1998, the program was expanded to incorporate troops from Mali,

86   Rothchild, 2001. A comprehensive study of US policy making during the genocide supports this conclusion, finding no evidence that the White House favored intervention or even that the president himself was involved in policy-making discussions on the subject. Cohen, 2007.

87   Clinton, 1996.

88   Baker, 1996; Ploch, 2011.

89   Committee on International Relations, 1997; Volman, 1998; Rothchild, 2001.

90   Omach, 2000.

91   When consulted, a number of African countries opposed the name because of the use of force. They preferred emphasizing a longer-term training and planning program and hence the term initiative rather than force. Henk and Metz, 1997.

Ghana, and Ethiopia. The initial ACRI was a five-year program, with $15 million allocated in FY97, $22 million in FY98, and similar levels through FY2000.[92]

The ACRI was seen by many in lieu of US military intervention, illustrating the ease of substitution between military instruments, as well as declining development assistance.[93] The Clinton administration later expanded upon the ACRI model in creating Operation Focus Relief (OFR), a response to several members of the UN Mission in Sierra Leone (UNAMSIL) being taken hostage in May 2000. In contrast to ACRI, OFR provided lethal training and materiel to Ghanaian, Senegalese, and Nigerian troops to be deployed to Sierra Leone. OFR expanded not only the scope of the training programs, but also the budget, costing an estimated $90 million over 15 months.[94]

Ongoing conflicts in Africa, difficulties using aid and trade policies, and failed peacekeeping policies then led to the search for new initiatives; and military engagement through ACRI was one substitute policy advanced. Given the problems arising in Sub-Saharan Africa, the president had few foreign policy instruments he could easily use because of domestic politics. One area where he was freer was the military, and as the administration faced opposition to aid, trade, and other policy instruments, the military option seemed to prevail increasingly.[95] Military action by the United States was not required by the problems in Africa; in fact, military assistance may have made the problems worse over time by fostering large powerful militaries that have intervened in politics frequently.[96] As one recent article notes, "Much U.S. effort has thus gone to training soldiers, not building health ministries or electoral commissions. The result has been to create strong armies in weak states."[97]

In sum, American policy in Sub-Saharan Africa became increasingly militarized over the 1990s. Problems on the continent turned into urgent humanitarian crises. Massive amounts of aid may have helped but were unavailable from Congress; so the president turned to military aid and intervention. Thus, while the initial withdrawal from Somalia suggested

92  Office of the Press Secretary, 1998; GlobalSecurity.org, 2012.
93  Committee on International Relations, 1997.
94  Berman and Sams, 2000.
95  One other notable use of military force in Africa came in the wake of two al Qaeda attacks on US embassies in Kenya and Tanzania on August 7, 1998. This case again shows how the president when confronted with a foreign problem can often use military means to address it very quickly and without many domestic constraints. His informational advantages often allow him much leeway domestically to employ military means. In retaliation for the bombings, President Clinton authorized unilateral air strikes against an al Qaeda-affiliated chemical weapons facility in southern Sudan on August 20. Ploch, 2011.
96  Hinshaw and McGroarty, 2014.
97  Ibid.

some congressional influence over military policy, in broader perspective it appears that the president's own preferences largely aligned with those in Congress who called for withdrawal. Though the president demonstrated ambivalence toward peacekeeping for much of his two terms, where he chose to engage he did so successfully in spite of congressional opposition in many cases. Moreover, in the realm of more traditional military engagement the president received clear support for his actions in Sudan. The president's relative success in military matters contrasts sharply with his frustration in the area of foreign economic assistance, which continued throughout his presidency. This indicates support for the hypothesis that in the realm of geopolitical aid and military deployment policy at least where ideological divisions are often less and distributive politics is weaker, Congress may be more likely to defer to the president's preferences.

## Sub-Saharan Africa Policy during the George W. Bush Administration (2001–2009)

During the Bush presidency, the terrorist attacks in the United States and the global war on terror (GWOT) accelerated the movement toward military involvement in Sub-Saharan Africa. The president tried to use many different policy instruments, but he too faced domestic constraints that limited his choices. As a Republican, it is not surprising that the president's favored policy bean was trade liberalization. Bush pushed trade policy forward initially, revising and expanding AGOA several times. But he faced domestic resistance to making AGOA an even larger element of US policy. Bush then turned more to aid and was able to increase aid to the continent, although never in the full amounts he desired. The Millennium Challenge Corporation (MCC) and PEPFAR were innovations in policy that were necessary to induce Congress and the public to resume aid to Sub-Saharan Africa. His administration also ended up substituting military engagement for greater aid and international trade due to American domestic political pressures. The US Africa Command (AFRICOM) represented the militarization of US policy in Sub-Saharan Africa. This military engagement encompassed not only the use of military means, but also diplomatic instruments and foreign assistance for economic development. It became easier domestically for Bush to engage on the African continent as he used the umbrella of AFRICOM to pursue his goals. Diplomacy and development aid were joined under the AFRICOM mandate rather than through the State Department and traditional aid sources like USAID.

Observers have noted the militarization of US policy toward Sub-Saharan Africa, especially under Bush.[98] Often this is presumed to be driven almost entirely by changes in the international environment. But our claim is that domestic politics is also responsible. The fact that aid and trade policy are much harder for presidents to control has led them to substitute military engagement for such non-military means.[99] As we noted elsewhere, trade and aid policy engage domestic interests and are resistant to presidential control of information. Military engagement, however, both minimizes such interest group pressures and plays to the president's asymmetrical information advantages. Wikileaks and the information leaked by Snowden make it clear that the White House developed and used very wide-ranging and powerful information collection techniques after 9/11 and that few outside the executive branch knew about these sources.[100] But these leaks make it evident that the president had very substantial informational advantages in foreign affairs and that Congress was excluded. Given presidential control over these informational sources, the executive could operate with greater latitude in the military area. Military engagement in Africa was thus easier for the president to secure support for at home, and this was further enabled by the rise of terrorist threats on the continent.

## Aid Policy

### AID POLICY CHANGES

Foreign assistance came to play a major role in US Africa policy during the Bush administration. As figure 7.1 shows, aid flows from the United States grew strongly during the Bush presidency, unlike the Clinton period. Bush, however, struggled to employ aid policy, just as Clinton did. Two things helped him: one, the geopolitical threat created by the 9/11 events, and two, the development of new aid institutions and policies to address Republican

98    Schirch and Kishbaugh, 2006; Ploch, 2011.

99    "One feature of the shifting U.S. policy focus after 9/11 was a new rhetorical emphasis on the strategic importance of Africa and on U.S. strategic interests there, outlined in the Bush administration's 2002 National Security Strategy, which identified weak and failed states as the central threat to global security emanating from the developing world. . . . Thus, chronic weaknesses that had previously attracted the attention mainly of humanitarians and development experts—poverty, joblessness, disease, illiteracy, corruption, weak governance—were discovered to have new strategic importance. This fed a tendency to conflate all forms of U.S. assistance to Africa—security, developmental, and humanitarian—with overriding counterterrorism 'objectives.'" Bellamy, 2009, pp. 15–16.

100    Posner and Vermeule argue strongly that especially in military affairs the president is no longer constrained by Congress or the public at all. Posner and Vermeule, 2010. In contrast, Goldsmith claims the fact that the secret information in Wikileaks was leaked shows how constrained the president actually is. Goldsmith, 2012.

objections to aid. Bush had to invent new aid institutions and practices that appeared less like development aid in order to employ this policy instrument. The president's struggles to use aid policy highlight the contentious nature of aid politics domestically. His difficulties were less apparent in the area of geopolitical assistance to which the administration increasingly turned toward the end of its first term. While trade and aid policy were tightly constrained by interest groups and partisan politics, geopolitical aid and deployments were less so.

The politics of the two major aid initiatives to emerge from this period, the President's Emergency Plan for AIDS Relief (PEPFAR) and the Millennium Challenge Account (MCA), demonstrated the limited ability of the president to steer the legislative process. Though PEPFAR is remembered as a presidential initiative, congressional Democrats had been pressing for AIDS legislation for some time before the Bush administration embraced the cause. While the president's imprimatur likely had a positive effect on conservative members of Congress, the overall success of the initiative seems to reflect the broad alignment of policy-maker preferences more than actual presidential influence. Indeed, when it came to funding the initiative, the president was unable to achieve his preferences. Ultimately, President Bush was forced to accept both a fivefold increase in funding for the UN's multilateral AIDS initiative (from $200 million to $1 billion) and a somewhat smaller increase in overall PEPFAR funds at the expense of his preferred initiative, the Millennium Challenge Account. These figures are consistent with data presented in chapter 5.

As in the area of trade policy, economic interests played a major role in these debates. The pharmaceutical industry was active not only in lobbying for PEPFAR's passage, but also in trying to shape the terms of the legislation in its favor. NGOs were also active, lobbying for passage, publicizing the AIDS crisis, and sounding the alarm over each aspect of the program with which they disagreed. Aid policy thus involved many economic and ideological interest groups, and they lobbied Congress and provided it with much information to counter the president's advantages. In describing the politics surrounding PEPFAR and then the MCC, we show that even though Bush had success with both, he had to battle with Congress despite the influence that the global war on terror gave his administration.

## ROLE OF CONGRESS (PEPFAR)

While the President's Emergency Plan for AIDS Relief (PEPFAR) is largely remembered as a presidential initiative, Congress was the initial proponent. Momentum for AIDS relief began to build in Congress long before the administration announced its intention of increasing relief funding. Beginning in 2001, lawmakers from both parties pressured the administration to increase foreign assistance directed at preventing and treating HIV/AIDS.

On January 28, 2003, during his annual State of the Union address, President Bush proposed the Emergency Plan for AIDS Relief, which was built on those already being ciculated in Congress. It called for $15 billion over five years for HIV/AIDS prevention and treatment, including $10 billion ($2 billion per year) in newly appropriated funds.[101] While Congress largely welcomed the president's support for AIDS funding, representatives were reluctant to accept presidential leadership on the issue. While the White House began drafting a legislative proposal in early 2003, members of the House of Representatives continued work on their own proposal, to the chagrin of the administration.[102]

This resistance in the Senate forced the administration to embrace the House version of the bill instead. Introduced by Representative Henry Hyde (R-IL) on March 17, 2003, the House measure was successfully voted out of committee on April 2, 2003. Following this initial authorization, Congress again asserted its preferences over those of the president during the appropriation process later that year. Though the president had initially proposed $3 billion in funding for FY2004, the same amount authorized in H.R.1298, the administration's FY2004 budget request included a proposed appropriation of only $2 billion, with only $1.5 billion in new money.[103] Democrats castigated the president for backing away from his initial commitment and unilaterally increased FY2004 funding to $2.4 billion at the expense of the president's preferred policy, the Millennium Challenge initiative (described in more detail below).[104] In its final form, PEPFAR also included a $1 billion donation to the UN Global Fund, which the administration had previously resisted.

Over the next five years, congressional appropriations continued to outstrip administration requests. By 2008, total PEPFAR funds allocated reached $19 billion, $4 billion higher than called for in Bush's initial State of the Union proposal. That year, Congress took up re-authorization. Although President Bush requested a new commitment of $30 billion over five years, Congress again expanded on this request, authorizing $50 billion instead.[105]

Overall, while PEPFAR represented a legislative victory for all involved, it also demonstrates the limits of presidential influence in foreign policy

---

101   Bush, 2003a.
102   Lefkowitz, 2009.
103   Rovner, 2003; Sun Reporter, 2003; Westside Gazette, 2003.
104   Rogers, 2003a.
105   Stolberg, 2008; Swenson, 2008.

when the majority in Congress holds competing objectives. Democrats in Congress had long pushed for a plan like PEPFAR. The president signed on later and helped push it through Republicans in Congress. And, interestingly in this case, Congress allocated more for the program than the president desired. In aid policy, we once again see the domestic constraints on presidents. These constraints derive in part from the distributive consequences of aid in terms of interest group activity as well as strong ideological divisions played out in partisan politics. We examine these pressures more below.

## ROLE OF INTEREST GROUPS AND DISTRIBUTIVE POLITICS

As in the area of trade policy, interest groups were important players in the policy-making process behind PEPFAR. A variety of interest groups, including economically motivated interest groups, actively lobbied in favor of greater AIDS funding. While doing so, these groups also provided detailed information to both the executive and legislative branches of government. Via this informational role, interest groups were able to influence the design of PEPFAR while supporting Congress in playing an assertive role in the policy-making process.

Pharmaceutical companies were vocal in pushing for increasing aid flows both before and after the introduction of PEPFAR. By 2001, the availability of generic AIDS medications began to drive down the cost of AIDS drugs worldwide. Under intense pressure from AIDS activists, pharmaceutical companies began to offer steep discounts on AIDS drugs to developing countries. Evidence also suggests that the pharmaceutical industry was active in lobbying President Bush directly. In June 2002, the Bush administration announced a new $500 million domestic initiative aimed at preventing mother to child transmission of HIV/AIDS. That same day, the president attended a fund-raiser sponsored by the CEO of GlaxoSmithKline, Jean-Pierre Garnier (and attended by numerous other pharmaceutical industry representatives) at the Mayflower Hotel while activists protested outside.[106]

This lobbying activity intensified following the president's announcement of PEPFAR in 2003. Two industry lobby groups (the Corporate Council on Africa's Task Force on AIDS and the Coalition for AIDS Relief in Africa) were formed early on and were both active in lobbying Congress to support the initiative. These groups counted Bristol-Myers Squibb, Abbott Laboratories, Pfizer, and other major players in the industry among their members.[107] A further signal of the pharmaceutical industry's influ-

106   Lobe, 2002.
107   Dietrich, 2007.

ence was President Bush's decision to nominate former Eli Lilly CEO, Randall Tobias, as the administration's first Global AIDS Coordinator, in spite of the fact that Tobias had no obvious expertise in either AIDS or Africa policy.[108]

Pharmaceutical companies were not the only private sector groups who lobbied in favor of greater AIDS funding. Other economic interest groups lobbied and provided Congress with much useful information. During a 2001 hearing before the House Committee on International Relations, the president of the Corporate Council on Africa Stephen Hayes stated: "The problem of HIV/AIDS is having a profound negative impact on American business in Africa."[109] Reflecting these concerns of US businesses, the Council's Task Force on AIDS (mentioned above) included many non-pharmaceutical companies in its membership, such as Halliburton, Ford Motor Company, and the Chevron Corporation.[110] In an example of the information-providing role of these interest groups, the Task Force released a report in July 2001 examining the AIDS crisis and providing guidance on private sector best practices for supporting relief efforts.[111]

PEPFAR received enthusiastic support from AIDS activists and humanitarian groups. Faith-based organizations generally welcomed the initiative and lobbied for its passage.[112] On September 16, 2003, a group of religious leaders and Bono (lead singer of the rock group U2 and global activist) held a press conference in the midst of the funding debate and urged the Bush administration and Congress to appropriate the full amount promised during the State of the Union address earlier in the year. Ultimately FBOs became another important element of PEPFAR's strategy for combating AIDS, with faith-based groups benefitting disproportionately from PEPFAR funding. In 2006, 23% of PEPFAR's partner organizations were faith-based groups.[113]

Thus in the course of lobbying for their preferred policies, interest groups provided Congress with crucial intelligence, enabling lawmakers to engage fully in the policy-making process. Notably, much of this testimony took place early in 2002, before the Bush administration began to seriously consider a new global initiative that summer. By the time administration officials began to formulate their proposed legislation, Congress was well-informed on many of what would become central components of the policy, including the provision of ARV therapies and the reliance on faith-based groups.

108   Ibid.
109   Committee on International Relations, 2001, p. 36.
110   PR Newswire, 2000.
111   Committee on International Relations, 2001, p. 39.
112   Dietrich, 2007; Enda, 2008.
113   Dietrich, 2007; Enda, 2008.

## ROLE OF CONGRESS (MCA)

The Bush administration's approach to foreign assistance in Africa was profoundly shaped by the experience of the 9/11 terror attacks and the view that long-term poverty and weak state institutions in Afghanistan had played an important role in facilitating the attacks. In a March 2002 address at the Inter-American Development Bank, President Bush described the link between poverty and terrorism, saying: "Poverty doesn't cause terrorism ... Yet persistent poverty and oppression can lead to hopelessness and despair. And when governments fail to meet the most basic needs of their people, these failed states can become havens for terror."[114] In keeping with this logic, the administration's new Africa policy emphasized building democratic institutions and promoting economic development in an effort to defuse potential support for terrorist organizations.

During the same speech cited above, President Bush outlined his first major initiative, the Millennium Challenge Account (MCA), pledging to seek $10 billion in new foreign assistance funds over three years. In a departure from traditional models of foreign assistance, Bush announced that disbursements of this new aid would be tied to economic and political governance as well as insulated from US political considerations. The proposed model not only alleviated traditional conservative concerns about accountability in foreign aid, but also provided important leverage to the administration in its aims of promoting democracy abroad.[115]

The White House submitted its legislative proposal for the Millennium Challenge Account (MCA) to Congress on February 11, 2003.[116] The proposal enjoyed broad support initially, both from Democrats who supported foreign assistance on principle and, unusually, from Republican lawmakers who frequently invoked national security concerns as justification for their support.[117] While Congress supported the MCA proposal in concept, lawmakers—particularly Democrats—were far less supportive of funding the initiative at the level requested by the Bush administration. The Millennium Challenge Act of 2004 incorporated most of the policy elements forwarded by the Bush administration, but included an initial appropriation of only $650 million (50% of the initial $1.3 billion requested by the Bush administration).[118] Congress was not willing to go along with the president's plan for aid. The president included only $2 billion in PEPFAR funds in his initial budget request, down from the $3 billion he had proposed earlier in the year.

---

114    Bush, 2002, p. 409.
115    Ibid.; Philipps and van de Hei, 2002.
116    Bush, 2003b.
117    Committee on Foreign Relations, 2003b.
118    Bush, 2003b; Consolidated Appropriations Act, 2004.

**Table 7.1.** Millennium Challenge Account Funding, 2004–2008

|  | FY2005 | FY2006 | FY2007 | FY2008 | FY2009 |
|---|---|---|---|---|---|
| Administration Request (bn) | 2.500 | 3.00 | 3.00 | 3.00 | 2.225 |
| Enacted Appropriation (bn) | 1.488 | 1.752 | 1.752 | 1.544 | 0.875 |
| Enacted Appropriation as Percentage of Request | 59.5 | 58.4 | 58.4 | 51.5 | 39.3 |

As noted earlier, House Democrats were enraged by this failure to request the full $3 billion in AIDS relief as promised. Lawmakers, led by Representative Nita Lowey (D-NY) of the House Subcommittee on Foreign Operations as well as the Congressional Black Caucus, retaliated by cutting funding from the MCA in order to expand PEPFAR.[119] President Bush strongly opposed these cuts, at one point threatening to veto the entire spending bill if MCA funds were reduced any further. Condoleezza Rice also undertook a last-minute, and ultimately unsuccessful, lobbying campaign in order to restore MCA funding to its requested levels.[120] Following this initial appropriation, funding for MCA continually fell short of the Bush administration's requests, never exceeding 60% of what the president asked for, as shown in table 7.1.[121] Bush's initial MCC proposal envisioned building up to a $5 billion annual commitment within three years. Instead, MCC funds peaked in FY2006 with a commitment of $1.75 billion before receding to a low of $875 million in FY2009. Also, while the House Foreign Relations Committee began work toward re-authorization of the program in 2006, the effort was abandoned early on and has yet to be taken up again.[122]

## ROLE OF INTEREST GROUPS AND DISTRIBUTIVE POLITICS (MCA)

Interest groups were also active in lobbying around the president's Millennium Challenge Account (MCA). While development experts and NGOs welcomed the MCA proposal, enthusiasm was tempered by concerns that the governance criteria would exclude some developing countries most in need of development assistance.[123] The MCA also received some support from the business community, though accounts of this are scarcer. Where business organizations did lend support to the proposal, they criticized important elements of it just as the NGOs had done. The Business Council for

119  Morgan, 2003; Rogers, 2003b; Rogers and Dreazen, 2003.
120  Rogers, 2003a; Stolberg, 2003.
121  Adapted from Tarnoff, 2013.
122  Ibid.
123  Catholic Relief Services, 2002; Mathews, 2003; St. Charles Pastoral Center, 2003.

International Understanding (BCIU) supported the initiative, but vocally opposed the creation of a new agency to administer it, arguing that funds should be dispersed through traditional channels at USAID.[124] This preference might reflect another key feature of the MCA proposal, which emphasized reliance on local businesses and organizations in the field, limiting the involvement of US personnel and potentially contractors who would otherwise benefit from the initiative.[125] Overall, there were a variety of interest groups in the United States who took an active role in lobbying and pushing for the MCC and other various aid packages directed to Africa mostly. These groups communicated information to Congress and helped shape policy, often to the detriment of the president and his preferences.

## PRESIDENTIAL POWER

Following the launch of MCA and PEPFAR in 2004, the Bush administration began to turn toward a more militarized foreign assistance policy. Frustration with Congress over MCC and PEPFAR led the Bush administration to develop a stronger military-oriented strategy toward Sub-Saharan Africa. One important milestone in this trajectory was the FY2006 National Defense Authorization Act (passed January 6, 2006) which, at the request of the administration, granted DoD broad, new powers to disburse foreign assistance independent of the Department of State. Section 1206 of the Act authorizes DoD to provide training and equipment to foreign military forces engaged in counterterrorism or stability operations. Also included in Section 1206 is the authority to provide counterterrorism training and equipment to foreign maritime forces. This was a very significant expansion of aid but through military channels; from FY2006 to FY2012, DoD disbursed $1.8 billion in Section 1206 funds globally. Section 1206 was also the first time Congress had granted such global power to DoD since the Foreign Assistance Act of 1961 placed military assistance under the authority of the Secretary of State.[126] In this light, Section 1206 represented a significant expansion of DoD's authority as well as its ability to engage in the state-building activities that were seen as central to countering global terrorism. This strategy was also a means for the executive branch to gain greater control over aid policy.

Another indication of a general re-orientation toward military assistance is the 2005 launch of the Trans-Sahara Counterterrorism Partnership (TSCTP). TSCTP grew out of a narrower military training program, the two-year, $7 million Pan Sahel Initiative (PSI), administered by the Depart-

---

124   Nowels, 2003.
125   Committee on Foreign Relations, 2003b.
126   Serafino, 2013.

ment of State beginning in 2003. Where the PSI provided limited training in counterterrorism and border control to military units in four West African countries, the new TSCTP encompassed a broad array of both development initiatives and military training programs in ten West African countries. Also, while the Department of State remained the primary coordinator of TSCTP (as it had been for PSI), DoD's role was dramatically expanded through the initiative's military counterpart, Operation Enduring Freedom-Trans Sahara (OEF-TS). At its outset, and for most of the years of the Bush administration, TSCTP was not funded by a congressional budget line but rather was funded from discretionary accounts within each agency. Since its inception, TSCTP has received around $100 million per year in funding.[127] This demonstrates DoD's growing role both in Africa policy and specifically in African development policy.

The increasingly intertwined nature of development and military assistance can also be seen within the traditional foreign aid bureaucracy whose own programs came to emphasize the role of the military. One area where this change is apparent is in the evolution of the administration's approach to democracy promotion. As development experts have noted, the Millennium Challenge Account emphasized consolidation of democratic rule, rather than the establishment of new democratic regimes.[128] From 2003 to the end of the Bush administration, this emphasis on the consolidation of democratic rule gave way to an emphasis on the stabilization of conflict areas, an approach that naturally dovetailed with military engagement. This transition was reflected both in the structure of foreign assistance disbursements and within the bureaucratic organization of USAID. For example, by 2007 five African countries consumed 60% of USAID's budget for "democracy promotion": Sudan, Liberia, Sierra Leone, Democratic Republic of Congo, and Somalia. Of these, Liberia and Sierra Leone are the only two that could be considered "good prospects for democracy," while the others were host to some of the longest running military conflicts in the world. Within USAID, the Office of Democracy and Governance, traditionally the focal point for democracy promotion, was moved under the purview of a new bureau for Democracy, Conflict, and Humanitarian Assistance.[129]

In each of these military aid initiatives, the Bush administration maintained much greater control over the policy-making process overall. And there was little involvement by special interest groups around these issues. Moreover, this shift toward a more militarized development policy reflected a strategic substitution away from traditional economic aid. As mentioned earlier, the MCA was intended as an instrument of democracy promotion in

---

127   Boudali, 2007; U.S. Government Accountability Office, 2008; Ploch, 2011.
128   Barkan, 2009.
129   Ibid.

order to mitigate the threat of terrorism emanating from Africa. These later initiatives in military (and development) assistance served a similar purpose though with a much enhanced role for the military. As is discussed in more detail below, the US military's growing role in development policy was an important justification for the establishment of a permanent combatant command for Africa. Hence the implications of this initial militarization of US aid policy toward Sub-Saharan Africa were far-reaching.

## Trade Policy

### TRADE POLICY CHANGES DURING THE GEORGE W. BUSH ADMINISTRATION

Republicans tend to favor trade policy as a foreign policy instrument relative to economic aid, and President Bush was no exception. US-Sub-Saharan Africa trade policy advanced during the early years of the Bush administration. The president enjoyed broad support among members of his own party who for much of the period held a majority in both the House and Senate. With the backing of Republican lawmakers and continuing support from the bipartisan architects of AGOA, the president successfully expanded and extended the African Growth and Opportunity Act on three occasions from 2001 to 2006. After becoming the first president to secure fast-track trade promotion authority in nearly a decade, President Bush also launched FTA negotiations with the Southern African Customs Union (SACU) and pursued shallower trade accords (TIFAs) with several other states in the region.

After this early momentum, the president's free-trade agenda came to an abrupt halt in 2006 when Democrats won a majority of seats in both the House and Senate. From this point forward, Democratic lawmakers concerned about the distributional effects of free trade adopted an antagonistic stance toward the president, blocking any new liberalizing measures for the remainder of his time in office. The contrast in support for the president's trade agenda pre- and post-2006 highlights the difference in presidential influence between members of his own party and those of the opposition. Partisan and interest group politics played a large role in curbing presidential influence in trade.

A second important feature of this period is the prominence of distributional concerns in debates over trade policy making. Economically motivated special interest groups demonstrated a high level of organization in lobbying both the president and Congress for their preferred positions. Finally, trade policy was an important issue in the 2006 mid-term elections, a key turning point in trade policy during this period. The Democratic takeover led subsequently to the frustration of the president's free-trade agenda.

## ROLE OF CONGRESS

For much of the Bush administration, Congress demonstrated an unusual willingness to cooperate with the president's trade policy priorities. This reflects both a Republican majority broadly supportive of the president's goals and continuing bipartisan support specifically for Africa trade as it evolved during the Clinton years. An examination of trade policy during this period provides an early example of presidential influence with members of his own party. The Trade Act of 2002, passed on August 1, 2002, contained the first set of amendments to the African Growth and Opportunity Act as well as, for the first time since 1994, authorization of "fast-track" trade promotion authority (TPA). The inclusion of TPA was controversial and the measure (H.R. 3009; Roll Call #370; July 27, 2002) passed the House by a slim margin of 215-212, driven mostly by Republican support for the measure.[130] In the Senate, the Act passed by a vote of 64-34, again with particularly strong support among members of the president's own party.[131]

Congress was similarly amenable to the president's 2003/2004 initiative to extend AGOA benefits beyond their initial end date of 2008. On January 15, 2003, President Bush announced his intent to request an extension from Congress during a videotaped broadcast at the annual AGOA forum in Mauritius.[132] During a Senate Foreign Relations Committee hearing on AGOA held June 25, 2003, Senator Richard G. Lugar (R-IN) described the initiative as a "notable success" and joined the president in calling for extension beyond 2008. Lugar also emphasized the importance of extending the LDC third-party fabric provision through which poor countries were allowed to export textiles made from non-Sub-Saharan Africa fabric and which was set to expire in 2004. Extension of the LDC third-party rule would become one of the more contentious aspects of the debate over AGOA III due to opposition from textile lobbies who feared import surges. On November 20, 2003, Lugar introduced S. 1900, a measure to extend AGOA benefits until

---

130   Among Republicans the vote was 189-27 in favor. Tyler, 2002; Jones and Williams, 2012.

131   On the Democratic side two important senators who came to support the measure were Senator Tom Daschle (D-SD) and Senator Max Baucus (D-MT). While Daschle's support for TPA may in part have been a result of the strong agricultural interests in his state, he also played an important role in negotiating concessions from Republicans over Trade Adjustment Assistance, which ultimately helped pass the bill. Alden, Mann, and Williams, 2002; Aubrey, 2002; Kirchhoff, 2002a; Kirchhoff, 2002b; Tonelson, 2002. Meanwhile, following a wake of more protectionist measures by the administration earlier in the year, Senator Baucus expressed support for the bill as it showed the United States's commitment to free trade. Alden and de Jonquieres, 2002; Dougherty, 2002a; Dougherty, 2002b. Nonetheless, several other Democrats such as Byron Dorgan (D-ND) or Richard Gephardt (D-MO) continued to oppose the measure, fearing adverse effects on industries in their states. Aubrey, 2002; Kirchhoff, 2002a.

132   Bumiller, 2003.

2015 and the LDC third-party rule until 2008. A similar measure, H.R. 3572, was introduced in the House on November 21, 2003. Both measures died in committee, but the following year Representative Bill Thomas (R-CA) introduced a new, nearly identical version on April 1, 2004. Thomas and McDermott led a bipartisan campaign in favor of passage and the measure, H.R. 4103, was successfully approved (by voice vote) on June 14, 2004.[133] Some expressed concerns that passage in the Senate would prove more complicated both due to resistance from textile-oriented legislators, particularly Senator Ernest Hollings (D-SC), and unrelated amendments. Confounding expectations though, the Senate approved the measure with unanimous consent on June 24, clearing the way for President Bush to sign it into law on July 13, 2004.[134]

In 2006, Congress agreed to one last set of amendments, again extending AGOA's special rule for LDCs, this time to 2015.[135] However, support for the president's trade policy agenda came to an abrupt halt following the 2006 mid-term elections in which Democrats took over the majority in the House and Senate. During these elections roughly two dozen seats "turned partly on Democrats' protectionist platforms."[136] A *Wall Street Journal* article identified sixteen Republican free-traders in the House and five in the Senate who lost their seats to protectionist Democrats.[137] From this point forward, Democratic legislators demonstrated strong opposition to the administration's trade policy, refusing to renew TPA in 2007 or to vote on significant trade deals which USTR had already negotiated with Korea, Panama, and Colombia.[138] Congress's ability to confound the president's agenda by refusing to pass already-negotiated trade agreements highlights the limits of presidential power when faced with an ideologically hostile majority and distributive concerns from interest groups.

## ROLE OF INTEREST GROUPS AND DISTRIBUTIVE POLITICS

The success of each round of AGOA amendments is partially attributable to interest groups that organized in support of the legislation, countering the influence of narrowly focused textile and apparel lobbies. These groups were active in lobbying both the president and Congress. During a 2003 hearing before the Senate Committee on International Relations, Assistant USTR for Africa Florizelle Liser noted that the administration was "working with industry" to develop its policy toward extension, mentioning the

133 Langton, 2004.
134 Africa Analysis, 2004a.
135 Jones and Williams, 2012.
136 Hitt and King Jr., 2006, p. A1.
137 Ibid.
138 Mekay, 2004; Hitt and King Jr., 2006; Chorev, 2009.

AGOA III Action Committee as one such partner.[139] Made up of mainly US corporations with operations in Africa, the AGOA III Action Committee was founded "to draft, promote and see enacted and implemented critically needed enhancements to the African Growth and Opportunity Act."[140]

African leaders were also active in lobbying for extension. In May 2004 a coalition of African former heads of state from Cape Verde, Ghana, Mauritius, Tanzania, Benin, and Botswana held a press conference in London urging Congress to extend overall AGOA preferences.[141] Uganda, Kenya, Swaziland, and Lesotho were particularly active in lobbying for extension of the third-party fabric provision.[142]

Interest groups were also engaged in a second major trade policy issue during this period, involving negotiations of a free trade agreement with the Southern African Customs Union (SACU). USTR Robert Zoellick announced that the administration would pursue negotiations with SACU in November 2002. Responding quickly to the initiative, the US-South African Business Council established an FTA advocacy coalition in December 2002 to lobby for an agreement. The agreement also received support from the Corporate Council on Africa, a US-based organization dedicated to increasing trade and investment ties with Sub-Saharan Africa. During a public hearing held by USTR on December 16, 2002, representatives of the retail, food distribution, and metal imports industries voiced support for the agreement. Particularly, these industries advocated the reduction of US tariffs on goods originating in SACU member-countries. Representatives from the service industries and the recycled clothing industries lobbied for the reduction of SACU tariff and non-tariff barriers.[143] Opposition to the agreement came from producers of canned fruits and vegetables (particularly the California peach and apricot industries), rubber footwear, the American Sugar Alliance, and various types of metal (silicon, manganese, and ferrovanadium).[144]

## PRESIDENTIAL POWER

The Bush administration tried to engage with Africa on trade policy (and foreign investment) beyond AGOA, but was often stymied in this by both domestic and international factors. During the early years of the Bush

139   Committee on Foreign Relations, 2003a, p. 7.
140   Whitaker Group, 2003.
141   Schwab, 2004.
142   Africa Analysis, 2004b; BBC, 2004; Kelley, 2004. In contrast, South Africa lobbied against the provision, favoring greater emphasis on local yarn and fabric production.
143   Langton, 2008.
144   Journal of Commerce Online, 2003; Langton, 2008.

administration, trade was an important issue for the White House. As already noted, President Bush presided over the extension and amendment of the African Growth and Opportunity act on three separate occasions between 2002 and 2006. On each of these pieces of legislation, the president enjoyed the support mainly from his own party.

Beyond the AGOA amendments, the Bush administration also launched FTA negotiations with the Southern African Customs Union (SACU) and pursued less ambitious trade agreements with numerous other partners. In spite of widespread support from business groups, the SACU FTA negotiations quickly stalled and were postponed indefinitely in 2006.[145] Instead of the hoped-for FTA, the Bush administration concluded a Trade, Investment, and Development Cooperative Agreement (TIDCA, similar to a TIFA) on July 16, 2008, which established a high-level "Consultative Group on Trade and Investment" intended to act as a forum for future trade negotiations.[146]

The administration did not lose interest in engaging with Africa on trade issues post-2006. Where it was not blocked by Congress, it continued to pursue trade policy as a foreign policy instrument, but it could not do anything major that would have involved congressional approval. Congress effectively blocked the president on advancing trade relations after the 2006 election. The SACU TIFA was one of many that the Bush administration concluded from 2001 to 2009 with countries throughout the region. In contrast to the difficulties the administration experienced post-2006 in convincing Congress to ratify its trade agreements, TIFAs do not require Senate approval and thus the administration was able to pursue its trade policy in this manner even after the Democratic takeover. But the president was blocked from signing major trade accords and thus unable to use the foreign policy instruments he most preferred.[147]

In conclusion, while the president enjoyed early support for his trade policy, his free-trade agenda was stymied once a Democratic majority, with its own economic and ideological interests, came to power. Using a mechanism to avoid congressional voting, the TIFA, Bush was able to keep trade policy with Sub-Saharan Africa moving forward. The government signed numerous TIFAs with African countries (as shown in table 7.2), even though these are much weaker and less deep trade agreements than he would have preferred. This process nevertheless helped advance America's economic engagement with Africa.

145  Langton, 2008.
146  Cooperative Agreement between the United States of America and the Southern African Customs Union to Foster Trade, Investment and Development, 2008.
147  Committee on Foreign Relations, 2010; Office of the United States Trade Representative, 2011.

**Table 7.2.** Economic Agreements Concluded
by the Bush Administration

| PARTNER | AGREEMENT TYPE | DATE SIGNED |
| --- | --- | --- |
| COMESA | TIFA | October 29, 2001 |
| WAEMU | TIFA | April 2002 |
| Nigeria | TIFA | February 16, 2005 |
| Mozambique | TIFA | June 21, 2005 |
| Rwanda | TIFA | June 7, 2006 |
| Mauritius | TIFA | September 18, 2006 |
| Liberia | TIFA | February 15, 2007 |
| Rwanda | BIT | February 19, 2008 |
| EAC | TIFA | July 16, 2008 |
| SACU | TIFA | July 16, 2008 |

## Military Policy

### CHANGES IN MILITARY POLICY DURING THE GEORGE W. BUSH ADMINISTRATION

Over the course of President Bush's eight years in office, American military engagement in Africa underwent significant expansion. Initially, the president resisted broad military engagement. By the end of his first term in office, however, the president began to pursue a markedly more militarized policy on the continent. The timing of this shift suggests that it may have been a reaction to the mixed success of the president's earlier initiatives such as the Millennium Challenge Account, where congressional politics undermined funding available for democracy promotion. Once again, the president was pushed to substitute a more military-oriented approach to foreign policy as a result of domestic constraints.

In contrast to foreign assistance or trade policy during this period, Congress largely deferred to the president's priorities once the administration shifted to an emphasis on military engagement. This cooperation is notable given Congress's earlier combativeness over foreign assistance and, post-2006, over trade policy as well. Also notable is the apparent absence of interest group activity in the policy-making process. While some NGOs did lobby around military issues, economic interests were largely absent. The low profile of special interests seems in keeping with predictions that military policy generates fewer distributional concerns. Congress's acquiescence also suggests support for the idea that ideological divisions were limited. Under these conditions, we expect information asymmetries to be strong and presidents to be more powerful and more able to achieve their objectives.

## ROLE OF CONGRESS

For most of the Bush administration's time in office, Congress seems to have been relatively compliant with the wishes of the administration, granting the president leeway to implement military policy as he chose. Even when representatives disagreed with the administration's approach, their complaints had little effect on the overall direction of US policy. Little distributive politics were apparent, and ideological divisions were muted in this area. While Congress held numerous hearings on topics including terrorism in Africa, energy security, and conflict resolution, there is little evidence that any high-profile initiatives emerged from these activities or that they had a significant effect on overall US policy.

Congressional cooperativeness increased in 2006 when the administration began planning for a fully independent combatant command for the continent. Soon after, Senator Russ Feingold (D-WI) introduced an amendment to the 2007 National Defense Authorization Act requiring DoD to complete a feasibility study on the establishment of a new Africa Command.[148] This initiative was directly in line with the president's own preferences by this point, since the administration had increasingly turned toward a militarized development policy. The proposed Africa Command received strong support from members of both parties when it was finally announced on February 6, 2007.[149] In a June 5, 2007 report, the Senate Armed Services committee welcomed the initiative and "commended" DoD "for its acknowledgment of the strategic and humanitarian importance of Africa to the interests of the United States."[150]

The cooperative approach to AFRICOM stands in stark contrast to the combative stance of Congress toward the administration in other policy areas, particularly trade. However, it also contrasts with congressional obstruction over foreign assistance during the early years of the Bush administration. In the area of military policy, the administration was quickly granted authorization to pursue its preferred policy, even though African problems did not require military solutions.

## ROLE OF INTEREST GROUPS AND DISTRIBUTIVE POLITICS

While not entirely absent, interest groups had a much more muted presence in the area of military policy in keeping with expectations. Those special in-

---

148 Copley, 2006; Feingold, 2006.
149 Cahlink, 2007; Lobe, 2007.
150 Committee on Armed Services, 2007, p. 418.

terests who did participate in the policy-making process were largely NGOs rather than economic interests. These NGOs largely opposed AFRICOM, arguing that it would continue the trend of militarization of humanitarian services to which many career humanitarians were vehemently opposed.[151] Mark Malan of Refugee International testified before the Senate Subcommittee on African Affairs that "the specter of integration [of US military and humanitarian objectives] is unnerving for humanitarians; they cannot be supportive of the new command as long as [humanitarian work is subsumed into the realm of military strategy]."[152] Unlike in the areas of trade and foreign assistance, however, these voices appear to have had little effect on the direction of US military policy.

## PRESIDENTIAL POWER

Although he quickly embraced military options in Afghanistan and Iraq, with few exceptions, the president resisted the use of the military in Africa during his early years in office. Thus, rather than expend precious military resources in Africa, the administration chose foreign assistance, and, to a lesser extent, trade as its primary instruments to combat the rising extremism on the continent. Where it did choose to engage the military, the Bush administration maintained a narrow focus, avoiding any potential for broader engagement. This early aversion to the use of military policy began to erode around the beginning of the administration's second term.

Though proposals for a new combatant command with sole responsibility for Africa appeared within DoD as early as 2003, the idea received little attention until 2006. By that time, the trends in foreign assistance discussed earlier led to a much-heightened profile for DoD on the African continent. By 2006, US European Command (EUCOM) officers reported spending up to half of their time on Africa issues, up from nearly none in 2003.[153] EUCOM did not oversee operations in the Horn of Africa, which fell instead under US Central Command's area of responsibility. This means that increased EUCOM activity on the continent was not driven by the most obvious security threat—instability and religious extremism in Somalia—but rather by trends related to energy security, development, and counterterrorism operations, particularly in West Africa.

Nonetheless, events taking place in the Horn of Africa around this time highlight the executive branch's informational advantage over Congress in matters of military instruments of statecraft. They also set the stage for a key component of AFRICOM's mission: the gathering of secret intelligence across Africa. In Somalia policy, the executive branch held a particular informational advantage over Congress since violence in the country limited access by most

---

151 Volman and Tuckey, 2008.
152 Committee on Foreign Relations, 2007, pp. 35–36.
153 Ploch, 2011.

foreigners. Press accounts suggest though that the US intelligence community actively carried out surveillance of the region, possibly providing a rare source of information about the political situation on the ground.[154]

Following congressional approval of the initiative, the administration moved quickly to establish the new command. The Bush administration made its plans public on February 6, 2007 and formally launched AF-RICOM as a unified sub-command under EUCOM on October 1, 2007. A year later, on October 1, 2008, AFRICOM assumed the status of full-fledged regional combatant command.

Though public information is limited, secret intelligence gathering has been an important element of AFRICOM's portfolio since its start. In a 2012 report, the *Washington Post* described an ongoing, extensive surveillance campaign carried out through the use of turboprop aircraft disguised as private planes. According to a former senior commander involved with the operation, DoD began establishing a network of secret air bases around the continent in 2007 (coinciding with the launch of AFRICOM).[155] During a June 2012 speech, head of Africa Command General Carter Ham acknowledged the role of AFRICOM in intelligence-gathering, noting, "Do we collect information across Africa? Yes, we do."[156]

At the same time, AFRICOM has been referred to by DoD officials as a "combatant command plus" reflecting a broad engagement with soft-power issues, such as humanitarian assistance and capacity building, in addition to its traditional combat-oriented responsibilities.[157] Thus AFRICOM represents not only a militarization of Africa policy, but also the deep integration of the military into development and humanitarian affairs. With many of Bush's trade and aid initiatives stymied by Congress, his administration turned increasingly to military engagement. This militarization of policy resulted from both fears about threats emanating from Africa and domestic politics surrounding foreign policy in the United States.

## Conclusion

This case study of US policy toward Sub-Saharan Africa reveals evidence in support of a number of our claims. First, it shows that foreign policy instruments differ in their politics domestically. Some are much more like traditional domestic political ones where Congress and interest groups are heavily involved and presidential power is limited. Distributional concerns

154   Royce, 2006.
155   Whitlock, 2012.
156   Quoted in Baldor, 2012.
157   Ploch, 2011.

raise the attention of interest groups who lobby and inform Congress of their interests and concerns with presidential initiatives. Areas with deep ideological divisions also activate Congress and spark partisan battles. Foreign aid and trade policy both have this type of character. And this does not differ much between the two presidents, even though they represented different parties and agendas. Other policy instruments, especially those concerned with the military, have a different character. They involve fewer distributional concerns domestically and hence have fewer interest groups attending to them. With fewer interest groups, Congress is also less likely to get information about them. This gives the executive branch an added advantage and gives the president greater capacity to pursue his desired policy in these areas. And in some cases these have weaker ideological divisions that also contribute to presidential power. The case of Sub-Saharan Africa shows how this can occur in the areas of military aid and deployment.

Finally, the case illustrates how the militarization of foreign policies can happen. As the presidents faced rising constraints from Congress and interest groups in trade and aid policy, they shifted more and more to one of military engagement. And this was even true when their central stated foreign policy goals were for economic development and democratization in Africa. Ironically, despite the end of the Cold War, US policy in Africa became increasingly militarized in this period. Events in Africa did not require a military-oriented policy by the United States, and it is not clear that such a policy achieved what has been hoped for. Other countries like China have advanced their goals on the continent without the use of military aid and deployments. Much of this was due to domestic politics in the United States. And as recent events have shown, this militarization continues, albeit under another president—Obama—as well.[158]

Of course, American foreign policy toward an entire region is complex and difficult to capture in one chapter. We have only scratched the surface of what could be written about it.[159] Our goal was to focus on the different policy instruments and how presidents have tried to use them, and how domestic US politics affected this. In doing so, we do not deal with a range of issues, including the specificities of country within the region or the history of interactions between the United States, Africa, and former colonial powers. These factors clearly matter for African American relations. Our case illuminates our key themes, but it does not offer conclusive evidence that our arguments extend spatially or temporally. Of course, other experts may read the details of this case in contrasting ways. Coupled with the evidence in preceding chapters, we believe this case provides further concrete support for our larger theory.

158   Schmitt, 2014.
159   Clough, 1992; Herbst, 1992; Tieku, 2012; Cooke and Downie, 2014.

# 8

# CONCLUSIONS

## Our Argument and Findings

In this chapter we summarize our argument and findings first. We then discuss some ramifications of our book for international relations theory and the study of foreign policy. Next we discuss some of the shortcomings of our study and how future research could overcome them. We conclude with observations about our study's implications for American foreign policy and how it is conducted. We explore broader policy considerations relating to the future of American foreign policy. In particular, we address important questions: (1) Will American foreign policy remain guided by a grand strategy of liberal internationalism? (2) What factors contribute to US foreign policy being successful or not? (3) How do changes in the distribution of information between the president and Congress affect US policy? And what effect does the new massive intelligence collection within the US government have on foreign policy? (4) Is more presidential power beneficial for US foreign policy?

Before we begin our conclusions, it is worth returning to the first page, where we began with quotes about the Obama administration and its plans for foreign policy, one by President Obama and one about his announced plans. How has the administration's performance compared to its stated goals? Much as our book predicts, it has been hard for him to turn away from military instruments of statecraft. His *desire* to do so was made clear in his 2014 commencement speech at West Point. Obama stated, "Here's my bottom line: America must always lead on the world stage. If we don't, no one else will. The military that you have joined is, and always will be, the backbone of that leadership. But US military action cannot be the only —or even primary—component of our leadership in every instance. *Just because we have the best hammer does not mean that every problem is a nail.*"[1] This quote illustrates both Obama's awareness of the need to consider and use many policy instruments and his reluctance to further militarize US foreign policy.

Like other presidents, Obama has desired to use a panoply of instruments to achieve his foreign policy goals. But domestic politics—distributional and ideological disputes—has gotten in his way. On economic aid, little has been possible due to ideological battles over the federal budget and

1   Obama, 2014.

continued funding of the government's debt. The sequester legislation of 2011 and 2012 effectively halted any growth in foreign aid, and the actual sequestration cut USAID's budget by 4%.[2] On the trade front, the president has also been stalled. Despite extensive negotiations with US trading partners toward regional trade agreements, such as the Trans-Pacific Partnership (TPP) and the Transatlantic Trade and Investment Partnership (TTIP), it was extremely difficult for Obama to get trade negotiating authority and so the agreements remain unfinished with many hurdles ahead as of the summer of 2015.[3] In terms of immigration policy, ideological battles within and between the parties in Congress prevented any action there as well prior to 2015. Indeed, in September 2014 Obama relinquished the idea of taking executive action to move the agenda forward on immigration, in part due to concerns about congressional races in November 2014.[4]

This inability to make use of foreign aid, trade, or immigration as instruments of foreign policy has left Obama with only military means to employ. And despite his desire not to use these types of instruments, as evidenced in his quote, he has been forced on many foreign policy issues to consider these instruments and often to employ them. There are numerous examples: the military surge in Afghanistan in 2009, the air support campaign in Libya in 2011, Obama's desire to not intervene in Syria but the recent decision to bomb there, the bombing in Iraq and addition of US troops to deal with the terrorist group ISIS in 2014, the drone attacks in Africa and the Middle East throughout his presidency, and even the sending of US troops to deal with the Ebola crisis in Liberia in 2014. In addition, Obama has been able to implement sanctions in a number of cases, but especially on the Russians over the Ukrainian crisis in 2014. Our theory sheds light on why this tendency to use military and coercive policy was likely, despite the president's preferences.

Our central focus has been on the process of American foreign policy making. Through this we provide a better understanding of how and why it gets made the way it does. We explored in particular the forces that affect the role of the president and executive branch in foreign policy making. Given America's many resources, its presidents have many different policies they could potentially use in any situation, but they choose one particular set. Why is this set chosen from among the wide variety of options they have? The answer lies in large part with America's political institutions, which make a big difference to how policy is made in the United States. Notably, the powerful role of Congress and the salience of interest groups and public opinion, as we show, critically influence American foreign policy. And this

2   Morales, 2013.
3   Akhtar and Jones, 2014; Cooper, 2014; Jolly, 2014.
4   Davis and Parker, 2014.

leads to a bias in policy toward military instruments as presidents try to sidestep the politics generated by these groups.

We addressed several more specific questions in the book. The first concerned presidential power in foreign policy making. When, and why, can the president get what he wants in terms of making and implementing foreign policy? Presidential influence in foreign policy is sometimes great and sometimes minor. We developed a theory about when and how it varies and then tested the propositions that derive from that theory. Presidential power is important because the president is the main conduit for foreign policy pressures to enter the domestic system. In addition, the president has been the main advocate for a grand strategy of liberal internationalism since World War II. When the president is weaker, this strategy is less likely to prevail. International engagement needs presidential leadership to extract sufficient resources from domestic politics and to be able to make reliable foreign commitments. The extent to which the United States can and will pursue an internationalist strategy in world politics depends greatly on presidential power.

Second, how and when are different foreign policy instruments chosen? To deal with a foreign policy problem, why do presidents decide to use force or economic aid or trade, or some combination of them? This decision, and the constraints that shape it, matter since some policy instruments, or combinations of policy instruments, are likely to be more successful than others in particular international relations situations. But distributional and ideological battles clash with presidential evaluations of the necessary foreign policy strategies. As a result, domestic politics, through its impact on the choice of policies, ultimately affects how successful US foreign policy is.

Third, when are presidents able to substitute one policy instrument for another? When are they constrained and unable to do this? Such policy substitution is critically important in foreign affairs. When constrained by domestic politics, presidents are not able to craft the best combination of policies to address the international problem or opportunity that the United States faces. An internationalist strategy and ultimately American global influence depends on policy substitution and its domestic politics.

We then contrasted the politics around different foreign policy instruments. We see the differences across policies and the instruments they involve as being critically important to the long-term direction of American foreign policy. In particular, this book focused on economic aid, trade, immigration, geopolitical aid, sanctions, domestic military spending, and military deployments, which we see as key pillars of American foreign policy.

Our theory engages with the debate about the role of the president in US foreign policy. Many theories, such as the "two presidencies," claim that the president has great influence over and power to determine foreign policy, especially in comparison to his role in domestic policy. Presidents, they aver, can readily shape foreign policy and thus can easily substitute one policy for another or combine them. We laid out arguments as to why these claims are contestable. Different foreign policy instruments have different political and economic characteristics. Presidential power varies across policy instruments, just as it may vary over time. The president's influence is moderated by two characteristics of policy instruments: the extent of distributional politics associated with the presence of large, concentrated costs or benefits for domestic groups (versus public goods types of qualities without large, concentrated benefits or costs) and the degree of ideological divisions. Hence we argue that interests and ideas are both important.

The distribution of information about policy is also important. When information asymmetries exist in favor of the executive, he will be more powerful. These asymmetries are more likely when distributional conflicts are smaller. These two features affect presidential influence and policy substitution. We reach this conclusion controlling for the influence of the international system in many of our analyses. We do not take the strong position that the international system has no influence on US foreign policy; instead our analytical strategy is to take a tighter focus on the ways domestic politics do.

Other attempts to understand differences in foreign policy instruments often rely on simpler categories. One example is the differentiation of foreign policy into "high" and "low" politics. All things related to the military are seemingly part of high politics, which is all about protecting national security through the threat or use of force. The designation of high politics appears to have something to do with the nature of the threat from the international environment and how much it affects state survival. Our step beyond this is to show what makes foreign policy instruments differ and to examine how domestic politics fits into this. Most American uses of force since World War II have not had much to do with the survival of the country. Hence designating any use of military statecraft as one of high politics seems misconstrued. Furthermore, within the military, politics tend to differ greatly across different instruments. Military deployments, at least ex ante, tend to give presidents the most discretion and to concern domestic groups the least, while domestic military spending is very similar to other domestic policy areas where interest groups and Congress are active. Geopolitical aid lies somewhere in between these two cases. On the other hand, trade, economic aid, and diplomacy can be invoked when a country is worried about its survival. For instance, in 2013–14, Ukraine's integrity as a state was helped greatly by economic aid from the West, diplomacy by the EU and United States, and certainly involved the trade agreement with the EU. We think foreign policy instruments differ less because of some inherent connection to national security, since they are all connected to it; and they differ more because of the domestic politics—the specter of distributional and ideological politics—that we identify.

In summary, presidential influence over foreign policy is greatest when distributional politics around a foreign policy instrument are low and when the president has more information than Congress and other social actors. In addition, presidential power rises as ideological divisions over a policy instrument decrease. This setting best characterizes policy making surrounding geopolitical aid, sanctions, and military deployments. In contrast, presidents are weakest when distributional politics and ideological divisions surrounding a policy instrument are prominent and no informational asymmetries exist in favor of the president. Under these conditions interest groups tend to be very active, and their lobbying transmits much information to Congress. This type of policy making characterizes economic aid, trade, and immigration. It is also very typical for military procurements and other domestic spending. This view is supported by a wide variety of evidence in the empirical chapters.

Our first empirical chapter focused our attention on interest groups and US foreign policy. Interest groups and distributional politics are intimately linked to particular policy instruments. We hypothesized that groups would have variable influence given the policy instrument at hand. Where organized groups can obtain highly concentrated benefits or may have to pay highly concentrated costs, economic interest groups on both sides of an issue will be active and lobby fiercely. Interest groups will also have an incentive to collect information and lobby Congress in order to overcome the executive's informational advantages. These distributional battles make policy highly contested and polarize debate so that it is more costly for presidents to realize their desired policies. For other foreign policy instruments, distributive politics will be much less prominent and interest groups less active. In areas that appear more similar to public goods, with few excludable benefits or costs, we expect fewer economic interest groups to be involved. But other groups, such as NGOs and ethnic or diaspora groups, who may be affected by the policy, will be more prominent. Interest group activity varies by policy instrument as well.

Chapter 3 showed how interest groups operate differently across the foreign policy instruments we have identified. We developed a new idea about interest group targeting, that is, how and whom different interest groups will lobby to realize their preferences. They target Congress or the executive branch depending on the policy instrument. In immigration, trade, economic aid, and military spending, the important distributive consequences of policy mean that economic interest groups organize, lobby, and testify before Congress frequently, paying less attention to the president. When the content of the lobbying dealt with distributional goods (e.g., parts of a budget), the president was more likely to be bypassed in favor of Congress, as expected. The purpose of this lobbying was to provide information to Congress about particular policies and their implications, as well as to push for preferred policies. But in areas where the material consequences are much less apparent, like geopolitical aid, deployments, and sanctions, we do not see so much organization and lobbying by these types of groups. We see less interest group activity overall in these two areas; when there was activity, it was led by different types of groups, mainly NGOs, ethnic groups, and especially representatives from the executive branch (including the military).

In chapter 4 we turned to Congress itself and examined two different types of data about elite behavior: executive agency budget data comparing presidential requests to congressional allocations and roll call voting in the US Congress. This chapter focused on the key decisions by the elites who put US foreign policy into place. Our theory suggested that the president's influence in the budgetary process would not be the same for all foreign affairs policy areas. The president gets more of what he wants in areas of the budget that deal most heavily with military-related issues, but less of what he wants in other foreign policy areas where distributive politics and ideological divisions were more important and the president had little informational advantage. We then looked at roll call votes in the House. Our analysis of these data showed that the influence of the president, as well as local constituency-level variables, varied across different types of foreign policy instruments. The president is better able to compel legislators in his party to vote his preferred way when the issues had fewer distributional effects and greater asymmetries of information favoring the president. Thus the president had more influence on his co-partisans in military deployments, sanctions, and geopolitical aid than in the other areas. Part of this is explained by the different role of interest groups and the amount of presidential control over the bureaucracies that deal with these issues.

In addition, we looked at the correlates of legislative voting for pro-international engagement policies, which are ones the president tends to favor. We presented two sets of results. First, we examined the extent of ideological divisiveness. Liberal legislators were more likely than conservative legislators to support economic aid and immigration liberalization; they were less supportive of geopolitical aid, military deployment, trade liberalization, and domestic military spending. However, ideological divisions varied across these instruments as well. Ideological divisions were much weaker for military aid, sanctions, and troop deployments. Presidents, wishing to use all of these instruments of statecraft, therefore face different patterns of support and opposition domestically to these foreign policy instruments, thus affecting his ability to substitute policies. However, our theoretical expectation that immigration would not be very ideologically divisive was not supported. Immigration is highly ideologically divisive.

Second, legislative voting on some types of foreign policy is strongly correlated with constituency interests. Consistent with economic models showing the distributive consequences of policies, legislative support in the House for foreign economic aid and trade liberalization was more likely when a legislator came from a district that was well endowed with a relatively high-skilled constituency. Domestic military spending at the district level was also predictive of legislative voting. Economic interests and ideological divisions matter for legislative voting.

In chapter 5 we focused on the design and historical evolution of the US foreign policy bureaucracy. The patterns of presidential power across different policy instruments that we theorize about are also present in the bureaucracy. To develop and implement foreign policy, the nation must have a bureaucracy that is capable of doing the many tasks that are required for this. Few studies of American foreign policy focus on the bureaucracy. But as American politics experts know, the bureaucracy is a critical source of power for the president and controlling it is a major way for Congress to exert influence. Over the last sixty years, the United States has built a vast bureaucracy to deal with foreign policy. Were these agencies established under tight presidential control or with considerable oversight and supervision by Congress? Congress plays a much stronger role over institutions that dealt with trade and economic aid than with military deployments and geopolitical aid. Our analysis of the bureaucracy data supports this claim, with greater institutional control by the president over these instruments. The biggest anomaly was the higher than expected degree of control by the president over agencies involved heavily in domestic military spending. Furthermore, when Congress is dissatisfied with the policies coming out of the executive branch, it may respond by *trying to* restructure the bureaucracy. Our case studies show this phenomenon in action, but with different success depending on the different foreign policy instruments.

Our final empirical analysis examined public opinion data. We believe public opinion matters for US foreign policy. Citizens believe that the informational advantage the president has varies across policy instruments in ways consistent with our theory. American citizens also recognize that the informational advantage depends on the local consequences of these instruments. And finally citizens recognize that the president has greater control over instruments that have fewer distributional effects and ideological cleavages. These findings provided micro-foundations for our arguments about when and why the president has greater ability to exert influence over policy.

But which citizens support and oppose the different policy choices for engaging with the international system? This chapter also focused on the role of ideology and the extent of ideological divisions across policy instruments. Previous research shows that the American public exhibits differences in their foreign policy preferences across the left-right ideological spectrum, but we show how some issues are more ideologically divisive on average than others, which we also demonstrate in our analysis of congressional roll call voting. These ideological divisions create problems for the president in making policy. Since he wants to be able to use all the foreign policy instruments available to him, he needs to be able to substitute and package together different types of policies. But these ideological divisions mean that he faces more complicated constraints in this process of substitution. He will have difficulty building political coalitions that allow him to utilize different sets of policies.

In chapter 7 we presented an extensive case study of US foreign policy in order to explore our theory and hypotheses in greater dynamic detail. We focused on US policy toward Sub-Saharan Africa over the course of two presidencies, Bill Clinton and George W. Bush, from 1993 to 2009. Presidents tried to use many policy instruments to deal with the serious problems arising in Africa after the end of the Cold War, but faced domestic political resistance. President Clinton (1993–2001) was blocked by the Republican-controlled Congress from using economic aid as he wanted and he had to turn first to trade policy and finally to a more military-oriented strategy. Then President Bush (2001–2009) tried to use trade and aid, again only to find Congress making this very difficult as the Democrats took over. And so he too turned to a more militarized policy for the continent. The cleavages around ideology and material interests shaped debates and policies, and control of information was important in this process. The case then provided vivid illustrations of our main themes.

In sum, domestic politics matter for foreign policy; both ideas and interests play an important role in shaping foreign policy. Governments have many policy instruments they can use to address foreign relations. American presidents have to negotiate and interact strategically with Congress and interest groups to enact the foreign policies they prefer. Different policy instruments have different politics associated with them. Two aspects are very important in shaping those politics: the nature of the distributional impact that policies have and the degree of ideological division over a policy instrument. The asymmetry of information between the president and Congress is also important, but this depends greatly on the distributional nature of the policy instrument. These features affect how powerful the president will be, and thus whether he can pursue his internationalist agenda. The different politics across policy instruments are key to understanding what policies are chosen and why. These decisions are shaped by the interactions of the president, interest groups, bureaucracies, and Congress. This is a fairly novel approach to foreign policy analysis, highlighting the role of distributional politics, ideology, and patterns of information provision.

# Important Implications for IR Theory

## The External Environment and International Politics

We have paid attention mainly to the domestic political process in making foreign policy and not to the behavior of other countries or the nature of international problems as factors shaping American policy. But we make two assumptions about international politics that in effect make them part of our theory. First, we assumed that presidents and the executive branch are the main conduits for bringing the pressures and problems of the international environment into the deliberations about policy in the United States. The president negotiates and interacts with foreign leaders frequently; he and his bureaucracy are the main points of US governmental contact with foreign governments. The president in effect transmits the international environment into the domestic process of policy making. His perceptions and views on what the international environment is like tend to dominate the domestic policy process. In the two-level game models, for instance, it is the president or chief executive who is the pivot between the domestic and international levels.[5] And this is how we see him as well.

The executive branch bureaucracy, including the departments of State, Defense, and Treasury and agencies like the CIA, are the main sources of information and intelligence about foreign countries and problems arising outside the United States. They are one of the main ways that information about the external environment enters the domestic political system. The executive branch, because of this informational advantage, sets the tone for how the international environment is perceived domestically. In addition, however, interest groups sometimes perform this function. Given their links to the international environment, interest groups bring the perspectives and preferences of external actors into the domestic policy process. Economic interest groups, for instance, develop preferences that take their position in the international economy into account. Export industries and American multinational corporations may well bring the concerns of the foreign countries they deal with into the American policy process through their lobbying, PAC contributions, and congressional testimony. Diaspora and ethnic identity groups operating in the United States also represent the interests of groups outside and inside the United States. Hence in this sense

5  Putnam, 1988; Milner, 1997.

we include the international environment and its pressures and opportunities via the preferences of domestic actors as they experience them.

Many scholars in IR theory suggest this process of bringing international influences into the foreign policy decision making of a country. They would probably agree that the international structure does not give decision makers clear indications of what constitutes good foreign policy; rather, leaders' perceptions and domestic politics shape policy choices. Threats from the outside—as well as opportunities—have to be perceived by domestic actors.[6] In most cases, the executive branch will be the first to appreciate such threats or opportunities, giving the executive the instruments and institutional capacity to develop knowledge about foreign affairs. But non-state actors within a country will also be important in transmitting international pressures and opportunities into domestic politics. Economic interest groups and diaspora groups are key sources of external inputs into foreign policy making. Hirschman's recognition long ago that increased connections with the international system created domestic groups with vested interests in those connections is an important element of foreign policy.[7]

The focus of much research on psychology in foreign relations also supports this notion of how domestic politics connects to the international environment. A range of studies examine the important role of threat perception and its role in foreign policy.[8] But oftentimes these studies focus on the role of individuals in the executive office. Studies, such as those on the operational code of presidents or national role theory, gather evidence about how the president and other foreign policy elites view the external environment and other states because they see these perceptions as shaping foreign policy.[9] His perception of the external environment is seen as a major influence on how policy is set.[10]

The role of psychological variables, of course, does not stop with the president. Others have pointed out that the members of the Republican and Democratic parties approach the international environment with fun-

6  Jervis, 1976; Walt, 1987; James and Hristoulas, 1994.

7  Hirschman, 1980 (1945).

8  Stein, 2013.

9  National Role Conceptions have been utilized as independent variables to explain foreign policy decisions. Holsti, 1970; Walker, 1987; Breuning, 1995; Grossman, 2005; Catalinac, 2007; Cantir and Kaarbo, 2012.

10  Bzostek and Robison emphasized the importance of a psychological variable assessing the president's view of foreign relations, which they measure as whether "the U.S. president perceives the world as a friendly place, where others can be trusted, or as a dark, Hobbesian domain, where others are hostile and will exploit weakness or naïveté." Bzostek and Robison, 2008, p. 361. And other work goes even further to understand how presidential illnesses can affect these perceptions, which underlines the centrality of presidents to US foreign policy. McDermott, 2007.

damentally different psychological theories.[11] This has implications for thinking about presidential behavior, as these theories may frame the same structural, external situation in very different ways, such as viewing strategic interaction more as an assurance game versus a prisoner's dilemma.[12] In our view, domestic actors actively perceive the external environment and the behavior of other states and interpret that information; they then bring their perceptions and preferences to the domestic political process. Our focus has then been on this domestic process, but it includes international influences.

## Change over Time and Change across Issues

In this book, we focus on differences across foreign policy instruments and the issue areas they connect to. We attend less to changes over time and longitudinal differences. This is a distinctive way of looking at American foreign policy. Changes over time clearly matter.

Our study does have implications for temporal changes. As we note, any weakening of the president and the executive branch in foreign policy is likely to make a robust strategy of international engagement less possible and less likely. Domestic political changes that limit the president or force him to reveal information collected by his intelligence agencies will shift the internal balance of power away from him. Rising ideological cleavages, such as those prognosticated by studies about partisan polarization, will also likely weaken the president. And rising distributional pressures as the United States grows ever more deeply tied to the global economy may also undermine his influence over foreign policy. If any of these become persistent temporal trends, then we will see large changes in US policy.

Moreover, the processes we identify in this book lead to a tendency for the militarization of American policy to exist. When certain policies are blocked, the president will default to others, creating a bias in favor of military instruments. This can occur at each decision point in time; however, as we show in chapter 7, this also occurs over time. As a result, without

11   Others have suggested background sets of genetic variables that are associated with the heritability of foreign policy preferences which would color the perceptions of external events. Cranmer and Dawes, 2012.

12   For example, Rathbun argues that, "Democrats, assuming the trustworthiness of their partners, framed the strategic situation after World War II less in terms of a prisoner's dilemma and more in terms of an assurance game, as they believed that cooperation would be reciprocated. . . . Republicans, in contrast, largely framed the same structural situation as a prisoner's dilemma game in which other countries would take advantage of American cooperation. They therefore preferred unilateralism in which the United States would retain full discretion over its foreign policy." Rathbun, 2011, p. 3. He goes on to say, "I use political party affiliation as a proxy for ideology, although the latter is the real manifestation of generalized trust." Ibid., p. 9.

proper attention US foreign policy could become less internationalist but more militaristic in character.

## Domestic Politics, Foreign Policy, Polarization, and Bipartisanship

One trend that has gained recent attention in American politics is increasing partisan polarization. Some scholars studying American politics identify a monotonic upward trend in partisan polarization.[13] Increased polarization over domestic policy has accompanied changes like rising income inequality, and may be related. One question that arises is whether foreign policy is affected by this trend. Partisan polarization might lead to declining bipartisanship and thus a loss of foreign policy flexibility. Some scholars do lament the passing of an era of bipartisanship in US foreign policy as a result of this trend.[14] Interestingly, it is often claimed that international events create bipartisanship; that is, external events, and threats especially, create domestic consensus and support for the president and his policy choices.[15] If this is the case, we would expect bipartisanship to wax and wane given the international situation. In contrast, increased polarization due to domestic politics would have a long-run effect on foreign policy, making all instruments of foreign policy harder to employ.

We do not, however, see any monotonic changes in foreign policy making as a result of underlying temporal changes in partisan polarization, at least at this point. Chaudoin, Milner, and Tingley show that bipartisanship in foreign policy has not seen a steady monotonic decline over time.[16] The much heralded increase in polarization in domestic politics does not have the exact same analog in foreign policy. Rather, our theory suggests that bipartisanship should vary across foreign policy instruments. For those issues that seem the most like domestic political ones, where distributional concerns are strong and informational asymmetries do not favor the president, declining bipartisanship over time may be more manifest. Those issues where ideological divisions are strong may also tend toward increasing partisanship. But other instruments with different characteristics may avoid this polarization. This is the pattern we see in the data. Starting from the universe of votes that we used in chapter 4, we created categories of votes

13   McCarty, Poole, and Rosenthal, 2006.
14   E.g., Kupchan and Trubowitz, 2007.
15   "Bipartisanship ought to be most prevalent when political developments outside Washington create for Republicans and Democrats, and Congress and the White House, a shared perception of common political goals." Meernik, 1993, p. 573. In contrast, Flynn argues instead that it is domestic politics that matters for bipartisanship, a least in executive branch appointments. Flynn, 2014.
16   Chaudoin, Milner, and Tingley, 2010.

that represent the use of the military or geopolitical aid, spending for the military, foreign aid, trade, and immigration. We then calculated for each vote whether it would be considered bipartisan.[17] We found that 66% of votes dealing with the usage of the military and related security agencies were bipartisan compared to a domestic policy baseline of 52%. Trade votes were slightly more bipartisan (58%) than domestic votes, while foreign aid votes, military spending, and immigration were slightly less bipartisan on average.[18] By and large, then, we see the expected differences across foreign policy instruments but few longitudinal trends.[19]

## How Does Our Argument Apply to Other Countries?

Our argument and data focus on the United States. How would our approach fare in other contexts? The United States is, of course, a special case in many ways. Internationally, it is a great power and for the last twenty or more years has been the hegemonic power in the system. Domestically, it is also rather different, being a presidential system with two parties and first-past-the-post voting. Combined with strong federalism, this makes the American political system non-representative among Western democracies. Do we expect any of our arguments to hold elsewhere?

In some respects we do. Our focus has been on three factors that shape foreign policy making. The first of these is the extent of distributive politics generated by the policy instrument. It seems likely that this is fairly constant across countries. All countries experience the costs and benefits associated with trade flows, for example. Obviously, some countries do more so than others and in different ways given their endowments. The United States is among the least globalized countries in the world, so others may experience this much more. But how distributive pressures are translated into politics

17    Mellow and Trubowitz, 2005. We also regressed this measure on indicators for each of the categories, with the excluded category being domestic votes. We clustered standard errors at the yearly level and estimated models with and without year fixed effects. In all models we excluded procedural votes. We find the same results as the simpler percentages reported in text.

18    These results hold whether we subset the data to be post-1970 (when rule changes in the House occurred) or use the full sample of votes from 1953–2008. Analysis using linear time trends uncovered no systematic changes, partly because some of the highest periods of bipartisanship surrounding the use of military tools of statecraft were in the post-2000 era.

19    Gridlock in Congress is another measure of partisan polarization's effects. The amount of congressional gridlock is the percentage of issues that needed to be addressed but were not. Binder, 2007. If foreign policy gridlock were increasing, we could conclude that domestic divisions were damaging American abilities to pursue a liberal internationalist foreign policy. Chaudoin et al. show that gridlock on foreign policy issues has not increased since the end of the Vietnam War or the end of the Cold War. Chaudoin, Milner, and Tingley, 2010.

differs because of the political institutions that aggregate preferences.[20] In the United States, legislators tightly represent their geographically defined constituencies and are much less bound to party discipline. Local interests and distributive politics generally get translated into politics more easily in this type of system.

In terms of information, the US Congress will have more sources of information than most legislatures because it is more institutionalized than others, having large staffs and powerful committees. But it is likely to be the case that presidents and prime ministers elsewhere also have well-developed bureaucracies that collect and report information about foreign affairs to them and do not share this information with their legislatures. Hence we anticipate that information asymmetries favoring the executive branch would be even stronger in most other countries.

We also expect ideology and partisanship to play a strong role in other countries. For many legislators in other types of systems, the role of the party is critical; they serve at their party's behest. Ideological divisions often represented in parties will be an important factor in foreign policy and will affect some instruments more than others. Scholars have remarked on the important role of political parties in shaping foreign policy in other democracies.[21] Hence our model will be broadly relevant in other democratic contexts. The executive in those systems will be more influential over policy in areas where distributive politics is less strong, information is more asymmetrically distributed in his favor, and party divisions over the instrument are weaker. Most countries compared to the United States will have fewer resources to devote to foreign policy generally; and their executives will be more limited by resources than in the United States. But many of the features that distinguish foreign policy instruments in the United States should be operative elsewhere.

It would be particularly interesting to examine the political dynamics underlying European Union foreign policy. The EU is often seen as a "soft power" foreign policy actor, employing promises of accession, economic aid, trade, diplomacy, and other economic measures rather than military ones.[22] The contrast with the United States is often made. Future research might consider how, if true, this difference arises in part from different domestic politics. For example, consider how more corporatist-style business-government relationships influence foreign policy decisions in Europe.[23] American relations with interest groups are often characterized in very

20  McGillivray, 2004; Hankla, 2006.
21  Milner and Judkins, 2004; Noel and Therien, 2008; Tingley, 2010.
22  Kagan, 2002; Cooper, 2004; Nye, 2004.
23  Katzenstein, 1985; Risse-Kappen, 1991.

different terms, as being more legalistic and antagonistic.[24] Interestingly, the recently announced "Transparency Register" will provide key data on interest group behavior in the EU to match the lobbying data now available in the United States. Future research should look at how these differences affect foreign policy in these two major powers.

## Limitations and Future Research

In light of these implications for international relations, we pause and take stock of the limitations in our analysis. In this book we theorize and collect data in a way that enables us to engage with American foreign policy at a broad level. This is different from scholarship that pays most attention to specific aspects, periods, or instruments of American foreign policy, which can allow more specific theorizing and empirical testing. As a result both our theory and empirics have weaknesses, but are also suggestive of future research that could not only address these weaknesses but also open up new research avenues for scholars of American foreign policy.

Our theory leaves several important issues unaddressed. First, we have been very general about the type of information that can bring advantages to the president. But it is useful to examine in more detail what types of information matter most and when they do so. A second concern focuses on ideology. Where do ideological preferences come from? Too little research, including our own, focuses on the origins of ideology and how, exactly, it interacts with economically driven preferences.

We bring together more actors than is usually the case in studies of foreign policy. Legislators and the executive branch interact in our theory, with the president often trying to impose his preferences on them. Informational advantages in his favor make this more likely, while ideological divisions across the parties make it less likely. Bureaucracies also matter in shaping this interaction. But we do not explicitly model how bureaucracies and the executive and legislative branches interrelate. And we theorize that such interactions vary across agencies and policy instruments. A more systematic model of this bureaucratic politics could be useful.

Our empirical approach has been to use a wide range of data to explore our theory. We report results from hundreds of thousands of lobbying reports, hundreds of carefully chosen substantive roll call votes as well as the universe of House roll call voting on foreign affairs, hundreds of bureaucratic agencies, and many thousands of survey respondents (including from international relations scholars). We also provide an intensive case study

24   Kagan, 2001; Kelemen, 2008.

of US foreign policy in Sub-Saharan Africa over a period of nearly twenty years. But as we discussed in each chapter, each of these data sources has its limitations.

Our analysis of interest group activity in American foreign policy introduces a new dataset spanning the universe of lobbying reports between 2007 and 2012. While rich, any new dataset comes with limitations. These data are affected by strategic interaction among the actors that we cannot see generally, and hence it may be affected by selection bias in which some groups do not appear and others appear more than they actually account for. Another obvious one is that it does not extend to earlier years because the exact data we use are not yet digitized pre-2007. Future work could consider analyzing the lobbying report data before 2007. Fortunately, chapter 3 also uses a new dataset of congressional testimony that does extend back in time. But these data face their own challenges, such as our not controlling who is invited, or who agrees to testify, and how this might be related to strategic interaction or even social desirability concerns.

One area that is more challenging for our theory and results deals with the role of diaspora lobbies, such as the pro-Israel Jewish lobby. Some scholars have argued that these groups have a disproportionate impact on US foreign policy.[25] US foreign policy is much broader than policy toward any particular region, and furthermore it also involves policy instruments that go beyond those pertinent to the Israeli case. Such groups are often highly organized and seek selective benefits that accrue to a large extent overseas rather than the benefits we focus on, which are domestic. Nevertheless, we recognize the electoral effects and political power of these groups, suggesting a broader understanding of the ethnic- and identity-based motivations of diaspora lobbies in light of our theoretical structure and empirical evidence.

In chapter 4 we examine the dynamics of budgetary requests and appropriations between the president and Congress as well as the determinants of roll call voting in the US House of Representatives. While in many respects this chapter lets us examine a number of our core propositions most directly, it is also a type of data for which we should expect strategic behavior to be highly likely, which lessens our ability to make confident causal inferences. Presidential position-taking is not random, nor are budget requests. Hence we explored a variety of different ways of looking at the data. No method was perfect, but all pointed toward similar conclusions.

One significant question involves presidential endorsement of policies and votes in Congress. We need to get a better sense from key decision makers about the importance and timing of presidential position-taking. We have not relied upon direct interviews in part because interviewees have

25  Mearsheimer and Walt, 2007.

strategic incentives too, but we would be naïve to suggest that a closer engagement with decision makers would not be revelatory. It would also be interesting to try to explore how long-lasting information asymmetries are. Future research should also examine policy instruments that we do not consider as directly, such as diplomacy.

Our work on the institutional design of bureaucracies in chapter 5 may also be improved in different ways. In order to speak to the existing literature, we have restricted our attention to a set of large and powerful bureaucratic agencies. However, the US federal government is vast, and making similar measurements for smaller agencies could reveal additional variation. Finally, there may exist additional ways to measure presidential versus congressional influence. We try to causally identify presidential influence using statistical controls that absorb the effect of other variables that do not, for example, vary within a president's term. This is one way to isolate presidential influence, but it is not perfect. And some of the variation over time may be of interest. For instance, as we show in chapter 5 with USAID, there can be change over time in the de facto extent of control between Congress and the president.

In chapter 6 on public opinion we recognize that it is difficult to establish causally a link between public opinion and actual government policies. Linking policies to institutional design features (such as those discussed in chapter 5) is also difficult because many agencies were established long ago. Furthermore, interest groups (such as those discussed in chapter 3) clearly have an important role that could crowd out the voice of the public. It is for these reasons that our evidence about public opinion is accompanied by other empirical explorations. But even within our study of public opinion we face questions. Some of these are measurement based. For example, an ideal measurement of preferences across multiple foreign policy instruments would let respondents trade off the expected costs of using different instruments. Individuals may impute monetary (or other) costs to *using* different instruments which might be distinct from their underlying *support* for using the instrument. Future research should employ designs to trace out individual preferences across policy instruments in a more systematic manner.

Our case study chapter brings the analysis closer to actual events, decisions, and individual decision makers. American relations with the many countries in Sub-Saharan Africa are complex and cannot be described in a single chapter. But we have tried to focus on the ways in which presidents tried to use various foreign policy instruments and the domestic politics that affected their use. Other factors such as the particular country, time period, or history of interactions clearly matter, but are not our focus. The case illuminates themes; it does not prove anything. And others may read aspects of the case differently than we do. But it provides needed detail and illustrates change over time that aligns with our claims.

Finally, there are other institutions and decision makers that we have neglected completely or partially. For example, we do not focus at all on the role of the judicial system. Its role in recent years has become more important, as judges have been asked to rule on the legality of different policies. This may very well become increasingly important as debates about cyber-security touch on broader issues such as privacy. The media and its presentation of foreign affairs may also matter. Future research should engage with the role of the judiciary and media in US foreign policy.

# Implications for American Foreign Policy

## Militarization

The differences we identify among policy instruments have critical implications. Some of these instruments, such as geopolitical aid, sanctions, and deployments, give the president greater freedom from domestic constraints and thus he can more readily deploy them and use them as substitutes. For any foreign policy problem, then, the president may be tempted to use military instruments of statecraft because he may find it easier to persuade Congress to authorize the use of such instruments, while authorization for other instruments would be difficult if not impossible to obtain. Why are the domestic costs and benefits likely to favor military means? The president has more discretion here and more access to information. Other instruments may face greater political contestation, stronger legislative constraints, more interest group opposition, more ideological divisions, and thus less presidential discretion. On policies like sanctions, military deployments, and geopolitical aid, Congress is less likely to constrain him because distributional issues and ideological divisions are less important and hence domestic groups are less activated to contest the president. And he has a national intelligence bureaucracy that is built to provide him with information, which gives him a strong advantage in the domestic political game. Partisan politics driven by ideological divisions may also be less constraining. Domestic politics generates a bias in policy toward military-oriented instruments of statecraft.

Thus, while non-military means of statecraft may be less expensive to employ and sometimes more likely to yield positive results, presidents may choose not to use them because of their greater domestic political costs. Militarization implies the injection of military forces and planning into all aspects of foreign policy making. If the use of military means is very costly internationally, then presidents will be forced to try other instruments.[26]

---

26  Clark and Reed point to more international factors in influencing policy substitution, although they do mention domestic politics. Clark and Reed, 2005.

But the difficulty of foreign policy substitution in the American political system is such that military means and solutions have become easier instruments for the president to employ. If, time after time, military means are less costly for the president, then the military option is more likely to be chosen. It is not inevitable in the American system, but there is a tendency toward it given the domestic political constraints on other foreign policy instruments. Other scholars have noted the tendency toward the "militarization" of American foreign policy.[27] Others focus on the substantial negative consequences of it with respect to combating terrorist organizations like ISIS.[28] And others have noted that such investment and use of military means can make the probability of war more likely.[29]

External pressures may also push presidents toward militarization, but these have been well discussed. Militarization thus reflects domestic politics as well as international relations.[30] Our point about militarization arising from the internal politics of a country is more provocative. Our claim here is suggestive since we do not provide dispositive empirical evidence that presidents employ foreign policy instruments based on their domestic political costs.

### Will the United States Remain Liberal Internationalist? Should It?

As Brooks, Ikenberry, and Wohlforth maintain, "Since the end of World War II, the United States has pursued a single grand strategy: deep engagement. In an effort to protect its security and prosperity, the country has promoted a liberal economic order and established close defense ties with partners in Europe, East Asia, and the Middle East. . . . The details of U.S. foreign policy have differed from administration to administration . . . , but for over 60 years, every president has agreed on the fundamental decision to remain deeply engaged in the world."[31] We also find strong support for this claim in our research.[32] But a number of recent studies have argued that the United States may turn its back on its longtime strategy of liberal

27  Sherry, 1995; Bacevich, 2002; Walt, 2005; Bacevich, 2007; Bacevich, 2010; Posen, 2013. "As early as World War II, the U.S. began squandering its diplomatic tools—and the net effect has been a collective amnesia: the only effective option we seem to remember is the military option. Militarization of U.S. foreign policy had been creeping up for decades." DeGennaro, 2014.

28  Kristof, 2014.

29  Slantchev, 2011; Debs and Monteiro, 2014.

30  President Obama in his 2014 commencement speech lamented the militarization of foreign policy, and the pressures put on him to do so. While he did not explicitly say so, the restrictions he has faced with other foreign policy tools from Congress we feel have contributed to this.

31  Brooks, Ikenberry, and Wohlforth, 2013, p. 130.

32  Chaudoin, Milner, and Tingley, 2010.

internationalism.[33] Some have argued that increased partisanship may lead to a declining internationalist orientation.[34]

According to our analysis, the United States is likely to remain internationally engaged as long as the president can play an important role in shaping US foreign policy. Should the president's role in setting foreign policy diminish while that of Congress increases, American foreign policy might veer away from liberal internationalism. Instead, US foreign policy could be replaced by domestic ideological and distributive struggles and an unwillingness to let the president take advantage of US resources when shaping foreign policy. This domestic battle could translate into an inability of the United States to engage and to negotiate successfully on the international stage, and an overreliance on military tools. International cooperation requires that the US government be able to credibly represent the United States in international negotiations, to be able to make commitments to use (or not use) certain policy instruments, and to implement the agreements reached. Congressional resistance to climate change agreements and to regional trade agreements recently shows the domestic constraints that can block American engagement globally and hinder US leadership abroad.[35] As distributive and ideological conflicts rise around foreign policy, these steps become more difficult for a president. As the two-level game logic points out, domestic politics can play a large role in fostering or preventing international cooperation.[36]

A second question is whether the United States should continue a strategy of liberal internationalism. The world has changed over the past seventy years since World War II when this strategy began to be defined and implemented. Some observers have made a normative plea for a more restrained role for the United States. For example, Barry Posen notes that Republican and Democrat consensus on the importance of US domination of the world has generated a "liberal hegemony," which he claims has been disastrous for the United States, calling it an "undisciplined, expensive, and bloody strategy [that] has done untold harm to U.S. national security."[37] He concludes, "It is time to abandon the United States' hegemonic strategy and replace it with one of restraint. This approach would mean giving up on global reform and sticking to protecting narrow national security interests."[38]

---

33  MacDonald and Parent, 2011; Brooks, Ikenberry, and Wohlforth, 2012; Craig, Friedman, Green, et al., 2013; Montgomery, 2014.

34  Kupchan and Trubowitz, 2007; Kupchan and Trubowitz, 2010.

35  Congressional and Republican resistance to any climate change commitments globally has persisted even in the recent Lima agreement of December 2014, while Democratic resistance to regional trade agreements has also been present. Catanoso, 2014; Ritter, 2014.

36  Putnam, 1988; Milner, 1997.

37  Posen, 2013, p. 117.

38  Ibid.

American politics has changed during this time as well. We noted earlier that the increasing polarization of American politics could, in the eyes of some analysts, make it impossible for the United States to pursue a policy of liberal internationalism. But we think the future foreign policy challenges facing the United States are less likely to be political deadlock and more likely to be how to deal with its rising competitors, like China, without starting a war—especially when using military means to solve international problems may seem easier domestically, but may end in disaster on the international scene.

### Success or Failure in American Foreign Policy?

Many scholars and analysts have claimed that US foreign policy was a success in the Cold War period.[39] They note that the United States in effect "won" the Cold War when the USSR dissolved into a much smaller Russia with many fewer resources and less influence, ending the bipolar contest. America's strategy of promoting a liberal internationalist order seemed to have been successful in preventing world war, achieving economic growth within the alliance, and deterring the spread of authoritarianism, especially in a communist guise. American goals of containing communism and spreading capitalism and democracy were being achieved. Liberal internationalism was a success, at least until 2001.

On a smaller scale, one can also name the foreign policy choices that seem to have brought success to the United States. In an interesting article, Walt identifies a number of successful and failed American foreign policies since World War II.[40] He mentions as examples of successes the Marshall Plan, NATO, GATT/WTO, the Bretton Woods monetary system, the non-proliferation regime, the opening to China, the Egyptian-Israeli Peace Treaty, and German reunification. These were all policies designed to engage internationally to promote a liberal global system. And he asks what all of these successes have in common:

> [T]hey were all primarily *diplomatic* initiatives, where the use of force played little or no direct role. This stands in sharp contrast to US foreign policy today, where the preferred response to many problems tends to be some form of "kinetic action" (in the form of drone strikes, special operations, covert action, large-scale bombing raids, or in a few cases, all-out invasions). . . . But our poor track record in recent years is also due to a tendency to shoot first and talk later, and to use military force to solve problems for which it is ill-suited. Just look at

---

39  Fukuyama, 2006.
40  Walt, 2013.

the recurring debate over whether the United States should even talk to Iran, and you get an idea of how much we have devalued diplomacy and privileged military power.[41]

The biggest failure in American foreign policy after World War II and before 2001 was probably the Vietnam War. It is the fourth largest war the United States had fought as ranked by US military and combat deaths (after the Civil War and the two world wars) and one of the longest (1955–1975).[42] The war ended with roughly 47,400 US military dead, 10,800 non-combatant deaths, 153,300 wounded, and 10,100 captured.[43] The American military devastated both North and South Vietnam, inflicted nearly 1 million casualties upon their peoples, and brought environmental catastrophes to large parts of the region. And it failed to achieve any of the American goals. Since 2001, the biggest failures have probably been the second Iraq war begun in 2003 and then perhaps the Afghanistan invasion after 9/11, which is now estimated to cost the United States $1 trillion.[44] While neither of these has resulted in the number of US battle deaths close to the Vietnam War, they have been hugely expensive, drawn-out conflicts that do not seem to have achieved many of the United States's original goals.[45]

What causes foreign policy failures like these? Jervis in an interesting review points out several key sources of foreign policy mistakes: "Many mistakes follow from leaders' failures to correctly assess the distribution of power. Others follow from the failure to properly diagnose the situation and the nature and intentions of others. States may then err by doing too little or too much to oppose others, and by acting too soon or too late."[46] It is interesting to note that in Jervis's understanding, these mistakes largely follow from how domestic leaders interpret international events and other states, and how they fail to "properly diagnose" what is going on outside the

41    Ibid.
42    Leland and Oboroceanu, 2010, pp. 2–4.
43    Ibid., p. 11.
44    Dyer and Sorvino, 2014.
45    As Fallows notes, "Although no one can agree on the exact figure, our dozen years of war in Iraq, Afghanistan, and neighboring countries have cost at least $1.5 trillion . . . Yet from a strategic perspective, to say nothing of the human cost, most of these dollars might as well have been burned. 'At this point, it is incontrovertibly evident that the U.S. military failed to achieve any of its strategic goals in Iraq,' a former military intelligence officer named Jim Gourley wrote recently . . . 'Evaluated according to the goals set forth by our military leadership, the war ended in utter defeat for our forces.'" Fallows, 2015, p. 77.
46    Jervis, 2012, p. 143. See Walker and Malici, 2011. As Jervis points out in foreign policy, although "many mistakes follow from misplaced certainty and that to minimize this, leaders should adopt flexible, contingent, and reversible stances, [this underplays] the possible bargaining advantages of taking irreversible moves, and, more importantly, underestimates the ambiguity that is likely to be present at all stages of an interaction, and, indeed, to remain in retrospect." Jervis, 2012, p. 144.

United States. It is thus crucial to understand that foreign policy is created through the lenses of domestic actors as they understand the external environment; they then bring this understanding and their preferences into the domestic political battleground.

For us, the sources of policy failure often lie in domestic politics and its interaction with the international environment. Political leaders may correctly perceive the international environment and other states' goals and actions, but they may be prevented by domestic politics from using the best policy instruments or finding the best combination thereof. Scholars often point to lack of fungibility of power resources as a source of policy failure.[47] But the ability to use different instruments and to substitute one for another will also be affected by domestic politics. And hence this reveals another source of infungibility among policy instruments and perhaps another potential source of policy failure.

Indeed, in the United States, presidents may be driven strongly toward the use of military force at all times.[48] American domestic politics may then exacerbate the "security dilemma" that all states face.[49] President Obama's recent foreign policy and its domestic critics illustrate this. Facing crises in Syria and Ukraine, many critics in the United States have pushed President Obama to employ military force to "solve" these problems.[50] His public approval ratings have fallen as the criticisms have mounted.[51] Obama has tried to use other foreign policy instruments that he feels will be more effective. He has pushed for large trade negotiations with Asian and European allies; he has signed new defense agreements; he has worked to put into place multilateral sanctions against Russia; he has tried to use diplomacy and aid to make progress in the Israeli-Palestinian peace negotiations; and he used diplomacy to get Syria to give up its chemical weapons. As Obama himself said, "Why is it that everybody is so eager to use military force? After we've just gone through a decade of war at enormous cost to our troops and to our budget. And what is it exactly that these critics think would have been accomplished [by using force in Syria or Ukraine]?"[52]

The pressures to use the military are accompanied by constraints on using other foreign policy instruments. Congress has made international trade negotiations difficult since there is not enough support to delegate

47   Baldwin, 1986.
48   The relative ease of using the military is also associated with the "military-industrial complex" that Eisenhower railed against in 1961. As he noted, military-industrial complex has a "total influence—economic, political, even spiritual—[that] is felt in every city, every State house, every office of the Federal government." Eisenhower, 1961.
49   Jervis, 1978; Glaser, 1997; Glaser, 2010.
50   Landler, 2014.
51   Hook, 2014.
52   Quoted in Landler, 2014, p. A1.

trade authority to the president. The fiscal austerity imposed by Congress has made increasing foreign aid very difficult. Immigration policy has been blocked in Congress. Sanctions face interest group resistance in the United States and elsewhere in a globalized economy, but at least provide some leverage for the president internationally.[53] When it is very difficult to get approval to employ these other foreign policy instruments and easier to use military force, it is no wonder that US policy has become militarized. And this, we fear, is a major source of American foreign policy failures. While many scholars focus on how international relations can exacerbate the security dilemma, we note here that domestic politics can also contribute to this.[54]

### Intelligence and Presidential Power

In chapter 5 we discussed how the president has systematic control over US intelligence agencies, even though Congress has on occasion tried to wrest some of this control away from him. Does more information lead to better policy by increasing certainty? Some research seems to advocate this position.[55] But the answer to this may be no, not always, and maybe not even most of the time. As Clausewitz said, "We know more, but this makes us more, not less uncertain."[56] And as Jervis notes, "It simply is not true that intelligence always can—or should—increase certainty. One reason policymakers often cringe when they get a good intelligence briefing is that at its best, intelligence is likely to disturb prevailing policy and increase rather than decrease uncertainty. It often tells those in charge that their ideas may not be right and that several possibilities are plausible."[57]

53  The politics surrounding the use sanctions regarding Iran represents a rather intriguing set of politics vis-à-vis questions about congressional versus presidential power. As of spring 2015, the Obama administration has been negotiating with Iran regarding its nuclear program, with the main "carrot" offered being the removal of sanctions. Some Republicans in Congress oppose the lifting of sanctions, and even sent a letter to the Iranian government stating that any deal could be overturned with a new president. While in part this may be seen as a challenge to presidential authority, it also underscores the centrality of the presidency as an institution when it comes to applying sanctions. Of course, as this case highlights, the control of sanctions is contested and hence represents a more intermediate policy instrument in terms of presidential power. A somewhat similar discourse emerged with the Obama administration announcing the normalization of relations with Cuba, including the lifting of some sanctions. While parts of the Cuban diaspora community in the United States opposed the move, other parts of the community as well as business interests have stepped up pressure on Congress to follow the president's lead.

54  Glaser, 2010.
55  Fingar, 2011.
56  von Clausewitz, 1976, p. 102.
57  Jervis, 2012, p. 145.

Our point in this book is not that more information creates more certainty or makes decisions better. Rather, having more information gives an actor more influence in the policy process domestically. The public, Congress, and the president seem to realize this. Congress is more likely to defer to the president and the public more likely to support this deference when the president is seen as having more information about a policy instrument. And interest groups, especially when they want to counter the president, are highly motivated to collect information and provide it to Congress for this same reason.

What we notice in many cases is that the president and executive branch jealously guard their information, and Congress diligently works to try to pry it out. Battles over access to information are common, as we expect, where Congress attempts to assert greater authority over information sources while the executive tries equally hard to prevent this. These battles are more salient in military affairs since this is where the president has his biggest informational advantages. As we show in chapter 5 on the bureaucracy, the president often manages to win these battles. The reasons given—the need for secrecy from foreign actors, the desire to avoid surprises from the external environment, and the necessity of timely if not rapid decision making—usually lend the president powerful support for his asymmetric access to information.[58] But this is also related to the characteristics of several military-related instruments and the lower level of distributive politics and ideological divisions in them.

This pattern of information asymmetry is not likely to change much in the United States. Executives jealously guard their control over intelligence sources, and it is usually only when policy fails (often in a spectacular fashion) that Congress can try to wrest control over or access to these sources. It remains an open question whether and how, in the wake of Wikileaks and Snowden, Congress will cut back on presidential control of information sources.[59]

This book has focused much on the conditions under which the president has influence over policy. We have shown how variations across policy instruments and the issue areas they affect differ in terms of the president's ability to get his preferred policy. We argued that this was important because presidents are most likely to choose a policy of international engagement. Implicit is this argument was a sense that such engagement was beneficial overall for the United States, and thus that presidential influence was beneficial as well. We know that this latter point has been much debated.

---

58 In other political systems with weaker parliaments, it is even more likely that the executive has a strong monopoly on information about foreign affairs.

59 Recent examples include the USA Freedom Act. However, even with the limitations imposed that grew out of the meta-data surveillance programs reviewed by Snowden, the president was able to have key provisions changed. Savage, 2014.

## Presidential Power and Foreign Policy

There is a long tradition in the study of American politics and political theory that asks what the best or right amount of presidential influence is for American democracy. The Founders feared executive power and thus tried to use checks and balances to deter executive tyranny. That is, of course, one reason why the United States has a powerful, independent legislature. We will not summarize the long and complex debate over the virtues and vices of presidential power here.[60] But we can note that it may be problematic for the president's influence to vary by policy instrument and this has implications for patterns in US international engagement. When the president has one instrument he can control more than another, he may "overuse" that first instrument. In this sense it would be preferable for the president to have roughly the same amount of influence over many different instruments of foreign policy. Given the differences across instruments, however, we doubt this is possible or likely.

On the other hand, it is hard to see how one could ideally set presidential influence given the structure of politics within different issues areas. Keeping information more firmly within the president's control on issues like trade or immigration seems quite difficult. Interest groups will push to collect and disseminate information in these areas. Restraining distributive politics is likely to require a wholesale change in political institutions, which is also unlikely. Making geographic representation less important and party control of the policy agenda more significant could alleviate some of the domestic pressures on presidents in these areas, as we noted above. But such changes seem beyond the imaginable currently. In sum, as we note below, there do not appear to be simple answers to these issues about presidential power on foreign policy making.

While some believe that key problems in foreign policy making could be resolved with more or better information or more perceptive or accurate decision making, many problems with US foreign policy rest in domestic politics. Jervis claims that "even if [foreign policy] strategies can be designed to probe the environment, great uncertainties will almost always remain. Even so, many mistakes do result from the failure to make a serious and unbiased effort to anticipate what others will do."[61] This is certainly true, but the problems entailed in making "serious and unbiased efforts to understand" what other countries or international actors will do may result more from domestic politics and less from human psychology or international relations.

60   How powerful the president really is or should be has also been debated often; for a recent round see Posner and Vermeule, 2010; and Goldsmith, 2012. Tatalovich and Engeman also have an interesting summary of this long debate. Tatalovich and Engeman, 2003.

61   Jervis, 2012, p. 144.

To build and sustain a liberal, internationalist world order, the US government has to be able to use not just its military and coercive instruments of statecraft. It must be able to use more cooperative instruments. It needs to be able to sign trade and investment agreements, to work with others on climate change policies, to reform the global institutions it created years ago, and to provide foreign aid to countries in need. But these types of policies are difficult to pass through the domestic political system. As a recent assessment of US foreign policy notes, "The US holds more cards than any other in shaping what the multipolar world will look like. It has more legitimacy than any potential rival—China in particular. But America's ability to address these vast challenges is stymied by domestic paralysis."[62] The tendency toward militarization and coercive instruments of statecraft is likely to exacerbate the "security dilemma" and could lead to more international conflict. Using other instruments of statecraft may be critically important as the global balance of power shifts.

What can be done about domestic politics in the United States to improve foreign policy making? At first blush, our research seems to suggest that one solution might be to further limit Congress's role, especially in the areas of trade, aid, and immigration. It is unlikely that Congress would willingly give up its influence in these areas, although in the past Congress has ceded some authority over foreign trade by giving the president foreign negotiating ability.[63] But we are not sure that this is a warranted conclusion. The issue is less about Congress's level of constraint on the president and more about the uneven nature of that constraint: a high constraint for some policy instruments and a low one in others. It is this unevenness that creates the tendency toward militarization. Congressional oversight of the president in foreign policy is probably just as warranted and important as in domestic affairs. Having to pass foreign policy through multiple screening processes domestically is probably a way to get better policy, as George, Lindblom, and others have long argued.[64] Justifying major actions that may cost many lives and much treasure is critical in a democracy and is likely to result in better policy in the long run. Perhaps, as we discuss below, allowing greater presidential influence on economic aid and trade (for example) in return for more congressional oversight on military instruments, would be a warranted compromise.

Limiting interest group lobbying and access to decision makers may also sound appealing. But this too seems like the wrong reform, not to mention an impossible one. Years ago, Krasner argued that insulating the executive from societal pressures produced better policy, at least in the United States.[65]

---

62    Luce, 2014.
63    Bailey, Goldstein, and Weingast, 1997.
64    Lindblom, 1965; George, 1980.
65    Krasner, 1978.

In doing this, the American government could pursue its national interest more fully. But again, interest groups convey information to Congress and the executive that may be very useful. And they also supply perceptions about foreign affairs and preferences informed by those perceptions that are important for the policy process to function well. It is not clear that blocking interest group access to the foreign policy-making process, even if possible, would be desirable. Perhaps the opposite is warranted. Continued interest group access could be productive if coupled with more transparency about it, rather than burying it in lobbying reports or testimony transcripts.

If the problem is militarization—i.e., the overuse of military instruments of foreign policy—then how can US political institutions be reformed to avoid this? We spell out several different policy recommendations as a way to conclude the book. The critical point is that the institutions and resources devoted to the economic and diplomatic instruments of American statecraft should be fostered disproportionately to close the gap with American military institutions and capabilities. In the first chapter we showed the ever-growing gap between the State Department and the Defense Department in figure 1.1. This gap needs to close, not widen.

First, the president and Congress should agree to shift resources from the military to other agencies such as the State Department and USAID. Building capacity in both institutions and adding to their meager resources would be an extremely important move, especially in light of the massive discrepancy in their support now. For instance, reversing the trend that has sent increasing percentages of geopolitical aid through the military and returning this instrument fully to the State Department is essential. Adding more resources to other agencies, such as Treasury's foreign relations divisions and the US Trade Representative—which promote other instruments of policy—may also be a way to counterbalance the military establishment. Presidents have agreed that three key elements of foreign policy must be attended to: development, diplomacy, and defense. At this point, only American defense has been paid sufficient attention. Rebalancing capacity to enhance America's ability to foster development abroad and effectively use diplomacy is necessary.

Second, and somewhat relatedly, USAID should be reformed to have more institutional stature. One mechanism to do this would be to have the USAID administrator be a cabinet-level position.[66] While the USAID administrator reports to the State Department, the State Department, of course, deals with many other areas of foreign relations. Making economic development an equal partner with defense and diplomacy in US foreign policy requires that it have institutional autonomy de-coupled from immediate geopolitical concerns. The status quo practice of seeing USAID as an

---

66   Brainard, 2006; Hindery, Sachs, and Smith, 2008; Rodriguez, 2015.

implementing agency, rather than one at the table when priorities are developed, undercuts the role of economic aid in US foreign policy. Similarly, proposals for USAID to have a "policy shop" to help developing countries formulate better policies would be a welcome addition.[67]

Third, the United States needs to be able to help countries, especially allies, when they face crises or become so fragile that they are in danger of failing. Nation-building is not something the United States can avoid, but it needs to do this in coordination with the country itself and with civilian not military instruments. Some research suggests that putting US military assets into certain countries increases rather than decreases those countries' problems, and especially ones related to terrorism.[68] Using the military is not an optimal policy instrument in many cases. Currently, the failed states index shows that five countries are on very high alert for state failure and another eleven, including Afghanistan, Haiti, Pakistan, and Iraq, are on high alert.[69] The United States needs a civilian capacity to assist these governments in their efforts to avoid collapse. It needs a civilian capacity to assist countries when they face catastrophes like the 2004 Indian Ocean tsunami, the 2010 earthquake in Haiti, the 2014 Ebola crisis in West Africa, or the growing numbers of floods and droughts associated with climate change.[70] Such a civilian capacity would rely upon foreign aid, humanitarian relief, civilian assistance, and peacekeeping, both for short-term emergencies and longer term state-building.[71] The United States has limited capacity to do this now. One powerful way to change this would be the creation of a national service opportunity for all young Americans under the control of the State Department. These individuals should be well trained, as are those in the military, with a broad cross-section of skills, including health care, governance and law, cyberdefense, and environmental management. Developing a civilian corps to respond to emergencies and undertake longer term state-building is another way to build capacity for non-military interventions. Such a corps, for instance, could be deployed instead of the US military or private military contractors in cases like West Africa's recent Ebola crisis. This civilian capacity, however, depends on Congress to legislate and fund it. It may be costly, but the benefits could be substantial for US foreign policy.

Fourth, the weakening of congressional control over foreign policy should not be seen as the only option. Instead, real progress is needed toward putting

67  Birdsall and Schwanke, 2014.
68  Pape, 2003; Azam and Thelen, 2010; Jamal, 2012. We note that researchers must take special care in establishing these relationships empirically. For example, see Ashworth, Clinton, Meirowitz, and Ramsay, 2008.
69  Fund for Peace, 2014.
70  Guha-Sapir, Hoyois, and Below, 2014.
71  For a discussion of US current capacity for this, see Margesson, 2013.

more constraints on the president's ability to use military deployments or geopolitical aid. The War Powers Act was one attempt to do this. But it has not had the intended effect. Reinvigorating this constraint through stronger oversight and justification procedures in Congress for the president to use military means would be an important step.[72]

None of these reforms are easy, and some might lead to other unintended complications. But it is important to note the spirit of our proposal. Both Congress and the president would be giving up something, but in return getting things that they also want and in doing so creating the foundations for a better US foreign policy. For example, if there was a greater appreciation of the president needing trade negotiation authority and access to real economic development instruments, then there might be room for a deal that puts in place more effective constraints on using military options.

Domestic politics and constraints on the executive in foreign policy making need not lead to worse policies and outcomes for a country; they may strengthen its foreign policy and enhance national security in the long run. But they may also cause unintended effects, like those we documented here. Domestic politics is a reality that all presidents must contend with. Given the enduring importance of foreign policy, presidents should seek to craft the best foreign policy they can. We hope that we have clearly identified the domestic sources of foreign policy making so that the defects in the process can be better appreciated and avoided.

72   Following the emerging threat of ISIS, on February 11, 2015 the Obama administration proposed a new authorization for use of military force (AUMF). While the administration had already deployed military force against ISIS based on the 2001 authorization passed by Congress (with a House vote of 420-1), the new proposal was seen by some to contain elements that would restrict the powers of the president when it comes to the use of the military. However, consistent with many of the themes in this book, a number of commentators noted that the proposal actually did not constrain the president. For example, one commentator argued that, "(t)o summarize the matter bluntly, the administration's draft fails—and intentionally fails—to address the relationship between this new authorization and the 2001 authorization . . . The result is that its authorities are, optics notwithstanding, simply additive with respect to presidential authority." See Schulberg, 2015. Even the Obama administration admitted that their proposal was intentionally vague so as to safeguard presidential power. Also see Sink, 2015. Our hope is that the administration can work with congressional leaders to establish a clearer authorization that better establishes a precedent for involving Congress. But as discussed earlier, we also think that Congress should recognize the importance of making it easier for the president to pursue foreign policy objectives with other instruments, such as trade and economic aid. In our view, a narrow debate on the authorization of use of military force forecloses a broader compromise that would lead to a more balanced US foreign policy.

# WORKS CITED

Abowd, John M., and Richard B. Freeman (Eds.) (1991). *Immigration, Trade, and the Labor Market*. Chicago: University of Chicago Press.

Abramowitz, Alan I., and Kyle L. Saunders (1998). Ideological Realignment in the U.S. Electorate. *Journal of Politics* 60(3): 634–652.

Africa Analysis (2004a). AGOA III Could Be Delayed. *Africa Analysis*, p. 15, June 25, 2004.

—— (2004b). Hopes and Fears for Future AGOA. *Africa Analysis*, p. 15, March 5, 2004.

Akhtar, Shayerah Ilias, and Vivian C. Jones (2014). *Proposed Transatlantic Trade and Investment Partnership (T-TIP): In Brief*. CRS Report No. R43158. Washington, DC: Congressional Research Service. June 11, 2014. Retrieved from http://fas.org/sgp/crs/row/R43158.pdf.

Alden, Edward, and Guy de Jonquieres (2002). A Deal, At Last. *Financial Times*, p. 14, August 1, 2002.

Alden, Edward, Michael Mann, and Frances Williams (2002). Bush Set to Win Fast-Track Trade Fight. *FT.com*. London: The Financial Times Ltd. Retrieved from http://search.proquest.com/docview/228623891

Aldrich, John H., Christopher Gelpi, Peter Feaver, Jason Reifler, and Kristin Sharp (2006). Foreign Policy and the Electoral Connection. *Annual Review of Political Science* 9(1): 477–502.

Aldrich, John H., John L. Sullivan, and Eugene Borgida (1989). Foreign Affairs and Issue Voting: Do Presidential Candidates "Waltz Before a Blind Audience?" *American Political Science Review* 83(1): 123–141.

Alesina, Alberto, and David Dollar (2000). Who Gives Foreign Aid to Whom and Why? *Journal of Economic Growth* 5(1): 33–63.

Alexander, Lamar (2014). *$335 Million for Uranium Processing Facility Ensures Project Comes in 'On Time and on Budget*. Press Release. Washington, DC: US Senate. June 18, 2014. Retrieved from http://www.alexander.senate.gov/public/index.cfm/2014/6/alexander-335-million-for-uranium-processing-facility-ensures-project-comes-in-on-time-and-on-budget.

Allison, Graham T. (1969). Conceptual Models and the Cuban Missile Crisis. *American Political Science Review* 63(3): 689–718.

Almond, Gabriel A. (1977). *The American People and Foreign Policy*. Westport, CT: Greenwood Press.

Alvarez, R. Michael, and Jonathan Nagler (1995). Economics, Issues and the Perot Candidacy: Voter Choice in the 1992 Presidential Election. *American Journal of Political Science* 39(3): 714–744.

Ansolabehere, Stephen, and Philip Edward Jones (2010). Constituents' Responses to Congressional Roll-Call Voting. *American Journal of Political Science* 54(3): 583–597.

Ansolabehere, Stephen, James M. Snyder, and Charles Stewart, III (2001a). Candidate Positioning in U.S. House Elections. *American Journal of Political Science* 45(1): 136–159.

—— (2001b). The Effects of Party and Preferences on Congressional Roll-Call Voting. *Legislative Studies Quarterly* 26(4): 533–572.

Art, Robert J. (1973). Bureaucratic Politics and American Foreign Policy: A Critique. *Policy Sciences* 4(4): 467–490.

Ashworth, Scott, Joshua D. Clinton, Adam Meirowitz, and Kristopher W. Ramsay (2008). Design, Inference, and the Strategic Logic of Suicide Terrorism. *American Political Science Review* 102(2): 269–273.

Atkinson, Carol L. (2014). *Military Soft Power: Public Diplomacy through Military Educational Exchanges*. Lanham, MD: Rowman & Littlefield.

Aubrey, Allison (2002). *Analysis: Trade Promotion Authority for the President*. Morning Edition. Washington, DC: National Public Radio. August 2, 2002.

Austen-Smith, David (1987). Interest Groups, Campaign Contributions, and Probabilistic Voting. *Public Choice* 54(2): 123–139.

—— (1993). Information and Influence: Lobbying for Agendas and Votes. *American Journal of Political Science* 37(3): 799–833.

Austen-Smith, David, and John R. Wright (1992). Competitive Lobbying for a Legislator's Vote. *Social Choice and Welfare* 9(3): 229–257.

—— (1996). Theory and Evidence for Counteractive Lobbying. *American Journal of Political Science* 40(2): 543–564.

Azam, Jean-Paul, and Véronique Thelen (2010). Foreign Aid Versus Military Intervention in the War on Terror. *Journal of Conflict Resolution* 54(2): 237–261.

Baack, Ben, and Edward Ray (1985). The Political Economy of the Origins of the Military-Industrial Complex in the United States. *Journal of Economic History* 45(2): 369–375.

Bacevich, Andrew J. (2002). *American Empire: The Realities and Consequences of US Diplomacy.* Cambridge, MA: Harvard University Press.

—— (2005). *The New American Militarism: How Americans Are Seduced by War.* New York: Oxford University Press.

—— (2007). *The Long War: A New History of U.S. National Security Policy since World War II.* New York: Columbia University Press.

—— (2010). *Washington Rules: America's Path to Permanent War* (1st ed.). New York: Metropolitan Books.

Bai, Jushan (2009). Panel Data Models With Interactive Fixed Effects. *Econometrica* 77(4): 1229–1279.

Bailey, Michael A., and David Brady (1998). Heterogeneity and Representation: The Senate and Free Trade. *American Journal of Political Science* 42(2): 524–544.

Bailey, Michael A., Judith L. Goldstein, and Barry R. Weingast (1997). The Institutional Roots of American Trade Policy: Politics, Coalitions, and International Trade. *World Politics* 49(3): 309–338.

Baker, Peter (1996). U.S. Near Approval of Mission to Aid Central Africa Refugees, *Washington Post*, p. A39, November 28, 1996.

—— (2009). Obama Reverses Rules on U.S. Abortion Aid, *New York Times*, p. A13, January 24, 2009.

Baldor, Lolita C. (2012). U.S. Expanding Military Aid, Intelligence in Africa. *Washington Times.* Washington, DC: Washington Times LLC. Retrieved from http://www.washingtontimes .com/news/2012/jun/25/us-expanding-military-aid-intelligence-in-africa/

Baldwin, David (1986). *Economic Statecraft*. Princeton, NJ: Princeton University Press.

Baldwin, Robert E., and Christopher S. Magee (2000). Is Trade Policy for Sale? Congressional Voting on Recent Trade Bills. *Public Choice* 105(1–2): 79–101.

Balistreri, Edward J. (1997). The Performance of the Heckscher-Ohlin-Vanik Model in Predicting Endogenous Policy Forces at the Individual Level. *Canadian Journal of Economics / Revue canadienne d'Economique* 30(1): 1–17.

Ball, Richard, and Christopher Johnson (1996). Political, Economic, and Humanitarian Motivations for PL 480 Food Aid: Evidence from Africa. *Economic Development and Cultural Change* 44(3): 515–537.

Barkan, Joel D. (2009). Advancing Democratization in Africa. In Jennifer G. Cooke and J. Stephen Morrison (Eds.), *U.S. Africa Policy beyond the Bush Years* (pp. 91–110). Washington, DC: Center for Strategic and International Studies.

Barnett, Michael (1990). High Politics Is Low Politics: The Domestic and Systemic Sources of Israeli Security Policy, 1967–1977. *World Politics* 42(4): 529–562.

Baron, David P. (1989). Service-Induced Campaign Contributions and the Electoral Equilibrium. *Quarterly Journal of Economics* 104(1): 45–72.

—— (1994). Electoral Competition with Informed and Uniformed Voters. *American Political Science Review* 88(1): 33–47.

Barrett, Christopher B., and Daniel Maxwell (2005). *Food Aid After Fifty Years: Recasting its Role*. New York: Routledge.

Bartels, Larry M. (1991). Constituency Opinion and Congressional Policy Making: The Reagan Defense Build Up. *American Political Science Review* 85(2): 457–474.

—— (2005). Homer Gets a Tax Cut: Inequality and Public Policy in the American Mind. *Perspectives on Politics* 3(1): 15–31.

Bas, Muhammet A., and Andrew J. Coe (2012). Arms Diffusion and War. *Journal of Conflict Resolution* 56(4): 651–674.

Bauer, Raymond Augustine, Ithiel de Sola Pool, and Lewis A. Dexter (1972). *American Business and Public Policy: The Politics of Foreign Trade* (2nd ed.). Chicago: Aldine-Atherton.

Baum, Matthew A. (2002). The Constituent Foundations of the Rally-round-the-flag Phenomenon. *International Studies Quarterly* 46(2): 263–298.

—— (2004a). Going Private: Presidential Rhetoric, Public Opinion, and the Domestic Politics of Audience Costs in U.S. Foreign Policy Crises. *Journal of Conflict Resolution* 48(5): 603–631.

—— (2004b). How Public Opinion Constrains the Use of Force: The Case of Operation Restore Hope. *Presidential Studies Quarterly* 34(2): 187–226.

Baum, Matthew A., and Tim J. Groeling (2010). *War Stories: the Causes and Consequences of Public Vews of War*. Princeton, NJ: Princeton University Press.

BBC (2004). Ugandan president writes to Bush on extension of fabric export to US markets. *BBC Monitoring Newsfile*, London: British Broadcasting Company. Retrieved from https://global.factiva.com/redir/default.aspx?P=sa&an=BBCMNF0020040402e04200001&cat=a&ep=ASE.

Beaulieu, Eugene (2002a). Factor or Industry Cleavages in Trade Policy? An Empirical Analysis of the Stopler-Samuelson Theorem. *Economics & Politics* 14(2): 99–131.

—— (2002b). The Stolper-Samuelson Theorem Faces Congress. *Review of International Economics* 10(2): 343–360.

Beaulieu, Eugene, and Christopher S. Magee (2004). Four Simple Tests of Campaign Contributions and Trade Policy Preferences *Economics & Politics* 16(2): 163–187.

Beaulieu, Eugene, Ravindra Yatawara, and Wei Guo Wang (2005). Who Supports Free Trade in Latin America. *World Economy* 28(7): 941–958.

Beckmann, Matthew N. (2010). *Pushing the Agenda: Presidential Leadership in US Lawmaking, 1953–2004*. New York: Cambridge University Press.

Bellamy, William Mark (2009). Making Better Sense of U.S. Security Engagement in Africa. In Jennifer G. Cooke and J. Stephen Morrison (Eds.), *U.S. Africa Policy Beyond the Bush Years: Critical Challenges for the Obama Administration* (pp. 9–33). Washington, DC: Center for Strategic and International Studies.

Bendor, Jonathan, and Thomas H. Hammond (1992). Rethinking Allison's Models. *American Political Science Review* 86(2): 301–322.

Bennet, James (1998). U.S. Cruise Missiles Strike Sudan and Afghan Targets Tied to Terrorist Network, *New York Times*, p. A1, August 21, 1998.

Bennett, D. Scott, and Timothy Nordstrom (2000). Foreign Policy Substitutability and Internal Economic Problems in Enduring Rivalries. *Journal of Conflict Resolution* 44(1): 33–61.

Berinsky, Adam (2007). Assuming the Costs of War: Events, Elites, and American Public Support for Military Conflict. *Journal of Politics* 69(4): 975–997.

Berinsky, Adam, Gregory Huber, and Gabriel Lenz (2012). Evaluating Online Labor Markets for Experimental Research: Amazon.com's Mechanical Turk. *Political Analysis* 20(3): 351–368.

Berman, Eric G., and Katie E. Sams (2000). *Peacekeeping in Africa: Capabilities and Culpabilities.* New York: United Nations.

Bermeo, Sarah Blodgett, and David Leblang (2010). *Foreign Interests: Immigration and the Allocation of Foreign Aid.* Unpublished Manuscript. Durham, NC: Duke University. November 9, 2010.

—— (Forthcoming). Migration and Foreign Aid. *International Organization.*

Bernstein, Michael A., and Mark R. Wilson (2011). New Perspectives on the History of the Military–Industrial Complex. *Enterprise and Society* 12(1): 1–9.

Bertrand, Marianne, Matilde Bombardini, and Francesco Trebbi (2014). Is It Whom You Know or What You Know? An Empirical Assessment of the Lobbying Process. *American Economic Review* 104(12): 3885–3920.

Binder, Sarah A. (2007). Taking the Measure of Congress: Reply to Chiou and Rothenberg. *Political Analysis* 16(2): 213–225.

Birdsall, Nancy, and Beth Schwanke (2014). Raj Shah's Legacy—and What about President Obama's? *Global Development: Views from the Center.* Washington, DC: Center for Global Development. Retrieved from http://www.cgdev.org/blog/raj-shah%E2%80%99s-legacy.

Bond, Jon R., and Richard Fleisher (1984). Presidential Popularity and Congressional Voting: A Reexamination of Public Opinion as a Source of Influence in Congress. *Political Research Quarterly* 37(2): 291–306.

—— (1990). *The President in the Legislative Arena.* Chicago: University of Chicago Press.

Bonica, Adam (2014). Mapping the Ideological Marketplace. *American Journal of Political Science* 58(2): 367–386.

Borjas, George J. (1989). Immigrant and Emigrant Earnings: A Longitudinal Study. *Economic Inquiry* 27(1): 21–37.

—— (1999a). *Heaven's Door: Immigration Policy and the American Economy.* Princeton, NJ: Princeton University Press.

—— (1999b). Immigration and Welfare Magnets. *Journal of Labor Economics* 17(4): 607–637.

—— (2003). The Labor Demand Curve Is Downward Sloping: Reexamining the Impact of Immigration on the Labor Market. *Quarterly Journal of Economics* 118(4): 1335–1374.

—— (2006). Native Internal Migration and the Labor Market Impact of Immigration. *Journal of Human Resources* 41(2): 221–258.

Borjas, George J., and Richard B. Freeman (Eds.) (1992). *Immigration and the Work Force: Economic Consequences for the United States and Source Areas.* Chicago: University of Chicago Press.

Boudali, Lianne K. (2007). *The Trans-Sahara Counterterrorism Partnership.* West Point, NY: U.S. Military Academy; The Combating Terrorism Center. April 2007.

Brainard, Lael (2006). Organizing Foreign Assistance to Meet Twenty-First Century Challenges. In Lael Brainard (Ed.), *Security by Other Means: Foreign Assistance, Global Poverty, and American Leadership* (pp. 33–66). Washington, DC: Brookings Institution.

Brakman, Steven, and Charles Van Marrewijk (1998). *The Economics of International Transfers.* Cambridge, UK: Cambridge University Press.

Brecher, Michael, Blema Steinberg, and Janice Stein (1969). A Framework for Research on Foreign Policy Behavior. *Journal of Conflict Resolution* 13(1): 75–101.

Breuning, Marijke (1995). Words and Deeds: Foreign Assistance Rhetoric and Policy Behavior in the Netherlands, Belgium and the United Kingdom. *International Studies Quarterly* 39(2): 235–254.

Briggs, Vernon M. (2001). *Immigration and American Unionism.* Ithaca, NY: Cornell University Press.

Bristol, Nellie (2011). Foreign Aid and National Security. *CQ Researcher* 21(23): 529–552.

Broad, William J., and David E. Sanger (2014). U.S. Ramping Up Major Renewal in Nuclear Arms, *New York Times*, p. A1, September 22, 2014.

# WORKS CITED

Brody, Richard A. (1991). *Assessing the President: the Media, Elite Opinion, and Public Support.* Palo Alto, CA: Stanford University Press.

Brooks, Stephen G. (2005). *Producing Security: Multinational Corporations, Globalization, and the Changing Calculus of Conflict.* Princeton, NJ: Princeton University Press.

—— (2013). Economic Actors' Lobbying Influence on the Prospects for War and Peace. *International Organization* 67(04): 863–888.

Brooks, Stephen G., G. John Ikenberry, and William C. Wohlforth (2012). Don't Come Home, America: The Case against Retrenchment. *International Security* 37(3): 7–51.

—— (2013). Lean Forward: In Defense of American Engagement. *Foreign Affairs* 92(1): 130–142.

Brooks, Stephen G., and William C. Wohlforth (2008). *World Out of Balance: International Relations and the Challenge of American Primacy.* Princeton, NJ: Princeton University Press.

Broz, J. Lawrence (2005). Congressional Politics of International Financial Rescues. *American Journal of Political Science* 49(3): 479–496.

—— (2008). Congressional Voting on Funding the International Financial Institutions. *Review of International Organizations* 3(4): 351–374.

—— (2011). The United States Congress and IMF Financing, 1944–2009. *Review of International Organizations* 6(3–4): 341–368.

Broz, J. Lawrence, and Michael Brewster Hawes (2006). Congressional Politics of Financing the International Monetary Fund. *International Organization* 60(2): 367–399.

Brulliard, Nicolas (2010). Pakistan Textile Exports: Call for Wider Lifting of U.S. Tariffs Intensifies, *Washington Post,* p. A08, December 24, 2010.

Bueno de Mesquita, Bruce, and Alastair Smith (2007). Foreign Aid and Policy Concessions. *Journal of Conflict Resolution* 51(2): 251–284.

—— (2009). A Political Economy of Aid. *International Organization* 63(2): 309–340.

Bumiller, Elisabeth (2003). Bush Says He Will Ask Congress to Extend Africa Trade Benefits, *New York Times,* p. A4, January 16, 2003.

Burns, Peter, and James G. Gimpel (2000). Economic Insecurity, Prejudicial Stereotypes, and Public Opinion on Immigration Policy. *Political Science Quarterly* 115(2): 201–225.

Burnside, Craig, and David Dollar (2000). Aid, Policies and Growth. *American Economic Review* 90(4): 847–868.

Busby, Joshua W., and Jonathan Monten (2008). Without Heirs? Assessing the Decline of Establishment Internationalism in U.S. Foreign Policy. *Perspectives on Politics* 6(3): 451–472.

Bush, George W. (2002). *Remarks at the Inter-American Development Bank.* Public Papers of the Presidents. Washington, DC: Government Printing Office. March 14, 2002.

—— (2003a). *Address Before a Joint Session of the Congress on the State of the Union.* Public Papers of the Presidents. Washington, DC: Government Printing Office. January 28, 2003.

—— (2003b). *Legislative Proposal for the Millennium Challenge Act of 2003: Communication from the President of the United States.* House Document No. 108-37. Washington, DC: Government Printing Office. February 5, 2003.

Buzan, Barry, Ole Wæver, and Jaap de Wilde (1998). *Security: A New Framework for Analysis.* Boulder, CO: Lynne Rienner.

Bzostek, Rachel, and Samuel B. Robison (2008). U.S. Policy toward Israel, Iraq, and Saudi Arabia: An Integrated Analysis, 1981–2004. *International Studies Perspectives* 9(4): 359–376.

Cadei, Emily (2010). Backers Say Time Is Ripe for Foreign Aid Overhaul, *CQ Weekly,* pp. 1728–1729, July 19, 2010.

Cahlink, George (2007). New Africa Command Would Mark Major Shift, *CQ Weekly,* pp. 305–306, January 29, 2007.

Caldwell, Dan (1991). *The Dynamics of Domestic Politics and Arms Control: The SALT II Treaty Ratification Debate.* Columbia: University of South Carolina Press.

Campbell, Colton C., Nicol C. Rae, and John F. Jr. Stack (2003). *Congress and the Politics of U.S. Foreign Policy.* Upper Saddle Ridge, NJ: Prentice Hall.

Campbell, John (2014). *U.S. Policy to Counter Nigeria's Boko Haram*. Council Special Report No. 70. New York: Council on Foreign Relations. November 2014. Retrieved from http://www.cfr.org/nigeria/us-policy-counter-nigerias-boko-haram/p33806.

Campbell, Kurt, and Brian Andrews (2013). *Explaining the US 'Pivot' to Asia*. Americas 2013/01. London: Chatham House. August 2013. Retrieved from http://www.chathamhouse.org/sites/files/chathamhouse/public/Research/Americas/0813pp_pivottoasia.pdf.

Canes-Wrone, Brandice (2006). *Who Leads Whom? Presidents, Policy, and the Public*. Chicago: University of Chicago Press.

Canes-Wrone, Brandice, David W. Brady, and John F. Cogan (2002). Out of Step, Out of Office: Electoral Accountability and House Members' Voting. *American Political Science Review* 96(1): 127–140.

Canes-Wrone, Brandice, William G. Howell, and David E. Lewis (2008). Toward a Broader Understanding of Presidential Power: A Re-Evaluation of the Two Presidencies Thesis. *Journal of Politics* 70(1): 1–16.

Canes-Wrone, Brandice, William G. Howell, David E. Lewis, and Terry M. Moe (1999). *The Two Presidencies in the Legislative and Executive Arenas*. Prepared for the Annual Meeting of the Midwest Political Science Association, Chicago, April 15–17, 1999.

Cantir, Cristian, and Juliet Kaarbo (2012). Contested Roles and Domestic Politics: Reflections on Role Theory in Foreign Policy Analysis and IR Theory. *Foreign Policy Analysis* 8(1): 5–24.

Carney, Dana R., John T. Jost, Samuel D. Gosling, and Jeff Potter (2008). The Secret Lives of Liberals and Conservatives Personality Profiles, Interaction Styles, and the Things They Leave Behind. *Political Psychology* 56(6): 453–484.

Carter, Jimmy (1982). *Keeping Faith: Memoirs of a President*. Toronto; New York: Bantam Books.

Carter, Ralph G. (1985). Presidential Effectiveness in Congressional Foreign Policy Making: A Reconsideration. In David Kozak and Kenneth Ciboski (Eds.), *The American Presidency: A Policy Perspective from Readings and Documents* (pp. 311–325). Chicago: Nelson-Hall.

—— (1986). Congressional Foreign Policy Behavior: Persistent Patterns of the Postwar Period. *Presidential Studies Quarterly* 16(2): 329–359.

Catalinac, Amy L. (2007). Identity Theory and Foreign Policy: Explaining Japan's Responses to the 1991 Gulf War and the 2003 U.S. War in Iraq. *Politics & Policy* 35(1): 58–100.

Catanoso, Justin (2014). Kerry: The Climate Crisis Is Here, and Republicans Are Threatening Us All. *Business Insider*. New York: Business Insider Inc. Retrieved from http://www.businessinsider.com/kerry-the-climate-crisis-is-here-2014-12.

Catholic Relief Services (2002). *Improving Effectiveness: Recommendations for the Millennium Challenge Account*. Baltimore, MD: Catholic Relief Services. June 24, 2002. Retrieved from http://reliefweb.int/report/world/improving-effectiveness-recommendations-millennium-challenge-account

Cavanaugh, John J., III (1980). Development Banks: Contract Strategy, Business America (publication), *Congressional Record*, Vol. 126, Part 4, pp. 4963–4967, March 6, 1980. Washington, DC.

CCFR (1975/1979/1982). *American Public Opinion and US Foreign Policy, National Leaders*. Chicago: Chicago Council on Foreign Relations.

Cha, Victor D. (2012). *The Impossible State: North Korea, Past and Future* (1st ed.). New York: Ecco.

Chace, James (1998). *Acheson: the Secretary of State Who Created the American World*. New York: Simon & Schuster.

Chapman, Frank (1998). TransAfrica Speaks Out Against Africa Trade Bill, *People's Weekly World*, p. 3, March 28, 1998.

Chase, Kerry A. (2005). *Trading Blocs: States, Firms, and Regions in the World Economy*. Ann Arbor: University of Michigan Press.

Chaudoin, Stephen, Helen V. Milner, and Dustin H. Tingley (2010). The Center Still Holds: Liberal Internationalism Survives. *International Security* 35(1): 75–94.

Chicago Council (2005). Global Views 2004: American Public Opinion and Foreign Policy. *Chicago Council on Foreign Relations*.

Chiswick, Barry R. (2000). Are Immigrants Favorably Self-Selected? An Economic Analysis. In Caroline B. Brettell and James F. Hollifield (Eds.), *Migration Theory: Talking across Disciplines* (pp. 61–76). New York: Routledge.

Chorev, Nitsan (2009). International Trade Policy under George W. Bush. In Andrew Wroe and Jon Herbert (Eds.), *Assessing the George W. Bush Presidency* (pp. 129–146). Edinburgh: Edinburgh University Press.

Citrin, Jack, Donald P. Green, Christopher Muste, and Cara Wong (1997). Public Opinion Toward Immigration Reform: The Role of Economic Motivations. *Journal of Politics* 59(3): 858–881.

Citrin, Jack, and John Sides (2004). *The Discreet Charm of the Bourgeoisie: Why the Educated Favor Immigration.* Prepared for the Annual Meeting of the American Political Science Association, Chicago, September 2–5, 2004.

Clad, James C., and Roger D. Stone (1992). New Mission for Foreign Aid. *Foreign Affairs* 72(1): 196–205.

Clark, David H., Timothy Nordstrom, and William Reed (2008). Substitution Is in the Variance: Resources and Foreign Policy Choice. *American Journal of Political Science* 52(4): 763–773.

Clark, David H., and William Reed (2005). The Strategic Sources of Foreign Policy Substitution. *American Journal of Political Science* 49(3): 609–624.

Clark, John F. (1998). The Clinton Administration and Africa: White House Involvement and the Foreign Affairs Bureaucracies. *Issue: A Journal of Opinion* 26(2): 8–13.

Clarke, Duncan L., and Steven Woehrel (1991). Reforming United States Security Assistance. *American University Journal of International Law and Policy* 6(2): 217–249.

Claude, Inis L., and Donald E. Nuechterlein (1997). America's Future in World Affairs: Aloofness or Involvement. In Kenneth W. Thompson (Ed.), *Presidency and Foreign Policy* (pp. 117–129). Lanham, MD: University Press of America.

Clinton, Joshua D., Anthony Bertelli, Christian R. Grose, David E. Lewis, and David C. Nixon (2012). Separated Powers in the United States: The Ideology of Agencies, Presidents, and Congress. *American Journal of Political Science* 56(2): 341–354.

Clinton, Joshua D., David E. Lewis, and Jennifer L. Selin (2013). Influencing the Bureaucracy: The Irony of Congressional Oversight. *American Journal of Political Science* 58(2): 387–401.

Clinton, William J. (1996). *Remarks Announcing Participation in Missions in Bosnia and Zaire and an Exchange with Reporters.* Public Papers of the Presidents. Washington, DC: Government Printing Office. November 15, 1996.

—— (1998). *Address Before a Joint Session of the Congress on the State of the Union.* Public Papers of the Presidents. Washington, DC: Government Printing Office. January 27, 1998.

Clough, Michael (1992). *Free at Last? U.S. Policy toward Africa and the End of the Cold War.* New York: Council on Foreign Relations Press.

Cohen, Jared A. (2007). *One Hundred Days of Silence: America and the Rwanda Genocide.* Lanham, MD: Rowman & Littlefield.

Cohen, Jeffrey E. (1982). A Historical Reassessment of Wildavsky's "Two Presidencies" Thesis. *Social Science Quarterly* 63(3): 549–555.

—— (1999). *Presidential Responsiveness and Public Policy-Making: The Public and the Policies that Presidents Choose.* Ann Arbor: University of Michigan Press.

Committee on Appropriations (1995). *Foreign Operations, Export Financing, and Related Programs Appropriations for Fiscal Year 1996.* Subcommittee on Foreign Operations, Export

Financing, and Related Programs. Washington, DC: Government Printing Office. February 16, 1995–May 18, 1995.

—— (1996). *Foreign Operations, Export Financing, and Related Programs Appropriations, FY97*. Subcommittee on Foreign Operations, Export Financing and Related. Washington, DC: Hrg-1996-SAP-0009. March 20, 1996–June 5, 1996.

Committee on Armed Services (2007). *National Defense Authorization Act for FY2008*. Washington, DC: Government Printing Office.

Committee on Banking, Housing, and Urban Affairs (2009). *Minimizing Potential Threats from Iran; Assessing Economic Sanctions and Other U.S. Policy Options*. Washington, DC: Government Printing Office. July 30, 2009.

Committee on Foreign Affairs (1993). *Foreign Assistance Legislation for FY94 (Part 7)*. Subcommittee on Africa. Washington, DC: Government Printing Office. April 29, 1993–May 12, 1993.

Committee on Foreign Relations (1992). *U.S. Security Issues in Africa*. Subcommittee on African Affairs. Washington, DC: Government Printing Office. May 7, 1992.

—— (1995). *Trade and Investment in Africa*. Subcommittee on African Affairs. Washington, DC: Government Printing Office. February 16, 1995.

—— (2003a). *African Growth and Opportunity Act*. Washington, DC: Government Printing Office. June 25, 2003.

—— (2003b). *Millennium Challenge Account: A New Way to Aid*. Washington, DC: Government Printing Office. March 4, 2003.

—— (2007). *Exploring the U.S. Africa Command and a New Strategic Relationship with Africa*. Subcommittee on African Affairs. Washington, DC: Government Printing Office. April 1, 2007.

—— (2010). *Investment Treaty with Rwanda (Treaty Doc. 110-23)*. Executive Report 111-8. Washington, DC: U.S. Senate. December 22, 2010.

Committee on Government Operations (1975). *Interception of Nonverbal Communications by Federal Intelligence Agencies*. Subcommittee on Government Information and Individual Rights. Washington, DC: Government Printing Office. October 25, 1975.

Committee on International Relations (1995). *Trade and Investment Opportunities in Africa*. Subcommittee on International Economic Policy and Trade. Washington, DC: Government Printing Office. March 8, 1995.

—— (1996). *Review of the Clinton Administration's Performance in Africa*. Subcommittee on Africa. Washington, DC: Government Printing Office. September 26, 1996.

—— (1997). *Africa Crisis Response Initiative*. Subcommittee on Africa. Washington, DC: Government Printing Office. October 8, 1997.

—— (2001). *United States' War on AIDS*. Washington, DC: Government Printing Office. June 7, 2001.

Committee on Ways and Means (1996). *U.S. Trade with Sub-Saharan Africa*. Subcommittee on Trade. Washington, DC: Government Printing Office. August 1, 1996.

—— (1997). *Expanding U.S. Trade with Sub-Saharan Africa*. Subcommittee on Trade. Washington, DC: Government Printing Office. April 29, 1997.

Condit, Doris M. (1988). *History of the Office of the Secretary of Defense* (Vol. II: The Test of War, 1950–1953). Washington, DC: Office of the Secretary of Defense.

Congressional Quarterly (1972). Defense Appropriations: $70.5-Billion for Fiscal 1972. *CQ Almanac* (27th ed.). Washington, DC: CQ Press. Retrieved from http://library.cqpress.com/cqalmanac/cqal71-1253240.

—— (1976a). $90.5-Billion Defense Funding Bill Approved. *CQ Almanac* (31st ed., pp. 873–887). Washington, DC: CQ Press. Retrieved from http://library.cqpress.com/cqalmanac/cqal75-1212781.

—— (1976b). U.S. Intelligence Agencies Probed in 1975. *CQ Almanac* (31st ed., pp. 387–413). Washington, DC: CQ Press. Retrieved from http://library.cqpress.com/cqalmanac/cqal75-1214373.

—— (1981). *Congress and the Nation, 1977–1980* (Vol. 5). Washington, DC: Congressional Quarterly.

—— (1985). *Congress and the Nation, 1981–1984* (Vol. 6). Washington, DC: CQ Press.

—— (1995). Intelligence Agencies Face Review. *CQ Almanac* (50th ed., pp. 458–463). Washington, DC: CQ Press. Retrieved from http://library.cqpress.com/cqalmanac/cqal94-1102485.

—— (1997). *Congress and the Nation, 1993–1996* (Vol. 9). Washington, DC: CQ Press.

—— (2005). *Congress and the Nation, 2001–2004* (Vol. 11). Washington, DC: CQ Press.

—— (2009). Bush Vetoes FY '08 Intelligence Bill. *CQ Almanac* (64th ed., pp. D-10–D-11). Washington, DC: CQ Press. Retrieved from http://library.cqpress.com/cqalmanac/cqal08 -1090-52016-2174403.

Congressional Record (1973). Conference Report on S. 1443, Foreign Assistance Act of 1973, *Congressional Record*, Vol. 119, Part 30, pp. 39313–39318, December 4, 1973. Washington, DC.

Consolidated Appropriations Act, 2004, Public Law No. 108-199, 118 Stat. 3. Enacted January 23, 2004.

Cooke, Jennifer G., and Richard Downie (2014). *Launching a New Chapter in U.S.-Africa Relations: Deepening the Business Relationship*. Washington, DC: Center for Strategic and International Studies.

Cooper, Robert (2004). The Goals of Diplomacy, Hard Power, and Soft Power. In David Held and Mathias Koenig-Archibugi (Eds.), *American Power in the 21st Century* (pp. 167–180). Cambridge, UK: Polity.

Cooper, William H. (2014). *Trade Promotion Authority (TPA) and the Role of Congress in Trade Policy*. CRS Report No. RL33743. Washington, DC: Congressional Research Service. January 13, 2014. Retrieved from http://fas.org/sgp/crs/misc/RL33743.pdf.

Cooperative Agreement between the United States of America and the Southern African Customs Union to Foster Trade, Investment and Development, Treaties and Other International Acts Series (T.I.A.S) 08-716.2. Enacted July 16, 2008.

Copley, Gregory R. (2006). US Tries to Create Africa Command Before Mid-Term Elections. *Defense & Foreign Affairs Strategic Policy* 34(9): 12.

Copson, Raymond W. (1995). *Africa: U.S. Foreign Assistance Issues*. CRS Issue Brief No. IB95052. Washington, DC: Congressional Research Service. October 18, 1995.

—— (2000a). *Africa: U.S. Foreign Assistance Issues*. CRS Issue Brief No. IB95052. Washington, DC: Congressional Research Service. May 12, 2000.

—— (2000b). *African Development Bank and Fund*. CRS Report No. RS20329. Washington, DC: Congressional Research Service.

Cornelius, Wayne A., Thomas J. Espenshade, and Idean Salehyan (Eds.) (2001). *The International Migration of the Highly Skilled: Demand, Supply, and Development Consequences in Sending and Receiving Countries*. Boulder, CO: Lynne Rienner.

Cornelius, Wayne A., and Marc R. Rosenblum (2005). Immigration and Politics. *Annual Review of Political Science* 8(1): 99–119.

Corwin, Edward S. (1940). *The President: Office and Powers*. New York: NYU Press.

Cox, Gary W., and Mathew D. McCubbins (2005). *Setting the Agenda: Responsible Party Government in the U.S. House of Representatives*. Cambridge, UK: Cambridge University Press.

CQ Weekly (1989). Foreign Governments April 1989 Lobby Registrations, *Congressional Quarterly Weekly*, p. 2341, September 9, 1989.

Crabb, Cecil V., and Pat M. Holt (1989). *Invitation to Struggle: Congress, the President, and Foreign Policy*. Washington, DC: Congressional Quarterly Press.

Craig, Campbell, Benjamin H. Friedman, Brendan Rittenhouse Green, Justin Logan, Stephen G. Brooks, G. John Ikenberry, et al. (2013). Debating American Engagement: The Future of U.S. Grand Strategy. *International Security* 38(2): 181–199.

Crane, Barbara B., and Jennifer Dusenberry (2004). Power and Politics in International Funding for Reproductive Health: The US Global Gag Rule. *Reproductive Health Matters* 12(24): 128–137.

Cranmer, Skyler J., and Christopher Dawes (2012). The Heritability of Foreign Policy Preferences. *Twin Research and Human Genetics* 15(1): 52–59.

Crawford, Neta C., and Catherine Lutz (2014). *Costs of War Project*. Providence, RI: Watson Institute for International Studies, Brown University. Retrieved from http://www.costsofwar.org/.

Crawford, Vincent P., and Joel Sobel (1982). Strategic Information Transmission. *Econometrica* 50(6): 1431–1451.

Dagne, Theodros (1996). *Africa Trade and Development: Clinton Administration Policy and Issues for U.S.–Sub-Saharan Africa Trade Relations*. CRS Report No. 96-639F. Washington, DC: Congressional Research Service. July 16, 1996.

—— (1998). *Africa: Trade and Development Initiatives by the Clinton Administration and Congress*. CRS Report No. 98-92F. Washington, DC: Congressional Research Service. March 2, 1998.

Davis, Julie Hirschfeld, and Ashley Parker (2014). Political Shift Stalls Efforts to Overhaul Immigration, *New York Times*, p. A11, September 8, 2014.

Debs, Alexandre, and Nuno P. Monteiro (2014). Known Unknowns: Power Shifts, Uncertainty, and War. *International Organization* 68(1): 1–31.

Defense Institute of Security Assistance Management (2007). International Training. In Defense Institute of Security Assistance Management (Ed.), *The Management of Security Assistance* (pp. 14-11–14-32). Wright-Patterson AFB, OH: DISAM.

DeGennaro, Patricia (2014). Diplomacy Is the Way to Beat the 'Islamic State.' *Time.com*, New York: Time, Inc. Retrieved from http://time.com/3274038/diplomacy-is-the-way-to-beat-the-islamic-state/.

Demirgüç-Kunt, Asli, and Harry P. Huizinga (1993). Official Credits to Developing Countries: Implicit Transfers to the Banks. *Journal of Money, Credit and Banking* 25(3): 430–444.

Desch, Michael C. (2008). America's Liberal Illiberalism: The Ideological Origins of Overreaction in U.S. Foreign Policy. *International Security* 32(3): 7–43.

Destler, I. M. (1972). *Presidents, Bureaucracies and Foreign Policy*. Princeton, NJ: Princeton University Press.

Devroy, Ann (1994). Clinton Assembles Bipartisan Support for Trade Pact, *Washington Post*, p. A4, November 29, 1994.

Dewar, Helen (1999). Senate Deal Allows Votes on Trade, Wage Bills, *Washington Post*, p. A16, October 30, 1999.

Dietrich, John W. (2007). The Politics of PEPFAR: The President's Emergency Plan for AIDS Relief. *Ethics & International Affairs* 21(3): 277–292.

Dinkins, David (1997a). Congress Should Approve Africa Trade Bill, *New York Amsterdam News*, p. 13, November 6, 1997.

—— (1997b). Many Favor African Trade Bill, but Will Congress Ever Vote?, *Christian Science Monitor*, p. 20, November 19, 1997.

Doherty, Carroll J. (1996). Clinton with Veto Pen Poised, Gets Agency-Cutback Bill, *Congressional Quarterly Weekly Report*, p. 895, March 30, 1996.

Dollar, David, and Victoria Levin (2006). The Increasing Selectivity of Foreign Aid, 1984–2003. *World Development* 34(12): 2034–2046.

Dorussen, Han, and Michaell Taylor (Eds.) (2002). *Economic Voting*. London: Routledge.

Dougherty, Carter (2002a). Bush to Get New Start on Trade, *Washington Times*, p. C08.

—— (2002b). House, Senate Agree on Trade Bill; 'Fast-Track' Nears Final Approval, *Washington Times*, p. A01, July 27, 2002.

Dreier, David (1994). GATT Approval Proves The Two Parties Can Tango, *Christian Science Monitor*, p. 18, December 13, 1994.

Drezner, Daniel W. (2000). Ideas, Bureaucratic Politics, and the Crafting of Foreign Policy. *American Journal of Political Science* 44(4): 733–749.

Duch, Raymond M., and Randolph T. Stevenson (Eds.) (2008). *The Economic Vote: How Political and Economic Institutions Condition Election Results*. New York: Cambridge University Press.

Dudley, Leonard, and Claude Montmarquette (1976). A Model of the Supply of Bilateral Foreign Aid. *American Economic Review* 66(1): 132–142.

Dugger, Celia W. (2005). Poverty Memo; African Food for Africa's Starving Is Roadblocked in Congress, *New York Times*, p. 4.

Dustmann, Christian, and Ian P. Preston (2007). Racial and Economic Factors in Attitudes to Immigration. *B.E. Journal of Economic Analysis & Policy: Advances* 7(1): 1–39.

Dyer, Geoff, and Chloe Sorvino (2014). $1tn Cost of Longest US War Hastens Retreat from Military Intervention. *FT.com*, London: The Financial Times Ltd. Retrieved from http://www.ft.com/intl/cms/s/2/14be0e0c-8255-11e4-ace7-00144feabdc0.html.

Edwards, George C., III (1986). The Two Presidencies: A Reevaluation. *American Politics Quarterly* 14(3): 247–263.

—— (1989). *At the Margins: Presidential Leadership in Congress*. New Haven, CT: Yale University Press.

—— (2003). *On Deaf Ears: The Limits of the Bully Pulpit*. New Haven, CT: Yale University Press.

Eisenhower, Dwight D. (1961). *Farewell Radio and Television Address to the American People*. Washington, DC: White House. January 17, 1961. Retrieved from http://www.eisenhower.archives.gov/all_about_ike/speeches/farewell_address.pdf.

Emmerich, Herbert (1971). *Federal Organization and Administrative Management*. Tuscaloosa: University of Alabama Press.

Enda, Jodi (2008). Negotiating with People's Lives. *Conscience* 29(3): 21–24.

Epstein, David, and Sharyn O'Halloran (1994). Administrative Procedures, Information, and Agency Discretion. *American Journal of Political Science* 38(3): 697–722.

—— (1995). A Theory of Strategic Oversight: Congress, Lobbyists, and the Bureaucracy. *Journal of Law, Economics & Organization* 11(2): 227–255.

—— (1996). The Partisan Paradox and the U.S. Tariff, 1877–1934. *International Organization* 50(2): 301–324.

—— (1999). *Delegating Powers: A Transaction Cost Politics Approach to Policy Making under Separation of Powers*. Princeton, NJ: Princeton University Press.

Erikson, Robert S., Michael B. MacKuen, and James A. Stimson (2002). *The Macro Polity*. New York: Cambridge University Press.

Espenshade, Thomas J., and Charles A. Calhoun (1993). An Analysis of Public Opinion toward Undocumented Immigration. *Population Research and Policy Review* 12(3): 189–224.

Esterling, Kevin M. (2004). *The Political Economy of Expertise: Information and Efficiency in American National Politics*. Ann Arbor: University of Michigan Press.

Evangelista, Matthew (1989). Issue-Area and Foreign Policy Revisited. *International Organization* 43: 147–171.

Evans, Thomas B., Jr. (1981). Contribution to the International Development Association, *Congressional Record*, Vol. 127, Part 23, p. 30793, December 11, 1981. Washington, DC.

Facchini, Giovanni, and Anna Maria Mayda (2008). From Individual Attitudes towards Migrants to Migration Policy Outcomes: Theory and Evidence. *Economic Policy* 23(56): 651–713.

—— (2009). Does the Welfare State Affect Individual Attitudes toward Immigrants? Evidence across Countries. *Review of Economics and Statistics* 91(2): 295–314.

Facchini, Giovanni, Anna Maria Mayda, and Prachi Mishra (2011). Do Interest Groups Affect US Immigration Policy? *Journal of International Economics* 85(1): 114–128.

Facchini, Giovanni, and Max Friedrich Steinhardt (2011). What Drives U.S. Immigration Policy? Evidence from Congressional Roll Call Votes. *Journal of Public Economics* 95(7–8): 734–743.

Facchini, Giovanni, and Gerald Willmann (2005). The Political Economy of International Factor Mobility. *Journal of International Economics* 67(1): 201–219.

Faini, Riccardo, and Alessandra Venturini (1993). Trade, Aid and Migrations: Some Basic Policy Issues. *European Economic Review* 37(2–3): 435–442.

Fallows, James (2002). The Military-Industrial Complex. *Foreign Policy* 133: 46–48.

—— (2015). The Tragedy of the American Military. *The Atlantic* 315(1): 72–90.

Fariss, Christopher J. (2010). The Strategic Substitution of United States Foreign Aid. *Foreign Policy Analysis* 6(2): 107–131.

Fearon, James D. (1995). Rationalist Explanations for War. *International Organization* 49(3): 379–414.

Federation of American Scientists (1996). The Evolution of the U.S. Intelligence Community: An Historical Overview *Intelligence Resource Program.* Washington, DC: FAS.org. Retrieved from http://www.fas.org/irp/offdocs/int022.html.

Feingold, Russell D. (2006). To Require a Report on the Feasibility of Establishing a United States Military Regional Combatant Command for Africa, *Congressional Record*, Vol. 152, Part 82, p. S6383, June 22, 2006. Washington, DC.

Fenno, Richard F. (1978). *Home Style: House Members in Their Districts*. Boston: Little, Brown.

Fetzer, Joel S. (2000). *Public Attitudes toward Immigration in the United States, France, and Germany*. New York: Cambridge University Press.

Fidler, Stephen, and Mark Suzman (1998). US Presents United Front Despite Doubt, *Financial Times*, p. 3, August 21, 1998.

Fingar, Thomas (2011). *Reducing Uncertainty: Intelligence Analysis and National Security*. Stanford, CA: Stanford University Press.

Fisher, Louis (1995). *Presidential War Power*. Lawrence: University Press of Kansas.

—— (1998). *The Politics of Shared Power: Congress and the Executive* (Vol. 1). College Station: Texas A&M University Press.

—— (2007). The Law: Presidential Inherent Power: The "Sole Organ" Doctrine. *Presidential Studies Quarterly* 37(1): 139–152.

Fleck, Robert K., and Christopher Kilby (2001). Foreign Aid and Domestic Politics: Voting in Congress and the Allocation of USAID Contracts across Congressional Districts. *Southern Economic Journal* 67(3): 598–617.

—— (2006). How Do Political Changes Influence US Bilateral Aid Allocations? Evidence from Panel Data. *Review of Development Economics* 10(2): 210–223.

Fleisher, Richard, and Jon R. Bond (1988). Are There Two Presidencies? Yes, But Only for Republicans. *Journal of Politics* 50(3): 747–767.

Flynn, Michael E. (2014). The International and Domestic Sources of Bipartisanship in U.S. Foreign Policy. *Political Research Quarterly* 67(2): 398–412.

Franck, Thomas M. (1981). *The Tethered Presidency: Congressional Restraints on Executive Power*. New York: New York University Press.

Franck, Thomas M., and Edward Weisband (Eds.) (1974). *Secrecy and Foreign Policy* (2nd ed.). New York: Oxford University Press.

Frieden, Jeffry A. (1991). Invested Interests: The Politics of National Economic Policies in a World of Global Finance. *International Organization* 45(4): 425–451.

Frieden, Jeffry A., and Ronald Rogowski (1996). The Impact of the International Economy on National Policies: An Analytical Overview. In Robert O. Keohane and Helen V. Milner (Eds.), *Internationalization and Domestic Politics* (pp. 25–47). New York: Cambridge University Press.

Fukuyama, Francis (2006). *The End of History and the Last Man*. New York: Simon & Schuster.

Fund for Peace (2014). *Fragile States Index 2014*. Washington, DC: Fund for Peace. Retrieved from http://ffp.statesindex.org/rankings-2014.

Gailmard, Sean, and John W. Patty (2013). *Learning while Governing: Expertise and Accountability in the Executive Branch*. Chicago: University of Chicago Press.

Gaston, Noel, and Douglas R. Nelson (2000). Immigration and Labour-Market Outcomes in the United States: A Political-Economy Puzzle. *Oxford Review of Economic Policy* 16(3): 104–114.

Gawande, Kishore, Pravin Krishna, and Marcelo Olarreaga (2009). What Governments Maximize and Why: The View from Trade. *International Organization* 63(3): 491–532.

Gawande, Kishore, Pravin Krishna, and Michael J. Robbins (2006). Foreign Lobbies and U.S. Trade Policy. *Review of Economics and Statistics* 88(3): 563–571.

George, Alexander L. (1980). *Presidential Decisionmaking in Foreign Policy: The Effective Use of Information and Advice*. Boulder, CO: Westview Press.

Gerber, Alan S., Gregory A. Huber, David Doherty, Conor M. Dowling, and Shang E. Ha (2010). Personality and Political Attitudes: Relationships across Issue Domains and Political Contexts. *American Political Science Review* 104(1): 111–133.

Gerring, John (1997). Ideology: A Definitional Analysis. *Political Research Quarterly* 50(4): 957–994.

Gibbs, David N. (1995). Secrecy and International Relations. *Journal of Peace Research* 32(2): 213–228.

Gimpel, James G., and James R. Edwards (1999). *The Congressional Politics of Immigration Reform*. Boston: Allyn and Bacon.

Glaser, Charles L. (1997). The Security Dilemma Revisited. *World Politics* 50(1): 171–201.

—— (2010). *Rational Theory of International Politics: The Logic of Competition and Cooperation*. Princeton, NJ: Princeton University Press.

GlobalSecurity.org (2012). Africa Crisis Response Initiative (ACRI). *GlobalSecurity.org*, Alexandria, VA: GlobalSecurity.org. Retrieved from http://www.globalsecurity.org/military/ops/acri.htm.

Goldin, Claudia Dale (1994). The Political Economy of Immigration Restriction in the United States, 1890 to 1921. In Claudia Dale Goldin and Gary D. Libecap (Eds.), *The Regulated Economy: A Historical Approach to Political Economy* (pp. 223–258). Chicago: University of Chicago Press.

Goldsmith, Jack L. (2012). *Power and Constraint: the Accountable Presidency after 9/11*. New York: W.W. Norton.

Goldstein, Judith L. (1993). *Ideas, Interests and American Trade Policy*. Ithaca, NY: Cornell University Press.

Goldstein, Judith L., and Robert Gulotty (2014). America and Trade Liberalization: The Limits of Institutional Reform. *International Organization* 68(02): 263–295.

Goldstein, Judith L., and Robert O. Keohane (1993a). *Ideas and Foreign Policy*. Ithaca, NY: Cornell University Press.

—— (1993b). Ideas and Foreign Policy: An Analytical Framework. In Judith Goldstein and Robert O. Keohane (Eds.), *Ideas and Foreign Policy: Beliefs, Institutions, and Political Change* (pp. 3–30). Ithaca, NY: Cornell University Press.

Goshko, John M., and Thomas W. Lippman (1993). Foreign Aid Shift Sought by Clinton, *Washington Post*, November 27, 1993.

Goshko, John M., and Daniel Williams (1994). U.S. Policy Faces Review by Helms; State Dept. Nemesis to Flex Muscle As Chairman of Foreign Relations, *Washington Post*, p. A01, November 13, 1994.

Goss, Carol F. (1972). Military Committee Membership and Defense-Related Benefits in the House of Representatives. *Western Political Quarterly* 25(2): 215–233.

Gould, Erica R. (2006). *Money Talks: The International Monetary Fund, Conditionality, and Supplementary Financiers*. Stanford, CA: Stanford University Press.

Government Printing Office (2009). *Historical Budget Tables: Outlays by Function and Subfunction*. Washington, DC: GPO. Retrieved from http://www.gpoaccess.gov/usbudget/fy08/sheets/hist03z2.xls.

Gowa, Joanne S. (1988). Public Goods and Political Institutions: Trade and Monetary Policy Processes in the United States. *International Organization* 42(1): 15–32.

—— (1998). Politics at the Water's Edge: Parties, Voters, and the Use of Force Abroad. *International Organization* 52(02): 307–324.

—— (1999). *Ballots and Bullets: The Elusive Democratic Peace*. Princeton, NJ: Princeton University Press.

Grant, Richard, and Jan Nijman (Eds.) (1998). *The Global Crisis in Foreign Aid*. Syracuse, NY: Syracuse University Press.

Gries, Peter Hays (2014). *The Politics of American Foreign Policy: How Ideology Divides Liberals and Conservatives over Foreign Affairs*. Palo Alto, CA: Stanford University Press.

Grimmer, Justin, and Brandon M Stewart (2013). Text as Data: The Promise and Pitfalls of Automatic Content Analysis Methods for Political Texts. *Political Analysis* 21(3): 267–297.

Grimmett, Richard F. (1995). *Multinational Peacekeeping Operations: Proposals to Enhance Congressional Oversight*. CRS Issue Brief No. IB95006. Washington, DC: Congressional Research Service. October 4, 1995.

Grossman, Gene M., and Elhanan Helpman (1994). Protection for Sale. *American Economic Review* 84(4): 833–850.

—— (2002). *Interest Groups and Trade Policy*. Princeton, NJ: Princeton University Press.

Grossman, Michael (2005). Role Theory and Foreign Policy Change: The Transformation of Russian Foreign Policy in the 1990s. *International Politics* 42(3): 334–351.

Guha-Sapir, Debarati, Philippe Hoyois, and Regina Below (2014). *Annual Disaster Statistical Review 2013: The Numbers and Trends*. Brussels: Center for Research on the Epidemiology of Disasters, Université catholique de Louvain. September 2014. Retrieved from http://www.cred.be/sites/default/files/ADSR_2013.pdf.

Guisinger, Alexandra (2009). Determining Trade Policy: Do Voters Hold Politicians Accountable? *International Organization* 63(3): 533–557.

Hagen, James M., and Vernon W. Ruttan (1988). Development Policy under Eisenhower and Kennedy. *Journal of Developing Areas* 23(1): 1–30.

Hainmueller, Jens, and Michael J. Hiscox (2006). Learning to Love Globalization: Education and Individual Attitudes Toward International Trade. *International Organization* 60(2): 469–498.

—— (2007). Educated Preferences: Explaining Attitudes toward Immigration in Europe. *International Organization* 61(2): 399–442.

—— (2010). Attitudes toward Highly Skilled and Low Skilled Immigration: Evidence from a Survey Experiment. *American Political Science Review* 104(1): 61–84.

Halperin, Morton H., and Priscilla Clapp (2006). *Bureaucratic Politics and Foreign Policy* (2nd ed.). Washington, DC: Brookings Institution Press.

Halperin, Morton H., Priscilla Clapp, and Arnold Kanter (1974). *Bureaucratic Politics and Foreign Policy*. Washington, DC: Brookings Institution.

Hamilton, Alexander (1791). Report on Manufactures.

Hankla, Charles R. (2006). Party Strength and International Trade A Cross-National Analysis. *Comparative Political Studies* 39(9): 1133–1156.

Hanson, Gordon H., Raymond Robertson, and Antonio Spilimbergo (2002). Does Border Enforcement Protect U.S. Workers from Illegal Immigration? *Review of Economics and Statistics* 84(1): 73–92.

Hanson, Gordon H., Kenneth F. Scheve, and Matthew J. Slaughter (2007). Public Finance and Individual Preferences Over Globalization Strategies. *Economics & Politics* 19(1): 1–33.

Hanson, Gordon H., and Antonio Spilimbergo (1999). Illegal Immigration, Border Enforcement, and Relative Wages: Evidence from Apprehensions at the US-Mexico Border. *American Economic Review* 89(5): 1337–1357.

—— (2001). Political Economy, Sectoral Shocks, and Border Enforcement. *Canadian Journal of Economics / Revue canadienne d'Economique* 34(3): 612–638.

Hartz, Louis (1955). *The Liberal Tradition in America; an Interpretation of American Political Thought Since the Revolution* (1st ed.). New York: Harcourt.

Haus, Leah A. (2002). *Unions, Immigration, and Internationalization: New Challenges and Changing Coalitions in the United States and France* (1st ed.). New York: Palgrave Macmillan.

Henehan, Marie T. (2000). *Foreign Policy and Congress: An International Relations Perspective*. Ann Arbor: University of Michigan Press.

Heniff, Bill Jr., Megan Suzanne Lynch, and Jessica Tollestrup (2012). *Introduction to the Federal Budget Process*. CRS Report No. 98-721. Washington, DC: Congressional Research Service.

Henk, Daniel W., and Steven Metz (1997). *The United States and the Transformation of African Security: The African Crisis Response Initiative and Beyond*. Carlisle, PA: U.S. Army War College, Strategic Studies Institute.

Henriksen, Thomas H. (2012). *America and the Rogue States*. New York: Palgrave Macmillan.

Herbst, Jeffrey Ira (1992). *U.S. Economic Policy toward Africa*. New York: Council on Foreign Relations Press.

Hibbs, Douglas A., Jr. (1982). The Dynamics of Political Support for American Presidents among Occupational and Partisan Groups. *American Journal of Political Science* 26: 312–332.

Hicks, Raymond, Helen V. Milner, and Dustin Tingley (2014). Trade Policy, Economic Interests and Party Politics in a Developing Country: The Political Economy of CAFTA. *International Studies Quarterly* 58(1): 106–117.

Hinckley, Barbara (1994). *Less than Meets the Eye: Foreign Policy Making and the Myth of the Assertive Congress*. Chicago: University of Chicago Press.

Hinckley, Ronald H. (1992). *People, Polls, and Policymakers: American Public Opinion and National Security*. New York: MacMillan.

Hindery, Leo, Jr., Jeffrey D. Sachs, and Gayle E. Smith (2008). *SAIS Review of International Affairs* 28(2): 49–54.

Hinshaw, Drew, and Patrick McGroarty (2014). The Return of Africa's Strongmen, *Wall Street Journal*, p. C1, December 6, 2014.

Hirschman, Albert O. (1980 [1945]). *National Power and the Structure of Foreign Trade* (Expanded ed.). Berkeley: University of California Press.

Hiscox, Michael J. (1999). The Magic Bullet? The RTAA, Institutional Reform and Trade Liberalization. *International Organization* 53(4): 669–698.

—— (2002a). Commerce, Coalitions, and Factor Mobility: Evidence from Congressional Votes on Trade Legislation. *American Political Science Review* 96(3): 593–608.

—— (2002b). *International Trade and Political Conflict: Commerce, Coalitions, and Mobility*. Princeton, NJ: Princeton University Press.

—— (2006). Through a Glass and Darkly: Attitudes Toward International Trade and the Curious Effects of Issue Framing. *International Organization* 60(3): 755–780.

—— (forthcoming). *High Stakes: The Political Economy of U.S. Trade Sanctions, 1950–2000*. New York: Cambridge University Press.

Hitt, Greg, and Neil King Jr. (2006). Slow Track: Democratic Gains Raise Roadblocks to Free-Trade Push; Party's Majority in Congress, Helped by Trade Critics, May Hamper Pending Deals; Early Tests: Peru, Colombia, *Wall Street Journal*, p. A1, November 11, 2006.

Holshek, Christopher (2014). Getting Past the Way of the Gun. *FP: Foreign Policy*, Washington, DC: FP Group. Retrieved from http://www.foreignpolicy.com/articles/2014/11/14/getting_past_way_gun_islamic_state_united_states_military_strategy_peace.

Holsti, Kalevi J. (1970). National Role Conceptions in the Study of Foreign Policy. *International Studies Quarterly* 14(3): 233–309.

Holsti, Ole R. (2004). *Public Opinion and American Foreign Policy*. Ann Arbor: University of Michigan Press.

Hook, Janet (2014). Americans Want to Pull Back From World Stage, Poll Finds. *Wall Street Journal*, New York: Dow Jones & Company. Retrieved from http://online.wsj.com/article/ SB10001424052702304163604579532050055966782.html.

Hook, Steven W. (1998). 'Building Democracy' through Foreign Aid: The Limitations of United States Political Conditionalities, 1992–96. *Democratization* 5(3): 156–180.

Hoskin, Marilyn B. (1991). *New Immigrants and Democratic Society: Minority Integration in Western Democracies*. New York: Praeger.

Hoskin, Marilyn B., and William Mishler (1983). Public Opinion Toward New Migrants: A Comparative. *International Migration* 21(4): 440–462.

Howell, William G. (2011). Presidential Power in War. *Annual Review of Political Science* 14(1): 89–105.

—— (2013). *Thinking about the Presidency: The Primacy of Power*. Princeton, NJ: Princeton University Press.

Howell, William G., Saul P. Jackman, and Jon C. Rogowski (2013). *The Wartime President*. Chicago: University of Chicago Press.

Howell, William G., and Jon C. Pevehouse (2005). Presidents, Congress, and the Use of Force. *International Organization* 59(1): 209–232.

—— (2007). *While Dangers Gather: Congressional Checks on Presidential War Powers*. Princeton, NJ: Princeton University Press.

Huber, John D., and Charles R. Shipan (2002). *Deliberate Discretion: the Institutional Foundations of Bureaucratic Autonomy*. Cambridge, UK; New York: Cambridge University Press.

Hughes, Thomas L. (1978). Carter and the Management of Contradictions. *Foreign Policy* 31: 34–55.

Human Rights Campaign (2013). Uniting American Families Act. Washington, DC: Human Rights Campaign. Retrieved from http://www.hrc.org/resources/entry/uniting-american -families-act.

Ikenberry, G. John (2009). Liberal Internationalism 3.0: America and the Dilemmas of Liberal World Order. *Perspectives on Politics* 7(01): 71–87.

Ikenberry, G. John, David A. Lake, and Michael Mastanduno (1988). Introduction: Approaches to Explaining American Foreign Economic Policy. *International Organization* 42(1): 1–14.

Ingwerson, Marshall (1994). Vote on Global Trade Pact Puts Bipartisanship to Test on Hill, *Christian Science Monitor*, p. 3, November 29, 1994.

International Security Advisory Board (2013). *Report on Security Capacity Building*. Washington, DC: Department of State. January 7, 2013.

Iqbal, Wasim (2014). Talks on BIT require new template, US tells Pakistan. *Business Recorder*, Karachi: Business Recorder. Retrieved from http://www.brecorder.com/business -a-economy/189/1152925/.

Irwin, Douglas A. (2006). *Historical Aspects of U.S. Trade Policy*. NBER Reporter: Research Summary. Cambridge, MA: National Bureau of Economic Research. Summer 2006.

Irwin, Lewis G. (2000). Dancing the Foreign Aid Appropriations Dance: Recurring Themes in the Modern Congresses. *Public Budgeting & Finance* 20(2): 30–48.

Isaacson, Walter (1992). *Kissinger: A Biography*. New York: Simon & Schuster.

Jabara, Cathy, Jean Harman, Roger Corey, Andrea Gash, Peter Pogany, Lori Brown, et al. (1996). *U.S.–Africa Trade Flows and Effects of the Uruguay Round Agreements*. ITC Publication No. 2938. Washington, DC: U.S. International Trade Commission. January 1996.

Jackman, Saul P. (2012). *Policy and Power: How the President Uses Governing Tools to Pursue Short- and Long-Term Goals*. Prepared for the Annual Meeting of the American Political Science Association, New Orleans, LA, May 23, 2012. http://papers.ssrn.com/sol3/papers .cfm?abstract_id=2107325.

Jackson, David J., and Steven T. Engel (2003). Friends Don't Let Friends Vote for Free Trade: The Dynamics of the Labor PAC Punishment Strategy over PNTR. *Political Research Quarterly* 56(4): 441–448.

Jacobs, Lawrence R., and Benjamin I. Page (2005). Who Influences U.S. Foreign Policy? *American Political Science Review* 99(1): 107–123.

Jamal, Amaney A. (2012). *Of Empires and Citizens: Pro-American Democracy or No Democracy at All?* Princeton, NJ: Princeton University Press.

James, Patrick, and Athanasios Hristoulas (1994). Domestic Politics and Foreign Policy: Evaluating a Model of Crisis Activity for the United States. *Journal of Politics* 56(02): 327–348.

James, Patrick, and John R. Oneal (1991). The Influence of Domestic and International Politics on the President's Use of Force. *Journal of Conflict Resolution* 35(2): 307–332.

Jasper, William F. (2013). Dangers of the Trans-Pacific Partnership (TPP) Secret 'Trade' Agreement (Video). *The New American*, Appleton, WI: John Birch Society. Retrieved from http://www.thenewamerican.com/usnews/foreign-policy/item/17182-dangers-of-the-trans-pacific-partnership-tpp-secret-trade-agreement-video.

Jentleson, Bruce W. (1990). American Diplomacy: Around the World and along Pennsylvania Avenue. In Thomas E. Mann (Ed.), *A Question of Balance: The President, the Congress, and Foreign Policy* (pp. 146–200). Washington, DC: Brookings Institution.

Jervis, Robert (1976). *Perception and Misperception in International Politics.* Princeton, NJ: Princeton University Press.

——— (1978). Cooperation under the Security Dilemma. *World Politics* 30(2): 167–214.

——— (2005). *American Foreign Policy in a New Era.* New York: Routledge.

——— (2012). Review of "U.S. Presidents and Foreign Policy Mistakes," Stephen G. Walker and Akan Malici; "Reducing Uncertainty: Intelligence Analysis and National Security," Thomas Fingar. *Political Science Quarterly* 127(1): 143–146.

Jessee, Stephen A. (2009). Spatial Voting in the 2004 Presidential Election. *American Political Science Review* 103(01): 59–81.

Johnson, Loch K. (1984). *The Making of International Agreements: Congress Confronts the Executive.* New York: New York University Press.

Jolly, David (2014). More Hope than Headway in U.S.-Europe Trade Talks, *New York Times*, p. B3, March 15, 2014.

Jones, Vivian C., and Brock R. Williams (2012). *U.S. Trade and Investment Relations with sub-Saharan Africa and the African Growth and Opportunity Act.* CRS Report No. RL31772. Washington, DC: Congressional Research Service. November 14, 2012.

Jost, John T. (2006). The End of the End of Ideology. *American Psychologist* 61(7): 651–670.

Jost, John T., Mahzarin R. Banaji, and Brian A. Nosek (2004). A Decade of System Justification Theory: Accumulated Evidence of Conscious and Unconscious Bolstering of the Status Quo. *Political Psychology* 25(6): 881–919.

Jost, John T., Jack Glaser, Arie W. Kruglanski, and Frank J. Sulloway (2003). Political Conservatism as Motivated Social Cognition. *Psychological Bulletin* 129(3): 339–375.

Journal of Commerce Online (2003). Trade Scene: More U.S. FTA's on the Way, *Journal of Commerce*, p. 1, March 18, 2003.

Kabugi, Njuguna (1999). House Approves Africa Trade Bill, *Washington Informer*, p. 1, July 28, 1999.

Kaempfer, William H., and Anton D. Lowenberg (1988). The Theory of International Economic Sanctions: A Public Choice Approach. *American Economic Review* 78(4): 786–793.

——— (1989). The Theory of International Economic Sanctions: A Public Choice Approach: Reply. *American Economic Review* 79(5): 1304–1306.

——— (1992). *International Economic Sanctions: a Public Choice Perspective.* Boulder, CO: Westview Press.

Kagan, Robert (2002). Power and Weakness. *Policy Review* 113(June/July): 3–28.

Kagan, Robert A. (2001). *Adversarial Legalism: The American Way of Law*. Cambridge, MA: Harvard University Press.

Kaplan, Lawrence S., Ronald D. Landa, and Edward J. Drea (2006). *History of the Office of the Secretary of Defense* (Vol. V: The McNamara Ascendancy, 1961–1965). Washington, DC: Office of the Secretary of Defense.

Katzenstein, Peter J. (1985). *Small States in World Markets: Industrial Policy in Europe*. Ithaca, NY: Cornell University Press.

Kelemen, R. Daniel (2008). The Americanisation of European Law? Adversarial Legalism a La Européenne. *European Political Science* 7(1): 32–42.

Kelley, Kevin J. (1998). Africa: Clinton's Africa Bill Suffers a Major Blow. *The East African*, Nairobi: BDAfrica. Retrieved from http://allafrica.com/stories/199808030201.html.

——— (2004). U.S. Agoa Backers Ask for Three-year Extension, *New York Beacon*, p. 16, May 6, 2004.

Kelly, Andrew P., and Robert P. Van Houweling (2011). *Roll Calls, Representation, and Agenda Control*. Prepared for the CSDP American Politics Colloquium, Princeton, NJ, November 17, 2011.

Kemp, Murray C. (1995). *The Gains from Trade and the Gains from Aid: Essays in International Trade Theory*. London; New York: Routledge.

Keohane, Robert O. (1983). Theory of World Politics: Structural Realism and Beyond. In Ada W. Finifter (Ed.), *Political Science: The State of the Discipline*. Washington, DC: American Political Science Association.

——— (1986). Reciprocity in International Relations. *International Organization* 40(1): 1–27.

Keohane, Robert O., and Joseph S. Nye (1977). *Power and Interdependence: World Politics in Transition*. Boston: Little, Brown and Company.

Kernell, Samuel (1993). *Going Public: New Strategies of Presidential Leadership* (2nd ed.). Washington, DC: Congressional Quarterly Press.

Kerr, William R., William F. Lincoln, and Prachi Mishra (2014). *The Dynamics of Firm Lobbying*. Working Paper Number 1072 Ann Arbor, MI: William Davidson Institute. January 2014.

Kessler, Alan (2001). *Immigration, Economic Insecurity, and the "Ambivalent" American Public*. CCIS Working Paper No. 41. La Jolla: University of California–San Diego. September 2001.

Kiewiet, D. Roderick, and Mathew D. McCubbins (1991). *The Logic of Delegation: Congressional Parties and the Appropriations Process*. Chicago: University of Chicago Press.

Kim, In-Song (2013). *Political Cleavages within Industry: Firm Level Lobbying for Trade Liberalization*. Princeton, NJ: Princeton University. October 7, 2013. Retrieved from http://www.princeton.edu/~insong/research/exporters.pdf.

Kindleberger, Charles P. (1973). *The World in Depression*. Berkeley: University of California Press.

King, Gary, Robert O. Keohane, and Sidney Verba (1994). *Designing Social Inquiry: Scientific Inference in Qualitative Research*. Princeton, NJ: Princeton University Press.

Kingdon, John W. (1989). *Congressmen's Voting Decisions* (3rd ed.). Ann Arbor: University of Michigan Press.

Kirchhoff, Sue (2002a). Bush Urges Lawmakers to Pass Trade Bill, *Boston Globe*, p. D1, July 27, 2002.

——— (2002b). Senate OK's Trade Measure Bill, Expands Power of the President in Negotiating Pacts, *Boston Globe*, p. E1, August 2, 2002.

Kirshner, Jonathan (2007). *Appeasing Bankers: Financial Caution on the Road to War*. Princeton, NJ: Princeton University Press.

Krasner, Stephen D. (1972). Are Bureaucracies Important? (Or Allison Wonderland). *Foreign Policy* 7: 159–179.

——— (1978). *Defending the National Interest: Raw Materials Investments and US Foreign Policy*. Princeton, NJ: Princeton University Press.

Kriner, Douglas L. (2010). *After the Rubicon: Congress, Presidents, and the Politics of Waging War*. Chicago: University of Chicago Press.

Kriner, Douglas L., and Andrew Reeves (forthcoming). *The Particularistic President*. Cambridge, UK: Cambridge University Press.

Kristof, Nicholas (2014). What ISIS Could Teach the West, *New York Times*, p. A31, October 2, 2014.

Kupchan, Charles A., and Peter L. Trubowitz (2007). Dead Center: The Demise of Liberal Internationalism in the United States. *International Security* 32(2): 7–44.

—— (2010). The Illusion of Liberal Internationalism's Revival. *International Security* 35(1): 95–109.

Ladewig, Jeffrey W. (2006). Domestic Influences on International Trade Policy: Factor Mobility in the United States, 1963 to 1992. *International Organization* 60(1): 69–103.

Lake, David A. (2009). Open Economy Politics: A Critical Review. *Review of International Organizations* 4(3): 219–244.

Lancaster, Carol (2000). *Transforming Foreign Aid: United States Assistance in the 21st Century*. Washington, DC: Institute for International Economics.

Landler, Mark (2014). Ending Asia Trip, Obama Defends His Foreign Policy, *New York Times*, p. A1, April 28, 2014.

Landler, Mark, and Mark Mazzetti (2013). For Obama's Global Vision, Daunting Problems, *New York Times*, p. A1, May 25, 2013.

Langton, Danielle (2004). *AGOA III: Amendment to the African Growth and Opportunity Act*. CRS Report No. RS21772. Washington, DC: Congressional Research Service. April 5, 2004.

—— (2008). *United States–Southern African Customs Union (SACU) Free Trade Agreement Negotiations: Background and Potential Issues*. CRS Report No. RS21387. Washington, DC: Congressional Research Service. July 24, 2008.

Lapinski, John S. (2013). *The Substance of Representation: Congress, American Political Development, and Lawmaking*. Princeton, NJ: Princeton University Press.

Lee, Frances E. (2009). *Beyond Ideology: Politics, Principles, and Partisanship in the U.S. Senate*. Chicago: University of Chicago Press.

Lee, Frederick Paul (1980). "The Two Presidencies" Revisited. *Presidential Studies Quarterly* 10(4): 620–628.

Lefkowitz, Jay P. (2009). AIDS and the President—An Inside Account. *Commentary Magazine* New York: Commentary Magazine. Retrieved from https://www.commentarymagazine.com/articles/aids-and-the-president-an-inside-account/

Legro, Jeffrey W. (2005). *Rethinking the World: Great Power Strategies and International Order*. Ithaca, NY: Cornell University Press.

Leidy, Michael P. (1989). The Theory of International Economic Sanctions: A Public Choice Approach: Comment. *American Economic Review* 79(5): 1300–1303.

Leland, Anne, and Mari-Jana Oboroceanu (2010). *American War and Military Operations Casualties: Lists and Statistics*. CRS Report No. RL32492. Washington, DC: Congressional Research Service. February 26, 2010.

LeLoup, Lance T. (2008). Reflections on Carol F. Goss's 1972 Article, "Military Committee Membership and Defense-related Benefits in the House of Representatives." *Political Research Quarterly* 61(39): 39–42.

LeLoup, Lance T., and Steven A. Shull (1979). Congress versus the Executive: The 'Two Presidencies' Reconsidered. *Social Science Quarterly* 59(4): 704–719.

Leogrande, William M., and Philip Brenner (1993). The House Divided: Ideological Polarization over Aid to the Nicaraguan "Contras." *Legislative Studies Quarterly* 18(1): 105–136.

Lewis-Beck, Michael S., and Martin Paldam (2000). Economic Voting: An Introduction. *Electoral Studies* 19(2–3): 113–122.

Lewis, David E. (2003). *Presidents and the Politics of Agency Design.* Redwood City, CA: Stanford University Press.

Lindblom, Charles (1965). *The Intelligence of Democracy: Decision Making through Mutual Adjustment.* New York: Free Press.

Lindsay, James M. (1992). Congress and Foreign Policy: Why the Hill Matters. *Political Science Quarterly* 107(4): 607–628.

—— (1994). *Congress and the Politics of U.S. Foreign Policy.* Baltimore, MD: Johns Hopkins University Press.

Lindsay, James M., and Randall B. Ripley (1992). Foreign and Defense Policy in Congress: A Research Agenda for the 1990s. *Legislative Studies Quarterly* 17(3): 417–449.

Lindsay, James M., and Wayne P. Steger (1993). The "Two Presidencies" in Future Research: Moving beyond Roll-Call Analysis. *Congress & the Presidency: A Journal of Capital Studies* 20(2): 103–118.

Lippman, Thomas W. (1994). Administration Sidesteps Genocide Label in Rwanda, *Washington Post*, p. A1, June 11, 1994.

Lobe, Jim (2002). New Bush AIDS Plan Outrages Activists. *AlterNet*, San Francisco: Independent Media Institute. Retrieved from http://www.alternet.org/story/13421/new_bush _aids_plan_outrages_activists.

—— (2007). Africa to Get Its Own U.S. Military Command. *Inter Press Service*, Montevideo: Global Network Content Services LLC. Retrieved from http://www.antiwar.com/ lobe/?articleid=10443.

Lohmann, Susanne, and Sharyn O'Halloran (1994). Divided Government and U.S. Trade Policy: Theory and Evidence. *International Organization* 48(4): 595–632.

Long, Clarence (1977). Investment in International Development Association, *Congressional Record*, Vol. 123, Part 17, p. 20572, June 23, 1977. Washington, DC.

Lowi, Theodore J. (1964). American Business, Public Policy, Case Studies and Political Theory. *World Politics* 16(4): 677–715.

Lowrey, Annie (2013). House Stalls Trade Pact Momentum, *New York Times*, p. B1, November 13, 2013.

Lü, Xiaobo, Kenneth F. Scheve, and Matthew J. Slaughter (2010). Inequity Aversion and the International Distribution of Trade Protection. *American Journal of Political Science* 56(3): 638–655.

Luce, Edward (2014). Uncertainty, not China, Is Replacing US Power. *FT.com.* London: Financial Times Ltd. Retrieved from http://www.ft.com/intl/cms/s/0/b7a1964c-d121-11e3-bdbb -00144feabdc0.html#axzz30xxz3WJ4

Lumsdaine, David H. (1993). *Moral Vision in International Politics: The Foreign Aid Regime, 1949– 1989.* Princeton, NJ: Princeton University Press.

Lupia, Arthur (1994). Shortcuts Versus Encyclopedias: Information and Voting Behavior in California Insurance Reform Elections. *American Political Science Review* 88(1): 63–76.

Lyman, Rick (2014). U.S. Denial of Visas for 6 in Hungary Strains Ties, *New York Times*, p. A11, October 21, 2014.

MacDonald, Paul K., and Joseph M. Parent (2011). Graceful Decline? The Surprising Success of Great Power Retrenchment. *International Security* 35(4): 7–44.

MacKinnon, Michael G. (2000). *Evolution of US Peacekeeping Policy Under Clinton: A Fairweather Friend?* New York: Routledge.

Magee, Christopher S. (2010). Would NAFTA Have Been Approved by the House of Representatives under President Bush? Presidents, Parties, and Trade Policy. *Review of International Economics* 18(2): 382–395.

Magee, Stephen P., William A. Brock, and Leslie Young (1989). *Black Hole Tariffs and Endogenous Policy Theory.* New York: Cambridge University Press.

Mages, Lisa (2007). *US Armed Forces Abroad: Selected Congressional Votes.* CRS Report No. RL31693. Washington, DC: Congressional Research Service. September 7, 2007.

Mahoney, Christine, and Frank Baumgartner (2008). Converging Perspectives on Interest Group Research in Europe and America. *West European Politics* 31(6): 1253–1273.

Malloy, Michael P. (2000). *United States Economic Sanctions: Theory and Practise.* The Hague (Netherlands): Kluwer Law International.

Manger, Mark (2009). *Investing in Protection: The Politics of Preferential Trade Agreements between North and South.* New York: Cambridge University Press.

Mann, Thomas E. (Ed.) (1990). *A Question of Balance: The President, the Congress, and Foreign Policy.* Washington, DC: Brookings Institution.

Manning, Bayless (1977). The Congress, the Executive and Intermestic Affairs: Three Proposals. *Foreign Affairs* 55(2): 306–324.

Mansbach, Richard W., and John A. Vasquez (1981). *In Search of Theory: A New Paradigm for Global Politics.* New York: Columbia University Press.

Mansfield, Edward D., and Diana C. Mutz (2009). Support for Free Trade: Self-Interest, Sociotropic Politics, and Out-Group Anxiety. *International Organization* 63(3): 425–457.

Margesson, Rhoda (2013). *International Crises and Disasters: U.S. Humanitarian Assistance Response Mechanisms.* CRS Report No. RL33769. Washington, DC: Congressional Research Service. August 1, 2013. Retrieved from http://fpc.state.gov/documents/organization/212995.pdf.

Marshall, William P. (2008). Eleven Reasons Why Presidential Power Inevitably Expands and Why It Matters. *Boston University Law Review* 88(2): 505–522.

Mathews, Jodi (2003). Bread for the World Begins New Push to End Hunger. *EthicsDaily.com,* Nashville: EthicsDaily.com. Retrieved from http://www.ethicsdaily.com/bread-for-the-world-begins-new-push-to-end-hunger-cms-2298.

Mathis, Marvin Dawson (1978). Limitation on United States Contribution to the International Financial Institutions, *Congressional Record,* Vol. 124, Part 19, p. 25958, August 14, 1978. Washington, DC.

Matishak, Martin (2014). Asia Pivot on Track, Pentagon Says. *The Hill,* Washington, DC: Capitol Hill Publishing Group. Retrieved from http://thehill.com/policy/defense/215177-asia-pivot-remains-on-track-pentagon-says.

Mayda, Anna Maria (2006). Who Is Against Immigration? A Cross-Country Investigation of Individual Attitudes Toward Immigration. *Review of Economics and Statistics* 88(3): 510–530.

Mayda, Anna Maria, and Dani Rodrik (2005). Why Are Some People (and Countries) More Protectionist than Others? *European Economic Review* 49(6): 1393–1430.

Mayer, Wolfgang, and Pascalis Raimondos-Møller (2003). The Politics of Foreign Aid: A Median Voter Perspective. *Review of Development Economics* 7(2): 165–178.

Mazzetti, Mark (2014). After Scrutiny, C.I.A. Mandate Is Untouched, *New York Times,* p. A1, December 27, 2014.

Mazzetti, Mark, and David E. Sanger (2013). Tap on Merkel Provides Peek at Vast Spy Net, *New York Times,* p. A1, October 31, 2013.

McCarty, Nolan M. (2004). The Appointments Dilemma. *American Journal of Political Science* 48(3): 413–428.

McCarty, Nolan M., Keith T. Poole, and Howard Rosenthal (2006). *Polarized America: The Dance of Ideology and Unequal Riches.* Cambridge, MA: MIT Press.

McCormick, James M., and Michael Black (1983). Ideology and Senate Voting on the Panama Canal Treaties. *Legislative Studies Quarterly* 8(1): 45–63.

McCormick, James M., and Eugene R. Wittkopf (1990). Bipartisanship, Partisanship, and Ideology in Congressional-Executive Foreign Policy Relations, 1947–1988. *Journal of Politics* 52(4): 1077–1100.

McCubbins, Mathew D., Roger G. Noll, and Barry R. Weingast (1987). Administrative Procedures as an Instrument of Political Control. *Journal of Law, Economics and Organization* 3(243–277).

—— (1989). Structure and Process, Politics and Policy: Administrative Arrangements and Political Control of Agencies. *Virginia Law Review* 75(2): 431–482.

McCubbins, Mathew D., and Thomas Schwartz (1984). Congressional Oversight Overlooked: Police Patrols and Fire Alarms. *American Journal of Political Science* 28(1): 165–179.

McDermott, Rose (2007). *Presidential Leadership, Illness and Decision Making*. New York: Cambridge University Press.

McGillivray, Fiona (2004). *Privileging Industry: The Comparative Politics of Trade and Industrial Policy*. Princeton, NJ: Princeton University Press.

McKinlay, Robert D., and Richard Little (1977). A Foreign Policy Model of US Bilateral Aid Allocations. *World Politics* 30(1): 56–86.

—— (1978). A Foreign-Policy Model of the Distribution of British Bilateral Aid, 1960–70. *British Journal of Political Science* 8(3): 313–331.

—— (1979). The US Aid Relationship: A Test of the Recipient Need and the Donor Interest Models. *Political Studies* 27(2): 236–250.

McLean, Elena V. (2015, Winter). Multilateral Aid and Domestic Economic Interests. *International Organization* 69(02): 97–130.

McMaster, Herbert R. (1997). *Dereliction of Duty: Lyndon Johnson, Robert McNamara, the Joint Chiefs of Staff, and the Lies that Led to Vietnam* (1st ed.). New York: HarperCollins.

Mearsheimer, John J. (2001). *The Tragedy of Great Power Politics*. New York: W. W. Norton.

—— (2011). *Why Leaders Lie: The Truth about Lying in International Politics*. New York: Oxford University Press.

Mearsheimer, John J., and Stephen M. Walt (2007). *The Israel Lobby and US Foreign Policy*. New York: Farrar Straus & Giroux.

Meernik, James (1993). Presidential Support in Congress: Conflict and Consensus on Foreign and Defense Policy. *Journal of Politics* 55(3): 569–587.

—— (1994). Presidential Decision Making and the Political Use of Military Force. *International Studies Quarterly* 38(1): 121–138.

Meernik, James, and Elizabeth Oldmixon (2008). The President, the Senate, and the Costs of Internationalism. *Foreign Policy Analysis* 4(2): 187–206.

Meirowitz, Adam (2007). Communication and Bargaining in the Spatial Model. *International Journal of Game Theory* 35(2): 251–266.

Meirowitz, Adam, and Kristopher W. Ramsay (2010). *Investment and Bargaining*. Economic Theory Center Working Paper No. 007-2010. Princeton, NJ: Princeton University. December 21, 2010.

Mekay, Emad (2004). U.S.: Support Ebbs for Trade and Farm Subsidies—Poll, *Global Information Network*, p. 1, January 23, 2004.

Mellow, Nicole, and Peter L. Trubowitz (2005). Red versus Blue: American Electoral Geography and Congressional Bipartisanship, 1898–2002. *Political Geography* 24(6): 659–677.

Mendelsohn, Matthew, Robert Wolfe, and Andrew Parkin (2002). Globalization, Trade Policy and the Permissive Consensus in Canada. *Canadian Public Policy / Analyse de Politiques* 28(3): 351–371.

Meyer, Jeffrey A. (1988). Congressional Control of Foreign Assistance. *Yale Journal of International Law* 13(69): 69–110.

Michaels, Marguerite (1992). Retreat from Africa. *Foreign Affairs* 72(1): 93–108.

Middlemass, Keesha, and Christian Grose (2007). The Three Presidencies? Legislative Position-taking in Support of the President on Domestic, Foreign, and Homeland Security Policies in the 107th Congress. *Congress and the Presidency* 34(2): 57–80.

Migration Policy Institute (2014). *U.S. Immigration Trends*. Washington, DC: MPI. Retrieved from http://www.migrationpolicy.org/programs/data-hub/us-immigration-trends.

Miller, Erin, Gary LaFree, and Laura Dugan (2011). *Global Terrorism Database*. College Park: University of Maryland. Retrieved from http://www.start.umd.edu/gtd.

Miller, Warren E., and Donald E. Stokes (1963). Constituency Influence in Congress. *American Political Science Review* 57(1): 45–56.

Milner, Helen V. (1988a). *Resisting Protectionism: Global Industries and the Politics of International Trade*. Princeton, NJ: Princeton University Press.

—— (1988b). Trading Places: Industries for Free Trade. *World Politics*. April.

—— (1991). The Assumption of Anarchy in International Politics: A Critique. *Review of International Studies* 17(1): 67–85.

—— (1997). *Interests, Institutions, and Information: Domestic Politics and International Relations*. Princeton, NJ: Princeton University Press.

—— (2006). Why Multilateralism? Foreign Aid and Domestic Principal-agent Problems. In Darren G. Hawkins, David A. Lake, Daniel L. Nielson and Michael J. Tierney (Eds.), *Delegation and Agency in International Organizations* (pp. 107–139). New York: Cambridge University Press.

Milner, Helen V., and Benjamin Judkins (2004). Partisanship, Trade Policy, and Globalization: Is There a Left–Right Divide on Trade Policy? *International Studies Quarterly* 48(1): 95–119.

Milner, Helen V., and Dustin H. Tingley (2008a). *The Economic and Political Influences on Different Dimensions of United States Immigration Policy*. Prepared for the Annual Meeting of the American Political Science Association, Boston, August 28–31, 2008. http://www.princeton.edu/~hmilner/working%20papers/The%20Economic%20and%20Political%20Influences%20on%20Different%20Dimensions%20of%20United%20States%20Immigration%20Policy.pdf.

—— (2008b). *Preferences Toward Openness: The Economic and Political Influences on Immigration Policy in the US*. Prepared for the Annual Meeting of the American Political Science Association, Boston, August 28–31, 2008.

—— (2010). The Political Economy of U.S. Foreign Aid: American Legislators and the Domestic Politics of Aid. *Economics & Politics* 22(2): 200–232.

—— (2011). Who Supports Global Economic Engagement? The Sources of Preferences in American Foreign Economic Policy. *International Organization* 65(1): 37–68.

—— (2013a). The Choice for Multilateralism: Foreign Aid and American Foreign Policy. *Review of International Organizations* 8(3): 313–341.

—— (2013b). Public Opinion and Foreign Aid: A Review Essay. *International Interactions* 39(3): 389–401.

—— (Eds.) (2013c). *Geopolitics of Foreign Aid*. Cheltenham: Edward Elgar.

Moe, Terry M. (1982). Regulatory Performance and Presidential Administration. *American Journal of Political Science* 26(2): 197–224.

Money, Jeannette (1999). *Fences and Neighbors: The Political Geography of Immigration Control*. Ithaca, NY: Cornell University Press.

Montgomery, Evan Braden (2014). Contested Primacy in the Western Pacific: China's Rise and the Future of U.S. Power Projection. *International Security* 38(4): 115–149.

Morales, John Alliage (2013). Sequestration's Effect on U.S. Aid. *Inside Development*, Washington, DC: Devex. Retrieved from https://www.devex.com/news/sequestration-s-effect-on-us-aid-80420.

Morgan, Dan (2003). AIDS Funding Advances on Hill; Bush Is Cautioned Against Inflating Promises of Money, *Washington Post*, p. A15, July 11, 2003.

Morgan, T. Clifton, Navin A. Bapat, and Yoshiharu Kobayashi (2013). *Threat and Imposition of Sanctions (TIES) Data 4.0 Users' Manual: Case Level Data*. Chapel Hill: University of North Carolina. June 2013. Retrieved from http://www.unc.edu/~bapat/TIES.htm.

Morgan, T. Clifton, and Glenn Palmer (2000). A Model of Foreign Policy Substitutability: Selecting the Right Tools for the Job(s). *Journal of Conflict Resolution* 44(1): 11–32.

Morgenthau, Hans J. (1960). *Politics among Nations: The Struggle for Power and Peace* (3rd ed.). New York: Knopf.

Morrissey, Oliver (1996). *Business Interests and Aid Policy*. Prepared for the Meeting of Directors of the European Development Policy Institutes, Copenhagen, November 11–12, 1996.

Morrow, William L. (1968). Legislative Control of Administrative Discretion: The Case of Congress and Foreign Aid. *Journal of Politics* 30(4): 985–1011.

Most, Benjamin A., and Harvey Starr (1984). International Relations Theory, Foreign Policy Substitutability, and 'Nice' Laws. *World Politics* 36(3): 383–406.

—— (1989). *Inquiry, Logic, and International Politics*. Columbia: University of South Carolina Press.

Moynihan, Daniel P. (1994). Conference Agreement on the Uruguay Round, *Congressional Record*, Vol. 140, Part 18, p. 24999, September 21, 1994. Washington, DC.

Murphy, Kevin M., and Robert H. Topel (2013). Some Basic Economics of National Security. *American Economic Review* 103(3): 508–511.

Muskie, Edmund S., Kenneth Rush, and Kenneth W. Thompson (Eds.) (1986). *The President, the Congress, and Foreign Policy*. Lanham, MD: University Press of America.

Neumayer, Eric (2005). Is the Allocation of Food Aid Free from Donor Interest Bias? *Journal of Development Studies* 41(3): 394–411.

Neustadt, Richard E. (1960). *Presidential Power, the Politics of Leadership*. New York: Wiley.

New York Voice (1998). Senate May Insult Africa With Trade Measure, *New York Voice*, p. 13, August 12, 1998.

Newhouse, John (2009). Diplomacy, Inc.: The Influence of Lobbies on U.S. Foreign Policy. *Foreign Affairs* 88(3): 73–92.

Nincic, Miroslav (2010). Getting What You Want: Positive Inducements in International Relations. *International Security* 35(1): 138–183.

—— (2012). External Affairs and the Electoral Connection. In James M. McCormick (Ed.), *The Domestic Sources of American Foreign Policy* (6th ed., pp. 139–156). Lanham, MD: Rowman & Littlefield.

Nixon, Ron (2013). Obama Administration Seeks to Overhaul International Food Aid, *New York Times*, p. A13, April 5, 2013.

Noel, Alain, and Jean-Philippe Therien (1995). From Domestic to International Justice: The Welfare State and Foreign Aid. *International Organization* 49(3): 523–553.

—— (2002). Public Opinion and Global Justice. *Comparative Political Studies* 35(6): 631–656.

—— (2008). *Left and Right in Global Politics*. Cambridge: Cambridge University Press.

Nowels, Larry (2000). *Debt Reduction: Initiatives for the Most Heavily Indebted Poor Countries*. CRS Issue Brief No. RL30214. Washington, DC: Congressional Research Service. February 1, 2000.

—— (2003). *The Millennium Challenge Account: Congressional Consideration of a New Foreign Aid Initiative*. CRS Report No. RL31687. Washington, DC: Congressional Research Service. August 26, 2003. Retrieved from http://fpc.state.gov/documents/organization/39340.pdf.

—— (2007). Foreign Aid Reform Commissions, Task Forces, and Initiatives: From Kennedy to Present. In Lael Brainard (Ed.), *Security by Other Means: Foreign Assistance, Global Poverty, and American Leadership* (pp. 255–276). Washington, DC: Brookings Institution.

Nye, Joseph S. (2004). Hard Power, Soft Power, and 'The War on Terrorism.' In David Held and Mathias Koenig-Archibugi (Eds.), *American Power in the 21st Century* (pp. 114–133). Cambridge, UK: Polity.

O'Rourke, Kevin H., and Richard Sinnott (2001). The Determinants of Individual Trade Policy Preferences: International Survey Evidence. *Brookings Trade Forum*: 157–206.

O'Rourke, Kevin H., and Jeffrey G. Williamson (1999). *Globalization and History: The Evolution of a Nineteenth-Century Atlantic Economy* (Vol. 1). Cambridge, MA: MIT Press.

O'Sullivan, Meghan L. (2003). *Shrewd Sanctions: Statecraft and State Sponsors of Terrorism*. Washington, DC: Brookings Institution Press.

Oatley, Thomas H. (2002). *Commercial Banks and the International Monetary Fund: An Empirical Analysis*. Unpublished Manuscript. Chapel Hill: University of North Carolina. July 2002.

Obama, Barack H. (2013). *Remarks by the President at the National Defense University*. Washington, DC: White House. May 23, 2013. Retrieved from http://www.whitehouse.gov/the-press-office/2013/05/23/remarks-president-national-defense-university.

—— (2014). *Remarks by the President at the United States Military Academy Commencement Ceremony*. Washington, DC: White House. May 28, 2014. Retrieved from http://www.whitchouse.gov/photos-and-video/video/2014/05/28/president-obama-speaks-west-point-graduates#transcript.

Obey, David R. (1993). Foreign Operations, Export Financing, and Related Programs Appropriations Act, 1994, *Congressional Record*, Vol. 139, Part 9, p. 13158, June 17, 1993. Washington, DC.

Office of Management and Budget (2014). *Historical Tables: Table 5.2—Budget Authority by Agency, 1976–2019*. Washington, DC: White House. Retrieved from http://www.whitehouse.gov/omb/budget/Historicals.

Office of the Press Secretary (1998). *Fact Sheet: African Crisis Response Initiative (ACRI)*. Washington, DC: White House. April 1, 1998.

Office of the United States Trade Representative (2011). *United States, Rwanda Ratify Bilateral Investment Treaty*. USTR Press Release. Washington, DC: Executive Office of the President. December 2, 2011.

—— (2014). *Israel Free Trade Agreement*. Washington, DC: Executive Office of the President. Retrieved from http://www.ustr.gov/trade-agreements/free-trade-agreements/israel-fta.

Ogden, Robert E., and David A. Anderson (2008). US Foreign Policy toward North Korea: A Way Ahead. *Strategic Studies Quarterly* 2(3): 72–119.

Oldfield, Duane M., and Aaron Wildavsky (1989). Reconsidering the Two Presidencies. *Society* 26(5): 54–59.

Olson, Mancur (1965). *The Logic of Collective Action*. Cambridge, MA: Harvard University Press.

Omach, Paul (2000). The African Crisis Response Initiative: Domestic Politics and Convergence of National Interests. *African Affairs* 99(394): 73–95.

Organisation for Economic Co-operation and Development (2006). *The United States: Development Assistance Committee (DAC) Peer Review*. Paris: OECD.

Osgood, Iain (2013). Differentiated Products, Divided Industries: A Theory of Firm Preferences over Trade Liberalization. Working Paper.

Ottaviano, Gianmarco I. P., and Giovanni Peri (2008). *Immigration and National Wages: Clarifying the Theory and the Empirics*. NBER Working Paper No. 14188. Cambridge, MA: National Bureau of Economic Research. July 2008. Retrieved from http://www.nber.org/papers/w14188.

Overby, L. Marvin (1991). Assessing Constituency Influence: Congressional Voting on the Nuclear Freeze, 1982–83. *Legislative Studies Quarterly* 16(2): 297–312.

Page, Benjamin I., and Robert Y. Shapiro (1983). Effects of Public Opinion on Policy. *American Political Science Review* 77(1): 175–190.

—— (1992). *The Rational Public: Fifty Years of Trends in Americans' Policy Preferences*. Chicago: University of Chicago Press.

Palmer, Glenn, and Archana Bhandari (2000). The Investigation of Substitutability in Foreign Policy. *Journal of Conflict Resolution* 44(1): 3–10.

Palmer, Glenn, Scott B. Wohlander, and T. Clifton Morgan (2002). Give or Take: Foreign Aid and Foreign Policy Substitutability. *Journal of Peace Research* 39(1): 5–26.

Pape, Robert A. (2003). The Strategic Logic of Suicide Terrorism. *American Political Science Review* 97(3): 343–361.

Paxton, Pamela, and Stephen Knack (2012). Individual and Country-level Factors Affecting Support for Foreign Aid. *International Political Science Review* 33(2): 171–192.

Peabody, Alvin (1995a). Black Summit Defends United States Aid to Africa, *Washington Informer*, p. 11, February 8, 1995.

—— (1995b). Jackson Rebukes Tarzan Approach to U.S. African Policy, *Washington Informer*, p. 1.

—— (1998). U.S. House Passes African Trade Bill, *Washington Informer*, p. 1, March 18, 1998.

Peppers, Donald (1975). The Two Presidencies Eight Years Later. In Aaron Wildavsky (Ed.), *Perspectives on the Presidency* (pp. 462–471). Boston: Little, Brown.

Perlez, Jane (1992). After the Cold War: Views From Africa; Stranded by Superpowers, Africa Seeks an Identity, *New York Times*, p. 1, May 17, 1992.

Peters, Margaret E. (2014). Trade, Foreign Direct Investment, and Immigration Policy Making in the United States. *International Organization* 68(4): 811–844.

—— (2015). Open Trade, Closed Borders: Immigration Policy in the Era of Globalization. *World Politics* 67(1): 114–154.

Peterson, Paul E. (1994). The President's Dominance in Foreign Policy Making. *Political Science Quarterly* 109(2): 215–234.

Pevehouse, Jon C., and Felicity Vabulas (2012). *The Role of Informational Lobbying in US Foreign Aid: Is US Assistance for Sale?* Prepared for the 2012 International Political Economy Society Conference, Charlottesville, VA, November 9–10, 2012.

Philipps, Michael M., and Jim van de Hei (2002). Foreign-Aid Boosts Set Off Confusion within White House, *Wall Street Journal*, p. A2, March 20, 2002.

Philips, Matthew (2013). How Washington Quietly Withholds Egypt's Military Aid. *Bloomberg Businessweek*, New York: Bloomberg. Retrieved from http://www.businessweek.com/articles/2013-08-22/how-washington-quietly-withholds-egypts-military-aid.

Ploch, Lauren (2011). *Africa Command: U.S. Strategic Interests and the Role of the U.S. Military in Africa*. CRS Report No. RL34003. Washington, DC: Congressional Research Service. July 22, 2011.

Policy Agendas Project (2014). *Congressional Roll Call Voting Data Codebook*. Austin: University of Texas. Retrieved from http://www.policyagendas.org/.

Pollin, Robert, and Heidi Garrett-Peltier (2011). *The U.S. Employment Effects of Military and Domestic Spending Priorities: 2011 Update*. Amherst, MA: Political Economy Research Institute, University of Massachusetts. November 28, 2011. Retrieved from http://www.peri.umass.edu/236/hash/0b0ce6af7ff999b11745825d80aca0b8/publication/489/.

Pollins, Brian M. (2002). Politics, Markets, and Grand Strategy: Foreign Economic Policies as Strategic Instruments. By Lars S. Skålnes. Ann Arbor: University of Michigan Press, 2000. 272pp. $54.50. *American Political Science Review* 96(02): 476–477.

Pomper, Miles A. (2001). Bill to Waive Pakistan Sanctions Clears Over Protests From Appropriators And Supporters of India, *CQ Weekly*, pp. 2484–2486, October 20, 2001.

Poole, Keith T., and Howard L. Rosenthal (2006). *Ideology and Congress*. Somerset, NJ: Transaction Publishers.

Posen, Barry R. (2013). Pull Back: The Case for a Less Activist Foreign Policy. *Foreign Affairs* 92(1): 116–128.

Posner, Eric A., and Adrian Vermeule (2010). *The Executive Unbound: After the Madisonian Republic*. New York: Oxford University Press.

Potter, William C. (1980). Issue Area and Foreign Policy Analysis. *International Organization* 34(3): 405–427.

Powell, G. Bingham, and Guy D. Whitten (1993). A Cross-National Analysis of Economic Voting: Taking Account of Political Context. *American Journal of Political Science* 37(2): 391–414.

PR Newswire (2000). American Businesses Unite to Fight Spread of HIV/AIDS in Africa. *PR Newswire*, New York: PR Newswire Association LLC. Retrieved from http://www.prnewswire.com/news-releases/american-businesses-unite-to-fight-spread-of-hivaids-in-africa-73271187.html.

Program on International Policy Attitudes (2005). *Americans on Promoting Democracy*. Chicago Council on Foreign Relations/Program on International Policy Attitudes. College Park: University of Maryland. September 29, 2005. Retrieved from http://www.worldpublicopin ion.org/pipa/pdf/sep05/Democratization_Sep09_rpt_revised.pdf.

Prokop, Andrew (2014). Why Counting Executive Orders Is an Awful Way to Measure Presidential Power. *Vox.com*, Washington, DC: Vox Media, Inc. Retrieved from http://www.vox .com/xpress/2014/11/22/7260059/president-executive-orders-chart.

Putnam, Robert D. (1988). Diplomacy and Domestic Politics: The Logic of Two-Level Games. *International Organization* 42(3): 427–460.

Rathbun, Brian C. (2011). The 'Magnificent Fraud': Trust, International Cooperation and the Hidden Domestic Politics of Postwar American Multilateralism. *International Studies Quarterly* 55(1): 1–21.

Rearden, Steven L. (1984). *History of the Office of the Secretary of Defense* (Vol. I: The Formative Years, 1947–1950). Washington, DC: Office of the Secretary of Defense.

Regan, Patrick M. (2000). Substituting Policies during U.S. Interventions in Internal Conflicts: A Little of This, a Little of That. *Journal of Conflict Resolution* 44(1): 90–106.

Renka, Russell D., and Bradford S. Jones (1991a). The 'Two Presidencies' in the Reagan and Bush Administrations. In Steven A. Shull (Ed.), *The Two Presidencies: A Quarter Century Assessment* (pp. 158–178). Chicago: Nelson-Hall.

—— (1991b). The 'Two Presidencies' Thesis and the Reagan Administration. *Congress & the Presidency* 18(1): 17–35.

Rentfrow, Peter J., John T. Jost, Samuel D. Gosling, and Jonathan Potter (2009). Statewide Differences in Personality Predict Voting Patterns in 1996–2004 U.S. Presidential Elections. In John T. Jost, Aaron C. Kay and Hulda Thorisdottir (Eds.), *Social and Psychological Bases of Ideology and System Justification* (pp. 314–347). New York: Oxford University Press.

Rice, Susan E. (1997). Africa: Rice Says 'Wave Of Change' Rolling Across Africa. *AllAfrica.com*, Cape Town: AllAfrica. Retrieved from http://allafrica.com/stories/199711280107.html.

Risse-Kappen, Thomas (1991). Public Opinion, Domestic Structure, and Foreign Policy in Liberal Democracies. *World Politics* 43(4): 479–512.

Ritter, Karl (2014). Washington Takes Heat at UN Talks over Targets. *The Big Story*, New York: Associated Press. Retrieved from http://bigstory.ap.org/article/33284f7202104c558f e8723612e27cb9/washington-takes-heat-un-talks-over-targets.

Rivers, Douglas, and Nancy L. Rose (1985). Passing the President's Program: Public Opinion and Presidential Influence in Congress. *American Journal of Political Science* 29(2): 183–196.

Robbins, Carla Anne, and Thomas E. Ricks (1998). Striking Back: American Forces Hit Alleged Terrorist Bases in Afghanistan, Sudan—Citing Embassy Bombings, Possible New Attacks, U.S. Targets Bin Laden—Support, Mostly, in Congress, *Wall Street Journal*, p. A1, August 21, 1998.

Roberts, Margaret E., Brandon M. Stewart, and Dustin H. Tingley (2014). stm: R package for Structural Topic Models. www.structuraltopicmodel.com.

Roberts, Margaret E., Brandon M. Stewart, Dustin H. Tingley, Christopher Lucas, Jetson Leder-Luis, Bethany Albertson, et al. (2014). Structural Topic Models for Open-Ended Survey Responses. *American Journal of Political Science* 58(4): 1064–1082.

Rodriguez, Andrea (2015). *Organizational Structure, Aid, and Reduction of Poverty*. Princeton, NJ: Princeton University Press.

Rogers, David (2003a). Agreement Is Near on a $17.3 Billion Foreign-Aid Budget, *Wall Street Journal*, p. A2, November 18, 2003.

—— (2003b). Bush's Tax Cuts Now Are Hitting Foreign-Aid Plan, *Wall Street Journal*, p. A6, July 25, 2003.

Rogers, David, and Yochi Dreazen (2003). House Media Vote Signals Fight Over Ownership, *Wall Street Journal*, p. A2, July 23, 2003.

Rogowski, Ronald (1987). Political Cleavages and Changing Exposure to Trade. *American Political Science Review* 81(4): 1121–1137.

—— (1989). *Commerce and Coalitions: How Trade Affects Domestic Political Alignments*. Princeton, NJ: Princeton University Press.

Rohde, David W. (2004). *Roll Call Voting Data for the United States House of Representatives, 1953–2004.* Compiled by the Political Institutions and Public Choice Program. East Lansing: Michigan State University. July 27, 2005.

—— (2010). *Political Institutions and Public Choice House Roll-Call Database*. Durham, NC: Duke University. June 16, 2010.

Rohde, David W., and Dennis M. Simon (1985). Presidential Vetoes and Congressional Response: A Study of Institutional Conflict. *American Journal of Political Science* 29(3): 397–427.

Roscoe, Douglas D., and Shannon Jenkins (2005). A Meta-Analysis of Campaign Contributions' Impact on Roll Call Voting. *Social Science Quarterly* 86(1): 52–69.

Rose, Gideon (1998). Neoclassical Realism and Theories of Foreign Policy. *World Politics* 51(1): 144–172.

Rose, Sarah (2014). *Congress Is Right about Honduras and Tunisia, But Wrong to Micromanage the MCC Board*. Ideas to Action: Independent Research for Global Prosperity. Washington, DC: Center for Global Development. January 22, 2014. Retrieved from http://www.cgdev.org/blog/congress-right-about-honduras-and-tunisia-wrong-micromanage-mcc-board.

Rosenau, James N. (1966). Pre-Theories and Theories of Foreign Policy. In R. Barry Farrell (Ed.), *Approaches to Comparative and International Politics* (pp. 27–92). Evanston, IL: Northwestern University Press.

—— (1967). Foreign Policy as an Issue-Area. In James N. Rosenau (Ed.), *Domestic Sources of Foreign Policy* (pp. 11–50). New York; London: Free Press; Collier-Macmillan Ltd.

Ross, Wendy S. (2000). Clinton Signs Africa-Caribbean Trade Bill: Measure Aims to Expand Two-way Trade, Encourage Reform, *Washington Informer*, p. 8, June 7, 2000.

Rostenkowski, Daniel D. (1994). Signing of Uruguay Round Trade Agreements, *Congressional Record*, Vol. 140, Part 6, pp. 7475–7476. Washington, DC.

Rothchild, Donald S. (2001). The U.S. Foreign Policy Trajectory on Africa. *SAIS Review* 21(1): 179–211.

Rourke, John (1983). *Congress and the Presidency in U.S. Foreign Policymaking: A Study of Interaction and Influence, 1945–1982*. Boulder, CO: Westview Press.

Rovner, Joshua (2011). *Fixing the Facts: National Security and the Politics of Intelligence*. Ithaca, NY: Cornell University Press.

Rovner, Julie (2003). *Analysis: Some Controversy Surrounding what President Bush Has Promised to Help Fight AIDS in Africa and what his Administration Has Actually Requested from Congress*. All Things Considered. Washington, DC: NPR. July 12, 2003.

Royce, Ed (2006). Pentagon Imperative: A Spotlight on Africa, *Christian Science Monitor*, p. 9, November 14, 2006.

Rudalevige, Andrew (2005). *The New Imperial Presidency: Renewing Presidential Power after Watergate*. Ann Arbor: University of Michigan Press.

Ruffin, Roy J. (1984). International Factor Movements. In Ronald W. Jones and Peter B. Kenen (Eds.), *Handbook of International Economics* (Vol. 1, pp. 237–288). Amsterdam: Elsevier.

Sanger, David E. (2014). U.S. Hopes Face-Saving Plan Offers a Path to a Nuclear Pact with Iran, *New York Times*, p. A4, September 20, 2014.

Sarkesian, Sam C., John Allen Williams, and Stephen J. Cimbala (2008). *US National Security: Policymakers, Processes, and Politics* (4th ed.). Boulder, CO: Lynne Rienner.

Sartori, Anne E. (2005). *Deterrence by Diplomacy*. Princeton, NJ: Princeton University Press.

Saunders, Elizabeth N. (2011). *Leaders at War: How Presidents Shape Military Interventions*. Ithaca, NY: Cornell University Press.

—— (2013). *The Electoral Disconnection in U.S. Foreign Policy*. Washington, DC: George Washington University. January 7, 2013.

Savage, Charlie (2014). Changes to Surveillance Bill Stoke Anger, *New York Times*, p. A20, May 21, 2014.

Schattschneider, E. E. (1935). *Politics, Pressures and the Tariff*. New York: Prentice-Hall.

Scheve, Kenneth F., and Matthew J. Slaughter (2001a). Labor Market Competition and Individual Preferences Over Immigration Policy. *Review of Economics and Statistics* 83(1): 133–145.

—— (2001b). What Determines Individual Trade-policy Preferences? *Journal of International Economics* 54(2): 267–292.

—— (2004). Economic Insecurity and the Globalization of Production. *American Journal of Political Science* 48(4): 662–674.

Schiff, Maurice (1994). How Trade, Aid, and Remittances Affect International Migration. *World Bank: Policy Research Working Paper 1376*.

Schilling, Warner R. (1981). US Strategic Nuclear Concepts in the 1970s: The Search for Sufficiently Equivalent Countervailing Parity. *International Security* 6(2): 48–79.

Schirch, Lisa, and Aaron Kishbaugh (2006). *Leveraging '3D' Security: From Rhetoric to Reality*. Foreign Policy in Focus Policy Brief, Vol. 11, No. 2. Washington, DC: Institute for Policy Studies. November 15, 2006.

Schlesinger, Arthur M., Jr. (1973). *The Imperial Presidency*. Boston: Houghton, Mifflin.

—— (2004). *The Imperial Presidency* (1st ed.). New York: Mariner Books.

Schmitt, Eric (1998). Bill to Push Africa Trade Is Approved, *New York Times*, p. A9, March 16, 1998.

—— (1999a). House Supports Trade Benefits to Aid Africa, *New York Times*, p. A1, July 17, 1999.

—— (1999b). Impasse in Senate Delays Action On Africa-Caribbean Trade Bills, *New York Times*, p. A4, October 30, 1999.

—— (1999c). Senate Passes Trade Bills for Caribbean and Africa, *New York Times*, p. A11, November 4, 1999.

—— (2014). U.S. Training Elite Antiterror Troops in Four African Nations, *New York Times*, p. A1, May 27, 2014.

Schneidman, Witney, and Zenia A. Lewis (2012). *The African Growth and Opportunity Act: Looking Back, Looking Forward*. Washington, DC: Brookings Institution. June 2012.

Schoultz, Lars (1987). *National Security and United States Policy Toward Latin America*. Princeton, NJ: Princeton University Press.

Schrodt, Philip A., and Omur Yilmaz (2007). *CAMEO: Conflict and Mediation Event Observations Codebook, Version 0.9b5*. Lawrence: University of Kansas. September 2007. Retrieved from http://eventdata.parusanalytics.com/data.dir/levant.html.

Schuck, Peter H. (1998). The Re-Evaluation of American Citizenship. In Christian Joppke (Ed.), *Challenge to the Nation-State: Immigration in Western Europe and the United States* (pp. 191–230). Oxford: Oxford University Press.

Schulberg, Jessica (2015). Legal Experts Tell Congress Obama's New War Authorization Fails to Limit Power. HuffingtonPost.com. New York: Huffington Post, Inc. Retrieved from http://www.huffingtonpost.com/2015/02/26/obama-aumf-congress_n_6764080.html.

Schwab, Jeremy (2004). Africans Lobby to Continue Trade Pact, *Bay State Banner*, p. 3, May 6, 2004.

Seidman, Harold (1998). *Politics, Position, and Power: The Dynamics of Federal Organization* (5th ed.). New York: Oxford University Press.

Serafino, Nina M. (2006). *Peacekeeping and Related Stability Operations: Issues of U.S. Military Involvement*. CRS Issue Brief No. IB94040. Washington, DC: Congressional Research Service. May 18, 2006.

—— (2013). *Security Assistance Reform: 'Section 1206' Background and Issues for Congress*. CRS Report No. RS22855. Washington, DC: Congressional Research Service. April 19, 2013.

Shah, Rajiv (2011). Remarks by USAID Administrator Dr. Rajiv Shah at the Center for Global Development. Washington, DC: USAID. Retrieved from http://www.usaid.gov/news-infor mation/speeches/remarks-usaid-administrator-dr-rajiv-shah-center-global-development.

Shah, Shahid (2006). Pakistan Gets Praise, But No U.S. Trade Deal: Backing for Washington's War on Terrorism Fails to Stitch Up a Hoped-for Textile Accord, *Wall Street Journal*, p. A6, May 2, 2006.

Shanker, Thom, and Eric Schmitt (2011). Three Terrorist Groups in Africa Pose Threat to U.S., American Commander Says, *New York Times*, p. A8, September 15, 2011.

Sharp, Jeremy M. (2014). *Jordan: Background and U.S. Relations*. CRS Report No. RL33546. Washington, DC: Congressional Research Service. December 2, 2014. Retrieved from http://fpc.state.gov/documents/organization/234976.pdf.

Sherry, Michael S. (1995). *In the Shadow of War: The United States since the 1930s*. New Haven, CT: Yale University Press.

Shull, Steven A. (Ed.) (1991). *The Two Presidencies: A Quarter Century Assessment*. Chicago: Nelson-Hall.

Shull, Steven A., and Lance T. LeLoup (1981). Reassessing the Reassessment: Comment on Sigelman's Note on the 'Two Presidencies' Thesis. *Journal of Politics* 43(2): 563–564.

Sigal, Leon V. (1998). *Disarming Strangers: Nuclear Diplomacy with North Korea*. Princeton, NJ: Princeton University Press.

Sigelman, Lee (1979). A Reassessment of the Two Presidencies Thesis. *Journal of Politics* 41(4): 1195–1205.

——— (1981). Response to Critics. *Journal of Politics* 43(2): 565–565.

Simmons, Beth A. (1994). *Who Adjusts? Domestic Sources of Foreign Economic Policy During the Interwar Years*. Princeton, NJ: Princeton University Press.

Simon, Julia (2013). Egypt May Not Need Fighter Jets, but the U.S. Keeps Sending Them Any- way. *Planet Money*, Washington, DC: NPR News. Retrieved from http://www.npr.org/tem plates/transcript/transcript.php?storyId=209878158.

Sink, Justin (2015). Obama Aide: ISIS War Powers Language "Intentionally" Vague. TheHill .com. Washington, DC: Capitol Hill Publishing Corp. Retrieved from http://thehill.com/ policy/defense/232476-obama-aide-war-powers-language-intentionally-vague.

Skålnes, Lars S. (2000). *Politics, Markets, and Grand Strategy: Foreign Economic Policies as Strategic Instruments*. Ann Arbor: University of Michigan Press.

Skowronek, Stephen (2008). *Presidential Leadership in Political Time: Reprise and Reappraisal*. Lawrence: University Press of Kansas.

Slantchev, Branislav L. (2005). Military Coercion in Interstate Crises. *American Political Science Review* 99(4): 533–547.

——— (2011). *Military Threats: The Costs of Coercion and the Price of Peace*. New York: Cambridge University Press.

Smith, Tony (2000). *Foreign Attachments: The Power of Ethnic Groups in the Making of American Foreign Policy*. Cambridge, MA: Harvard University Press.

Snider, L. Britt (2008). *The Agency and the Hill: CIA's relationship with Congress, 1946–2004*. Washington, DC: Center for the Study of Intelligence; Central Intelligence Agency.

Sniderman, Paul M., Richard A. Brody, and Philip E. Tetlock (1991). *Reasoning and Choice: Explorations in Political Psychology*. New York: Cambridge University Press.

Snyder, Glenn H. (2002). Mearsheimer's World—Offensive Realism and the Struggle for Secu- rity: A Review Essay. *International Security* 27(1): 149–173.

Souva, Mark, and David Rohde (2007). Elite Opinion Differences and Partisanship in Congres- sional Foreign Policy, 1975–1996. *Political Research Quarterly* 60(1): 113–123.

Spanier, John W., and Joseph L. Nogee (Eds.) (1981). *Congress, the Presidency, and American Foreign Policy*. New York: Pergamon Press.

St. Charles Pastoral Center (2003). *Rise to the Challenge: End World Hunger*. Romeoville, IL: Catholic Diocese of Joliet. March 15, 2003.

Starr, Harvey (2000). Substitutability in Foreign Policy: Theoretically Central, Empirically Elusive. *Journal of Conflict Resolution* 44(1): 128–138.

Stasavage, David (2004). Open-Door or Closed-Door? Transparency in Domestic and International Bargaining. *International Organization* 58(04): 667–703.

Stein, Janice Gross (2013). Threat Perception in International Relations. In Leonie Huddy, David O. Sears, and Jack S. Levy (Eds.), *The Oxford Handbook of Political Psychology* (2nd ed., pp. 364–394). Oxford: Oxford University Press.

Stewart, Brandon M. (2014). *Latent Factor Regressions for the Social Sciences*. Cambridge, MA: Harvard University. November 30, 2014. Retrieved from http://scholar.harvard.edu/files/bstewart/files/tensorreg.pdf

Stokes, Donald E. (1963). Spatial Models of Party Competition. *American Political Science Review* 57(2): 368–377.

Stolberg, Sheryl Gay (2003). House Approves a Smaller Measure of $2 billion for AIDS, *New York Times*, p. 9, July 25, 2003.

—— (2008). In Global Battle on AIDS, Bush Creates Legacy, *New York Times*, p. A1, January 5, 2008.

Sullivan, Terry (1991). A Matter of Fact: The 'Two Presidencies' Thesis Revitalized. In Steven A. Shull (Ed.), *The Two Presidencies: A Quarter Century Assessment* (pp. 143–157). Chicago: Nelson-Hall.

Sun Reporter (2003). Congressional Report: Lee Rips Bush On Slow AIDS Funding, *Sun Reporter*, p. 1, July 17, 2003.

Suzman, Mark (1998). Critics Join in Support for Missile Strikes; Doubts Remain; Approval Rating of More than 60%. *Financial Times*, p. 3, August 22, 1998.

Swenson, Scott Blaine (2008). AIDS Fight Requires More than Politics As Usual, *Westside Gazette*, p. 13A, March 20, 2008.

Symington, James W. (1971). Department of Defense Appropriations, 1972, *Congressional Record*, Vol. 117, Part 33, pp. 49243–49253, November 23, 1971. Washington, DC.

Taliaferro, Jeffrey W., Steven E. Lobell, and Norrin M. Ripsman (2009). Introduction: Neoclassical Realism, the State, and Foreign Policy. In Steven E. Lobell, Norrin M. Ripsman and Jeffrey W. Taliaferro (Eds.), *Neoclassical Realism, the State, and Foreign Policy* (pp. 1–41). New York: Cambridge University Press.

Tarnoff, Curt (2013). *Millennium Challenge Corporation*. CRS Report No. RL32427. Washington, DC: Congressional Research Service. February 13, 2013.

—— (2014). *Millennium Challenge Corporation* CRS Report No. RL32427. Washington, DC: Congressional Research Service. April 8, 2014. Retrieved from http://www.fas.org/sgp/crs/row/RL32427.pdf.

Tarnoff, Curt, and Marian Leonardo Lawson (2011). *Foreign Aid: An Introduction to U.S. Programs and Policy*. CRS Report No. R40213. Washington, DC: Congressional Research Service. February 10, 2011.

Tatalovich, Raymond, and Thomas S. Engeman (2003). *The Presidency and Political Science: Two Hundred Years of Constitutional Debate*. Baltimore, MD: Johns Hopkins University Press.

Teitelbaum, Michael S. (1984). Immigration, Refugees, and Foreign Policy. *International Organization* 38(3): 429–450.

Therien, Jean-Philippe, and Alain Noel (2000). Political Parties and Foreign Aid. *American Political Science Review* 94(1): 151–162.

Thurber, James (Ed.) (1991). *Divided Democracy: Cooperation and Conflict between the President and Congress*. Washington, DC: CQ Press.

Tichenor, Daniel J. (2002). *Dividing Lines: The Politics of Immigration Control*. Princeton, NJ: Princeton University Press.

Tieku, Thomas Kwasi (2012). *U.S.–Africa Relations in the Age of Obama*. Occasional Paper Series No. 15. Ithaca, NY: Institute for African Development, Cornell University. Retrieved from http://iad.einaudi.cornell.edu/node/8194.

Tierney, Michael J., Daniel L. Nielson, Darren G. Hawkins, J. Timmons Roberts, Michael G. Findley, Ryan M. Powers, et al. (2011). More Dollars than Sense: Refining Our Knowledge of Development Finance Using AidData. *World Development* 39(11): 1891–1906.

Ting, Jan C. (2006). Immigration and National Security. *Orbis* 50(1): 41–52.

Tingley, Dustin H. (2010). Donors and Domestic Politics: Political Influences on Foreign Aid Commitments. *Quarterly Review of Economics and Finance* 50(1): 40–49.

—— (2013). Public Finance and Immigration Preferences: A Lost Connection? *Polity* 45(1): 4–33.

Tingley, Dustin H., Christopher Xu, Adam Chilton, and Helen V. Milner (2015). The Political Economy of Inward FDI: Opposition to Chinese Mergers and Acquisitions. *Chinese Journal of International Relations* 8(1): 27–57.

Tonelson, Alan (2002). Leviathan Gown on Free Trade Ideology, *Washington Times*, p. B03, July 21, 2002.

Trager, Robert F., and Lynn Vavreck (2011). The Political Costs of Crisis Bargaining: Presidential Rhetoric and the Role of Party. *American Journal of Political Science* 55(3): 526–545.

Trubowitz, Peter (1998). *Defining the National Interest: Conflict and Change in American Foreign Policy*. Chicago: University of Chicago Press.

Tucker, Robert W., Charles B. Keely, and Linda Wrigley (Eds.) (1990). *Immigration and U.S. Foreign Policy*. Boulder, CO: Westview Press.

Tyler, Gus (2002). Tyler, Too: How Farm Bloc Seeded Bush's Fast Track, *Forward*, p. 14, August 30, 2002.

U.S. Department of Defense (1995). *United States Security Strategy for Sub-Saharan Africa*. Washington, DC: Department of Defense. August 1995.

U.S. General Accounting Office (1983). *Political and Economic Factors Influencing Economic Support Fund Programs*. Report to the Chairman, Committee on Foreign Affairs, House of Representatives. Washington, DC: GAO. April 18, 1983.

—— (1995). *Multilateral Development Banks: Financial Conditions of the African Development Bank*. GAO Report No. NSIAD-95-143BR. Washington, DC: General Accounting Office. April 21, 1995.

U.S. Government Accountability Office (2008). *Combating Terrorism: Actions Needed to Enhance Implementation of Trans-Sahara Counterterrorism Partnership*. GAO Report No. 08-860. Washington, DC: Government Accountability Office. July 2008.

Umoren, Rose (1996). Africa–U.S.: Clinton's Africa Trade Policy Widely Faulted. *Inter Press Service*, Washington, DC: Inter Press Service News Agency. Retrieved from http://www.ipsnews.net/1996/05/africa-us-clintons-africa-trade-policy-widely-faulted/.

United Nations (2001). *Replacement Migration: Is It a Solution to Declining and Ageing Populations?* New York: United Nations.

United Nations Security Council (1995). *Angola Mission Approved, Delays in Troop Arrival*. SC/5995 Resumed 3499th Meeting, February 8, 1995 (PM summary). New York: United Nations.

United States Agency for International Development (2001). *Contracts and Grants and Cooperative Agreements with Universities, Firms and Non-Profit Institutions by Country/Region Active as of October 1, 1999*. USAID Yellowbook Fiscal Year 2001. Washington, DC: USAID: Office of Procurement. June 18, 2001.

—— (2014). *U.S. Overseas Loans and Grants*. USAID Greenbook. Washington, DC: USAID. March 28, 2014. Retrieved from http://gbk.eads.usaidallnet.gov/.

United States Census Bureau (2014). *State & County QuickFacts—USA*. Washington, DC: US Department of Commerce. Retrieved from http://quickfacts.census.gov/qfd/states/00000.html.

United States Department of Defense (2012). *2012 Demographics: Profile of the Military Community*. Washington, DC: Office of the Deputy Assistant Secretary of Defense. Retrieved from http://www.militaryonesource.mil/12038/MOS/Reports/2012_Demographics_Report.pdf.

van de Walle, Nicolas (2010). US Policy towards Africa: The Bush Legacy and the Obama Administration. *African Affairs*. 109(434): 1–21.

Vidal, John, and Suzanne Goldenberg (2014). Snowden Revelations of NSA Spying on Copenhagen Climate Talks Spark Anger. *TheGuardian.com*, London: Guardian News and Media. Retrieved from http://www.theguardian.com/environment/2014/jan/30/snowden-nsa-spying-copenhagen-climate-talks.

Volman, Daniel (1998). The Development of the African Crisis Response Initiative. *Africa Policy Report*, Washington, DC: AllAfrica Global Media. Retrieved from http://allafrica.com/stories/199804230158.html.

Volman, Daniel, and Beth Tuckey (2008). Militarizing Africa (Again). *Foreign Policy in Focus*, Washington, DC: Institute for Policy Studies. Retrieved from http://fpif.org/militarizing_africa_again/.

von Clausewitz, Carl (1976). *On War*. Princeton, NJ: Princeton University Press.

Waever, Ole (1995). Securitization and Desecuritization. In Ronnie D. Lipschutz (Ed.), *On Security* (pp. 46–86). New York: Columbia University Press.

Waithaka, Njeru (1998). The Final Frontier: Africa and the African Growth and Opportunity Act, *Network Journal*, p. 12, October 31, 1998.

Wala, Michael (1986). Selling the Marshall Plan at Home: The Committee for the Marshall Plan to Aid European Recovery. *Diplomatic History* 10(3): 247–265.

Walker, Martin (1994). It's No Trade, Say Odd Couple: Washington on an Unlikely Crusade to Derail the Gatt Deal. Rhetoric Apart, There Are Signs that the WTO Could Be in Trouble, *The Guardian*, p. 40, July 16, 1994.

Walker, Stephen G. (Ed.) (1987). *Role Theory and Foreign Policy Analysis*. Durham, NC: Duke University Press.

Walker, Stephen G., and Akan Malici (2011). *U.S. Presidents and Foreign Policy Mistakes*. Stanford, CA: Stanford University Press.

Wallerstein, Mitchel B. (1980). *Food for War—Food for Peace. United States Food Aid in a Global Context*. Cambridge, MA: MIT Press.

Walt, Stephen M. (1987). *The Origins of Alliances*. Ithaca, NY: Cornell University Press.

—— (1998). International Relations: One World, Many Theories. *Foreign Policy* 110: 29–46.

—— (2005). Taming American Power. *Foreign Affairs* 84(5): 105–120.

—— (2013). Which Works Best: Force or Diplomacy. *FP: Foreign Policy*, Washington, DC: The FP Group. Retrieved from http://www.foreignpolicy.com/posts/2013/08/21/force_and_diplomacy.

Waltz, Kenneth N. (1979). *Theory of International Politics*. Reading, MA: Addison-Wesley.

Warburg, Gerald Felix (1989). *Conflict and Consensus: The Struggle between Congress and the President over Foreign Policymaking*. New York: Harper & Row.

Waters, Maxine (1998). An open letter from Congresswoman Maxine Waters: "Why we must now oppose the Omnibus Fast Track / African Trade Bill," *Hyde Park Citizen*, p. 9, August 13, 1998.

Watkins, Shanea J., and James Sherk (2008). *Who Serves in the U.S. Military? Demographic Characteristics of Enlisted Troops and Officers*. CDA Report No. CDA08-05. Washington, DC: The Heritage Foundation. August 21, 2008. Retrieved from http://s3.amazonaws.com/thf_media/2008/pdf/cda08-05.pdf.

Wawro, Gregory J., and Ira Katznelson (2014). Designing Historical Social Scientific Inquiry: How Parameter Heterogeneity Can Bridge the Methodological Divide between Quantitative and Qualitative Approaches. *American Journal of Political Science* 58(2): 526–546.

Wendt, Alexander E. (1992). Anarchy Is What States Make of It: The Social Construction of Power Politics. *International Organization* 46(2): 391–425.

Westside Gazette (2003). President Bush Urges Congress to Pass AIDS Bill Quickly, *Westside Gazette*, p. 5C, May 14, 2003.

Whitaker Group (2003). AGOA III 'Action Committee' Formed to Lobby to Extend Life of Trade Pact, Other Enhancements. Washington, DC: The Whitaker Group. Retrieved from http://allafrica.com/stories/200306240035.html

Whitaker, Rosa (1999). Africa-at-Large: Passage of African Trade Bill in 1999 'Top Priority.' Washington, DC: United States Information Agency. Retrieved from http://allafrica.com/stories/199901220001.html.

Whitlock, Craig (2012). Military Expands Spying in Africa, *Washington Post*, p. A01, June 14, 2012.

Wildavsky, Aaron B. (1966). The Two Presidencies. *Trans-Action* 4: 7–14.

—— (1991). *The Beleaguered Presidency*. New Brunswick, NJ: Transaction Publishers.

—— (Ed.) (1969). *The Presidency*. Boston: Little.

Williams, Michael C. (2003). Words, Images, Enemies: Securitization and International Politics. *International Studies Quarterly* 47(4): 511–531.

Wilson, James Q. (1973). *Political Organizations*. New York: Basic Books.

—— (1980). *The Politics of Regulation*. New York: Basic Books.

Wirls, Daniel (1992). *Build-up: The Politics of Defense in the Reagan Era*. Ithaca, NY: Cornell University Press.

Wittkopf, Eugene R. (1986). On the Foreign Policy Beliefs of the American People: A Critique and Some Evidence. *International Studies Quarterly* 30(4): 425–445.

—— (1990). *Faces of Internationalism: Public Opinion and American Foreign Policy*. Durham, NC: Duke University Press.

Wong, Carolyn (2006). *Lobbying for Inclusion: Rights Politics and the Making of Immigration Policy*. Stanford, CA: Stanford University Press.

Woodward, Robert U. (2004). *Plan of Attack*. New York: Simon & Schuster.

Woolley, John T., and Gerhard Peters (2014). *The American Presidency Project*. Santa Barbara: University of California–Santa Barbara. Retrieved from http://www.presidency.ucsb.edu/.

Wright, John R. (1996). *Interest Groups and Congress: Lobbying, Contributions, and Influence*. Boston: Allyn and Bacon.

—— (2002). *Interest Groups and Congress: Lobbying, Contributions and Influence*. London: Pearson Longman.

Wright, Joseph, and Matthew Winters (2010). The Politics of Effective Foreign Aid. *Annual Review of Political Science* 13(1): 61–80.

Yoo, John C. (1996). The Continuation of Politics by Other Means: The Original Understanding of War Powers. *California Law Review* 84(2): 167–305.

You, Hye-Young (2013). Three Essays on the Political Economy of Lobbying. Dissertation, Harvard University.

Zahariadis, Nikolaos, Rick Travis, and James B. Ward (2000). U.S. Food Aid to Sub-Saharan Africa: Politics or Philanthropy? *Social Science Quarterly* 81(2): 663–676.

Zeidenstein, Harvey G. (1981). The Two Presidencies Thesis Is Alive and Well and Has Been Living in the U.S. Senate since 1973. *Presidential Studies Quarterly* 11(4): 511–525.

Zimmerman, William (1973). Issue Area and Foreign-Policy Process: A Research Note in Search of a General Theory. *American Political Science Review* 67(4): 1204–1212.

Zolberg, Aristide R. (1990). Reforming the Back Door: The Immigration Reform and Control Act of 1986 in Historical Perspective. In Virginia Yans-McLaughlin (Ed.), *Immigration Reconsidered: History, Sociology, and Politics* (pp. 315–339). Oxford: Oxford University Press.

# INDEX

Note: Figures and tables are indicated by "f" and "t," respectively, following page numbers.